Routledge Revivals

Problems in Class Analysis

First published in 1983, *Problems in Class Analysis* presents a coherent theory of labour's domination by capital, based upon the notion of the capitalist nature of both the product relations and of the productive forces themselves, including science and technology. The author demonstrates that all knowledges are a product, direct or indirect, of economic relations, so that different knowledges will be the product of different social classes as determined by their position within economic production relations. By posing and re-solving fundamental problems in class analysis, Dr. Carchedi forms a bridge between the theory of the production process and contemporary debates in economics, sociology and epistemology.

Problems in Class Analysis

Production, knowledge, and the function of capital

G. Carchedi

Routledge
Taylor & Francis Group

First published in 1983
By Routledge & Kegan Paul

This edition first published in 2022 by Routledge
4 Park Square, Milton Park, Abingdon, Oxon, OX14 4RN
and by Routledge
605 Third Avenue, New York, NY 10017

Routledge is an imprint of the Taylor & Francis Group, an informa business

Publisher's Note
The publisher has gone to great lengths to ensure the quality of this reprint but points
out that some imperfections in the original copies may be apparent.

Disclaimer
The publisher has made every effort to trace copyright holders and welcomes
correspondence from those they have been unable to contact.

A Library of Congress record exists under LCCN: 83003157

ISBN: 978-1-032-39881-5 (hbk)
ISBN: 978-1-003-35532-8 (ebk)
ISBN: 978-1-032-40919-1 (pbk)

Book DOI 10.4324/9781003355328

PROBLEMS IN CLASS ANALYSIS

Production, knowledge, and the function of capital

G. CARCHEDI
University of Amsterdam

ROUTLEDGE DIRECT EDITIONS

Routledge & Kegan Paul
London, Boston, Melbourne and Henley

First published in 1983
by Routledge & Kegan Paul Plc,
39 Store Street, London WC1E 7DD,
9 Park Street, Boston, Mass. 02108, USA,
296 Beaconsfield Parade, Middle Park,
Melbourne, 3206, Australia, and
Broadway House, Newtown Road,
Henley-on-Thames, Oxon RG9 1EN
Printed in Great Britain by
Redwood Burn Ltd,
Trowbridge, Wiltshire
© G. Carchedi 1983

Library of Congress Cataloging in Publication Data

Carchedi, Guglielmo.
    Problems in class analysis.
    (Routledge direct editions)
    Bibliography: p.
    Includes index.
    1. Social classes - economic aspects. 2. Marxian
economics. 3. Socialism. 4. Capitalism. I. Title.
HT675.C374 1983   305.5   83-3157
ISBN 0-7100-9426-4 (pbk.)

CONTENTS

FOREWORD

Around the end of the 1960s a cycle in the antagonistic relations between capital and labour came to an abrupt end. The new epoch which started in the 1970s is marked by a long-term crisis not only of capital (perhaps not as violent in its form, but certainly as deep as that of the 1920s) but also of labour. Labour enters the 1970s leaving behind the broken illusions of 'realized socialism' (or, better said, of non-realized socialism) within a cultural and political climate on the Left increasingly hostile to the dominance of the Third International ideology. Let us mention some elements of this ideology: the concept of imperialism as a decaying economy and as being destructive of the productive forces; of the state as exclusively an instrument of coercion; of the proletariat as exclusively the 'manual' productive (in the Marxian sense) labourer; of the Party as the meeting point of the proletariat and of the traditional intellectuals, deserters of their own class; of tactics as the proletariat's domination over (and instrumentalization of) other classes and social groups. (1)

Two more themes are mentioned separately because of their fundamental importance in the context of the present book. First, the concept of the productive forces (and thus of science and technology) as basically socially neutral, i.e. not class determined in their content. This notion has suffered increasingly severe blows from the wave of anti-authoritarianism which swept the labour movement after the May 1968 events and to the related critique of the capitalist organization of production. In fact, if the (capitalist) production process is based upon supposedly neutral and 'rational' sciences and technologies and if coercion too is necessary for it, it follows that coercion is rational and necessary under any social system of production, and thus also under socialism. But, if this mode of production is recognized as capitalist in essence, if coercion is recognized as an element of class domination within production as well, if these machines objectify the fragmentation of positions and the expropriation of knowledge to which the individual producer is subjected under capitalism, then it is not so obvious any more that the technology, and thus the science, upon which the capitalist mode of production is based can be used within completely different social relations.

vii

The second theme, or element of Third International ideology, is the acceptance within Marxism of the fragmentation of science into independent areas of inquiry. These two elements are strictly related. This book has been written in the conviction that it is only through the development of an epistemology and history of science which stress the class content of knowledge that useful (for the struggle for socialism) outcomes in economic and social analysis and theory can be achieved. On the other hand, a correct approach to economic and social analysis, and especially to the process of production both in its material and in its mental aspects, is a necessary condition for the solution of important epistemological problems. To mention only one example: nowhere in Marx's work - nor in that of the leaders and theoreticians of the Marxist movement - can an analysis be found of what we will call the process of mental transformation which even approximates the depth and comprehensiveness of Marx's analysis of the capitalist production process producing material commodities. Yet, it is such a detailed analysis which is needed if we want to understand why a 'schoolmaster is a productive labourer, when in addition to belabouring the heads of his scholars, he works like a horse to enrich the school proprietor'. (2) In what kind of process does the schoolmaster engage, what does he transform, when is this process productive of surplus value? It is our contention in what follows that the answer to this and other important questions has not been satisfactorily given because of the two above-mentioned elements.

The thesis of the class content of the productive forces (of their determination by the production relations), is of the utmost political, and not only theoretical, importance. It is simply the thesis that this science (both natural and social) and this technology cannot be used in a different (socialist) system; that their class content is inherent in them (since they are functional for the reproduction of the capitalist production relations) and does not derive from a 'distorted' application. It is the determination, in the last instance, of the capitalist productive forces by the capitalist production relations which makes the former unsuitable for the construction of socialism. The theoretical development of these themes presupposes the development of a concept of determination rooted in the notion of class. Thus, neither an idealist notion of dialectics à la Hegel, nor an evolutionist one à la Popper, (3) would do. We need a different concept of dialectical determination. This concept must account for capitalism's determination of its own conditions of supersession as well as of (contradictory) reproduction; it must account for the capitalist productive forces being capitalist, i.e. non-neutral, fostering the development of the capitalist production relations; it must account for the development of science not as a unilinear, asymptotic approximation of an eternally valid truth, but as being the realization of one (or more) of a variety of possible conditions, on the ideological level, of reproduction of the economic system; it must account for social phenomena to be class determined and yet not class specific; for the new social subjects (women, unemployed, youth, etc.) and social movements to be expressions (and potential allies) of the proletariat, not in the sense of being temporary appendices of it, but as constitutive elements of a multiform, multidimensional revolutionary subject without abandoning

the principle of the determining role of the proletariat for the
struggle for socialism.

The problem of determination, important as it is, is only one
example of what is aimed at in what follows. The reflections
submitted in this book attempt to cope with some open questions,
theoretical lacunae, of Marxist theory, as, for example, the
theoretical status of those elements of knowledge which are shared
by more than one class (or society); the issue of verification;
the possibility for, and the conditions under which, the individual
production of knowledge reveals its class determination by becoming
a social phenomenon; the conditions under which mental transformation
is productive of surplus value; the variety of production processes
under capitalism; and the function of capital in its economic,
sociological, and epistemological significance. This latter is of
fundamental importance in the present book. The myth of the
neutrality of science and thus of the (capitalist) production process
has had the extremely grave theoretical consequence of preventing an
analysis not only of the capitalist nature of the labour process
under capitalism (as argued in chapter 5) but also of the coercive
element imposed upon the labour process and yet necessary for the
production process. This is what Marx calls the work of control and
surveillance, or non-labour, and is referred to here as the function
of capital. It is argued in the present book that consideration of
an element of capitalist production as important as the function of
capital cannot but have extremely important consequences not only at
the level of sociological analysis (as I have argued also in a
previous work published in 1977) but also at the economic and
epistemological level. It is the simultaneous development of, and
interaction among, the sociological, economic, and epistemological
areas of inquiry in the light of an analysis of the function of
capital which is one of the characteristic features of the approach
submitted in what follows.

But, as will be argued later, a form of theoretical appropriation
of the real concrete does not develop in a vacuum. It advances only
by replacing other forms, i.e. through ideological class struggle.
Thus, these reflections bear the marks of the theoretical conjuncture
in which they have taken form, a conjuncture which sees the widespread resurgence of idealism together with the 'crisis of Marxism'
which is in fact the crisis *of a type* of Marxism, that of the Third
International. Both the resurgence of idealism and the crisis of
Third International Marxism are aspects on the theoretical level of
the difficulties experienced by the proletariat in its struggle
against the bourgeoisie. Thus, the recognition of the existence of
real problem areas within Marxism is made more difficult by the
ideological denial, or tacit abandonment, of its basic tenets. But
this denial and abandonment can be effectively counteracted on the
theoretical level only on condition that those problems within
Marxism are successfully tackled and solved.

Finally, a few words on the Appendix by A. Baracca to be found
at the end of chapter 1. The thesis of the class determination of
knowledge is by no means restricted to the social sciences. This
book, even though basically concerned with the social sciences,
submits that this thesis is valid also for the natural sciences and
provides some examples to this effect, especially in the first

chapter. However, these examples are limited in number and extent, a consequence of the fact that the author of the present book is neither a professional historian of science nor a natural scientist. It is for this reason that an Appendix, written by A. Baracca, an author of several works in the history of physics and also engaged in research in that field, has been added. The usefulness of this Appendix is two-fold. First of all, the reader will find in it an up to date review of the recent Italian literature in the history of the natural sciences which has been one of the elements inspiring the present book. These works are of extreme inherent interest and yet beyond the reach of those who do not read Italian. But, even more important for our purposes, we believe that Baracca's original and detailed historical case studies will provide further and convincing evidence of the correctness of the thesis of the class determination of production in general and of the production of natural sciences in particular. (4) We believe that it is only on the basis of this thesis that a class analysis of basic methodological, epistemological, and socio-economic questions (as constituent elements of the same theoretical whole) can be attempted. And this is precisely the ultimate aim of this book.

Chapter 1

DIALECTICAL DETERMINATION, KNOWLEDGE, AND TRANSITION TO SOCIALISM

INTRODUCTION

Like any view of reality, ours too is based upon basic postulates the validity of which can only be shown by the validity (verification) of the theory based upon them. Let us make them explicit. First, the postulate of the material basis of life, or that the basis of life is material transformation. This postulate expresses the need people have (aside from any social conditioning) to transform material reality in order to reproduce themselves. People must engage, under any social circumstances, in the transformation of use values, and first of all of material use values, i.e. they must engage in a labour process. Second, the postulate of the social basis of material life: while the need to transform material reality is not socially determined, the way in which this transformation takes place is socially determined. The producers, those who transform reality, engage in relations with each other in the very act of production, in the production process: they enter into, and become carriers of, production relations. It is the content of these production relations which determines the way in which people reproduce themselves by producing their means of reproduction. There is thus no production valid for all epochs, but only specific modes of production. Or, while all societies must engage in a labour process, the labour process takes on a specific form according to the specific production relations of a specific epoch. Third, the postulate of the class basis of social life. While postulate 1 expresses an a-historical and a-societal need (even Robinson Crusoes engaged in the transformation of use values), and postulate 2 expresses the necessarily social determination of the satisfaction of that need, postulate 3 introduces a further restriction by focusing on a special type of society, the class divided one. Classes are first of all identifiable in terms of relations in which people enter when participating in the material transformation of reality. That is, all those people carrying the same aspects of production relations belong objectively to the same class. Classes become thus the basic units of social life. From this it follows that, since production relations are determinant of material transformation and since this latter is the basis of life, of social life in all societies, production relations are the most important of all social relations.

Particularly important for us is a *basic epistemological principle* which can be derived from these three postulates: since people need to transform material reality, they need to gain knowledge of it and they gain knowledge of it in the process of material transformation. Knowledge, or mental transformation, is determined by material transformation in the sense that the latter calls the former into existence (even though possibly in a very mediated way, i.e. even though the former is apparently unconnected with the latter). This is the general definition of determination as applied to the relation between material and mental transformation. This is not yet the definition of dialectical determination. This general definition, however, is sufficient to point out that material and mental transformation can be considered as elements or aspects of the same unity in determination, or societal labour process.

If material transformation is socially class-determined, so is mental transformation: classes, therefore, are not only the basic units of social life but also of knowledge. More specifically, from the basic epistemological principle we can draw the following three corollaries:

(a)   only those who deal with (participate in the transformation of) material (and thus social) reality can gain knowledge of it;

(b)   since it is classes which transform reality, it is they which are the subjects of knowledge, which can produce an independent vision of reality;

(c)   but since each class deals with reality (the same reality) in a different way, i.e. by engaging in different (aspects of) production relations, each class is bound to have a different (socially, class determined) knowledge of the same reality.

It is against this background that we will submit in the present chapter that knowledge, both of the natural and of the social world, is class determined; that even those forms of knowledge which apparently cross over class boundaries and modes of socio-economic organization can (and should) be shown to bear the marks of class; that knowledge's reaction upon the socio-economic context which has determined it cannot (similarly to its social origin) but be a factor of class domination; and that thus no illusion should be entertained about the possibility of building a socialist society by using sciences and techniques developed within the context of bourgeois hegemony. (1) Since this all revolves around the concepts of dialectic and class, the first task of this chapter is an attempt to ground the former on the latter and to show the theoretical potential of such a procedure not only for a theory of knowledge but also, implicitly, for a theory of transition to socialism.

If approaches stressing the social determination of knowledge (especially of social theories) enjoy now wide circulation, attempts to develop a theory of class determination of knowledge are few and far between and are usually cast within the Diamat version of the Abbildtheorie, with its positivist notion of abstraction as a-historical selection of the essential and with its evolutionist and continuist concept of progress in knowledge. (2) This cannot be consistent with a radical theory, with a concept of knowledge as class determined appropriation in thought of the concrete, i.e. as the structurally determined condition of class domination. The development of such a theory and concept hinges upon the development of the concept of determination. Our task is therefore, first of all, that of carving out this latter's specific elements, avoiding, at the same time, some of the pitfalls which mark recent Marxist attempts to come to grips with it. They range, if the social sciences are considered, from the economicist reduction of other spheres of society to a simple reflection of the economic, to the opposite, i.e. either the denial of determination in the last instance by the economic, (3) or the reduction of the economic to a simple reflection of the political; (4) from the 'critique of class reductionism' (5) to the structural-functionalist view of determination as structural condition of existence, (6) which glosses over the need to explain the possibility for the determinant instance to determine the conditions of its supersession as well as determining a multiplicity of forms of a certain type of determined instance. This latter approach, while correctly stressing the contradictory nature of the determinant instance, minimizes the role of individuals as social agents and fails to integrate organically, notwithstanding claims to the contrary, the concept of class struggle in its model of society. (7) Yet, the concept of determination as calling into existence is a useful one and we will start our inquiry from here. While we claim general interpretative validity for the concept of dialectical determination which we will submit, we will restrict its application here to the determination of knowledge. Not surprisingly, within this context we will have to deal with the 'bleibende' elements of knowledge, those elements (especially in the natural sciences and even more in mathematics) of human knowledge which seem to be bound to no society in particular nor to any class.

First of all, we should emphasize that for us determination is an epistemological concept. By epistemological calling into existence we mean first that certain instances call other instances into existence and, second, that this process is perceived as such by a class, the proletariat, not as a simple reflection in thought of a real process but as the objectively determined view specific to that class (which, however, as we will see in chapter 4, has the possibility of gaining a correct knowledge of reality). Class determination of knowledge means that we do not know whether determination actually takes place in reality as the proletariat depicts it, since this class only knows reality through that facet of the prism corresponding to its collocation in the social structure. In a sense, therefore, the proletariat imposes its view of reality upon this latter so that determination is first of all an epistemological concept rather than an ontological one. This, however, calls for neither idealism nor absolute relativism since, from the point of view of the proletariat, its view does come from (is determined by) concrete reality and has inherent in itself the possibility of knowing reality correctly, as shown by verification. In short, the point of view of the proletariat is that each class secretes its own knowledge (class determined relativism of knowledge) and that within this view only the proletariat has the possibility of gaining a correct knowledge of *all* (and not only some) aspects of reality because of this class's position in the societal labour process (class determined supersession of knowledge's relativism).

We do not claim that the proletariat depicts real processes as they take place in reality (reflection). But we do claim that this class's view has the objectively determined possibility of being correct, to find a 'match' with the reality it depicts, not in spite of, but because of, its being class determined. It is in this sense that determination can be referred to as an epistemological calling into existence. And it is in this sense that our view differs from the 'reflection' theory and can be called non-reflective realism: knowledge is not determined simply by material transformation, but by this transformation immersed in specific social contexts, that is, by the real concrete.

1   DETERMINATION IN THE LAST INSTANCE AND REALIZED DETERMINATION

The concept of determination submitted above takes on a specific meaning when it is immersed in the context of the Marxist 'Weltanschauung'. Within this context, determination must account theoretically for the possibility for the determinant instance to call into existence both the conditions of its own existence (or reproduction) and the conditions of its own supersession. If this were not the case, there would be no theoretical foundation explaining the possibility for a system to generate from within itself its own decay and replacement by another, fundamentally different, system. On the other hand, determination must account theoretically also for a range of types of such conditions and, with each type (e.g. the state) it must account for a range of forms (e.g. the liberal or the fascist state, both conditions of reproduction of capitalist production) as well as for the way in which some of these types and forms are 'selected' for realization. To tackle these two orders of problems, I distinguish between determination in the last instance (DLI) and realized determination. In this context, the specific meaning attached to 'to be determined in the last instance' is to be one of the several real possible conditions of existence (or reproduction) or of supersession of the determinant instance. (8) On this view, DLI does not explain realized determination, the specific form taken by a certain type of a determined instance (and, as we shall see, also by the determinant instance, due to over-determination). (9) DLI creates only possibilities. Therefore, the inquiry into a relation of DLI is only a precondition for an inquiry into the mechanism of a certain determined instance's concretization. Moreover, DLI should not be equated with mediated determination. The link of DLI tying the determinant and the determined instances can be both a mediated and an immediate one and owes its connotation to the functionality the latter instance has for the former one.

Thus, the inquiry into the class basis of ideas is not the same as the one into the process and mechanism through which these ideas are produced and become social phenomena. To this end we need not only a general theory of realization but also specific theories of realization, including one concerning the production of ideas. For example, an analysis of the class nature (DLI) of Weber's theory shows that the birth of the value judgments vs. statement of facts problematic was a condition (of the ideological type) of reproduction

of the bourgeoisie not only because, as Sorg mentions, it was this
class's interest to restrict the field of inquiry to what 'is'
and to exclude what 'ought to be'; (10) not only because by
submitting that no scientific choice could be made among different
value judgments, the choice for socialism was reduced implicitly
to an individual and voluntaristic act so that no scientific
ground was left to the proletariat as a class for choosing
socialism; but also because of Weber's legitimation in terms of
'rationality' of what has been called elsewhere the 'private
bureaucracy', i.e. of that complex of agents, hierarchically
and bureaucratically organized, which performs, on behalf of the
real owner of capital, the control and surveillance of the collective
worker; which, in other words, through the expropriation of surplus
value makes possible its appropriation by the real owner of
capital. (11) Yet, this is not sufficient if we want to understand
the particular form taken by Weber's mental production and the
mechanism through which this individual production becomes a social
phenomenon.

   DLI and concrete realization are thus two complementary but
different phases of logical analysis. Only the first of them will
be examined in detail in this chapter. As far as realization is
concerned, we will stress here only the general elements of our
theory (leaving to chapters 3 and 4 the task of applying this theory
to the realization of knowledge) and we will thus provide a justification for the argument that the actual concretization of one form
of a certain determined instance is due to the reciprocal influence
of all instances of society, due to the inner essence of these
instances, i.e. due to class struggle. In a sense, therefore, it is
correct to stress the importance of class struggle for an understanding of history. (12) But we should beware of interpretations
stressing that to account for variations in the determined instance
(as seen in its concrete realizations) we only need to inquire into
the different historical circumstances. This type of view achieves
only a superficial unity between historical and logical analysis (13)
and hides a theoretical gulf it cannot bridge. Only when a theory
of DLI and one of realization are provided and fused into a coherent
logical whole, can this latter be seen in its necessary complementarity with a historical analysis. Logical analysis can then provide
the interpretative framework through the concept of complex
dialectical unity (see next section), without which historical
phenomena could not be related to each other. From this point of
view historical analysis is nothing other than a logical analysis
carried out through time. But the adjudication of the determinant,
dominant, determined, etc., role to the specific, concretized
instances is a matter of historical analysis. From this point of
view logical analysis is nothing more than the flattening of the
several instances into an a-historical, a-temporal dimension.
Exclusive focus on either of these two views is foreign to Marxism
as is the notion that the difference between logical and historical
analysis is that the former is static while the latter is dynamic,
due to the introduction of the 'time element'. The latter can be
dynamic only inasmuch as the former is dynamic. What follows is
thus also a precondition for an historical analysis, both in general
and in particular as far as knowledge is concerned. It is a necessary

step if we wish to escape both the individualistic/psychological and the structuralist explanation of knowledge formation, if we wish, in short, to retain a dialectical approach based on the class determination of knowledge.

2 DIALECTICAL DETERMINATION AND DIALECTICAL UNITIES: SIMPLE AND COMPLEX

In 'On Contradiction' Mao Tse-Tung examines some characteristics of the unity of opposites, of the 'law of contradiction in things' (1967, p. 313), thus capturing some essential aspects of Marxian dialectics. He stresses correctly that 'external causes are the *conditions* of change and internal causes the *basis* of change and that internal causes become operative through external causes' (p.314, emphasis added). However, Mao seems to think that the only difference between a simple process, i.e. a process of development of a simple thing, of a unity of two mutually exclusive opposites, and a complex process, i.e. one which contains more than one of these simple dialectical unities, is that the latter is just a multiplication of the former. This functions as a theoretical stumbling block in the development of a concept of complex dialectical unity which must encompass the analysis of the relation not only between the determinant and the determined instance (i.e. between the basis and the conditions of change) but also among the several determined instances. Consequently, no theorization is offered of the plurality of possible and realized forms of a certain determined instance and thus of this latter's relative autonomy. The concept of complex dialectical unity (determination) that we submit below is meant to overcome these shortcomings. Let us call A the determinant instance and B and C the determined ones. Then:

1 Determination in the last instance means that A calls B and C into existence as conditions of A's own existence or supersession among a range of real possible conditions of existence or of supersessions (i.e. of other equally possible B's and C's). We focus here on the functional relation between A, on the one side, and B and C on the other. (14)

2 Relative autonomy means that B and C are not simple reflections of A since they are concretizations of one among the several possible forms of B and C. We focus here on the possibility that more than one B or more than one C can be conditions of reproduction or of supersession of A.

3 Concrete or realized determination means that of all possible B's and C's only one (or some) will realize itself (themselves).

4 Overdetermination means that B and C as concrete determinations react upon and thus tend to modify (or to prevent the modification of) A.

5 Correspondence or contradiction between the determinant and the determined instances means that the latter can respectively foster or hinder the reproduction of the former. The reproduction of the determinant instance is hindered only in case of antagonistic contradiction (a point to be further elaborated in section 9).

6 Domination means that one instance (either A, B or C) plays the

fundamental role in the reproduction or supersession of the determinant one.

7 Unity in complex determination means a unity of determinant and determined instances tied by a relation as depicted in points 1 to 6 above. (15)

8 Dialectical process (simple or complex) refers to the process of development of a simple or complex unity. In a complex unity it will be certain determined instances which will regulate this process. These are the laws of its development, to be examined in the next chapter.

Let us consider now three points of clarification. First, the question of the levels of abstraction: the role assigned to an instance as determinant or determined depends upon the level of abstraction at which we carry out our research. The process of descending to more concrete levels of abstraction is one of considering more 'details' or, to put it better, of considering, instead of just the 'simplest determination', the 'rich totality of many determinations and relations'. (16) For Marx, the simplest determinations are not reached by abstracting the a-historical essence but, on the contrary, by focusing on the 'essential difference', (17) by condensing in them what is historically specific. It is in this sense that the simplest determinations are the outcome of the journey from the real concrete to the concrete in thought (whose phases are analysed in chapter 3). And it is because of this specific, historical, and condensed character that the simplest determinations are also those which encompass already in nuce all other contradictions. And this is also the reason why they can serve as the point of departure for the reverse journey, i.e. that they can be the starting point for an increasingly complex depiction of reality (of the real concrete) through the unfolding of more and more of the contradictions already implicit in them (i.e. in the fundamental contradictions). (18) Thus this method of inquiry explains reality in terms of contradictions instead of explaining these away as mistakes or anomalies. This is the basic difference between a model of social reality based upon an assumption of equilibrium and a dialectical model. By starting from equilibrium, all inherent contradictions are excluded a priori, so that disturbances in equilibrium conditions can only come from outside the system. (19) On the other hand, a dialectical model has the ability to account for more and more 'details' (determination and relations), and for its own dynamic, from within itself and not by a process of mechanical addition of elements. Since we must isolate the most important elements of the analysis, the simplest determinations (problem of the method of inquiry), and since we cannot say everything at once (problem of method of presentation), we use the levels of abstraction (mental constructions devised to draw a line between those elements which should and those which should not (yet) be considered at this stage of analysis or presentation) as a convenient device to facilitate the solution of these two orders of problems. There is no question of a 'progressive addition of superstructural variables'. (20) In our model of determination, and thus of society, the determined - e.g. super-structural - instances are not simply added, but are from the very beginning contained in the determinant instance as conditions of its

own existence or supersession. Simply, some instances are taken
into consideration at a later stage in order to facilitate analysis
and/or presentation.

Second, we consider the epistemological status of the model. This
model rests upon the assumption that reality can be known but that
this knowledge is historically, and thus class, determined. The
historical condensations referred to above are generally valid just
because they are historical condensations, (21) because they are the
categories through which classes will see reality and history. (22)
And this does not mean that different societies, or classes, will
illuminate different parts of the same reality (23) (a sort of
Popperian searchlight generated by a class-powered battery). Rather,
it means that different subjects (classes) will provide different
pictures of the same reality, (24) all of them pragmatically 'true'
because able to lead conscious action on the real concrete. Different
epochs, or different classes, will work out different categories.
If our account must be fully reflexive, what just stated must apply
also to Marxism, (25) the proletariat's interpretative scheme for all
reality and history. (26) It becomes thus understandable why Marxism,
the science of the direct and indirect producers, gives the determinant role to the economic, production (materialism), so that history
becomes the history of several modes of production. But this aspect
(historical materialism) is deeply bound up with the view that the
condition for knowledge is to consider reality (both social and
natural) as the development of the unity of opposites (27) (dialectical materialism), so that history is also the history of class
struggle. History becomes the history of the producers' class
struggle. Thus the working class rewrites history as the history of
class struggle and considers reality in its own image and likeness,
i.e. as a movement (no class trying to achieve a radical societal
change could consider reality as static, could produce a knowledge
based upon a static view of reality) of two poles which can exist
only because the other exists ('in a unity') and yet are in mortal
antagonism ('of opposites'), just as the struggle between the
proletariat and the bourgeoisie is a movement within a unity of
opposites. In short, Marxism is self-reflective not only concerning
its origin (Abentroth, 1972) but also, and especially, concerning the
social content of its interpretative scheme.

Third, the dynamization of the model. This model can be set in
motion, as it were, turned into a dynamic interpretation of social
reality by introducing history's dynamic force, class struggle. We
regard class struggle as the mode of existence (28) of contradictory
structures, i.e. of social relations, and consequently of their forms
too, in class divided societies. The theoretical advantage of this
procedure is that we can find in the concept of class struggle the
logical tie between structures and agents. In fact, society is a
totality of mutually interacting structures which, however, could
not obviously exist, first, if people would not exist and become
carriers of those structures (agents), and, second, could not
obviously interact if people (agents) would not interact. As far as
contradictory structures are concerned, this interaction takes the
form of struggle, competition. Take the capitalist production
relations, for example. They are contradictory, a contradictory

structure, because they are, to begin with, a relation of ownership/
non-ownership. This structure cannot exist without the agents,
carriers of aspects of contradictory relations, without the owners
and the non-owners of the means of production, just as its
contradictory nature cannot exist but through the struggle between
these two types of agents, carriers of the contradictory aspects of
those relations (structure). Class struggle thus becomes part and
parcel of any social phenomenon.

3 PROLEGOMENA TO THEORIES OF REALIZATION

As already mentioned, we will consider here only the general
elements of a theory of realization. The analysis of the specific
mechanisms through which class determined forms of knowledge realize
themselves will be carried out in chapters 3 and 4. What we need to
account for theoretically is, *first*, the possibility for a structure
to determine the condition of its own supersession; *second*, the
possibility for a certain determined instance to take a variety of
forms; and, *third*, the principle through which some of these
possible forms realize themselves. Let us tackle the first point
through a discussion of an illustration already used in the previous
section: the ownership element of the capitalist production
relations. The owner is the carrier of the 'principal' aspect of
this relation because he is the carrier of that aspect which
characterizes 'the nature of things', (29) the nature of the
relation. The structure will tend to reproduce itself first of all
through the reproduction of its principal, determinant, aspect.
But this reproduction can take place only through the production
(determination) of the principal aspect's condition of existence,
i.e. to begin with, the secondary (determined) aspect, the non-
ownership of the means of production. In turn, this simple
dialectical unity can reproduce itself only by determining other
dialectical unities both on the economic level (e.g. the exploiter/
exploited relation) and on other levels (e.g. political and
ideological relations). Now, since structures exist only through
agents, it will be the task of the carrier of the principal aspect
of the ownership relation to create the conditions of reproduction
of this relation on the several levels. And, since the mode of
existence of this contradictory structure is class struggle, the
owner (as a class) will create these conditions through class
struggle with the non-owner (also a class), so that these conditions
materialize themselves as types and forms of class struggle (social
phenomena). But since class struggle is struggle for domination on
all levels, it is by creating the conditions of his domination upon
the non-owner that the owner creates also the conditions of
reproduction of the structure. (30) Moreover, the owner is not
only the carrier, the personification of an aspect of a social
relation, he is also a person, so that the realization of those
objective structural needs, i.e. of the conditions of reproduction
of the relation and thus of domination over the non-owner, will be
perceived by the owner as his own interest.
    Now the secondary aspect is the other pole of the antagonistic
relation and is thus antagonistic to the principal aspect and thus

to the relation as a whole. This means that this aspect is antagonistic to itself as an aspect of that relation. This aspect too will come to life through an agent, the non-owner. For him too class struggle will be his mode of existence and he too will aim at domination over the owner on all levels. But, because of the nature of the secondary aspect, the non-owner's fight to create the conditions of his domination will not be the fight to creat his conditions of existence as non-owner, since this would perpetuate one pole of the relation and thus the relation as a whole; since, in other words, he would fight for something to which he is antagonistic. The proletariat's structurally determined fight for domination will have to be directed towards the supersession of the relation, i.e. towards the replacement of that and other relations by a different set of relations. Thus struggle for domination will now be struggle for the introduction of new social relations, for the supersession of the system. Again, the creation of these conditions of domination, of supersession of the system, will be perceived by the non-owner as his own interest. (31) Therefore, to sum up, given a contradictory structure and agents (classes) carrying the contradictory aspects of that structure, it is by creating the conditions of their own domination upon other classes that classes create also the conditions of reproduction of or supersession of that structure. The realization of these conditions will be perceived by those agents as their own interests, for interests are the way in which the aspects of a relation motivate the agents to create those aspects' conditions of reproduction or of supersession and thus the conditions of those agents' domination. In short, interests are the personified expression of the structurally determined conditions of existence or of supersession of the structure. (32) It is in this sense that the Third Thesis on Feuerbach should be read: 'The coincidence of the changing of circumstances and of human activity can be conceived and rationally understood only as a revolutionary practice' (Marx and Engels, 1969, p.14). The conditions for the proletariat's domination (revolutionary practice) become thus the conditions for the supersession of those relations and thus of the proletariat itself. This is the profound meaning of the Third Thesis. Marx's dialectical genius allows us to escape the false dilemma between economicism and voluntarism. But this understanding is conditional upon the realization that the same structure, by tying together two antagonistic aspects, and thus two radically opposed forces, can express the conditions both of its supersession and of its reproduction.

Two important conclusions follow from our discussion of this first point. First, since structures create the conditions of their own existence or supersession through the struggle of the agents pursuing their own interests, we do not need to make any a-historical, anthropological assumptions about the reasons why, for example, carriers of certain social (production) relations resist the introduction of new ones (e.g. small peasants resisting the introduction of capitalist production relations). The reason resides not in any a-historical human nature. Simply, these carriers will perceive this resistance as their interest because the new production relations are the condition for the supersession of the relation which those

agents carry. Second, since the agents perceive as their interest
the creation of the conditions of existence or supersession of the
structure as determined by the structure itself, the Weberian
dichotomy between value judgments and statements of facts (33) is
shown to be false in one stroke. Science can and should help in
the choice of ends, i.e. in the clarification of class interests.
(34)

We now come to the second point mentioned above: the plurality
of forms taken by a certain determined instance. This presupposes,
on the one hand, a plurality of possible forms which can be taken
by a certain (type of a) determined instance and, on the other,
this latter's relative autonomy in the 'choice' of one or more of
these forms. Now, these possibilities are not a priori existing
ideas, already formed and waiting to be chosen by some mysterious
hand for realization on earth. Rather, they are contained in nuce
in the determinant instance, they are formless potentials contained
in the elements (aspects) of this latter instance (relation). This
latter, in order to reproduce itself, generates constantly new forms
of the determined instance. That some forms realize themselves does
not mean that other forms could not have come to life under different
circumstances, but this in turn does not mean that those unrealized
possibilities keep on wandering in the world of ideas waiting to be
chosen much the same as some books, and not others, are picked from
a bookshelf. These possibilities are not (in a structuralist
fashion) different combinations of the same, already existing,
somewhat pre-social, elements either. They can be truly new social
forms and yet contained in the determinant instance in the sense that
they are conditions of reproduction or of supersession of that
instance because they are conditions of domination of the antagonistic elements making up that instance. These possibilities are
inscribed in the actual composition, structure, nature of the
determinant instance, i.e. are real possibilities. It is in this
sense that 'reality contains alongside the existents, coexisting
in time, the world of potentials as well. Practice, in the first
instance, does nothing but alter the boundaries between things which
are already with us in existence or potential'. (35) For example,
there is a variety of ideologies, from racism to reformism
$(I_1 \ldots I_m)$, which can help the reproduction of capitalist production
relations. There are other types of ideologies, from co-operation
among economic units to distribution according to needs $(I_n \ldots I_z)$,
which are in antagonistic contradiction with those relations and yet
are an expression of them. But there are other types of ideologies,
from a theocratical political ideology to an ideology of decision-
making based upon witchcraft $(I_\alpha \ldots I_\beta)$, which are not inscribed in
capitalist production relations because they are not an expression
of (the interests of) any of the aspects of those relations (classes),
since they are not conditions of domination of any of the classes
structurally contained within the determined instance. These latter
are not real possibilities. The existence of the two ranges of
possibilities $I_1 \ldots I_m$ and $I_n \ldots I_z$ indicates the *autonomy* of the
determined instance, while the impossibility of the $I_\alpha \ldots I_\beta$ range
indicates the relative aspect of that autonomy. It is in this sense
that the determinant instance sets the limits of the determined

instance's variation and not in the structuralist - both Marxist and not - sense that the former determines only a range of possible conditions of existence.

It is now clear, from what has been said above, that only as an artificial didactical device can we separate the discussion of the plurality of possible forms which can be taken by the determined instance from the issue of their realization. This, our third and last point, implies also a discussion of the concept of over-determination. To begin with, let us again consider relative autonomy. To accept such a feature in our model of dialectical determination implies at the same time the acceptance also of both a reciprocal interaction of all the determined instances and of these latter's overdetermination upon the determinant one. The former because the determined instances, as conditions of domination, must interact with (attempt to dominate) each other. The latter because this interaction and reciprocal modification modifies the conditions of reproduction or supersession of the determinant instance and thus that instance itself in its form and/or nature. (36) Overdetermination, however, is not simple reaction upon the determinant instance, it is differential and mediated. It is differential because the determined instance is not a simple reflection of the whole (this could be the case if the determinant instance was an undifferentiated, unstructured, and non-contradictory whole) but, by being an expression of basically an aspect of the (contradictorily articulated) determinant instance, (37) reacts upon that instance by reacting differently upon the different, contradictory parts (aspects) of the determinant whole. But this impact is also mediated. In fact, each determined instance, e.g. B, by interacting and modifying other determined instances, e.g. C, affects the element of the determinant instance expressing C through C's modification, i.e. in a mediated way. Overdetermination is thus differential and mediated impact upon the different structural elements of the determinant instance. This amounts to saying that each determined instance realizes itself, takes on a specific form thus leaving the realm of formless potentials, in the process of being modified by, and modifying, all other determined instances and, through their overdetermination, the determinant instance as well. Thus, not only the concrete form taken by the determined instances but also the concrete form taken by the determinant one will be the result of this complex interrelation. This has nothing in common with simple mutual interaction. (38) Rather, this interaction is the determination in the last instance of certain realized determined instances which, in the process of this realization, take concrete form and also give concrete form to their own determinant instance.

To conclude, we can now mention briefly some of the advantages of our approach. First, it allows us to escape both determinism and reciprocal interactionism. Or, in other words, since the determinant instance is present in different ways in each of the determined instances already in the very act of their realization, there is no incompatibility between DLI and concrete realization through mutual interaction: on the contrary, the former realizes itself through the latter. (39) Second, through our approach it becomes possible to account for the uniqueness of particular, individual concretizations within the frame of DLI by the economic.

More specifically, the concept of the capitalist mode of production
is a necessary precondition for the analysis of concrete cases of
specific, individual determined instances. But this is possible
because already at this level, where a concrete capitalist society
is divested of its concrete, specific features so that only its
capitalist essence is considered, we have created the theoretical
possibility for a plurality of forms of the determined instances.
Third, the functional element (functional relationship) is not
rejected but superseded, integrated within a dialectical framework.
Fourth, we can theorize both the DLI of the several determined
instances by the same determinant one and the different forms taken
by this latter. (40) These different forms were not the necessary
starting point for a logical explanation of the different types and
forms of the determined instances, as would be the case for strict,
non-dialectical, economicist determination. Fifth, relative autonomy
is explained completely in terms of the model and no recourse to
exogenous, extra-social, or 'empirical' factors (41) is needed. For
example, we will not have to postulate an internal core in science –
not subject to external, social factors – to explain the relative
autonomy of scientific development. Sixth, the emphasis placed on
class struggle as the principle accounting for the concrete realization of social phenomena stresses the social scientist's participation in the class struggle as an element of the formation of the
phenomena he/she studies. This, together with the principle,
mentioned above, according to which only those who deal with reality
can know it, accounts for the fact that 'one can "foresee" to the
extent that one acts'. (42) Finally, as a consequence of the above-
mentioned points, there is no a priori inescapable necessity for any
one form of a determined instance in spite of its DLI. (43)

4   THE TRANS-EPOCHAL ELEMENTS OF KNOWLEDGE

Any theory of the class determination of knowledge must reckon with
those elements of knowledge which seem to be common to more than one
epoch or class. Marx is aware of this. 'The difficulty', he says,
for example in the *Grundrisse*, 'lies not in the understanding that
the Greek arts and epic are bound up with certain forms of social
development. The difficulty is that they still afford us artistic
pleasure' (1973, p.111). However, the explanation he offers, that
'the charm of their art for us ... is inextricably bound up ... with
the fact that the unripe social conditions under which it arises ...
can never return', is clearly inadequate and reveals a theoretical
gap. But there is in Marx's work no concession to the neutrality
of knowledge thesis. Engels's position is different. He concedes
that a part of the natural sciences, those 'concerned with inanimate
Nature' (1970, p.97) can achieve absolute knowledge, even though
this knowledge may remain incomplete for 'long successions of
generations and be completed only step by step'. For Engels, it is
only the discovery of this knowledge which is socially determined
(44) and not its content and significance, which will remain
immutable and valid under any social system. (45) Quite different,
however, is Engels's (1970, pp.344-5) and Marx's (1973, p.110)
approach as to why religion continues to survive in social systems

which have not determined it. In short, their answer is that religion is a condition of reproduction of all societies in which men are subject to forces, either natural or social, which they do not understand and thus cannot control: thus they take refuge in false, imaginary explanations. (46) Now, the hypothesis that we would like to submit is simply a generalization of Marx's and Engels's argument: there are elements of knowledge which are common to more than one society (or, within one society, to more than one class) because they can be conditions of reproduction or of supersession of more than one society, i.e. because they can be conditions of domination of more than one class. (47) In this sense, these trans-epochal elements of knowledge are class determined as far as their origin is concerned. (48) However, the fact that they survive from one system to another does not mean that they remain the same, i.e. that their nature has become neutral. A new development in science, due to a change in the productive forces, in turn determined by a change in the social (and, to begin with, in the production) relations, emerges neither from the simple and total negation of the previous body of knowledge, (49) nor simply from its different application, but from its supersession. A new body of knowledge will develop and certain elements of knowledge, the trans-epochal ones, will be retained, while others will not. However, those elements which will be retained will be placed in a different system of knowledge and will acquire a different significance. In this sense the trans-epochal elements of knowledge are class determined also as far as their social nature (and not only as far as their origin) is concerned because they will acquire a different meaning and significance due to immersion in a different context. (50)

We said that a new body of knowledge develops through the supersession of the old one. More specifically, if we apply the scheme of determination submitted above, we can advance the thesis that at each historical point in time there is a range of real possible developments of knowledge and that the realization of one or more of them depends upon the class struggle in all its types and forms. (51) By real possible developments we mean those which are all equally possible outcomes of the development of the existing body of knowledge and which are all conditions of reproduction or supersession of the complex capitalist economic structure. Through this approach we overcome the sterile contraposition between an internalist and an externalist approach. This contraposition would not be avoided if we adopted an internalist perspective as far as the possible developments of science are concerned and an externalist view concerning the choice of one or more of them. Scientific development would then become the combined effect on the one hand of science's internal dynamic, which is due to its internal contradictions and which finds expression in the plurality of possible theoretical outcomes, and on the other hand of the external (to science) contradictions which, in the form of class struggle, determine the choice among several possibilities. This would not be supersession of the idealist content of the internalist view nor of the mechanist view (which can take the form either of economicism or of sociologism) implied in the externalist view. Supersession cannot be a splitting of the problem into two sub-problems and an

application of the internalist criteria to the former and of
externalist criteria to the latter. Supersession means complete
transfiguration of the previous elements in an organically new
approach. For us, thus, the plurality of possibilities in the
development of science is a plurality of possible expressions of
the determinant instance's contradictory nature, it is a plurality
of possible conditions of existence or supersession of the determinant instance (the economic) even though all of them are possible
developments of science, it is a plurality of possible forms of
class domination on the ideological level. On the other hand, the
'choice' of one of these possibilities is due to the interrelationship of all social phenomena and thus also to the existing state of
scientific knowledge, i.e. also to 'internal' factors. While the
need to orient the development of science in one rather than another
direction obviously must be perceived and formulated somehow by the
scientists, it is social classes which in fact determine the direction
of development according to needs of which the scientists can be
unconscious or have a partial and distorted view.

The important question therefore becomes the overdetermining
effect of the trans-epochal (or trans-class) elements. Their changed
significance allows these elements to be functional for the reproduction of the new system. To return to religion, when it takes a
specific form, Calvinism, it becomes functional for the reproduction
of a class and of a social system, capitalism, or, to quote Engels,
it becomes the 'creed ... fit for the boldest of the bourgeoisie'
(52). Even the most obvious and indispensable elements of knowledge,
the so-called 'facts', are after all not so obvious and indisputable
since they can never be perceived outside of a theoretical frame
which provides meaningfulness to that perception. An apple, when
dropped, falls to the ground irrespective of the social system under
which this 'fact' takes place. Yet, doesn't this 'indisputable
fact' acquire a completely different significance according to
whether it is placed within a Newtonian or an Einsteinian framework?
(53)

The analysis of the determination of knowledge encompasses thus
both its being determined and its being an overdetermining factor.
The really crucial question becomes, therefore, whether there
exists a univocal relation between these two aspects of the determination of knowledge; whether a science which has been developed
within a certain social system and is functional for its reproduction
can have the same function for another system; in short, whether
capitalist science and technology can be used under socialism.
If we answer in the affirmative, the question of the social determination of knowledge becomes a purely academic one. Why should we
bother to inquire into the social (class) origin and content of
something if it can be used irrespectively of its origin and
content? The inquiry into the social (class) determination of
knowledge acquires relevance only in relation to its overdetermining
role. Our thesis is that each new mode of production determines a
new type of knowledge, both natural and social; that there are
elements of knowledge which lend themselves to function as conditions
of reproduction of different social systems (classes); that these
elements are those which are (or can be given a significance) in
correspondence or non-antagonistic contradiction with certain

features common to those systems; that these elements, however, will change significance when incorporated in a different body of knowledge; and that it is precisely through this change in significance that these elements can fulfil their trans-epochal function. This thesis will be illustrated in the following sections. Sections 5 and 6 consider the changes in significance undergone by trans-epochal elements of knowledge due to the advant of capitalism and how these elements only apparently remain the same and in fact become functional for the existence of the capitalist system and class because of this changed significance. Section 7 will consider the consequences for socialist theory (and thus practice) when the above criticized concept of the neutrality of knowledge (itself class determined) is accepted, by discussing in particular Lenin's and Gramsci's belief in the possibility of using the 'rationality' of the capitalist organization of labour for the construction of a socialist system. Section 8 will identify that element which lends its particularly capitalist character to the knowledge (both social and natural) developed under capitalism. Finally, section 9 will discuss the nature of antagonistic and non-antagonistic contradictions, a fundamental element in our discussion of the relation between social relations and knowledge.

5   AN EXAMPLE: IS THE CONCEPT OF 'ONE' DETERMINED BY CAPITALISM? (54)

In this section we will consider a trans-epochal concept, that of the number one, which seems to be a most obvious example of the neutrality, social boundlessness, of the natural sciences. Is 'one' not a number, and is not the number one the same under any social system? Our stratagy will be that of showing that, first, the interpretation of the nature of 'one' changed radically around the sixteenth century and, second, that this change is determined by the rise and development of capitalism. Consequently, we can show that only apparently do we have the same element of knowledge and that this change is a condition of existence and reproduction of the capitalist system and class.

Today, the notion that one is a number just as any other number seems to us to be quite natural. The reasoning we might adduce to prove this could be the following: since one is part of a number and since the part must have the same nature as the whole, one must be a number. This is, in fact, the line of reasoning following by the sixteenth century Dutch mathematician Simon Stevin. However, before that time and since the early Greek mathematics, 'one' was not a number. The ancient Greeks' reasoning was that since one generates both odd and even numbers, it must have elements of both, it must thus stand above the odd-even dichotomy, and cannot thus be a number. For the Greeks, it was quite natural that 'one' was not a number. As D. Bloor correctly remarks, both lines of reasoning are coherent and correct and no amount of explicit argument could show either one to be mistaken. The reason for the belief in the correctness of either of these two interpretations must thus be rooted in social factors. For the ancient Greeks numbers were always a number of (arithmos)

something, they always referred to collections of entities. As
J. Klein says, 'When Plato speaks of numbers which have "visible
and tangible bodies", this expression must be taken quite literally....
Just as there exists no triangle which is neither equilateral nor
scalene so there can be no decade which is not this or that ten
definite things.' (55) And, as Bloor remarks, the ancient Greeks'
knowledge of numbers was 'built up by observing objects when they
are subject to simple ordering and sorting operations'. (56) This
led to the development of a type of mathematical knowledge totally
different from ours. For example, since numbers were always numbers
of things, they could always be represented as numbers of dots,
which in turn can be arranged in triangular, square, oblong, etc.,
shapes. The Greeks then developed the notion of triangular, square,
etc., numbers (an absurd concept for us) and, on the investigation
of their properties and shapes, developed concepts such as the
'gnomon', an 'appropriately shaped number which, when added to one
of the above [mentioned] shapes, did not alter the general configuration' (p.106). Since numbers were always numbers of discrete
things, in this kind of mathematics numbers were basically used to
count and theoretical problems solved in order to find specific
solutions, definite numerical values, by following specific methods
for specific problems. These are the characteristics of the chief
work of Diophantus, for whom 'the algebraic processes are not used
with the same generality as we would use them. They are always
subordinated to numerical problems' (p.180). The unknown solution
is indicated by S, but S is not a variable, it is a specific unknown
number. In the words of Klein, 'the unknown [is] to be understood
as an "indeterminate multitude" only from the point of view of the
completed solution, namely as "provisionally indeterminate", and
as a number which is about to be exactly determined in its
multitude.' (57)

Why were then numbers used principally to count and classify
things and why, therefore, could 'one' not be a number? Because
this was the Greeks' way of symbolizing, and thus gaining knowledge
of, nature and society. Let us quote Klein again extensively.

The general point of view governing the efforts of the
Pythagoreans might be sketched out as follows: They saw the
true grounds of the things in this world in their *countableness*,
inasmuch as the condition of being a 'world' is primarily
determined by the presence of an *'ordered arrangement'* – and
this means a well-ordered arrangement.... [It is this] order
[which] determines the *very being* of things, and furthermore,
this orders rests in the final analysis on the possibility of
distinguishing things, i.e. of *counting* them. [Therefore] the
arithmetical properties of things concern their *being itself*....
Here the sequence of numbers represents not a linear chain whose
links are all 'of the same kind' but an 'ordering' in the sense
that each number precedes or follows in the order *of its being*,
i.e. is related as prior or posterior. Thus the science of the
Pythagoreans is an *ontology of the cosmos* [58] [and] ... whatever
special motives may have led to such a conception ... the basis
of its possibility is the 'natural' conception of the arithmos.
(59)

For the ancient Greeks, thus, any idea of number in general is just

impossible. The order and hierarchy of mathematics 'captured for
them both the unity of the cosmos and man's aspirations and role
in it.... The classification of numbers resonated with the classification of daily thought and life. Contemplation of the former was
a means of grasping in thought the true meaning of the latter. (60)

Underlying the notion of one as not being a number there is thus
the discontinuous nature of the act of counting, itself an integral
part of the ontological science of the ancient Greeks. This notion
lasted until the sixteenth century when it was challenged by
S. Stevin, among others. Stevin's underlying assumption of the
homogeneity of the part and the whole was becoming taken for granted,
'natural'. Numbers are now likened to a line. The (modern) concept
of variable, of something which can take a range of values and thus
can be represented as a line and not any longer simply as a dot, is
introduced. Since numbers are now seen as something continuous, the
part must have the same nature as the whole, one must be a number.
But why were this new concept of one and this new analogy (with a
line) introduced? Because numbers were now used not any longer
basically to count but also to measure, and the act of measuring
is a continuous one. Bloor makes this point very cogently.

> Stevin was an engineer. The major mathematical practitioners
> of the time all had preoccupations which were technological or
> applied. Their practical bias led them to use numbers not
> merely to count but also to measure.... Numbers came to perform
> a new function by indicating the properties of moving, active
> processes of change. For example, number and measurement become
> central to an intellectual grasp of ballistic, navigation and
> the use of machinery. (61)

Concerning Vieta's mathematical investigations (and the same holds
for Kepler, Descartes, Barrow, Newton, etc.), Klein shows that they
were closely connected with his cosmological and astronomical
interests.

> The *Canon mathematicus* ... gives, among other things, the
> *computational methods* used in the construction of the canon, and
> teaches in particular, the computation of plane and spherical
> triangles with the aid of the *general* trigonometric relations
> which exist between the different determining components of such
> triangles. (62)

The search for computational methods (in which modern mathematics,
unlike the ancient Greeks, is interested), for general relations,
for formulae, is only possible on the basis of a concept of number
separated from the things, the unit, whose number it happens to be.
It is on the basis of this (socially determined) separation that the
unit, one, becomes a number and that the number becomes a number in
general so that the letter (or symbol) which designates it refers
now to its general character of being a number. 'As soon as
"general number" is conceived and represented in the medium of
species as an "object" in itself, that is, symbolically, the modern
concept of "number" is born.' (63)

To sum up, the new concept of number, and thus of one, is clearly
related to the development of symbolic algebra which in turn is
related to the development of sixteenth-century technology. Now,
it is Hessen's merit to have shown, in his classical study of
Newton's 'Principia', that both the new technological needs and

the non-teleological view of science (and thus, we can add, the modern concept of number and of 'one') were functional for (determined by) the rise and development of capitalism. (64) Hessen shows very clearly how Newton's work addressed itself to solving those technical problems whose solution was a necessary condition for the development of manufacture and merchant capital, and that the solution of those problems (Hessen analyses the three areas of communication, industry, and war) required a new type of science, a science based on the knowledge of causes, i.e. a science able to reproduce phenomena experimentally and thus industrially. Moreover, since most of these problems were of a mechanical nature, the image used by Newtonian science was that of our planetary system as a huge mechanism. Often, the basic features of the determinant instance impress themselves on the determined one (in this case the new natural sciences) translated, as it were, in the language of the latter, i.e. in this case as mechanicism. (65) But, as Hessen stresses, the interpretative scheme in the 'Principia' is both mechanicist and religious and these two aspects are inseparable: a mechanism can be set in motion only by external forces, i.e. by God. Newton embodies the philosophical view of the English bourgeoisie of his time which waged ideological class struggle in the form of religion. The social effects of Newton's theory consist thus in reinforcing the capitalist production relations not only on the economic level, because it fostered a tremendous growth in the capitalist productive forces, but also on the ideological level because - aside from the legitimation of those relations through the growth of these forces - belief in the existence of God, a belief which is condition of class domination also under capitalism, (66) seemed now to be grounded in the most advanced form of science.

This illustration allows us to glimpse at the complexity of the social factors which determined a change in the notion of 'one' and the functionality of this changed notion for the rise and development of capitalism. Against this background, we can now conclude this section by commenting briefly on the status of the correct solutions in the natural sciences, i.e. on their social determination. Our thesis is that, given a certain problematic, and thus a standard of correctness, a solution to a problem posed within that problematic will be either correct or not. However, given that that problematic is socially class,determined, it will be social factors which, in the last analysis, will impose a certain solution as the correct one. The practical value of a solution, and more generally of knowledge, is therefore meaningful only within a certain social context, i.e. is significant only within the social nature of that solution. Moreover, even when a solution seems to have acquired the status of a trans-epochal element of knowledge, as, for example, in the case of mathematical proofs, its significance will vary according to the body of knowledge into which it will be integrated. Let us mention briefly two examples to illustrate our case: (1) that in case of conflicting alternative problematics the choice of 'the' correct solution will be dependent upon social factors, and (2) that, when a solution to a problem posed and solved within a certain problematic is transplanted within another problematic, the interpretation of that solution will change thus changing the nature of the solution itself. To begin with this

latter, we refer again to Bloor and more specifically to his
discussion of the square root of two. Aristotle's proof that
this root is not a rational number holds today just as when it was
first produced. Yet, for us square root of two is an irrational
number, for the Greeks it was no number at all. Actually, Aristotle
did not proove that root of two is an irrational number nor that it
is no number. What Aristotle proved 'depends on the background
assumptions about number within which the calculation is viewed.
If number basically means counting number, a collection or pattern
of dots, then the calculation will mean something quite different
than if number has been intuitively blended with the image of the
continuous line' (1976, p. 109).

To illustrate the former point, concerning the social nature of
the choice of the correct solution, we will refer to the building of
the cathedral of Milan, which started in 1386. The cathedral,
envisaged within an 'architectural campaign called for building on a
scale calculated to rival the largest Gothic cathedrals of Western
Europe' (67) had, however, to be built not in the Gothic style,
whose cross-section was 'ad quadratum', but in the Lombard Gothic
style and thus with a triangular cross-section. This presented
new theoretical problems, not originated by architectural science's
inner dynamics but by social factors. One of these problems, for
example, was that, since the width and the height of an equilateral
triangle are incommensurable, the architects could not determine
beforehand the height of the main cross-section. (68) The foreign
experts regularly hired (and regularly dismissed) to solve these
problems 'simply draw upon their experience and on Gothic
tradition ... without consideration or understanding of the peculiar
structural requirements of the Cathedral'. (69) For those, who
carried the architectural knowledge of the time, i.e. the Platonic
one, the Dome was destined to certain ruin. For them, the Milanese
masons' construction was based only on technique (ars) but not on
scientific knowledge, i.e. their scientific knowledge (scientia).
As they put it, 'ars sine scientia nihil est'. From the point of
view of the knowledge of their time they were right. They could
have built a perfectly sound cathedral. Yet, 'the Milanese plod
stubbornly along'. (70) For these latter 'scientia sine ars nihil
est'. The fact that the cathedral still stands proves that their
solution was correct, at least as correct as that of the foreign
experts. As Ackerman shows, the choice of the Milanese masons'
solution was not due to their superior theory. This choice, as well
as the origin of the problem, was a socially determined one. (71)

6 ANOTHER EXAMPLE: IS BELIEF IN GOD DETERMINED BY CAPITALISM?

It is customary for the social sciences to develop views of society
(or parts of it) based on interpretative schemes in which natural
sciences' models are more or less surreptitiously imitated. (72)
The view criticized above which considers science as an accretion
of elements which are neutral in terms of their social content
and/or origin, is no exception to this rule in the sense that it
too has migrated to the social sciences. To take only one recent
examples: E. Laclau's proposition that 'ideological "elements"

taken in isolation have no necessary class connotation and ... this
connotation is only the result of the articulation of those elements
in a concrete ideological discourse' (1977, p.99). Belief in God,
for example, can then be an ideological element common to both
feudal and capitalist ideologies and has intrinsically no class
connotation. Of course, if one reaches this abstraction by
eliminating rather than accentuating the historical and class
specific nature of this phenomenon and if, even at this level, one
does not consider this phenomenon's functionality for class domination
in class divided societies, (73) then one must conclude that belief
in God is not class determined. Further, for Laclau, while the
elements have no class nature, the ideology does because of the class
nature of the 'articulating principle'. But, aside from the problems
posed by the implicit structuralist matrix (revolving around the
concept of different combinations or articulations of the same
elements), (74) either any element can fit into an ideology, but
then one has to explain where the class nature of the articulating
principle comes from, or certain elements (e.g. anti-semitism)
cannot fit into certain ideologies and then one has, in fact,
returned to the social nature content of those elements.

The problem posed by the trans-epochal elements in ideologies
(more generally, in the conceptions of the social world) is the
same as that in the natural sciences (or conceptions of the natural
world). Let us take, for example, belief in God, an element common
to both the Middle Ages and the Renaissance. Following Engels, we
can submit that in both cases this belief is functional for the
domination of one class over another (or more classes). In other
words, in both cases this element has the function of hiding the
real (oppressive) nature of society (of both types of society),
i.e. it corresponds to the fact that people have not yet gained an
understanding of the oppressive nature of their social systems.
But this is not enough. Our approach should allow us to detect
changes in the significance of this ideological element and to
relate these changes to radical modifications in the economic
structure. And, in fact, the scholastic belief in God, the belief
in a Creator of Nature, is not the same as the pantheistic belief
in the essential identify of God and Nature in the Renaissance.
When Nikolaus von Kues introduces, through his pantheism, the
principles of the material unity of the world, stresses the point
of view of the totality (i.e. it is the whole that determines the
knowledge of its parts), and ascribes to it a contradictory
existence (since everything, for him, consists of different parts
of different nature in which one dominates the other); and when
Pico della Mirandola stresses that it is the contradictory nature
of the world which explains its movement; then two of the conditions
of ideological domination of the emerging bourgeoisie, the
materiality of the world and its movement are expressed and they
take the form, due to the complex interrelation of all factors at
that time, of a religious doctrine. However, the dialectical
elements, i.e. the concept of the contradictory nature of the real
concrete and of the movement generated by these contradictions, and
pantheism, as we will see in a moment, are no such conditions and
will be discarded by this ascending class. Thus, 'belief in God'
is a condition of class domination in both social formations, but

it is not the same belief in God. Not only do we have in one case
a creationist and in the other a pantheistic notion of God, we
have here the introduction in the religious ideology of the Middle
Ages of the concepts of the materiality and movement of the world
and therefore a change in the notion of God. We have here an
ideological penetration of the emerging bourgeoisie into the
religious ideology of the Middle Ages (and not a simple addition of
new elements), a penetration which changes the class nature of that
ideology. If we focus on the fact that both the scholasticism of
the Middle Ages and the pantheism of the Renaissance believed in
God, we miss not only the historical specificity of this ideological
element but also the changed class nature of the ideology of which
this element is a part.

On the dialectical element of the new ideology one should take
distance from the 'official' Marxist interpretation as well,
according to which the objective dialectics of the social processes
could not be seen in the early stages of capitalist development
because this latter's internal contradictions were not yet fully
developed so that thought could not become conscious of them. In a
similar way, the objective dialectics in the natural world could
not be conceived of because of the low theoretical level and limited
collection of facts in the seventeenth and eighteenth centuries.
We recognize here not only Engels's dialectics of nature, (75)
from which we take distance, but also its continuist, evolutionist,
and teleological degradation. We must shift to social, class
determination of knowledge and stress that in the early stages of
capitalism (the Renaissance) it was the emerging bourgeoisie which
tended to create dialectical ideas but in a form (religious) which
was unsuitable for the proletariat. The belief in God is a
condition for the domination of the bourgeoisie over the proletariat,
i.e. of the existence of capitalism, and cannot be the condition of
the opposite domination. The proletariat was not yet developed in
its real subordination to capital (i.e. it was not yet fully a class
in itself) and could not express its own knowledge (dialectics) as
a condition of its own domination over the bourgeoisie. It is not
true that the stage of empirical research in the seventeenth and
eighteenth centuries was indispensable for the development of
dialectics in the natural sciences. Rather, both empirical metaphysics and Marxist dialectics are structural conditions of class
domination and the fact that dialectics did not fully develop
(even the metaphysical philosophical systems of Descartes, Spinoza,
and Leibnitz contain important dialectical features) until the
nineteenth century is due not to the inevitable historical necessity
of a previous metaphysical empirical stage but to the impossibility
of a not yet fully developed proletariat developing its conditions
of ideological domination. Dialectics is not the spontaneous
supersession of empirical metaphysics due to the development of
natural sciences. Rather, it is the theoretical elaboration of,
first, the ascending bourgeoisie and then, when this class has
established itself and thus lost interest in a view based on the
transiency and internal contradictions of all phenomena, of the
proletariat, but then no longer in combination with pantheism (or
any other form of religion, for that matter).

Let us dwell on this point a little longer. The natural philoso-

phers of the Renaissance (Francesco Patrizzi, Giordano Bruno,
Tommaso Campanella) created a dialectical view of the world within
a pantheistic frame. The new natural sciences, however, whose
capitalist determination can be seen from their tendency towards
the experimental-mathematical method, came into contradiction with
the pantheistic element of natural philosophy, which did not foster
the study of the parts. Moreover, the natural sciences and
philosophy of the seventeenth century rejected not only pantheism
but also the dialectics which went with it. They took the way of
metaphysical materialism not because dialectics had to liberate
itself from pantheism before it could become scientific, because,
that is, a period of careful inquiry into the details of the concrete
laws of existence and development of nature, of society, and of
thought was needed, (76) but because neither pantheism nor dialectics
were functional for bourgeois production and ideological domination.
In other words, there was a qualitative disagreement between the
emerging capitalist sciences and dialectics because there was a
qualitative disagreement between dialectics and the bourgeoisie,
since the former could not be used, in those circumstances, by the
latter; could not be transformed into a condition of the latter's
domination over the other classes. On the other hand, according to
the official interpretation, the dialectics present in the works of
the Renaissance, had to be discarded because it could not keep up
with the methodological demands posed by the developing natural and
social sciences. More specifically, according to this interpreation,
dialectics was first developed during the Renaissance because of
the initial development of capitalism, then it acquired a subordinate
character due to a halt in this process of development, and finally
became dominant starting from the end of the eighteenth century due
to strong capitalist development (Various Authors, 1979, p.321).
But, the development of science was necessary before dialectics
could become dominant, this time made its own by the proletariat.
We can now clearly see what are the consequences for class analysis
when the notion of the neutrality of science is accepted. Since
science is neutral (and not capitalist), if there is a qualitative
disagreement between science and dialectics, it is the latter which
must be abandoned and later re-built as scientific dialectics, i.e.
as based upon science. And since it is capitalism which brings
about a gigantic development in science (even though this latter
is neutral, a reflection, a reproduction of reality), dialectics
becomes the theoretical expression of capitalism rather than of
class struggle, i.e. its development is immediately tied to the
phases of economic development of capitalism rather than being the
theoretical expression of classes in their struggle.

7   THE NEUTRALITY OF SCIENCE AND CAPITALIST PRODUCTION

If the content of science (both social and natural) is class
determined (and there is no reason why this social phenomenon should
be given a privileged status), then no amount of a different application of this science will suffice to build a different social
system. The social determination of the myth of the neutrality of
science becomes then easily visible just as it becomes easy to see

how the overdetermining effect of this myth cannot but be that of
fostering and reproducing bourgeois domination. If the issue of
the neutrality vs the social determination of knowledge concerned
only the epistemologists, the social scientist could be excused if
he directed his attention to other areas of inquiry. Unfortunately
this is not the case. The myth of the social neutrality of science
penetrates socialist theory and practice and has devastating effects
on them. In this section we will be concerned with a particularly
powerful way in which that myth generates bourgeois domination,
that is, we will be concerned with its legitimating of, and serving
as an implicit theoretical support for, the belief in the neutrality
of the capitalist organization of production. If science is seen
as neutral and its development is seen in a linear, continuist
light, then this science can be seen as the most advanced one and
its application to the production process can serve to legitimate
this latter as the most rational one. The door is then open to the
acceptance of capitalist rationality as *the* rationality and of the
capitalist organization of production as *the* rational organization.
From here to the acceptance of the subjugation of the labourer
through fragmentation of tasks and coercion (the essence of capitalist
production) is a short step. Even Lenin and Gramsci fell victim
to this optical illusion, the former by favouring the introduction
of Taylorism, the latter by accepting the retention of coercion in
production.

The opinion according to which Lenin's approach to Taylorism
implies 'a naturalist conception of technique and a technical
conception of the relations of production' (77) seems to us to be as
unbalanced as the opposite one which stresses only the instrumenta-
lity of Lenin's attitude to Taylorism, its being dictated purely by
the disastrous economic conditions of the young Soviet state in the
hostile capitalist world. As R. Linhart convincingly argues (1976),
if it is true that 'scientific management' could have appeared to
Lenin as a method to increase both production and the discipline of
a labour force still basically of peasant origin, it is also true
that the ambiguities of Lenin's thoughts on Taylor go back to 1913
and 1914 when, in two articles published in 'Pravda', he attempted
the impossible task of separating the 'rational' aspects of Taylorism from its exploitative, capitalist nature. (78) These ambiguities
remained in the years between 1914 and 1918, as the then unpublished
'Notebooks on Imperialism' show, and re-appeared in the spring of
1918 when Lenin advocated the introduction of Taylorism. (79) They
were thus a constant of Lenin's thought. Even in that short-lived
conception of Lenin's which was the 'Soviet Taylorism' (i.e. first,
Taylorism had to be a sort of collective appropriation of knowledge
on the part of a working class in which the majority of the
individuals was unskilled and thus not liable to have knowledge
expropriated; second, the reduction of the working day, following
the introduction of productivity-raising Taylorism, had to find its
counterpart in an increased and massive participation of the working
class in the management of the state (Linhart, 1976, pp.110-14)),
there is no realization that Taylorism is bureaucratization within
the production process and that therefore it is impossible to fight
bureaucracy at the political level by retaining it at the economic
level. That a thinker, an unrelenting critic of capitalism, such as

Lenin could hope to separate the 'rational' from the 'capitalist'
aspects of Taylorism can only be accounted for if Lenin's belief
about the neutrality of natural sciences is taken into account.
To introduce Taylorism within a socialist context meant for Lenin
to liberate basically neutral productive forces and to use the
results for the construction of socialism. This is why, for Lenin,
the abolition of the division between 'mental' and 'manual' labour
will be basically the result of the development of the productive
forces rather than of the conscious action of the proletariat.
And this is why Lenin's critique of Taylor is focused on super-
exploitation, unemployment, and the formation of labour-aristocracies
but not on the dequalification of work and on the resulting subjugation of the individual labourer and complete abolition of the
workers' initiative and intellectual activity. (80)

Not dissimilarly to Lenin, Gramsci also believed that 'organization and capitalist division of labour are ... neutral productive
forces', (81) indeed, that they are good because they train the
workers to discipline. We will consider here only the writings of
the 1919-20 period, the 'Ordine Nuovo' period. (82) Given the
nature of these writings we can at most attempt a reconstruction of
the unstated theoretical frame from which they originate. No doubt,
we have here articles, most of them not longer that a couple of
pages, not only written under the impulse of the daily events and in
a journalistic fashion, but also showing the imprint of the objective
social conditions of those years, and thus also the emergency
conditions of the shattered post-First World War Italian economy.
The similarities with the young Soviet state are, from this point
of view, obvious and it can be little wonder then that Gramsci, like
Lenin, was concerned with the need to increase productivity to the
point of overlooking the fundamental (for the construction of
socialism) question of the social nature of the organization of the
production process. However, just as in Lenin, the overlooking of
this question is due just as much to the theoretical limits of
Gramsci's thought on this matter as to the immediate need to increase
production. These limits coagulate in the notion (never spelled
out explicitly, but leading a subterranean life in the 'Ordine
Nuovo' writings) of the neutrality of science and of the productive
forces and thus of the technical (capitalist) division of labour.
Thus, the emphasis laid by Gramsci on the need to change the mode
of ownership in order to build socialism is matched by an almost
complete silence on the need to transform radically the technique
and the division of labour born under capitalism. For Gramsci, a
change in the ownership of the means of production will bring about
a better distribution of tasks and of income (1975a, p.197), but no
mention is made of the fact that the abolition of capitalist
exploitation and supervision is much more than simply abolishing
one agent of the capitalist production process (i.e. the capitalist
as owner) and leaving the tasks of the other agents basically
unchanged.

Not by chance, in fact, is socialism, for Gramsci, the univer-
salization of the mode of existence of the proletariat (1975a,
p.412) rather than its abolition. Thus, socialism will foster the
further quantitative growth of the productive forces (p.123) but,
again, no mention can be found of the need to transform the

capitalist productive forces into socialist ones. Aside from a
couple of moments in which Gramsci's formulation could be interpreted
differently (pp.136 and 157), the underlying and unrevealed theme
is that of the neutrality of the productive forces and of the
division of labour. The three most obvious indications of this
conception are Gramsci's evaluation of the Communist Saturdays, of
the relationship between the division of labour and proletarian
solidarity, and of the need for, and nature of, discipline in the
work-place.

To begin with the effect of the capitalist division of labour on
class solidarity: for Gramsci, the former fosters the latter
(pp.325-6). For him, thus, the division of labour and thus the
productive forces are essentially neutral and thus applicable to
opposite social systems. If the technical division of labour were
capitalist in essence, how could a proletarian solidarity stem from
it? Gramsci's argument is as far from Marx as it is close to the
Durkheim of 'The Division of Labour in Society' (1964, p.389).
Second, it is for the same reasons that Gramsci can give an
uncritically positive evaluation of the Communist Saturdays, in this
faithfully following Lenin. As Linhart correctly points out, the
Communist Saturdays were a first attempt to overcome the difference
between mental and manual labourers but not between mental and
manual labour (1976, pp.148-9). In fact, the organization of labour
of the Communist Saturdays did not differ from the traditional
organization of the production process. Not only is there no
attempt to stimulate the inventiveness of the masses, it is the
military-like discipline which is praised by Lenin (Linhart, 1976,
p.146) and by Gramsci (1975a, p.143). No mention is made, either
by Lenin or by Gramsci, of the need to create a new organization,
a new structure of tasks. Thus Gramsci attaches great importance
to discipline, to order in production. The discipline which stems
from the organization of the production process is not, for him,
capitalist in nature. This discipline is a necessary consequence
of technical development. It is imposed nowadays upon the working
class by the capitalist because the latter owns the means of
production: tomorrow, under socialism, it will be accepted
spontaneously by a free proletariat. The notion that discipline,
coercion in the work-place, the work of control and surveillance -
an activity which nowadays is performed by a hierarchy of agents
instead of by only the capitalist - cannot denote or agree with
socialist production because it is in antagonistic contradiction
with socialist production relations, is absent from Gramsci's (and
Lenin's) thought.   It is this which functions as the third
indication of the neutrality thesis in Gramsci. This notion will
remain in Gramsci's work up to the 'Prison Notebooks' as the
following, written in the frame of his considerations on the
militarization of labour under the period of War Communism in the
Soviet Union shows: 'The principle of coercion, direct and indirect,
in the ordering of production and work, is correct.' (83) The
neutrality of science and technique is thus a recurrent theme also
in Gramsci's thought. (84)

8 NATURAL SCIENCE AND SOCIALISM

The social determination of the origin of science is today not an
unusual position, even with respect to the natural sciences. Much
less frequent, however, is a position stressing the class determination
of the content of science, and certainly of the natural sciences, and
its logical conclusion, the need for a socialist mode of production
to develop its own vision of the world, both natural and social. In
the previous sections we have developed a theory of the class
determination of both the origin and the content of knowledge, giving
no privileged status to the natural sciences. Our basic concern has
been the overdetermining effect of science (85) due to its class
determination. There have been attempts to develop theories which,
while recognizing the social determination of the content of science,
deny a specific social nature to its overdetermining effect. One
such example concerning the natural sciences is Sohn-Rethel's
'Intellectual and Manual Labour' (1978). (86) We will consider this
work briefly because this will give us the opportunity to tackle a
fundamental point of our theory. In fact, up to now we have argued
for the class determination of knowledge and have provided some
examples of the capitalist determination of science. However, we
have not yet specified what gives science its particularly bourgeois
character, what is the general feature which stamps bourgeois
knowledge and which realizes itself in the specific forms of
knowledge as, for example, not only the change in the notion of one
or of God, but also and above all as the creation of completely new
bodies of the social and natural sciences. Let us start from an
example of social determination which fits very nicely our theory,
that of the concept of inertia in physics. As Sohn-Rethel points
out, before capitalism inertia had always been conceived of as
rest and movement as being originated from an impetus coming from
outside the object (basically from man). This is 'in keeping with
a handicraft mode of production' (Sohn-Rethel, 1978, p.124). The
advent of capitalism brought with it new problems which transcended
those limits of human strength and skills which were also the
limits of the previous modes of production and which were the
determining factors behind the concept of inertia as rest. To solve
those problems, as, for example, the ballistics of gunnery 'which
in turn governed the entire range of military engineering and
architecture', Galileo worked out the concept of inertial motion,
i.e. the concept that 'a body in motion will continue to move, and
to persist in its rectilinear motion and given speed, so long as
nothing prevents it from doing so.' (1978, p.125). Now it is motion
which becomes the natural state of affairs. And this could hardly
be different in a system which, for the first time in history, is
based on continuous change. The non-empirical concept of inertial
motion then allowed Galileo to solve the calculation of the trajectory
of cannon balls. This is thus a clear example of not only social
but actually class determination of knowledge. Sohn-Rethel, however,
draws quite different conclusions from it. While this is an example,
perhaps the example 'that the rise of the modern science is ...
inherently connected with the rise of modern capitalism' (1978, p.125),
of how, we would say, the latter determines the content of the
former (a new concept of inertia), modern science's, 'findings are

valid irrespective of any particular relations. Inasmuch as it is
based on the mathematical and experimental method science is one
and only one' (1978, p.179). How can the social determination of
the content of natural science be reconciled with its trans-epochal
validity? This is possible, for Sohn-Rethel, because 'looking at
nature under the category of the commodity form, science affords
precisely the technology on which hinges the controlling power of
capital over production' (p.179). Therefore, what must be changed
under socialism is not science but its use, technology (p.181) and,
if we understand the argument correctly, it will be through this
different use that science will acquire a new significance (p.183).
It becomes thus clear that the social determination of science's
content and its neutrality as a social factor cannot be reconciled.
In order to maintain the latter, Sohn-Rethel must give up the
former, so that what is socially determined is the particular,
social way in which a-historical laws of nature have been discovered.
However, once discovered, this science has general and trans-epochal
validity and what will be subject to change will be only its use
(and thus significance). For Sohn-Rethel, it is the form of
eternally valid laws of nature which is socially determined, for us
these laws are equally eternally valid, but it is the content itself
of this knowledge which changes. Therefore, for Sohn-Rethel, the
different use of science will determine its different significance
and correspondence with a different social system, while for us
this different use will be probably very common in a transition
period while a new system will eventually generate a new view of
the natural world.

In spite of its theoretical differences, Sohn-Rethel's theory
comes very close, in its practical consequences, to the neutrality
of science position with its emphasis on the social determination
of technology and not of science. This author has, however, the
important merit of attempting the identification of that element
which lends its capitalist form to the natural sciences. For Sohn-
Rethel, this is the separation of the direct producer from the
means of mental production, of manual and intellectual labour.
The different use and significance of this science will come under
socialism from the reunification of mental and manual labourers,
from the abolition of what is ultimately characteristic of capitalist
production. Now, Sohn-Rethel's concern is in our view correct,
only we disagree on the indentification of what is ultimately
characteristic of capitalism and thus on the conclusion that it
will be science, and not only its use, that will have to be newly
developed under socialism. If the essential trait of capitalism
is identified in the separation of the producers from their means
of production, and thus in the labourer/non-labourer dichotomy,
(87) then the general element which lends a capitalist nature to
science is that in the natural sciences the producers must produce
knowledge with means of mental production belonging to the non-
producers. In fact, since knowledge of reality is possible only
inasmuch as one can deal with reality, it is the producer, the
labourer, which can produce knowledge; since it is material transformation which determines mental transformation, those who own
the means of material production own also the means of mental
production; and since as far as the production process is concerned,

it is the producer/non-producer dichotomy which characterizes the
capitalist mode of production, it is possible for the non-producers
to impose the breaking up and fragmentation of the production
process upon the producer and thus also the separation within the
labourers between material and mental labourers. (88) It follows
that under capitalism the producer of the natural world's knowledge
is not only separated from immediate material transformation, he
produces this knowledge on behalf of, i.e. with the means of mental
production, within the optics and according to the interests, of
the non-producer. (89) A different science, therefore, will spring
not only from the abolition of the separation between mental and
material labour (Sohn-Rethel's reunification of the indirect and
direct producer), but also and first of all from the abolition of
non-labour, i.e. of the private ownership of the means of production.
It is from this abolition, logically antecedent to that reunification,
that the radical change in the natural sciences, the possibility for
the labourers to develop their own means of mental production will
derive. The bourgeois character of the natural sciences (i.e. their
functionality for bourgeois domination) does not emanate in the
first instance from their being the product of intellectual
labourers separated from material labourers, but from their being
the product of intellectuals (labourers supervised by non-labourers)
(90) who, without being aware of it, produce a knowledge of the
natural world which fosters at the same time the domination of the
non-labourers over the labourers (quite aside from bourgeois
science's application for purposes of class domination and from its
legitimating function vis-à-vis capitalist social relations).
    Given this point's fundamental importance, let us dwell on it a
little longer and consider how the ownership of the means of
material production can determine the nature of the means of mental
transformation. If it is correct to stress that the mental
labourer produces knowledge in artificial isolation from material
transformation (the concepts of material and mental transformation
will be dealt with in detail and defined in chapters 3 and 5) and
that the material labourer transforms material reality in artificial
isolation (having had the knowledge necessary for it expropriated),
it is also necessary to stress that this is not enough. The
collective labourer (i.e. all those who transform the ensemble of
society's use values) has not only been divided into material and
mental labourer but also fragmented, within these two broad
categories, into a number of agents performing a myriad of different
(and mostly dequalified) tasks. The technical division of labour
is introduced also within the mental labourer, (91) science becomes
a collective effort either directly or indirectly related to
problems arising from material production (on this basis we will
draw a distinction in chapter 4 between practical and theoretical
knowledge). In the present stage of capitalist development science
is less and less the outcome of individual geniuses and more and
more of the combined effort of thousands of people. But even those
scientists dealing with problems directly connected with material
transformation do that in the context of a technical division of
labour in which elements of knowledge are worked upon in artificial
isolation from each other. The mental producers cannot thus achieve
a view functional for the producer's domination over the non-producer

not only because they are separated from material transformation, but also because of the technical division of labour within mental labour, because each one of them has a very limited, partial, and isolated exposure to the collective process through which knowledge is produced. It is through this double and interrelated aspect of the division of labour that the non-producer, having separated and fragmented the mental labourer, destroys this latter's ability to work out his own view of reality thus imposing at the same time the non-producer's point of view. Through this separation/fragmentation each individual scientist can be made to accept the optic of the non-labourer so that the recomposition of these separated elements of knowledge, i.e. the outcome of the collective mental labourer, cannot but be functional for bourgeois domination.

Notice that this is a theoretical account of the possibility for one class to impose its view on (at least a sector of) another class. The process of separation/fragmentation is whàt makes it possible for the bourgeois optic to be imposed upon the producers of the natural sciences as the collective mental labourer. This process is not the mechanism through which that imposition takes place. This mechanism is the penetration/incorporation mechanism to be discussed at length in chapter 4; it is the acceptance by an agent, belonging objectively, i.e. in terms of production relations, to a class, of an ideology (or of an element of knowledge) determined by another class. But the penetration of foreign ideological elements at the individual level does not account for the possibility that not only individual mental producers but also the mental producer as a whole can turn out a science functional for the (mental) producer's domination by the non-producer. It is thus correct to stress the internalization by the individual scientists (mental producers) of the bourgeois 'ideological assumptions [which] help to determine the very experimental designs and theories of scientists themselves'.(92) This is the specific way in which the penetration of bourgeois ideologies within the mental producers of natural sciences (who, objectively speaking, are members of the working class) happens in reality. But this can happen not only because of the separation of the mental producers from material production but also because of the fragmentation of mental production and its subjugation to (mental) non-labour. (This topic will be picked up again in chapter 4, section 1f, where the question will be tackled as to whether the proletariat can produce a 'correct' knowledge of the natural world with 'alien' means of mental production.)

But the producer, no matter how divided and fragmented, is the producer none the less, i.e. he must transform both material reality and the knowledge necessary for this transformation. Natural science does have thus a practical value but is a knowledge of the natural world deeply embedded in the world-view of the bourgeoisie. The abolition of the labourer/non-labourer dichotomy and thus the reunification of mental and material labour will thus result into a new organization of labour (to be discussed in chapter 5), into a new way for the producer to relate to the natural world, and thus into a new type of natural sciences. It is for this reason that the result of such an abolition cannot but be a radically different natural science and that statements such as 'the science indispensable for socialism is methodologically the same as the science in

capitalism' (93) are untenable from a Marxist point of view. A
proletarian science will not foster domination not because it will
be used differently (as partially in the case of the transition
period) but because it will be inherently different from a science
born within the context of exploitation and domination. In a fully
developed socialist society the claim to survival advanced by the
natural sciences developed under capitalism will appear as absurd
as a similar claim advanced by the science developed under feudalism
would appear today.

The bourgeois character of natural sciences derives thus from
their being determined by a societal production process in which both
labour and non-labour are necessary and which is carried out on
behalf of non-labour. It is for this reason that 'it was not
annexation by capital that first turned this science into an
instrument of domination and valorization; science already possessed
these characteristics - at least potentially - *prior* to its
application by capital'. (94) And it is also for the same reason
that the application of this science (technology) cannot but be
instrumental for the domination of non-labour over labour. The
bourgeois character of natural sciences becomes then visible in its
application, in that it 'combines human material and technological
constructions by strictly scientific procedures, namely, by
dissecting man into detailed mechanical parts so as to fit him into
the machine system'. (95) Or, the bourgeois character of technology
comes from within, not from the fact that it is applied within a
capitalist rather than within a socialist system. Just as the class
content of technology derives from the class content of science,
so, in the upside-down world of bourgeois ideology, the neutrality
of technology (technicism) is the logical consequence of the
neutrality of science's view. The neutrality of science and
technology does lead out of 'economic determinism', but it leads
also out of Marxism. (96) In short, as Panzieri puts it concisely
and effectively: 'it is precisely capitalist "despotism" which takes
the form of technological rationality'. (97) This being so, how can
this type of society, this mode of production, be considered to be
irrational? We will attempt an answer in the next section.

9 CORRESPONDENCE AND CONTRADICTIONS

The point that a science and technology developed under a certain
social system cannot be used as a condition of reproduction of
another system can now be expressed in more general terms (1) by
extending it from science and technology to the whole of the
productive forces as well as to their relation to the production
relations, and (2) by specifying what kind of contradiction exists
between these two elements of the economy. Let us begin first of
all by providing a typology of the three cases which can tie a
determinant and a determined instance: the case of correspondence,
the case of non-antagonistic contradiction (non-AC), and the case
of antagonistic contradiction (AC). In the case of correspondence,
the determinant instance calls into existence the determined one as
a condition of the former's existence and fosters the unfettered
concretization (i.e. development and utilization) of the latter.

Consequently, this latter fosters the non-contradictory reproduction of the determinant instance. Given the contradictory nature of the determinant instance, this case can at most be temporary and transitory. In the case of non-AC, the determinant instance calls into existence the determined one as a condition of the former's existence (just as in the previous case) but fosters the concretization of the determined instance in a contradictory way (and this is the difference from the case of correspondence), i.e. by constantly posing limits (fetters) to its development and utilization (other conditions of existence, contradictory to each other). These limits are constantly overcome only to reappear again in a different place and in a different form. In spite of this, and given that the two instances are qualitatively similar, the determined instance fosters the reproduction of the determinant one. In the case of the relation between the capitalist production relations and the capitalist productive forces, there is no qualitative contradiction (both have the same class nature), i.e. the contradiction is non-antagonistic. In this case the contradiction takes the form of a quantitative one within the productive forces. The increase in the productivity of human labour is not fully realized either ante festum (there is no full utilization of the existing productive forces) or post festum (due to the destruction of wealth due to crises of overproduction, wars, etc.). Yet, the main tendency remains the growth of the capitalist productive forces and their reinforcing effect (on all levels) on the reproduction of the capitalist production relations. We will go deeper into the concept of tendency in the next chapter. Finally, we have the case of AC. Here the determinant instance calls into existence the determined one against its own will, as it were; it calls into life, and at the same time hinders, what contributes to its supersession. It thus resists, it does not foster, as in the previous two cases, the concretization of the determined instance which, in turn, once it has come into existence, can grow and establish itself only at the expense of the determinant instance, only if this latter is reduced and disappears or if it survives in a radically transformed form. AC thus means that the determinant instance hinders the birth and development of what it itself calls into life and that this latter, in its turn, will tend to weaken and eventually destroy the determinant instance. This can be explained only if we start, as we have done in this chapter, from the inherently contradictory nature of the determinant instance.

Disregard of the difference between, or mistaken characterization of, AC and non-AC can have serious consequences, especially because of the possibility some contradictions have of changing their social (class) nature, i.e. of changing from non-AC into AC. More specifically, if we recall that the conditions of reproduction or of supersession in a social system express themselves as conditions of class domination, some conditions of domination of A (e.g. the capitalist class) cannot be transformed into a condition of domination of B (e.g. the proletariat) and thus of supersession of A. In this case, A's condition of domination must be replaced by B's own condition of domination. Coercion in production is an example already provided. In chapter 4 we will deal with another example, domestic labour. But there are other conditions of domination, say of A, e.g. social reforms, which can be transformed

in B's conditions of domination if they become part of B's radically
different economic, ideological and political praxis. By extending
what was submitted above concerning the trans-epochal validity of
certain elements of knowledge, we can say that these conditions of
domination can change their class character and thus significance
because they can become part of a different practice. Those
conditions of domination of A, which originally are in non-AC with
A and thus foster this latter's reproduction, can be transformed
by all other types and forms of class struggle into conditions of
domination of B, thus entering into AC with A.

Let us now return to the relation between the productive forces,
which we can now define in both a quantitative and a qualitative
(98) way, i.e. as the extent to which and the way in which it is
possible to produce under a certain mode of production, and
production relations. We can now see that what we have argued for
in this first chapter is that between capitalist productive forces
and capitalist production relations there is a relation of non-AC
which cannot be transformed into one of AC. There is contradiction,
but it is not a qualitative one. This contradiction will determine
all other contradictions which make possible a transition to
socialism, but since this contradiction cannot be transformed into
an antagonistic one, the development and use of the capitalist
productive forces will not be the basis upon which to build new,
socialist, production relations. Moreover, since this contradiction
is not, and cannot be transformed into, a qualitative one, the
development and use of the capitalist productive forces will continue
until when the capitalist production relations will exist. Former
theories stressing the impossibility for the forces of production
to be further developed under capitalism, as, for example, in
Lukàcs', (99) completely overlook the qualitative aspect of the
contradiction, thus making a double mistake. This author, on the
one hand, considers the natural sciences (but not the social ones)
and thus the productive forces as neutral, (100) thus introducing
within Marxism a fundamental element of bourgeois theory; (101)
on the other hand, the qualitative aspect of the productive forces,
absent because of the myth of their neutrality, reappears
surreptitiously in a quantitative form, i.e. in the form of the
impossibility of their further quantitative growth due to the
capitalist production relations. History has abundantly belied
this still fashionable view. (102) The contradiction between the
capitalist productive forces and the production relations, the
powerful limits posed by the latter to the development of the
former, limits which at times can be mistaken as the terminal
station of the former's development, only signals the fact that
the latter have exhausted their historical mission in the sense
that it has become possible for them to be replaced by new social
relations which in turn will necessitate new productive forces for
their reproduction. As far as the so-called 'backward' countries
are concerned, if it is correct to stress that they do not have to
develop first in a capitalist social system in order to achieve
socialism, it is also correct to keep in mind that no socialist
system can be achieved without the necessary material basis. (103)

In this light, the irrationality of the capitalist system takes
on a new connotation. This irrationality is to be understood neither

in a humanist way as a contradiction between the capitalist social relations and an abstract, a-historical 'human nature', nor in a traditional, 'third internationalist' way as a contradiction between essentially rational productive forces and exploitative (thus irrational) capitalist production relations. As A. Baracca, S. Ruffo, and A. Russo correctly remark, the notion still dominant nowadays among the trade unions and left-wing traditional parties is that the productive forces, of which science is a very important element, are intrinsically rational and determine the production relations which characterize a certain society. The development of the productive forces, and thus of science, becomes thus a sequence of stages common to all human communities. On this view, the productive forces are neutral even though (a) the choices consciously directing their development can steer this latter in non-progressive directions and (b) the use of the results of this development can be partial and contrary to the interests of humanity. (104) These 'irrational' choices and uses are then contrary to the intrinsically 'rational' nature of the productive forces and of their development. It is this contradiction, this irrationality, then, which becomes explosive and which will determine the revolutionary transformation of the production relations and thus of society. (105)

If this interpretation is rejected, and we have attempted to show that it should be rejected, then the concept of irrationality of the capitalist system changes too. The irrationality of the system is thus not measured against something essentially not socially determined and not socially determinable (an a-historical human nature or neutral forces of production), but against the system itself, within it. Irrational is a system which itself produces its own conditions of supersession. (106) The capitalist productive forces, even though in non-AC with the capitalist production relations, are not irrational for the system since they foster its development and reproduction. On the other hand, a socialist development of the productive forces implies a full development of the individual, something which is obviously not possible within the frame of capitalist production relations. A full development of the individual would obviously be in AC with the system of capitalist production relations and would be irrational with respect to that system. It would have as both cause and effect a new structure of human needs. From this point of view, the principle 'to each according to his needs' cannot mean that these productive forces will have grown to such an extent, or will be used in such a way, that these needs, as developed by capitalism, will be satisfied. A different society will have to develop new productive forces and thus new needs and, by not being contradictory, will have to develop those productive forces which will satisfy in a non-contradictory way those needs created by society itself. The contradictory satisfaction of the needs capitalist society creates in people is thus rational in terms of its own contradictory rationality, i.e. in terms of the system's conditions of reproduction. If the capitalist system generated only conditions of its own reproduction, even though of a contradictory nature, it would be perfectly rational in its own terms, in terms of a contradictory rationality. But whether the historical mission of a system has been completed or not can be judged in terms of AC and not in terms non-AC, in terms of whether a system from a certain moment on, starts digging its own grave. It is precisely the conceptualization of these objectively determined ACs that gives origin to those 'concrete utopias' which lead the proletariat's struggle. (107)

ON THE DEVELOPMENT OF PHYSICS AND CHEMISTRY AT THE TURN OF THE NINETEENTH CENTURY: EXAMPLES OF A HISTORICAL MATERIALIST ANALYSIS by A. Baracca

1 THE INFLUENCE OF SOCIAL DYNAMICS AND OF THE RELATIONS OF PRODUCTION ON SCIENCE

The influence of social dynamics and of the relations of production on the natural sciences has been treated, even in the Marxist tradition, differently from the influence on the social sciences. (1) In the latter case, it has long been generally accepted that the structure, the field of phenomena, the concepts and the tools of a specific discipline are built up in conformity with the concrete, material aims which people have to accomplish. These aspects have been carefully analysed by Carchedi in this book.

For the natural sciences, the situation is much more complex. On the one hand, it is presently widely accepted that social events have an influence on the development of the various disciplines. For example, mechanics developed in its modern form when the need to use tools and machines grew in the transition from a feudal to a capitalist economy; modern calculus took the form of an autonomous field of mathematics, with its own axioms and rules, when new criteria of scientific rigour were necessary in a new phase of development of industrial societies at the beginning of the nineteenth century and a similar and parallel need explains the development of thermodynamics in the same period; chemistry took its definite form and basis, as we will shortly analyse specifically under the pressure of the needs developed by production in the modern chemical industry at the end of the nineteenth century; the biological theory of evolution developed in the framework of a changing world-view imposed by the middle class as it established its position of power.

On the other hand, social events are often taken to influence the natural sciences only in the external aspects of a given discipline. As in the previous examples, they may largely determine the historical period in which it develops. They may also strongly influence the type of approach to the field, the type of vague ideas and interpretations that are put forward in the initial attempts to understand it (thus its specific development), the path through which it takes an autonomous structure as an independent discipline with its own principles, the development of the parallel need of scientific rigour or of use of sophisticated mathematical tools, and so on. But it is generally assumed as a strong criterion of historical interpretation that the kernel of a discipline, its fundamental facts and their 'true' interpretation remain completely independent from any external, non-natural factor.

This is fundamentally true also in the main Marxist tradition. When Engels analysed the structure of the natural sciences, he spoke of a pure dialectic of nature and excluded any possible interaction between human, social action and nature. Even in Lenin's analysis the concept of inexhaustibility of nature defines successive levels whose intimate structure is completely specified in a natural sense, while human social action determines at most the depth of investigation into them and the degree of understanding of them. In the subsequent Soviet tradition, the Diamat is petrified into a completely formal tool; finally, even the very original development of the idea of contradiction by Chinese Marxism has left the concept of natural sciences fundamentally untouched. (2)

Many new ideas and perspectives concerning a different point of view have emerged in recent years, following the social crisis and the struggles of 1968. A direct experience and participation in the Italian events, even if unavoidably filtered in a subjective way, are at the basis of what I shall write below.

Let me stress a central point in this sense. There is no doubt for me that, in a period when capitalistic domination passed through a real and deep crisis, all the social groups who fought in those years felt quite clearly that science and technology themselves are not the result of a pure process of gaining knowledge of nature. Knowledge itself is not neutral; it is instead the product of a particular way of looking at certain things. Both scientists and engineers have certain interests and aims, that substantially reflect those of the class which holds the economic power. Investigation for the purpose of increasing surplus value and the exploitation of the working class is basically different from investigation which puts the health of the producers first and which has in mind the production of use values rather than exchange values. These two directions lead to different kinds of scientific knowledge. It follows that science and technology, as they have developed historically in the framework of capitalistic society and industrialization, embody capital's domination, and are in themselves also instruments for the domination and exploitation of one class by another.

A characteristic aspect of this approach is that - as Carchedi has stressed clearly in this book - the productive forces themselves are not neutral at all, but are strongly and deeply determined by the relations of production in which they have been shaped, and, consequently, they are functional to class domination and exploitation. It is not my aim here to attempt an assessment of the past twelve years. But I think it is important to stress the specific, concrete basis of my conception concerning the lack of neutrality and the class determination of the natural sciences, technology and the productive forces in general.

2 A SURVEY OF RECENT ITALIAN LITERATURE

Since I shall limit myself to some examples that seem particularly
significant, it is important to mention the existing literature on
these positions and analyses which is not accessible to the English-
speaking world.

A report by Pancaldi (1980) has appeared in English giving an
account of the studies on the history of science in Italy and
discussing the general situation and role of the positions I am
trying to summarize here. It seems correct to recall that the first
occasion for the expression of this kind of analysis in a coherent
form was the new series of the journal, 'Sapere', directed by
G.A. Maccacaro from 1974. Maccacaro himself has made extremely
important contributions for a critical and political analysis in the
field of medicine and health (see, for example, Maccacaro, 1977)
together with his concrete activity, for instance in the movement
'Medicina Democratica' (which publishes a journal with the same
title).

The general framework for the approach to be put forward in what
follows has been carefully examined by Cicotti, Cini, De Maria and
Jona (1976); Baracca and Rossi (1976).

General surveys of the development of science since the eighteenth
century along these lines are contained in the detailed introduction
to the anthological volumes by Baracca and Livi (1976) and Baracca
and Rossi (1978).

The specific historical research started with the analysis of
the developments of science during the first industrial revolution
and the French revolution. The starting points were the analysis
of the deep difference between the empirical British and the mainly
rational, mathematical, French methodology during the eighteenth
century (Rossi, 1971, 1973) and the old but still extremely
stimulating inquiry by Hessen (1931) concerning the influence of the
emerging capitalist production on Newton's work. The following
investigations clarified how the completion of mechanics, the
introduction of the concepts of work and energy were largely
determined by the previously unknown needs of the industrialization
process and absorbed in their formulations specific characters of it:
Baracca and Rigatti (1974), Baracca (1974) and the clear formulation
of the two distinct theorems of vis vivae and impulse (Bergia and
Fantazzini, 1981; see also 1979, 1980).

The advances connected to the French revolution and the following
social and economic transformations were considered by Israel and
Negrini (1973), and Baracca and Rossi (1974).

An analogous study treated the development of thermodynamics,
which began with the first English industrial revolution and the
building and perfecting of the steam engine (Baracca and Rigatti,
1974; Baracca, 1974), and continued with a considerable change of
scientific practice, in post-revolutionary France (Baracca, 1981).
An outline of the above-mentioned items will be given in the first
two examples discussed below. The developments of theoretical and
practical science in the subsequent decades in Britain have been
analysed by Rossi (1974 and 1976).

The problem of extra-scientific causes in the revolution in
physical theories at the turn of the nineteenth century was posed

clearly by Ciccotti and Donini (1975) and by Battimelli (1974). The realization of the existence of extra-scientific causes stimulated the investigation further, and the above-mentioned theoretical transformations were connected to the change in scientific practice induced by the completely new structure and needs in the second industrial revolution in the second half of the nineteenth century mainly in the German chemical industry (Baracca, Ruffo and Russo, 1979). This constitutes the main example that we shall develop here. Parallel aspects were treated originally and more carefully by De Marzo (1978), while Battimelli (1974) and Bergis (1973, 1978, 1979a and 1979b) have analysed more specifically Einstein's contributions and the upheaval brought by his theory of special relativity. A scientific handbook in which the treatment of statistical mechanics is blended with the above-mentioned historical analyses is Baracca, 1980. The parallel developments in mathematics, in particular the process of abstract formalization, were considered by Marchetti, 1977; Boldrighini and Marchetti, 1977.

More recently the historical investigation has got more deeply into our century, mainly in connection with the appearance of the new journal 'Testi e Contesti' (published quarterly since 1979 by CLUP-CLUED in Milan; see the review in 'Isis' by Finocchiaro (1981), and with the organization of the International Conference 'The Recasting of Sciences between the two World Wars', held in Florence and Rome, 23 June - 3 July 1980. The first analysis to be mentioned in this respect is that of Tonietti (1976). The context of the upheaval corresponding to the final formulation of 'orthodox' quantum theory in Weimar Germany was studied by Donini (1979), Baracca, Livi and Ruffo (1979), De Maria and La Teana (1979 and 1981), Tonietti (1980).

The development of American science in the first decades of the century and the successive shift of scientific supremacy from Germany to the USA has been studied by Donini (1979a, 1979b and 1980), De Maria (1980), De Maria and Seidel (1979), Russo (1981). An account of the entire programme of research has been reported in the 'Radical Science Journal' (Baracca, Ciliberto, Livi, Lorini, Pettini, Ruffo and Russo, 1980).

Let us mention finally the extremely stimulating analysis made by Lorini (1979) of the first developments of the social sciences in the process of rapid industrialization of the USA at the beginning of this century. Israel (1977) has presented a very interesting study on the connections between the mathematical formulation of the Bourbaki school and the scientific management techniques. Baracca and Bergia (1975) tried a critical analysis of the mechanisms underlying the investigation in elementary particle physics, although some of the conclusions should be reconsidered in the light of the most recent advances in this field.

3   ON THE RELATION BETWEEN MAN AND NATURE

Our guiding concept is that each specific scientific practice, each process of scientific discovery, each piece of scientific research activity is historically determined. It must consequently be studied in the framework of the global historical situation in which the scientist and scientific group operate, taking into account all the motivations, factors and material conditions of their work.

We shall discuss some examples of how to go about such a study, while we shall not engage here in a more exhaustive discussion of the general basis of it, i.e. the specific adaptation of Carchedi's methodology to the case of the natural sciences. The position that we will develop here is essentially anti-epistemological, in the precise sense that it refuses systematically to classify each scientific practice into some general kind of 'scientific method' or of 'scientific discovery', characterized by specific - even if different in the various general cases - procedures of research, criteria of rigour, relation between theory and experiment, and so on. (3) In the historical analysis of each specific situation, one may ask how deeply the 'external' factors might influence the scientific practice and its product, i.e. scientific knowledge.

One might argue that scientific knowledge always concerns nature and that, consequently, nature determines in the last analysis the kind of final scientific knowledge, phenomena and laws. Such a point of view thereby reasserts the neutral character of science and productive forces. What is wrong with it, in my opinion, is the conception of nature as something given and determined once and for all, unchangeable and a-historical: like a reservoir from which man has simply to extract its 'true' content.

In Baracca and Rossi (1979) we have put forward a rather different point of view. What coule be, in fact, the sense of a nature invariable but inexhaustible, in the sense that man may approach its core but never know it completely? Maybe such a nature exists, but it could have only an indirect role in the production of knowledge, through the mediating role of the concrete activity of men. Its existence has only a speculative, metaphysical interest: it may be legitimate to investigate its bearing on the process of knowledge, but for us it is much more interesting and important to take a different attitude. Humankind, in its (material and conceptual) productive activity, establishes a relationship with nature. What humankind really experiences and what is knowable for it is just this relationship between nature and social activity. Nature, on the one hand, and society, on the other, appear, not as primitive essences, but exist for humankind and are experienced by it only as terms of this relationship. The relationship between them deeply modifies their characters, as experienced by humankind. Society, on the one hand, is severely restricted because of the existence of nature as a counterpart in the relationship. But also nature, as is knowable by humankind, is experienced in forms strongly dependent on specific human social activities and aims. In fact humankind, at a certain (historically determined) level of social organization, in its productive activity enters into a relationship with nature only at a certain (also historically determined) level. It is concerned only with certain aspects of nature and interacts with it at the level that corresponds to the kind of tools and development of the productive forces convenient for its social organization.

Obviously nature, as a counterpart, poses some restrictions, but the kind of things, relations and laws that are investigated is determined in the first place by the social (class) relations dominating at the social level. As an example, the fact that in dynamics force is proportional to acceleration and not, let us suppose, to its square or cube, is a natural feature; but this is not the most relevant aspect for our analysis. The most important aspects that must be understood are the material reasons for which, in a definite historical epoch, humankind has investigated motion as the effect of certain forces, rather than as a natural trend (as it had been for the Aristotelian science); while, in turn, the detailed study of motion in terms of kinetic and dynamical quantities preceded that in terms of work and energy concepts. We shall outline this kind of analysis in our first case study, but let us conclude the argument with a few more remarks.

The priority of the aspects of scientific practice on which we insist is not an obvious choice at all. I think that it derives from an essentially political choice. As we said, it is certainly legitimate to investigate the other aspects, e.g. the logical structure of science or the nature of the scientific laws, but the connection between science, technology and the social structure, the motivations determined by material production that are behind the scientific practice and impose specific choices, the class determination of science – all these aspects are most relevant from the point of view of the active transformation of society and consequently of the role of science and scientists in it.

Another remark concerns the distinction and the relation between science and technology. We think that the distinction between them is commonly overestimated and misunderstood. When one looks more deeply at a specific, historically determined process of knowledge, every definition or distinction introduced a priori fails to remain valid and to reproduce the facts. For example, although many treatises of history of science do not consider him as a 'scientist' at all, we shall stress the fundamental role of James Watt in the development of the science of thermodynamics. In other situations the relationship between science and technology appears as less direct, but, by disregarding it, one gains a very incomplete and probably wrong understanding of the development of science: we shall explicitly argue that the difference between science at the beginning and at the end of the nineteenth century cannot be understood without taking into account the change in the role and in the reciprocal dependence of science and technology; and that, for instance, the developments in chemistry and physics at the turn of the century intrinsically depended on the specific structure and needs of the German chemical industry. In general, we recommend abandoning any a priori definition and considering the scientific and the technological aspects and their connections as historically determined in every specific situation. In this way one understands the specific character of the lack of neutrality of the productive forces.

4 CASE STUDY 1: OUTLINE OF THE BIRTH OF THE CONCEPTS OF WORK AND
   ENERGY DURING THE FIRST INDUSTRIAL REVOLUTION

Mechanics, as developed by Newton, did not cover the entire field of this discipline as it is known today. In particular, Newton explicitly denied the validity of any conservation principle. He described motion in terms of the quantity of motion (in contrast with Locke's concept of vis viva (4)(for the quarrel between them see, for example, Koyre, 1957) and he concluded from his conception of the corpuscular composition of matter that, in the course of the motion and the interaction of bodies, the total quantity of motion cannot be conserved (this was in turn connected with Newton's particular conception of God: see again Koyre (1957)). Moreover, in Newton's mechanics the concept of work does not appear.

From our point of view, these aspects of early eighteenth century mechanics are particularly significant for judging the class character of the developments of science at the beginning of the capitalist production system. If science were absolutely neutral, the very nature of phenomena would determine the structure of the theory and concepts describing them. In modern treatises energy conservation is deduced from the laws of dynamics, and it is immediately seen that vis viva is the quantity to be used in this connection (as explained in note 4). How could it happen that Newton formulated the laws of dynamics, but denied some of their consequences? As a matter of fact, the part of mechanics developed by Newton was deeply related to the economic and technical needs of the emerging English middle class, as was carefully analysed by Hessen (1931). But in Newton's time no industrial production had yet developed. The dominant system in England for producing wool has already been carefully studied and has been called the domestic production system (see, for example, Mantoux, 1971; Dobb, 1971). A class of yeomen in the country possessed or hired a piece of land to till and added to their economic budget by working at home at a spinning wheel or a loom that they owned and selling the product to merchants. In such a class and production structure it is clear that the quantity of the product was determined by the working capacity of the producers and the need was hardly felt to measure the work done or the energy spent to perform it.

The situation changed rapidly in the subsequent decades with the establishment of a capitalistic production system and the parallel change of the class structure of the British society. The process cannot be discussed in detail here (see again Mantoux, 1971; Dobb, 1971; and the debate in Dobb et al., 1978). Essentially, from the growing volume of the economic exchanges a class of capitalists grew, who became owners of the means of production, while the producers were transformed into hired labourers. The profit of the former was by now made up by the difference between the value produced and the salary gained by the latter. Machines having the task of increasing the surplus value of the capitalists were introduced.

It is essential to understand that it now became a primary necessity to rigorously define and measure work and energy. It is significant that the first proper definitions and energy balances were done not in academic milieux, but by technicians working in contact with the new capitalistic class. Musson and Robinson (1969) have carefully documented the birth of the many scattered Literary and Philosophical Societies (the most famous of which was the Lunar Society of Birmingham) and the collaboration and scientific and technical progress which took place. Essentially, one may say that the new emerging class created its new institutions and mechanisms

in order to find satisfactory solutions for the completely new
needs and problems posed by industrial production.

One of the most pressing needs was connected with energy supplies:
at the beginning of the industrial revolution there was a real energy
crisis. For a long period water constituted the main energy supply:
in 1839 there were still, in the British textile industry, 2230
water wheels compared with 3051 heat engines, giving respectively
27,983 and 74,094 hp (Musson and Robinson, 1969, pp. 67-8). Water
wheels had been built for centuries, but no scientific study of them
had ever been done. Their use in the industrial production posed
the need of exploiting their power to the utmost.

John Smeaton (1724-92) was one of the outstanding technicians of
that 'heroic' period of the development of capitalism. His
investigations and practical projects covered an incredibly large
number of fields: experiments in pure mechanics (Smeaton, 1776,
1782), studies on water wheels and wind mills (Smeaton, 1759), the
design and construction of machines of every kind, heat engines,
ironworks, dams, harbours, bridges, channels, lighthouses, and so
on (Smeaton, 1812). Smeaton was a typical protagonist of the new
class, who embodied its firm belief in progress. Smeaton's work
requires a detailed discussion (see, for example, Smiles, 1861-2),
but we must limit ourselves to mentioning some of his contributions.
In the study communicated in 1759 to the Royal Society he contributed
to a substantial advance in the general understanding and the
practical technology of water wheels (Smeaton, 1759). He built a
small model of a water wheel and performed careful experiments in
order to determine the best operating conditions and to maximize
efficiency. It was this reasoning in terms of efficiency,
conforming to the aims of the industrial class, that imposed the
introduction of the concept of mechanical work and power: (5)
different operating conditions of a water wheel were compared by
measuring the speed at which a weight was raised to a certain
height. It is important to insist on the lack of neutrality, on
the class character of the concept thus introduced. On the one
hand, it corresponded without doubt to an objective aspect of the
processes considered. On the other hand, there were nevertheless
an extremely large class of processes involving energy exchanges
and transformations: among all of them, the above-mentioned
definition referred precisely to those that we could call the
'productive energy transformations'. Although it was understood
later that work and energy were expended even in processes in which
there was no moving force, for instance when I hold a weight, such
a process clearly could never provide a material product; consequently
it was of no interest to capitalist production. (6) For the
purposes of capitalist production, only a particular sample was
chosen and treated rigorously from the very large framework of
existing work and energy transformations, determining consequently
one particular development of the physical sciences among many that
were, in principle, possible.

Many comments should be added on the contributions of Smeaton and
other technicians. Here we shall limit ourselves to adding that his
point of view led him to understand the equivalence of mechanical
work and kinetic and potential energy, through the need to compare
the action of water while accompanying the descending paddles and

thus the wheel with that of water falling down freely and knocking against the paddles (7) (an equivalence in principle, that prescinds obviously from the inelastic, non-conservative deformation of water in the collision). From this Smeaton was led to formulate the fundamental principle of hydraulic technology, i.e. the necessity of avoiding shocks and differences of velocity between the water and the parts of the machine.

Another extremely relevant scientific contribution was given in a later experimental study (Smeaton, 1776) that clarified the difference between, and the proper use of, the concepts of energy and impulse (see also Bergia and Fantazzini, 1981; Baracca and Rossi, 1978).

5 CASE STUDY 2: OUTLINE OF THE BIRTH AND DEVELOPMENT OF THERMO-DYNAMICS

A number of detailed accounts exist of the history of the steam engines in the eighteenth and nineteenth centuries. Less attention has been devoted to the parallel beginning of thermodynamics as a science (Baracca and Rigatti, 1974; Baracca, 1974; Baracca and Rossi, 1976). The figure of James Watt (1735-1819) merits a careful discussion in this respect. He too was undoubtedly a typical representative of the new social and economic order, extremely sensitive to the above-mentioned emerging and urgent needs and involved also in the social events of his time. Let us simply mention that his son was in Paris during the French Revolution and became a supporter of Robespierre (for a lively account of Watt's life see Smiles (1861-2)).

In 1763 Watt had to repair a model of Newcomen's steam engine. He had to carry out exact measures (see, for example, Cardwell, 1971), in the course of which he understood, together with the chemist Blach, the difference between heat and temperature and the concepts of specific and latent heat. (8)

The 1769 patent of the separate condenser contained quite explicitly the principle that two heat sources at different tempera-tures were necessary in order to make a heat engine work: it was the first part of Lord Kelvin's formulation of the second law of thermodynamics of 1851. (9) At this time, and thanks to a man-made instrument - the steam engine - two phenomena, quite different in principle, were unified into aspects of the same principle, i.e. the spontaneous heat transference between two sources at different temperatures and the transformation of heat into mechanical work. (10) And as a matter of fact a heat engine is always conceptually used to prove the equivalence of different formulations of the second law.

Watt's subsequent studies and achievements were deeply entwined with the economic exploitation and protection of the patent and with his partnership with industrialists, mainly with Matthew Boulton (see mainly Musson and Robinson, 1969). It is likely that it was mainly under the pressure of economic requirements that Watt and his staff were led to a substantial development and enrichment of work and energy concepts, beyond the purely mechanical point of view. In line with an attitude that still conceived only

of mechanical and water engines and processes, the steam engine
in fact continued to be used only as a pump: in such a use the
power developed by the steam engine was measured by the already
discussed concept of the quantity of water raised to a certain
height in a given time. But Watt understood that it would have
been much more efficient to connect the steam engine to the machinery
of the factory and to make it work them directly. He had to solve
a lot of problems in order to transform alternating into rotary
motion; but he had also to convince the clients of the advantages of
this solution, and to change their old and deeply rooted mentality.
Still more important, since the clients paid the Boulton and Watt
firm a sum of money proportional to the saving of coal with respect
to a Newcomen engine having the same power, he had to determine the
power developed by his engines in the new operating conditions.
Since the friction of the factory machinery was unknown, the old
concepts of mechanical work and power were no longer adequate. He
understood that the work done by the steam making the engine work
was proportional to the volume and the instantaneous pressure inside
the cylinder. So he arrived at defining the new concept of thermodynamic work (11) and devising a method for measuring it, the
'indicator diagram' (Hills and Pacey, 1972; Baracca and Rigatti,
1974): it is clear that the introduction of this concept – in
spite of its purely dimensional and formal equivalence to that of
mechanical work – required a profound change in ideas in conformity
with the pressure of the economic and productive needs.

The subsequent history of thermodynamics is equally indicative of
the influence of social relations on the development of scientific
ideas. One has to shift from England to France and to take into
account the antithesis between the empirical attitude dominating in
the former country and the rational one characteristic of the
latter throughout the whole eighteenth century (Rossi, 1971, 1973)
and Baracca and Rossi, (1977). The emerging French middle class
absorbed the practical English achievements, inserting them into a
rational, systematic and mathematical framework that made possible
new advancements. In 1783 Lazare Carnot, who was later to have an
extremely important role in the events of the French Revolution
(Gillespie, 1971; Baracca and Rossi, 1974, 1977), wrote the first
treatise on the mechanics of machines: he put the advancements
Smeaton had made for hydraulic engines on a rigorous footing and
extended them to all mechanical engines (Carnot, 1783).

In the hands of the enterprising bourgoisie, new horizons opened
for science; the French Revolution and the Napoleonic age led to a
new relationship between science and production and to a different
conception and structure of the scientific disciplines. A
professionalization of scientists and a specialization of the
different branches into autonomous disciplines with new requirements
of rigour and precision took place in the new scientific and
educational institutions, the École Polytechnique, the Ecole Normale
Superieure, and so on (Israel and Negrini, 1973; Baracca and Rossi,
1974). It was the beginning of that marvellous epoch of French
science that went under the name of Positivism. Rossi (1974, also
in Baracca and Rossi, 1977) has shown the persisting difference in
the orientation of British science, by analysing the practical
achievements and conceptions of Boscovich. The further developments

of thermodynamics, mainly its configuration as an autonomous
discipline, with the contributions of Fourier (Herivel, 1975) and
Sadi Carnot, can be placed in the context of this French science.

While for mechanical engines the previous advancements in
mechanics had allowed the theoretical determination of the total
available energy (e.g. through the quantity of water in a supply
placed at a given height), the lack of such a possibility for heat
prevented the development of a real theory. Carnot now treated the
steam engine theoretically (Carnot, 1824). He relied on the only
analogy that he had at his disposal, that is, the hydraulic engine.
He therefore used an hydraulic analogy for heat, in which the latter
was conceived of as a fluid which may pass through different 'thermic
heights' and whose quantity is conserved. By now it was known from
Smeaton's studies that a perfect hydraulic engine had to avoid any
jump in the transference of water to the engine (because the shock
is inevitably inelastic and wastes energy: note 7). The hydraulic
analogy, even if physically incorrect, led Carnot directly to
determine the ratio between the initial thermic energy of heat and
its energy when it passed to the lower temperature supply through
the engine (Baracca, 1981).

It is not necessary to comment further on the fact that Carnot's
physical conception was intrinsically historically determined by the
technological and productive level reached at that time and by the
practical aim of the investigation: that of putting the technology
of heat on a sound basis. The heat engine as a productive force was
not simply the expression of purely natural laws, but was a human
product and had a dynamic of development that depended on social and
productive relations in an essential way. Carnot's theory of heat
was later found to be wrong (since heat is not a conserved fluid,
but can be transformed into work or other forms of energy) when the
field of known phenomena and practical applications widened, but it
led, nevertheless, to a substantially correct determination of the
efficiency of heat engines.

6 CASE STUDY 3: THE SCIENTIFIC CHANGE AT THE TURN OF THE NINETEENTH
   CENTURY

Now I want to discuss in more detail the breakdowns in the development of the natural sciences - with main reference to physics and
chemistry - in the second half of the nineteenth century and at the
beginning of the twentieth century. The main point that I want to
stress is that there was no pressing, purely scientific, need for
the changes I shall discuss; it would have certainly been conceivable
in principle to give answers to the open problems within the framework of the then existing scientific conceptions and theories.
The established practice and structure of science did not prevent
acceptable scientific advances, but rather these were becoming more
and more inadequate in a profoundly changing framework of relation-
ships between science and the system of production. Fundamental
changes were occurring in social relations and in the class and
production structure: in the new emerging order the existing
scientific and technical instruments were no longer adequate and
what was needed in the first place was a new dynamic of scientific

research, a new structuring of scientific conceptions, a more
flexible scientific practice more sensitive to new technological
needs.

Two features of science in the first half of the nineteenth
century must be stressed with reference to the previous case study.
In the first place, the development of the scientific conceptions
had followed that of technology. It was a form of relationship
between science and technology typical of the first phase of the
industrialization process. Technological advance occurred
principally on an empirical footing, and the new science had
essentially the role of understanding, and putting on a sound basis,
the principles of those technological realizations in order to get
rigorous methods for their further improvement. This kind of
scientific practice could hardly have led to really new technological
devices.

A second feature of positivistic science was connected with this
dependence on technological progress. The need for a rigorous,
objective description of nature and the reaction against the
indiscriminate use of metaphysical speculations in science in the
past had led to the prescription of limiting oneself to the known
and certain empirical facts. This attitude limited even more the
possibility of opening up really new fields of phenomena to knowledge.
Obviously this prescription, although explicitly assumed in principle,
was rarely completely followed in practice: we have seen how Sadi
Carnot based his study on a model for heat. Nevertheless even the
assumed hypotheses basically reflected the framework of developed
technology.

Both these aspects of early nineteenth-century science were to
reveal their complete inadequacy as the social situation and the
mode of production began to change.

Following the revolutions of 1848, the middle class definitely
established its power in western Europe: the next two decades were
those of 'The Age of Capital', as Hobsbawm (1975) has called them
in discussing in detail the spreading of the point of view of the
middle class into every aspect of cultural and practical life. The
final defeat of the old aristocratic class and the conquest of
economic power posed for capitalism not only the possibility, but
also the need for a step forward. Progress was made towards the
overcoming of protectionism, and an international area of free trade
was established. Free enterprise received a growing stimulus,
enhanced by the setting up of new forms of credit and by new
developments in the banking system. The two decades following the
1848 revolutions showed a spectacular increase in the rate of
technological inventions and innovations (see, for example, Landes,
1969). In fact, the technological basis on which the preceding
development had been founded revealed itself as increasingly limited
for the new rate of development and the new possibilities that were
opening up, now that a number of bottlenecks could be overcome.

Let us mention only two examples that are particularly relevant
for the following analysis. New techniques were developed for the
production of steel (Bessemer, Siemens, Gilchrist-Thomas), which
allowed this branch of industry to develop on a solid basis. Unlike
the British industry, which had already developed in the course of
the preceding century into a massive, rigid and difficult to reorganize

structure, the German steel industry was essentially born with these new methods: at the turn of the century the average size of German steelworks was about four times that of the British ones.

Something similar happened in soda production when Solvay introduced a new and much more efficient method of synthesis. Britain already had a large industry based on the old Leblanc process and was unable radically to renew itself. But the emerging German industry, with its inevitably less rigid structure, outdid British production in a few decades and, using flexibly the most advanced techniques, became the major world producer. The whole of chemical production advanced rapidly as well; for example, the rapid development of the new field of organic products, the role of which we shall discuss below.

In general, one might say that a process of radical redefinition of the relationship between man and nature started in these years, within which the old productive forces and the dynamics of technical innovation revealed themselves to be absolutely inadequate to the needs of the new enterprising industrial middle class. A radical change in the economic and technical basis of the production system was becoming increasingly necessary. In particular, leaving the process of innovation to haphazard activity or to the pure ingenuity of inventors became inadequate; and so did a kind of science no longer able to open up really new fields of phenomena and practical applications, and no longer able to be a solid guide to innovation. This inadequacy was the real basis of the change in the scientific disciplines that began around the middle of the century.

Science was more and more consciously required, not only to describe rigorously the known phenomena, but also to be able to suggest new connections, to indicate new laws and to make real predictions. It is within this framework that we interpret the birth of a new theoretical physics which (as in Clausius and Boltzmann's kinetic theory or in Lord Kelvin and Maxwell's electromagnetism) intensively used models and hypotheses, which treated them mathematically, and which extracted new, unknown conclusions - conclusions which could turn out to be right or wrong, but which in any case constituted a real advancement in the control of processes and phenomena.

This new science turned the practice of the preceding half of the century upside down. While the earlier science had limited itself substantially to known empirical facts, and had rejected the use of hypotheses and models as non-rigorous and not well founded, the new practice conceived of them precisely as tools to guide the discovery of new facts. To this end, they were not used in a speculative form, but instead were inserted into mathematical formalisms, so that scientific disciplines could then give them specific content and transform them into hypothetical-deductive systems: their postulates became a set of assumptions about the field of phenomena treated, the properties of which were deduced with a mathematical development of the model. Such a kind of science reached an effective predictive power.

Following this line of thinking, it is evident that science changed under the pressure of external factors and not on the basis of needs posed by the scientific problems themselves: disregard of the changes at the production and social level would lead to a very poor understanding of the origin of that scientific change.

Let us take an example of the effects of the above-mentioned transformation in the use of models from what we have called the new theoretical physics. Stokes completed the mathematical theory of physical optics, identifying light with waves propagating in a highly elastic fluid, called optical ether. A rather similar treatment was introduced by Lord Kelvin and developed by James Maxwell for electromagnetism. Maxwell broke unequivocally with the French tradition of the first half of the century, which had tried to formulate the laws of the empirical facts in terms of forces acting at a distance (this had been considered at that time as a natural explanation and not as an assumption). He explicitly recognized this aspect and, building on the conceptions introduced by Faraday on a mainly qualitative footing, developed a mathematical theory of the electromagnetic field in terms of a hypothetical fluid: it was a mechanistic model, in which the electromagnetic actions were identified with the pressure, stress, or torque inside the fluid. The model was formulated by analogy with a mechanical phenomenon the mathematical treatment of which was sufficiently developed. On these grounds Maxwell built up a mathematical theory, from which one could derive rigorously every possible quantitative physical consequence. Many of them, for instance the theory of the electromagnetic waves and the electromagnetic nature of light, were unknown at his times: whether or not predictions such as these turned out to be correct, their testing could push experimental investigation into completely new fields and would extend the control of man over nature and the possibilities of technical innovation. In the worst case one would have to formulate a different theory, but even then the phenomena found experimentally would none the less have been previously unknown. As a matter of fact, the discoveries that derived from Maxwell's theory opened up really new paths to technology, in addition to science.

Our analysis of the formulation of kinetic theory runs along similar lines. Parallel to the acceptance of the atomic theory of matter, a conception of thermodynamic quantities as the average effect of the properties of atoms and molecules started to impose itself. This use of a mechanical model implied a program of theoretical derivation of thermodynamic quantities and laws, which were determined only at a phenomenological level, and exemplified in itself the overcoming of the scientific practice of the previous decades. Kronig in 1856 and Clausius in 1857 derived the expression of the pressure in a perfect gas – and consequently the equation of state of the perfect gas – as the mean effect of the shocks of the molecules on the walls of the container; the mechanical character of the model is evident. In the following years, Maxwell and Boltzmann formulated in rigorous mathematical terms the kinetic model of a gas and systematically deduced all its properties. They found unexpected connections between them (e.g. the relationship between the transport coefficients) and laws that could not easily have been established by experiment. Finally, Boltzmann deduced the irreversibility implied by the second law of thermodynamics, which then became a consequence of the mechanistic model of the gas; a quantity was found which grew continuously when the gas was out of thermodynamic equilibrium and was constant when it reached the equilibrium state –

this quantity was shown to be proportional to the state function called entropy. (12)

An analysis along the previous lines could be extended to the other disciplines in the two decades following the mid-century. For instance, even in the biological theory of evolution, great advances were allowed by the use of a model that had basically a mechanistic nature.

The analysis of chemistry is particularly relevant, because in chemistry both the values and the limits of this new scientific methodology were to reveal themselves most clearly in the subsequent decades. The acceptance of the atomic theory (which, we recall, had been considered with suspicion in the previous decades as a non-verifiable hypothesis) inaugurated the birth of a methodology based on mechanistic models in chemistry as well. On the one hand, parallel to the growing consciousness of the existence of equilibria in chemical reactions, (13) Guldberg and Waage in 1864 formulated the concept of chemical equilibrium with a treatment similar to that of kinetic theory, i.e. in terms of the collisions between the reacting and final molecules. On the other hand, models displaying the disposition of the atoms constituting given molecules were made and the macroscopic properties of substances were connected to such structures. This permitted a great advance in technical and productive innovation, since it allowed a kind of 'molecular engineering', planning the building up of new molecular structures starting from certain known atomic groups and obtaining substances which contained the wanted chemical and macroscopic properties.

In all fields this mid-century turning point - with the adoption of mechanical models and obviously also of experimental techniques having a precision unknown in the past (an aspect that would merit particular attention) - opened completely new perspectives in the programming of scientific advance and technological innovation, based on an overturning of the relationship between science and technology.

Notwithstanding the great progress and the success of this new practice, the last three decades of the century did not show a steady development of these brilliant premises, and the scientific community was torn by heated debate. Profound difficulties arose in the interpretation of natural phenomena on the basis of the theories discussed above, and the turn of the century saw an upheaval in their structure and method, principally through the formulation of the special theory of relativity and quantum theory. The paradoxical aspects raised by what we called the new theoretical physics are well known. On the one hand, the electromagnetic ether, the fluid that was supposed to transmit the electromagnetic interactions, had to combine rigidity and penetrability (since it could not disturb the motion of bodies through it), properties which did not seem easy to reconcile. Even when deprived of its material nature by the growing formalization of physics epitomized by the purely mathematical model underlying Maxwell's equations (see, for example, Tarsitani, 1972), the ether still remained an absolute frame of reference; in this respect, one would expect to find effects of a 'wind of ether' (similar to the effect of moving through the standing atmosphere) - effects which were not found experimentally.

In the kinetic theory of gases, the paradoxical aspect lay in the fact that the irreversibility of thermodynamic processes implied by

the second law had been apparently derived from the principles of
mechanics alone, which are intrinsically reversible (a stone falling
freely by accelerated motion does go up again with a retarded
motion if its velocity is exactly reversed, but nobody has seen a
gas enter spontaneously into a small container).

My point is that such difficulties were not purely physical
problems concerning these theories; instead, they displayed two
particular aspects of a deeper change in point of view and in
scientific practice, which involved the very foundation of the
scientific developments that we have discussed. In short, once not
only the possibility, but the very need of using models was granted,
the restriction to mechanical models alone turned out to be too
limited. I think that the kernel of the debates and of the scientific
upheaval between the nineteenth and the twentieth centuries centred
on the prevailing mechanistic structure of nineteenth century
science; or, more generally, on its reductionist structure, in which
the general properties of phenomena were deduced from the interactions
between elementary constituents of matter or fields: such constituents
and interactions could indeed have a mechanical nature (as in the
cases analysed until now), but they also could have a different nature,
as we will see in specific examples. Although these kinds of limits
of such a scientific method were not recognized immediately in physics,
they soon became evident in chemistry, and here, as we will see, they
rapidly caused the above-mentioned upheaval.

One must refer to the socio-economic events of the second
industrial revolution. A scientific and technological basis had
accumulated until 1873, when the economic crisis and the 'great
depression' of 1873-96 caused much deeper economic and productive
changes. In brief, the end of the Civil War in the USA and the
unification of Germany in 1871 allowed the development of an industrialization process so rapid and so new as to take the form in the two
countries of an economic 'revolution', while Britain's old and huge
productive system was too rigid compared with such a rapid recasting
and change. Scientific development in these two leading countries
took different courses as a direct consequence of the profound
differences between socio-economic processes. German science took
the world leadership – at least in physics, chemistry and mathematics
(but probably in the whole domain of scientific research) – for half
a century. The USA, on the other hand, lagged behind until approxi-
mately the 1930s. The latter country developed a technicist and
pragmatic attitude, avoiding or disregarding general theoretical
frameworks and systematic investigation (see e.g. Noble, 1977;
De Maria and Seidel, 1979).

In Germany, the growing industrial system rested on advanced and
continually renewing processes, on intensive and programmed technological progress, and on scientific investigation explicitly
directed to industrial application. In this respect chemical
industry (especially organic chemistry, and in particular the dye
industry, which produced 85-90 per cent of the world output at the
end of the century) constituted the leading sector of the German
industrial structure. The modern chemical firms arose in these
decades (BASF, Hoechst, Geigy) and gradually shifted direction to
the research laboratory; it was here that industry assumed its
modern structure with programmed team-investigation. The modern

research laboratories were shaped in these science-based industries.
The percentage of workers with a university degree in the chemical
firms at the end of the century was comparable with that of today.
Very close contacts and collaboration were established by the firms
with the leading university investigators. Among the great technical-
scientific enterprises of the German chemical industry in this period
were BASF's seventeen-year investigation of the industrial synthesis
of indigo (costing one million pounds), and the fixation of nitrogen
(synthesis of ammonia) carried out in 1913 by the academic chemist
F. Haber and the BASF chemist Bosch, after more than ten years of
research. The latter process allowed Germany, while completely
surrounded, to continue to resist for years during the First World
War, since it could produce explosives and fertilizers (the only
other source being guano from Chile, which was subject to the control
of sea trade).

The education system in Germany was the most advanced in the
world, and it satisfied the growing need for the training of
specialized scientists and technicians. Besides the universities,
which modernized their laboratories and teaching methods, there was
a system of 'Technische Hochschulen' unknown in other countries.
At both levels the above-mentioned collaboration with the main firms
guaranteed close contact with the concrete problems of production.
German chemical schools became the most advanced in the world, and
almost all chemists wanting a thorough training went to study or to
specialize in Germany. The most lively reports on the advances of
German technical-scientific education may be found in the British
'Parliamentary Papers' of those years, as a witness to the alarm at
German progress. Much more should be said about these events, but
we shall limit ourselves to referring the reader to the general
history of economic and technical change of Landes, 1969; Braverman,
1974; and for the specific and comparative analysis of the German
chemical industry to Hohenberg, 1967; Beer, 1959; Baracca, Ruffo and
Russo, 1978.

For our aims one must remark that many crucial branches of physics
itself actually arose from the dynamics of technological innovation
in chemistry. The problem of black body radiation, to which the
quantum hypothesis was applied (see below), derived directly from
the spectroscopic method of chemical analysis introduced by Bunsen
and Kirchhoff in 1860. The study of the thermodynamic properties
of physical systems at high temperatures and pressures was pushed
forward by the realization of chemical reactions (such as the
synthesis of ammonia) that do not proceed in normal conditions; the
problems of cathalysis in such reactions stimulated the production
of new alloys (such as the chromium-nickel alloys of the Krupp firm)
and a better understanding of metallurgy. Research in the physics
of very low temperatures was pushed forward in turn by the problems
of the liquefaction of gases and the fractional distillation of air
in order to obtain cheap oxygen for the chemical industry.

But the first aspect that must be analysed in detail here is
connected to the new dynamics of development in chemistry itself.
The search for more and more refined compounds, more suitable for
manifold specific needs, became relentless: more complex molecules
had to be synthesized through sophisticated operations of 'molecular
engineering', which, because of increasingly difficult conditions of

chemical equilibrium, pushed towards uncommon conditions of temperature and pressure, in order to let the reactions proceed in the desired direction and with an acceptable speed.

Chemists were directly subject to a lot of pressure, and their work had to be aimed at the solution of urgent, a-typical problems of unprecedented difficulty. It was here that the old kinds of approaches revealed themselves as insufficient to cope with the rate and urgency of the new dynamics of innovation. In this changing general frame, in fact, the old mechanistic and reductionist scientific attitude was no longer fit for new, growing needs; the ideal and practice of building up the properties of all the phenomena from the interaction of the elementary components of matter turned out to be inadequate for the urgent problems of the chemical industry. Moreover, while mechanics was the natural reference frame in a world in which the technical basis of production and the organization of labour had a basically mechanical structure, the development of the productive cycle of the chemical (mainly organic) industry further limited the scientific elaboration that could be done on mechanics. For example, a chemical equilibrium certainly could be studied on the basis of mechanistic models (as in the above-mentioned Guldberg and Waage's approach), but the result was cumbersome and dependent on models which were applicable only for a given range of temperature and pressure. Thermodynamics, on the other hand, allowed a model-independent, direct determination of equilibrium and its dependence on temperature and pressure (a crucial point, since processes of growing complexity, such as synthesis of ammonia, could be carried out only in non-standard conditions). Moreover, the growing complexity of reactions and molecular structures would have led to an incredible complexity in the dynamics of molecular collisions; it would have been extremely difficult to take into account the various stages of decomposition and recombination of the intermediate molecules, or the effect of variation in pressure and temperature and of catalysts, whose 'mechanism' was so difficult to understand.

The shift from mechanics to thermodynamics as a basis for scientific research is the main point that must be stressed here. It is important to remark again that the mechanistic and reductionist methodology did not encounter a purely scientific limit. It suffered certainly from the already mentioned difficulties, but these were not at all insurmountable even in the framework of that methodology. The intrinsic limitation of the reductionist-like models revealed itself rather in its inability to keep up with the new rate of technical innovation and scientific understanding. There is never a unique theoretical context that can explain a given field of phenomena (we shall see this explicitly), but each theoretical explanation is suited to a different role of science in society, and mainly in its connection with the field of production.

Let us look a bit deeper at the change that took place in chemistry. Chemists, subject directly to the urgent needs of the production system, rediscovered the extreme flexibility of the thermodynamic laws. These had been originally established on a phenomenological ground and were in agreement with every particular model of the microscopic, unobservable constitution of the system. But now the thermodynamic laws were reformulated too; no longer assumed to be phenomenological laws, they were rather developed as

theoretical instruments for the prediction of the properties of the
systems that were studied.

A typical case was that of chemical equilibria. In the first
instance, the two laws of thermodynamics were developed mathematically,
in order to include all physical systems. (14) From these laws, it
was possible to obtain theoretically, and without the use of a
particular model, the equilibrium conditions of a chemical reaction
and also its dependence on macroscopic parameters, i.e. temperature
and pressure. Thermodynamics thus offered a less restrictive
framework in which to treat these processes more generally. The need
for introducing microscopic models for the reaction did not disappear;
although pure thermodynamics allowed the treatment of equilibrium,
it did not determine the speed at which the reaction proceeded. In
order to treat this problem – clearly important for practical use –
one had again to introduce models. This was not done on purely
mechanical grounds from the beginning, however, but only after a
thermodynamic approach had already given important results in a
compact form, unobtainable from a mechanistic treatment. In a word,
models and theories could now be conceived on the much less
restrictive basis of the requirements of thermodynamics, and the way
was also open for conceiving a different class of models and theories
from the mechanistic or reductionist ones.

I hope to have given an idea, even if schematic, of the revolution
in point of view and scientific practice of chemistry in the last
decades of the century, driven by the new rhythm of technological
innovation and production needs. The scientific practice shaped just
after the mid-nineteenth century was unable to fulfil these tasks;
the chemists forced its premises to the extreme, eliminated the
restrictions on which it was based through the shift from mechanics
to thermodynamics. For more details see Baracca, Ruffo and Russo,
1979.

What happened among the physicists? The new dynamics of production
was reflected in physics less directly and in a less stringent form.
In making a concrete historical reconstruction and in order to
evaluate correctly the debate that involved physicists, one should
keep in mind the complex links between structure and superstructure.
In the activities that were not directly connected with production,
the whole importance of the economic and social changes were not
perceived immediately. But physicists too lived in this changing
world. Not all the complex interconnections have been clarified yet,
and the application of Carchedi's method could allow a deeper
understanding. The emergence of a different spirit in all cultural
activities was clearly felt, and it was to clash with the old
persisting positions. A reshuffling of social groups in the positions
of power was taking place and, if some of these saw the changes as
a step forward, the old ones were to suffer their own loss of power,
and were to perceive that historical period as one of profound
crisis.

In physical research there were different and contrasting
positions. The rigidity of the mechanistic and reductionist practice
appeared in connection with more abstract problems and typically
epistemological aspects. And the debate developed more on the
legitimacy of the mechanistic description than on its limits. In
the last decades of the century essentially three contrasting
positions emerged.

First of all an opposition, but one with a reactionary flavour, appeared in the mechanistic kind of physics developed after mid-century (the one we named the new theoretical physics). It was clearly inspired by a substantial opposition to the new changes and the consequences that could have derived from them and was linked to the spirit of scientific research and the economic order of the previous half-century. Even if articulated in different positions, it had the common feature of returning to a refusal of the legitimacy of using models, and tried to go back to a kind of scientific practice limited to the consideration of experimental, certain facts alone. This retrenchment could not be a simple step backwards, however, and, in some exponents, it had a deep epistemological content and important consequences, as in the case of the criticism of the central role of mechanics (Einstein had to acknowledge his debt to Mach). On the one hand, the critical empiricism of Mach, Avenarius and others, explicitly posed a phenomenalistic and anti-mechanistic requirement, vindicating a return to 'pure experience' - the reduction of all that exists to sensations - and branding as metaphysical every conceptual description beyond that (including atomic theory and the very concept of matter). On the other hand, Ostwald's 'Energetics', a rougher but much more popular conception in the scientific community at that time, reconsidered the central role of thermodynamics in its earlier phenomenological form, and proposed an extension of its two laws to other forms of energy.

One of the concrete strengths of these positions of opposition to the post 1850 model-building and mechanistic new theoretical physics consisted in the fact that the latter encountered the difficulties and paradoxical aspects that we have discussed above. These problems, that could certainly have been solved by deepening the reductionist treatment of these phenomena, were instead considered by these adversaries as limits of the mechanistic and reductionist conception in itself. One must remark, for the sake of completeness, that such criticisms - as also the new chemical practice and the twentieth-century revolution in physics - developed mainly in Central Europe, where profound economic changes dominated the cultural and scientific atmosphere. Victorian Britain, proudly closed to this ferment, continued with the mechanistic type of physics.

A second route was the further development of the post-1850 mechanistic physics. On the Continent the founders and supporters of the new theoretical physics - chiefly Boltzmann - fought these criticisms and positions. Boltzmann, however, was obstinately locked into a defence to the last of the mechanistic position. One must insist again on the fact that the mechanistic and reductionist conceptions could have been able to provide conceptually satisfactory solutions to the problems. Boltzmann framed a solution to the difficulties of kinetic theory that enriched the mechanistic structure of the theory with probabilistic concepts: this promising route, formally embodied in the basically different structure of statistical mechanics, was stopped short by the conceptual revolution of the turn of the century.

For electromagnetism and the problem of ether, the situation developed even further. Lorentz worked out a theory of electrons, in which matter was supposed to be composed of elementary electric charges of corpuscular nature (an hypothesis that preceded the discovery of the electron by J. J. Thomson in 1897) and in which the basic equations were Maxwell's equations and the one for the inter-action of the charges with the field. It was a unitary theory of matter and field, built up from the interaction between the basic components: in a sense, an electromagnetic version of reductionist theories. The theory, which obviously embodied the concept of ether, was relatively successful. Lorenz even rigorously deduced from the form of the electromagnetic interacting forces of the constituents of matter a contraction of bodies in the direction of their motion through the ether, and thereby demonstrated that the mechanistically predicted 'ether wind' could not be shown experi-mentally. Thus, the failure to reveal it brilliantly confirmed the theory of electrons. This contraction of Lorentz was not an ad hoc hypothesis – as some authors have presented it – but a rigorous consequence of his theory. Since then, the elctron theory has explained all the facts as they were discovered, and was consequently completely equivalent to Einstein's special theory of relativity. How could it happen then that the latter superseded Lorentz's theory?

The answer to this question leads us finally to considering the third route in the development of physics – besides the already discussed phenomenistic and the reductionist positions – and the so-called revolution of the beginning of the twentieth century – the adoption of new principles, having thermodynamics as a guide. This overturning of physical theories was based on an anti-mechanistic and an anti-reductionist attitude that seemed inspired by the practice already adopted by chemists. Thermodynamics assumed a guiding role in the foundation and the advancement of physical theory as well. It was placed in a scientific practice different from previous ones. The new principles that were basic to a new conception of natural phenomena were extracted from a careful analysis of the phenomenological situation, were framed by non-reductionist criteria and were 'forced' to predict new possible principles that completed the physical description. Sometimes the new principles that were assumed as the basic ones were just those aspects that created the main problems to the reductionist theories. This is particularly clear in the theory of special relativity, where it is assumed that the velocity of light is independent of the reference frame and that the physical laws retain the same form for observers in relative uniform motion. In this way the problems related to the hypothesis of ether were not to be explained or solved, but – rather schemati-cally – were, so to say, simply eliminated from the beginning.

The structure of the theory of special relativity certainly presents a lot of stimulating epistemological aspects, and many pages have been written on them. But from our point of view the most interesting problem is to define the overturning of the reductionist perspective, and to single out the characteristics of the new scientific practice and the general role that it plays. Without doubt, the new theory, based on two postulates which are simply the formulation of experimental facts, has a quite different structure from Lorentz's reductionist theory. But on top of that, the very aim and the concept of scientific explanation has changed in it. Not only does Einstein start from general facts, rather than from the elementary constituents of nature, but also he is not really concerned with the problem of ether; his real concern is with the symmetry requirement of physical laws and the description of phenomena (these are the focus of the opening words of Einstein's 1905 paper), a concern which obviously has very little of a reductionist attitude. In this way Einstein was led to a very different, but also much simpler, theory than Lorentz's. In spite of the physical equivalence of the two theories, this simplicity is one of the main reasons for the immediate victory of the theory of relativity on the Continent (for further analysis, see Zahar, 1973; Battimelli, 1974; Bergia, 1978, 1979b) and for its being ignored for a certain time by the still reductionist-minded British scientists (Goldberg, 1970).

Let us come now to a discussion of the other branches of physics (for a deeper discussion see Baracca, Ruffo and Russo, 1979 and in Baracca, 1980). Boltzmann's attitude towards the problems of kinetic theory was not adequately developed, as mentioned above. The formulation of statistical mechanics by Gibbs (1902) and by Einstein himself (1903) formally embodied Boltzmann's probabilistic concepts, but substantially turned his view upside down. Bodies clearly continued to be conceived of as composed of atoms and molecules, but macroscopic laws were no longer built up starting from their microscopic interactions and collisions. Incorporating the already mentioned advances due principally to theoretical chemistry in the thermodynamic treatment of complex systems, abstract theoretical macroscopic laws for probability were related directly to thermodynamic functions. (15) The laws of thermodynamics were no longer built up, but rather were embodied in the very axiomatic foundation of the theory. In this way the latter was disconnected from classical mechanics and assumed a much more general validity: in fact the basic formalism was to remain the same for the quantum systems (which satisfy the same thermodynamic laws) provided that the values of energy were quantized and the integrals were replaced by sums.

Now let us come to the problem of black body, (16) into the treatment of which Planck first introduced the quantum hypothesis in 1900. It must be said immediately that Planck's first derivation of the famous formula did not include it. We cannot treat here the full story of the previous attempts to determine experimentally and theoretically the spectrum of black body radiation. The relevant thing is that, when in 1900 it was fully experimentally worked out, revealing that previous theoretical formulas were wrong, Planck used purely thermodynamic reasoning (the role of thermodynamics in Planck's thought was stressed first by Klein, 1966). He was able to reduce one of these earlier formulae, proposed by Wien, to a general thermodynamic expression of the entropy of the system, and, assuming the simplest generalization of this expression, was led to his famous formula, which agreed with the experimental facts.

The breakdown of the reductionist view in physics, first stressed by Ciccotti and Donini, 1975, broke away from the consideration of the fundamental structure of the system. With a striking analogy to the practice of chemists, Planck went on to try a 'microscopic' derivation of his thermodynamically based formula. Here he finally introduced the quantum of energy in order to count the number of microscopic configurations of the system and, consequently, their statistical weight. While he had been previously indifferent or suspicious towards Boltzmann's approach, and had always preferred thermodynaic reasonings (as he explicitly admits in his autobiography), he now used it pragmatically to 'justify' his own previous result, even though Boltzmann's formulae, derived rigorously for a gas, were far from firmly established for the case of the electromagnetic field.

The full discussion of Einstein's contributions to the quantum theory would be too complex and too long to be attempted here (see Bergia, 1979a; Baracca, Ruffo and Russo, 1979; Baracca, 1980). Let us limit ourselves to recalling the features which are most relevant from our point of view. First of all, one must stress the fundamental role of thermodynamics in Einstein's thought (first stressed by Klein, 1963, 1965, 1967). A second relevant aspect is the persisting care which Einstein, guided by thermodynamics, took to eliminate any asymmetry from the physical description of nature. The introduction of photons in 1905 was aimed at eliminating the asymmetry between the discrete corpuscular description of matter and the continuous description of a field: such a clearly non-reductionist requirement was justified on the basis of the formal identity of thermodynamic laws for a gas and for an electromagnetic field and his taking this identity as a sufficient reason for postulating a corpuscular structure for a field. He called these corpuscles photons.

A further asymmetry was discussed in 1907: since the mean energy of the corpuscular constituents of the field had already been determined by Planck in 1900 and satisfied the law he had determined in 1900 instead of the 'classical' equipartition theorem, Einstein tried to apply it also to the mean energy of the constituents of matter. He obtained theoretically a behaviour for specific heats of solid bodies which went to zero at zero absolute temperature. At that time no proof existed of such behaviour. But here the line of research on the new quantum theory joined concretely with the route coming directly from chemical research.

Walther Nernst was a chemist, engaged in the study of chemical equilibria and also in practical aspects connected with some chemical firms. He had realized that the presence of an arbitrary additional constant in thermodynamic functions prevented a complete theoretical determination of the dependence upon temperature of chemical equilibrium constants. This was a typical thermodynamic problem. In searching for a criterion for fixing universally the value of this constant, he was led in 1906 to the third law of thermodynamics. The most direct physical consequence of this new law was precisely the prediction that specific heats must go to zero at zero absolute temperature. This behaviour of the specific heats became a test of both the third law and the quantum conceptions, as Nernst himself explicitly recognized. He verified this feature and turned into one of the most convinced supporters of the quantum theory. The latter had fully paid its debt to chemistry.

Let us now summarize the fundamental lines of our analysis. The phenomenistic structure of science, which had been in a relation of subordination with respect to the empirical process of technological innovation and invention up to the first decades of the nineteenth century, was upturned around the mid-century, when the triumphing bourgeoisie posed the material basis for the take-off of a second phase of industrialization. The need for a firmer basis for a new, programmed development of technological innovation was the main reason for the shift to a new scientific practice. The new theoretical physics and the progress of chemistry in the period 1850-70 have been discussed as examples of this model-building, mechanistic science. The mechanistic, or reductionist, structure of this methodology marked the limits of the above-mentioned transformation. These limits emerged clearly in front of the economic events of the last decades of the nineteenth century. In fact, it is impossible to account in a satisfactory way for the full meaning of this sequence of transformations from within chemical or physical theory alone. The breakdown of the old scientific practice was not imposed by 'scientific', 'internal' needs, since the alternatives open at that time (and now) were showing promising results. One sees once more that humankind establishes a relation, not directly with nature itself, but indirectly, through choosing those aspects that are relevant to its activities and interests, and interpreting them in accordance with these interests and the main cultural trends. Mechanics had been the natural reference frame in a world in which the technical basis of production and the organization of labour had a basically mechanical structure. A new scientific practice was now needed in order to cope with the take-off of the second industrial revolution. The development of the production process of the German chemical (mainly organic) industry showed most clearly the limits imposed by mechanics upon scientific elaboration. A new world-view was associated with this upheaval. The chemical and physical theories of the turn of the century were not conceived to solve the problems encountered by the reductionist science: they simply turned the attention to different problems and assumed new principles for the interpretation of natural phenomena. Thermo-dynamics was the prototype of a non-mechanistic, more flexible and productive guide for scientific discovery, particularly consistent with the structure of the German chemical industry.

These are the lines for a specific explanation of the main scientific developments in physics and chemistry in that particular historical phase. We have mentioned that the history of American science shows different features. The pragmatic attitude which generally underlay the developments of science in the United States must be related to the specific structure of American economy and society (De Maria and Seidel, 1979; Russo, 1981). Reference must be made to scientific management and to the adoption of efficiency criteria in every activity. In this context, the need for social control explains also the developments of the social sciences and their specific structure and methods (Lorini, 1979, 1980; Baracca, Ciliberto, Livi, Lorini, Pettini, Ruffo and Russo, 1980). The last-cited reference gives also a synthetic account of the further upheaval in the physical sciences, which took place in the 1920s and 1930s, and whose main result was the formulation of the 'orthodox', or 'Copenhagen-Göttingen' quantum mechanics.

To conclude, we think that the point of view on science we have exemplified here is the only one which may overcome a subordinate rank with respect to the dominant ideology and practice of science and may be fit for an active transformation of the reality in which we live. Let us mention briefly only one example. The environmental and energetic problems which exploded dramatically in recent years cannot be efficiently tackled by a single disciplinary approach nor, above all, from a point of view strictly limited within these problems' own confines, i.e. without taking into consideration their social and political depth. In fact, the complex structure of these problems shows a deep and inextricable intertwining of physico-chemical, geological, ecological, economic, environmental and social aspects. This creates the need for a comprehensive approach capable of overcoming the narrow point of view of any individual discipline and of devising new practical and conceptual instruments. But, above all, the energetic and environmental problems show characteristics which are intrinsically and necessarily determined by the way in which human kind has previously related, and still relates, itself with natural resources, i.e. determined, in the last instance, by both the production and consumption structure characteristic of capitalist society and of its specific class structure. Nature has been considered as an inexhaustible reservoir of resources and has been exploited and pillaged by the social classes which hold economic power according to the logic of profit and to the interests of capital. No consideration has been given either to the needs of the exploited classes and of the countries subordinated to the industrial powers and to the multinationals, or to a correct balance between humankind and nature. From this point of view it becomes immediately evident that no discipline, or interlacing of scientific disciplines, will ever be able to tackle effectively and solve this type of problems. What is needed is, on the contrary and to begin with, clear-cut political choices carried out with the direct participation of those social subjects who have an interest in a radical trans-formation of the present structure and are willing to fight for it. These subjects will have to face the problem, first of all, of deciding what to produce, by means of which production processes, and what and how to consume, thus turning upside down the logic of production and consumption imposed by capital. This process of transformation - certainly painful and difficult - will make it possible to develop and utilize, in a correct and balanced way, the energetic and environmental resources and to find again a balance between humankind and nature. And, at the same time and without any doubt, the limits inherent in these scientific instruments and concepts - functional for the capitalist relations of domination - will emerge. It will then be possible, with the participation of everybody, to devise different instruments and conceptions, functional for a new social and production structure. The effort we are making to understand the class sediment which, in the course of history, has deposited itself in science will not be useless, we believe, for this process of transformation of science and society.

Chapter 2

SOCIAL PHENOMENA AND SOCIAL LAWS

1 SOCIAL PHENOMENA

The concept of dialectical determination developed in the previous
chapter is a tool for the study of social phenomena not in isolation
but in their mutual relation. But what are social phenomena, and
how is their production and reproduction regulated? More specifically,
do social phenomena have a specific nature, does our theory provide
guidelines for an objective classification of different types of
social phenomena, and do the determinant ones have a specific way of
regulating their own reproduction? The answer to these questions is
the task of this chapter. Let us begin by recalling a basic feature
of the approach expounded in chapter 1, an approach which we have
characterized as non-reflective realism, (1) i.e. that there are
several, class determined, possible interpretations of the real
concrete, none of them being either a simple reflection of, or an
arbitrary construction about, the real concrete. An immediate
corollary is that not only science in general but also its branching
out into specialized areas of science is class determined. This
subdivision is not purely arbitrary, it does not depend upon the
whims of individuals or of the scientific community: it is rather
the result (even though not the reflection) of real differences in
the world around us and of our class determined theorization of those
differences. And, to begin with, there is a real difference between
natural and social phenomena, since the former are essentially
independent of, while the latter are essentially dependent upon,
social life in its concrete manifestation. But even within these
two broad categories of phenomena there are subdivisions which are
clearly related to real differences. As far as social phenomena are
concerned, we will argue that the specialization in the different
·social sciences is related to real differences in the class structure
and thus to class struggle.
   A different nominalist approach would not take us very far. For
example, Karl Popper is of the opinion that 'we are perfectly
justified in calling a problem "physical" if it is connected with
problems and theories which have been traditionally discussed by
physicists'. (2) Popper's epistemology turns out to be something
with an object, science and the various sciences, not worth being

defined. (3) More still, for the 'greatest philosopher of science
there has ever been', (4) the origin itself of science cannot be
accounted for since the source of ideas, theories, etc. is a
psychological problem and thus not explicable in philosophical,
logical terms. (5) For this peculiar combination of conventionalism
and psychologism, the criterion to adopt in order to screen those
theories which are, from those which are not, to be the object of
science is therefore that 'we are not simply looking for truth, we
are after interesting and enlightening truth, after theories which
offer solutions to interesting problems. If at all possible, we are
after deep theories'. (6) One cannot help wondering how interesting,
enlightening, and deep Popper's own theory is.
    Let us go back to firmer grounds. Social pehnomena have been
distinguished from the natural ones because the former are, and the
latter are not, essentially dependent upon the concrete, historical
manifestations of social life. More specifically, given that social
life is based upon social relations, given that these latter manifest
themselves as specific concretizations, and given the relation of
dialectical determination used to interpret both the DLI and the
concrete determination of these relations and forms, we can define
social phenomena as social relations and the specific forms taken by
them in their relation of complex dialectical determination. (7)
On this basis, and keeping in mind what was said in chapter 1 about
complex dialectical determination, we can enunciate what we could
call the three basic methodological principles for the study of
social phenomena.
1 Consider social phenomena as determined both by the totality and
by the economic. Given that DLI is the determination by the economic
and concrete determination is the determination by the totality, it
should be clear that there is no incompatibility but a deep and
necessary interpenetration between these two aspects of social
phenomena's determination. (8) Without the complex interrelation of
all phenomena, the DLI cannot take concrete form, but without DLI
complex interrelation becomes theoretically meaningless. Social
phenomena's 'intelligibility developes in proportion as we grasp
their function in the totality to which they belong' (9) as well as
their relation to the economic.
2 Consider social phenomena as both structure determined and as
class determined. Given that it is structures (especially the
economic one) which play the determinant role in society, and given
that it is only through people that these structures can come to
life as social classes, there is again no separation, let alone
contradiction, between a structure-oriented and a class-oriented
analysis. (10) Of course, the first and the second principles are
deeply interrelated. We have stressed in chapter 1 the case of
contradictory structures. Because of their nature they can come to
life only through class struggle. To say, therefore, that social
phenomena concretize themselves in their reciprocal interrelation
means, in fact, that they are formed in the context of class
struggle. And, to say that social phenomena are determined in the
last instance by the economic means, in fact, that they are
functional for the domination of one of the classes structurally
definable in economic terms, i.e. in terms of production relations.
3 Finally, given that the first two principles are aspects of a

logical analysis and given that, as stressed in chapter 1, only a
historical perspective allows us, first to adjudicate the determinant,
etc., role to the various social phenomena, and, second, to give
historical specificity to our representations of social phenomena,
we can enunciate our third principle as: consider social phenomena
as both logically and historically determined.

Social phenomena have been defined as those phenomena which are
essentially dependent upon social life, i.e. which exist only because
people live in societies (11) and that therefore are independent of
the will of individuals as such. It is in this sense that social
phenomena are objective, as against the objectivity of natural
phenomena which derives from their being independent of the will of
individuals as well as of society. If we now consider class divided
societies, where, in our view, classes are the basic units of social
life (and thus of social analysis), it follows that social phenomena
are objective because they are independent of the will of individuals
but not of social classes. More specifically, social phenomena must
satisfy a double condition in order to be such, i.e. they must be,
first, socially determined (in the sense of being determined by
society, in its class structure and historical development) (12) as
well as, second, capable of affecting the concrete determination of
all other social phenomena and thus to overdetermine the determinant
phenomena. In short, social phenomena are such, i.e. objective,
when they are determined and when they not only are affected by, but
also affect, other social phenomena, thus overdetermining the
determinant instance. To take only one example, a theory - even
though the creation of an individual - is also a socially determined
phenomenon because that individual, as a carrier of social relations,
produces something which is functional for the domination of a class
definable in terms of production relations and whose concrete form
is the result of all social phenomena not only in the realm of the
ideological but also in all other spheres of society. This being
socially determined, however, is not yet enough to characterize
this phenomenon as a social one. And the fact that this phenomenon
becomes essentially independent of the will of his creator as an
individual, that it breaks the essential relation creator/created
by starting to live a life of its own (e.g. the circulation in other
individuals' heads), is not enough either for this phenomenon to
be objective in the social sense. This phenomenon becomes objective,
social, only when, because of that social determination and through
this break, it becomes something capable of affecting social
phenomena; when, by penetrating men's consciousnesses, it affects
social practice, class struggle. In the absence of this last
condition, or 'active role', a phenomenon does not trespass the
borders of subjectivity; it remains (or becomes again) a subjective
phenomenon because it is dependent for its existence (essentially
dependent) upon the will of the individual. (13)

What we have attempted to show is that the essence of social
phenomena (and thus their interrelation) is really different from
the essence of natural phenomena and that consequently, the method
to be followed in analysing social phenomena (as outlined in the
above-mentioned three principles) must be specific to them. But, as
anticipated at the beginning of this chapter, there are also real
differences among the different social sciences, differences related

to the class structure and thus class struggle of a certain society.
To identify these differences means, of course, to draw the border-
lines between the general study of society, on the one hand, and the
specific and specialized areas of study, on the other, as well as
between these latter. The general study of society, sociology, is
the study of the birth, reproduction, and supersession of social
phenomena in their relation of complex dialectical determination.
This study subdivides itself into branches, or specific social
sciences, whose objects are social phenomena which are at the same
time a special category of social phenomena. (14) The most important
categories of social phenomena (and thus the most important social
sciences) in class divided societies are the economic, the political,
and the ideological because these are the basic types of class
domination. It is in this sense that real differences underlie the
different social sciences. And it is because of these real differences
that each science has its own object, a certain field of study which
distinguishes it from all other sciences. As E. Durkheim says, a
science 'must take cognizance of a reality which is not in the domain
of other sciences'. (15) Of course, it is not the summation of
certain social phenomena, deemed in a conventionalist way to belong to
a certain field of study, which delimits this latter's contours.
Rather, it is by drawing certain contours on the basis of real
characteristics that certain phenomena fall within the scope of a
science. Thus, for example, economics is the study of production,
distribution, exchange and consumption relations and their forms,
or the study of the production, distribution, exchange, and consumption
of material and mental products as exchange values. (16) This delimits
the field within which social phenomena can be considered also as
economic phenomena. These limits are not arbitrary since these
economic relations are also a specific (economic) type of class
domination. For example, exploitation is the form of class domination
specific to capitalist production relations. Since these phenomena
are social, they must be studied by analysing the method typical of
the social sciences as outlined above. Since they are also economic,
i.e. since they belong to a specific area, with a specific object,
they are subject to a specific kind of dynamic, i.e. to specific
laws and mechanisms of birth, reproduction, and supersession which
will have to be discovered by applying the above-mentioned method.
Similarly, the political and the ideological are delimited by
respectively political and ideological relations (which are also two
different types of class domination) and their forms. Again, the
study of these two realms of social phenomena must strive to discover
the laws and mechanisms through which political and ideological
phenomena are born, reproduce themselves, and are finally superseded
as well as, of course, their interrelation with social phenomena
belonging to other realms of society. Important for our purposes
is the study of the ideological, i.e. of the production of knowledge
as a means of class domination, something which we will undertake
in chapter 4. To anticipate only one point, there we will see that
the production and distribution of knowledge takes place according
to a mechanism specific to this type of social phenomenon (mental
products), i.e. the penetration/incorporation mechanism, and that
it is through this mechanism that a certain mental product can
change its social content. In that chapter we will provide also an

example of a social phenomenon, the nuclear family, which does not fall (or does not fall exclusively) within any of the three basic social sciences. In these sort of cases the method to be followed is that of examining first the functionality of such a phenomenon for the economic, political, and ideological domination of one (or perhaps more than one) class identifiable in terms of production relations, and second the specific form taken by this phenomenon, i.e. the way these types of domination take a particular form, reproduce themselves, within that phenomenon.

We can now proceed to a categorization of phenomena. Given the importance of the concept of 'relation' and given the Marxist, and thus materialist, nature of our approach, the question is bound to arise as to the nature of social relations: are they material or not and, if they are not, are they of a different non-materiality than that of the products of the human mind? We will submit that social relations are not material and yet qualitatively different from consciousness, i.e. that within each of the three basic categories of social phenomena just mentioned, another subdivision is possible: that between social phenomena belonging to the real concrete, and yet non-material, and social phenomena which are mental products and thus of a totally different kind of non-materiality.

Let us begin by considering the nature of relations in general and of social relations in particular. To hold, as H. Korch (1980) does, that relations among physical bodies and production relations are material because they exist independently of consciousness means to call 'matter' what, in fact, for Marx, is the real concrete. On this basis, Korch introduces the distinction between matter (Materie) and forms of existence of it as, for example, substance (Stoff), field (Feld), and relations. These latter are thus material in this broad sense but not in the narrow sense of being made of substance. (17) This approach leads to an unnecessary strain on the concept of matter so that everything which does not originate in our minds must be material. This standpoint is probably due to the difficulty to give a general, philosophical definition of matter, given the generality of the concept. It is because of this that the definition of matter is related to the concept of consciousness. Matter becomes everything which is not consciousness. (18) On the other hand, social (including economic) relations are for us non-material and yet belong to the real concrete. What is, then, the status of relations within the concept of real concrete? Engels (1976) and Lenin ('Collected Works', No.38) have stressed that matter's mode of existence is movement and that matter exists only through the individual material things. If matter, the whole, exists only through the individual material things, then the latter, by being part of the whole, by co-existing within the whole, must be in relation with each other. The individual things, not as isolated entities but as parts of the whole, can realize their characteristics (and thus themselves) only in relation to each other. Therefore, relations are the mode of existence of the material parts of the whole (matter) or the mode of existence of matter in its quality of being internally differentiated, of being a complex of material things. But matter exists only as movement of matter. Thus the relation among specific material things is a specific form of movement. The relation between two bodies is expressed, for example, by the attraction of one by the other (the

fall of a body); or, the relation between two classes is expressed
by class struggle, again a particular form of movement. More
specifically, if movement is the form of existence of matter and if
matter's internal relations are its mode of existence as a complex
of parts, as a differentiated whole, then class struggle can be the
mode of existence of contradictory social relations (as submitted in
chapter 1) because social relations are the mode of existence of
matter (individuals) in the social context, of people as units (parts)
of society (the whole).

Against this background, we can now proceed to a categorization of
phenomena consonant, in our opinion, with both the explicit definitions
provided by Marx and with the spirit of his theory. The real concrete
is what exists independently from, and thus from a logical point of
view before, appropriation in thought. It is thus not only matter:
it is also relations, both in the social and in the natural world.
The appropriation in thought of the real concrete is called by Marx
imagined concrete ('a chaotic conception of the whole') and concrete
in thought (based upon 'the simplest determinations', i.e. the
essential elements of a model of reality which encompass in nuce all
the features of that model). We are not specifically interested here
in the distinction between these two stages of mental production (we
will deal with this distinction in the next chapter) and will give
the outcomes of both stages the general name of mental products.
Material and non-material phenomena are defined according to whether
they are made of matter (solid, liquid, or gaseous) or not. Natural
phenomena are that part of the real concrete which is essentially
independent of social life in the sense that they are independent of
both individuals and of social classes. Natural phenomena can be
both material and non-material. These latter are the relations among
the constituent parts of the material whole. Social phenomena are,
as we have seen, social relations and their forms in their interrelation. They can be either real concretes or mental products.
They are all those phenomena which are socially determined and which
have also the property of affecting all other social phenomena. The
social phenomena which belong to the real concrete can be both non-
material (since they are social relations or their, in this case
non-material, forms) or they can take a material form (e.g. a newspaper). In this latter case the social phenomenon needs a material
form to manifest itself (this particular case will be discussed
further in chapter 5). The non-materiality of this category of
social phenomena is completely different from the non-materiality of
the mental products, since the former belong to the real concrete
and the latter to the concrete in thought. Both, however, are
objective. Objective phenomena are those whose existence is
essentially independent of the will of the individuals (in the social
world, however, they are essentially dependent upon the will of
social classes) or also of classes (in the natural world). If their
existence is essentially dependent upon the will of the individuals,
they are subjective. Schematically, they are shown in Figure 2.1,
where the symbol => denotes determination (a process analysed in
detail in the next chapter as far as determination of mental production goes). Let us take a few examples. A physical body is a
material (made of matter), a natural (its existence is independent
of concrete social life), and a real concrete phenomenon (its

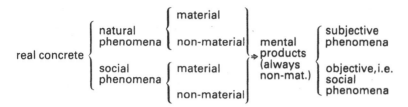

Figure 2.1

existence is independent of its appropriation in thought). The technical
division of labour is an example of a social (because socially determined
and affecting other social phenomena), real concrete (it is independent
of its appropriation in thought), and non-material phenomenon. The fall
of that physical body is an example of a non-material, natural, real
concrete phenomenon. The observation of that fall and the working out
of, for example, the law of gravity are examples of mental products,
therefore non-material phenomena. The same applies to a theory of the
division of labour in society. Both mental products can become
objective, social phenomena under the conditions specified above. The
difference is that the former belongs to the natural sciences and the
latter to the social ones. The next session will deal with the
difference between these two categories of science.

2   SOCIAL LAWS

The vantage point which has been taken in the first chapter is that
structures, when inherently antagonistic, create the conditions of
their reproduction or supersession because classes, the groups of
people through which structures come to life, create their conditions
of domination. But these conditions of reproduction or supersession
are not all on the same level. On the one hand, we have the difference
between the determinant (the economic) and the determined instances.
This means that a society's reproduction is basically the reproduction
of its determinant elements through the calling into existence (determination) of the determined instances, i.e. of the determinant
instances' conditions of reproduction. On the other hand, there are
also differences among the several determined instances. And this
not only, as we have seen, in the sense that there are different forms
and types of class domination (the three categories of social
phenomena, i.e. the economic, the political, and the ideological),
but also in the sense that a categorization can be drawn cutting
across these three basic types of social phenomena, and based upon
the specific way in which the determined instances contribute to the
reproduction or supersession of the determinant one. It is against
this background that the analysis of social laws, or laws of motion,
(19) should be placed. They are a particularly important type of
the production relations' conditions of reproduction. (20) Their
study is fundamental for the construction of verifiable hypotheses
about the rise, development, and disappearance of social phenomena.
   The basic Marxian hypothesis concerning social laws (as we
reconstruct it) is made up of two propositions, of which the first
is that there exist natural laws, laws independent of any historical

determination, the nature of which never changes. These laws are
called natural by Marx, and are natural phenomena, because, even
though they are essentially related to social life, they are not
only independent of the will of the individuals, (21) but also of
social classes and of the specific form of a society. One such law
is that in all societies men must engage in a labour process, in
the transformation of use values. This process is for Marx independent of any social determination:

> The process of production of capital is above all an *actual*
> *labour process*, considering its real aspect, or considering it
> as a process which forms new use-values by useful labour with
> use-values. As such, its moments, its conceptually determined
> constitutive parts, are those of the *labour process* at large -
> of *each labour process* on whatever level of economic development
> and on the basis of whatever mode of production happens to be
> proceeding. (22)

Another such law is that every society must distribute social labour
in a certain way and in certain proportions among products and
agents of production:

> Every child knows, too, that the masses of products corresponding
> to the different needs require different and quantitatively
> determined masses of the total labour of society. That this
> *necessity* of *distribution* of social labour in definite proportions
> cannot possibly be done away with by a *particular form* of social
> production but can only change the *mode* of its *appearance*, is
> self-evident. No natural laws can be done away with. What can
> change in historically different circumstances is only the *form*
> in which these laws assert themselves. (23)

But, second, since every society is characterized by certain social
(and especially production) relations, these natural laws become
social in nature, take on a specific social nature, according to
the specific nature of those social relations. (24) Under capitalism
the labour process, while remaining such, becomes also a surplus
value producing process, since use values are now produced as means
for the production of exchange values and thus of profit. (25) Or,
concerning the 'necessity of the distribution of social labour in
definite proportions',

> the form in which this proportional distribution of labour
> asserts itself, in a state of society where the interconnection
> of social labour is manifested in the *private exchange* of the
> individual products of labour, is precisely the exchange value
> of these products. (26)

More specifically, the need to distribute social labour in a definite
way and in definite proportions becomes, in simple commodity
production, allocation of social labour for production of commodities,
i.e. of value, and thus requires the exchange of products according
to the labour time which is necessary to produce them. Under
capitalist production, where 'a priori there is no conscious social
regulation of production' and where 'the rational and naturally
necessary asserts itself only as a blindly working average', (27)
the allocation of social labour takes place not any longer through
the law of value but through its modification and requires the law
of the equalization of the rate of profit and thus the exchange of
commodities at their price of production. Under socialism the

allocation of society's labour takes place according to the principal 'from each according to his ability, to each according to his needs'. The social (production) relations have changed and thus changes the mode of allocation of society's labour. This latter takes place through a production and distribution not any longer of value but of use value. (28) These, as well as many others, are all social laws, all social expressions of natural laws under certain systems of social relations. It is because they are social expressions of natural laws that they regulate the functioning of the social system, that they become the laws of motion of society. Thus, natural laws can manifest themselves only in specific social forms while retaining their character of necessity, of objectivity. In their socially determined form, they regulate the functioning, movement of the social system; they are social phenomena which regulate the production of other social phenomena (and of society), including the production and reproduction of those social phenomena (production relations) by which they are determined. Therefore, della Volpe's statement to the effect that

se ad es., dice Marx, esaminiamo la categoria economica della *produzione*, dobbiamo saper vedere che il suo carattere *generale* o comune è qualcosa di *articolato* o complesso, che si *diversifica* in numerose determinazioni. Taluni di questi elementi sono comuni a tutte le epoche, altri ad alcune soltanto (29)

is correct. But we can go further. We can specify why certain elements are 'common to all epochs' and what is the status of all these common elements. In line with what was expounded in the previous chapter, we can submit that, as to the first question, these elements (e.g. the production of use values) are common to all epochs, because they are conditions of existences of all societies, i.e. natural laws operating in the realm of human society. But, and this is the second question, these common elements can materialize themselves only in their social expression: the production of use values takes place under capitalism in its socially characteristic expression as production of exchange values. Thus, these natural laws are necessarily moulded in socially determined laws, become social laws. The object of science becomes, therefore, what is social about them, historically specific, e.g. in case of capitalist production 'science consists precisely in demonstrating *how* the law of value asserts itself'. (30)

But, to speak of the laws of motion under capitalism as the social expression of natural laws is not enough. This holds for all types of society. Capitalism, however, is a class divided society based on contradictory production relations. Thus, not only is capitalist society characterized by contradictions, it is characterized by specific contradictions due to the fact that social relations are contradictory already at the level of production. Social relations cannot but be contradictory and the mode of existence of this contradictory nature is, as we have seen above, class struggle. Now, since social laws are the 'translation' in society and by society of natural laws, and since this translation is determined by contra- dictory social relations, social laws must regulate the functioning of the system in a contradictory way. But this is not enough, because to say that social laws regulate the functioning of the system in a contradictory way, and thus through class struggle, means to stay at the level of class divided societies without considering the specificity of that particular type of class divided society which is capitalism. Social laws' way of contra-dictory regulation of capitalism's functioning is by their being: (a) tendential, in the sense that the basic tendency cannot be separated from the several countertendencies and that, as we will see shortly, at times the countertendencies can become dominant, something which manifests itself in the form of fluctuations in the phenomena observed; and (b) cyclical, in the sense that they affirm themselves, i.e. that the basic tendency affirms itself against the countertendencies, recurrently and cyclically. (31) For example, 'every special historic mode of production has its own special laws of population, historically valid within its limits alone'. (32) The law of population 'peculiar to the capitalist mode of production' is the production of relative surplus-population', i.e. 'surplus with regard to the average needs of self-expansion of capital', (33) or in other words is the production of the industrial reserve army. This tendency is, however, always accompanied by countertendencies, i.e. 'is always connected with violent fluctuations and transitory production of surplus population'. (34) These fluctuations, however, are not a-rhythmic, they are cyclical, they 'take on the form of periodicity', (35) since 'the varying phases of the industrial cycle recruit the surplus-population, and become one of the most energetic agents of its reproduction'. (36) Surplus population, therefore, disappears due to the countertendencies, only to reappear at a later stage in a roughly regular (cyclical) way. Similarly, wages are tendentially determined by the value of labour power but fluctuate according to 'the expansion and contraction of the industrial reserve army'. (37)

   The fact that social laws are not arbitrarily 'chosen', that they are the social form taken by natural laws and that this social form is contradictory, implies that the system is based upon fundamental social phenomena which are contradictory in nature, and thus that it is based upon fundamental contradictions. Social laws can therefore be regarded also as the expression of the fundamental contradictions of class divided society. We agree, thus, with neither A. Cutler et al. that 'there can be no laws of tendency'; (38) nor E. Balibar's reduction of the law of development to the status of tendency, (39) since, for us, the latter is a characteristic of the former due to the contradictory nature of the system; nor do we agree with M. Godelier, for whom social laws 'expriment les propriétés structurales inintentionnelles des rapports sociaux et leur hiérarchie et articula-tion propres sur la base de modes de production déterminés', (40) since implicit here is the concept of social laws as effects of the structure. (41) Moreover, the statement that social laws are an expression of the structure, even though correct, is incomplete and too general because, on the one hand, it does not recognize the existence of natural laws and, on the other hand, does not inquire into the nature of social laws under capitalism. Also, our approach differs, of course, radically from Max Weber's, since the counter-tendencies are not deviations from the basic tendency, as Weber's irrational action is a deviation from 'a conceptually pure type of rational action'. (42) Social laws are inherently tendential. On the other hand, for Weber, laws are 'typical probabilities confirmed

by observation to the effect that under certain given conditions an
expected course of social action will occur, which is understandable
in terms of the typical motives and typical subjective intentions
of the actors.' (43)   Finally, we take due distance also from
supposedly Marxist concepts of laws and tendency. For example, for
C. Helberger

> Unter einer Tendenz versteht man im allgemeinen eine Aussage
> über eine Anzahl von Ereignissen oder eine Regelmassigkeit, die
> nicht für jeden Zeitpunkt zutrifft, aber für die Gesamtheit der
> Fälle oder auf längere Sicht stimmt.' (44)

Given this definition - which has nothing further in common with
Marx - of tendency and of tendential laws ('Bei Tendenzaussagen
handelt es sich gewissermassen um Gesetze, zu denen Ausnahmen
zugelassen werden') it follows quite naturally that, for this author,
'"Tendenzen" sind also ausserordentlich vage Aussagen über einen
Gegenstand.' (45)   For us, on the other hand, social laws are of a
completely different nature. They are socially and historically
determined (even though they express natural laws). Also, the status
of a law changes according to the level of analysis so that, for
example, capital export can be either a countertendency when framed
in the analysis of the law of the falling rate of profit, or the
main tendency in an analysis of imperialism.

This discussion of social laws allows us to throw some light on
the difference between natural and social sciences. Our thesis has
been that this difference is not that social sciences are socially
determined while natural sciences are not. Neither the social nor
the natural scientist is free from social conditioning in the very
act of producing knowledge. The difference resides in the nature of
the phenomena studied. Natural science is socially determined
analysis of natural (i.e. non-socially determined) phenomena; social
science is socially determined analysis of social (i.e. socially
determined) phenomena. A further difference follows, i.e. that the
social sciences become, the moment they become social phenomena,
part of the real concrete which they study. Both social and natural
sciences are social phenomena, (46) but only the former becomes part
of the real concrete which it studies, through its action upon other
social phenomena. It is this difference which creates the illusion
of the (greater) objectivity of the natural sciences, objectivity
which is interpreted as lack of social determination of the natural
sciences whereas what is not socially determined is the phenomena
they study. (47)   This illusion, i.e. to consider natural sciences
as non-socially determined because of the non-social determination
of the phenomena they study and to consider these sciences as
objective because of their supposed lack of social determination,
reflects itself - in a typical ideological mechanism - upon the
social sciences which are then considered as objective (i.e.
scientific) only if not socially determined, i.e. only if they study
non-socially determined phenomena. Social laws - and phenomena in
general - typical of a certain society (capitalism) must then be
absolutized as laws and phenomena common to all societies (in order
for their study to be seen as 'objective') i.e. social laws are
generalized to a-historical natural laws, so that the laws of the
capitalist system (and thus the system itself) become eternal.

Notice, however, that when we say that natural sciences do not

affect natural phenomena we do not imply that human action does not
affect the natural environment, nature. Nature does change, due to
human action. Thus, what changes is both the nature of the interpretation of those laws and the natural environment. What does not
change, in the sense that it does not depend upon human action and
relations, is the nature of the natural phenomena, i.e. natural laws.
In the social sciences, on the other hand, both the nature of the
phenomena, the nature of the environment in which they are formed,
and the nature of their interpretation are subject to change, to
social determination. (48) This allows us to understand why it is
misleading to separate 'natural', 'objective', human needs from
those 'artificial' needs which are created by society. Let us take
as an extreme example a certain type of natural laws, the biological
ones, as for example the 'objective' law, or 'fact', that a certain
organism must have a certain minimum amount of food in order to
survive. No food, no life. This is true 'under any social system'.
Yet, since in the realm of human society natural laws can be known
only in their social shape, i.e. as social laws, biological needs
(e.g. the need for food) can be known and studied also only as they
are shaped by society. The hunger of the savage, says Marx, is
different from that which is satisfied by using fork and knife. And
this is not only so because of the different sorts, qualities, of
food and the different modes of production they presuppose. In
fact, what is the 'minimum quantity of food' above which this need
becomes unnatural? Minimum in relation to what? The need for a
certain minimum quantity of food necessary to keep a man (worker)
alive for an average of twenty-five years was natural during the
industrial revolution in England, but would be utterly unnatural
nowadays. Even the basic biological needs (not to speak of the
psychological ones) are known only in their socially determined
expression, form. True, certain needs, common to all societies,
must be satisfied under penalty of extinction; but it is society
which determines the shape taken by the needs and the way in which
they are satisfied.

3 TENDENCY, DETERMINATION, AND DIALECTICS IN SOCIAL LAWS

Against this background, we can account for the assertion made in
section 2 concerning the fundamental trait of social laws under
capitalism, that of being tendential in nature. If the concept of
dialectical determination accounts for the nature of social phenomena,
it must account also for the particular nature of those particular
social phenomena which are the social laws. Let us begin by
returning to the example provided in section 2 concerning the law of
population typical of capitalism, i.e. the production of relative
surplus population. What determines this social phenomenon? In our
view, it is the need that capital has to replace men with machines,
i.e. to increase its organic composition, since this is the way to
increase the production of relative surplus value. But the production
of relative surplus value can have also the opposite effect through
the search for new markets, the creation of new branches of production,
and thus the absorption of (a part of) the relative surplus population.
Both production and absorption of relative surplus population are thus

determined by the same determinant instance or, generally speaking, it is the same determinant instance which determines both the tendency and the countertendencies. It is, actually, precisely because of this logically contemperaneous determination that a certain phenomenon (in our example the production of relative surplus population) assumes a tendential nature, i.e. that it cannot realize itself (as a condition of reproduction of the determinant instance) apart from the realization of countereffects (equally conditions of reproduction of the same determinant instance). Or, in other words, the determinant instance – because of its contradictory nature – can reproduce itself only in a contradictory way, by creating contradictory conditions of its own reproduction. (49) The countertendencies are obstacles put in the way of the working of the main tendency. The interplay of the main tendency and of the countertendencies gives the contradictory nature of the dynamics of the capitalist system, i.e. shows how a social law regulates the development of the system in a contradictory way. The fact that these obstacles are overcome only to be posed, to appear, again in a different place under different forms, shows the recurrent and cyclical nature of the social laws. And the fact that at times the main tendency can be overcome by the combined effect of the countertendencies (when this is so is an object of conjunctural analysis) shows the tendential nature of social laws. Tendency is thus the particular way in which dialectical determination acts in those particular social phenomena which are social laws.

Implicit in our approach is the possibility that both types of determined instances have to be dominant, i.e. play the fundamental role in the reproduction of the determinant instance at each different conjunctural moment. It is thus not the determinant instance which assigns the dominant role to the determined one but it is the conjuncture, the complex interrelation of all social phenomena, of all forms of class struggle. (50) It is this complex interrelation which will 'select' for realization either the one (the tendency) or the other (the countertendency) social phenomenon. Empirical research can inform us on which one of the two is dominant, but no amount of empirical research can substitute itself to this dialectical analysis, not even if the tendency would appear less consistently than the countertendency in a given span of time. But, if both types of the two determined instances can be dominant, how can we be justified in calling the one the tendency and the other the countertendency? Can the conjuncture change the nature of the one into the other? Such a view would collapse one of the basic elements of Marxist analysis, the existence of structural tendencies, into a basically empiricist view. In fact, we do not have to step into this alien theoretical terrain. The identification of a structural tendency, of a tendency, that is, which in a certain form holds at least for a whole phase of development of a social system, is not essentially an empirical business, but depends upon the recognition that what characterizes the tendency, what causes the tendential phenomenon, reproduces itself within the countertendential phenomenon. In our example, the production of unemployment is the main tendency vis-à-vis the absorption of the labour force because the new branches of production (upon which such an absorption depends) will be immediately (from a logical, structural point of view) subjected to the same mechanism

of an increase in the organic composition of capital and thus will
reproduce the main tendency within themselves: the tendency to
unemployment will characterize also these new branches of production.
(51) It is precisely this power to force its way through within the
countertendencies, i.e. within the other determined instances, which
characterizes and defines the main tendency even at times when it is
the countertendencies which play the fundamental role for the
reproduction (or supersession) of the determinant instance. And it
is just because of this ability to re-appear within other determined
instances that these phenomena, tendencies, can regulate the working
of the system, can be the laws of movement of the system.

It follows that the laws of capitalist development, or fundamental
tendencies, are valid for all stages of capitalism even though they
might assume different forms in different stages of development.
For instance, export of capital is a tendency of the capitalist
economy but can take on the form of export of commodity or of money
capital. Similarly, the forms taken by capital concentration and
centralization change with the different phases of capitalist
development (52) and with them change the countertendencies, but
capital will always tend to concentrate and centralize itself.
Panzieri's view that 'the only constant is the tendency for capital's
domination over labour-power to increase' (53) seems therefore to be
unwarranted. Countertendencies in a certain phase cannot become
'dominant tendencies in the new situation'. (54) Rather, tendencies
remain such even though their form might change and even though at
times the countertendencies might become dominant. Panzieri's
correct concern to avoid 'falling into the "systematic" error of
fixing the representation of any moment, with its particularly
transitory laws, as the "fundamental mode" to which the system's
further development could only make more or less marginal corrections'
(55) should not result in the obliteration of the borders delimiting
the fundamental, structural laws - tendencies - of a certain socio-
economic system. Just as there is no contradictoriness but complementarity between determination in the last instance and the variety of
the realized (and realizable) forms of the determined instances, so
there is no contradictoriness but complementarity between the
determined character of social laws and their being, first, fundamental for the system's reproduction and, second, tendential in the
way they ensure this reproduction. The consequences of our position
as well as its specificity can best be brought into relief by
contrasting it with R. Bhaskar's recent work. This will be the topic
of the following section of this chapter.

4 DIALECTICS, OPEN AND CLOSED SYSTEMS, AND SOCIAL LAWS

Von Bertalanffy's article, The Theory of Open Systems in Physics and
Biology, published in 1950, (56) is widely regarded as having started
the systems thinking movement. In the words of F.E. Emery, scientific
interest was mobilized by von Bertalanffy's 'rigorous distinction
between open and closed systems'. (57) Whether this distinction can
be accredited this much or not, the fact remains that systems theory
has gained, since then, widespread popularity not only in terms of
its practical applications to the governmental and administrative

spheres but also in terms of its penetration in the realm of theory.
New disciplines, like cybernetics, information theory, communication
theory, operations research, and systems analysis have come to life
and old disciplines have developed branches based upon systems
thinking. This holds for many of the natural and social sciences as
well as for philosophy. (58) Common to all these applications is
the fundamental distinction between open and closed systems where,
to say it with von Bertalanffy, 'a system is closed if no material
enters or leaves it; it is open if there is import and export and,
therefore, change of the components'. (59) No wonder, then, that in
the wake of systems theory's seeming success and impressed by
systems theory's seeming scientific rigour, many authors fall into
the temptation to borrow (either consciously or not) essential
elements of this approach and first of all the closed system/open
system distinction. By way of illustration, we will consider
shortly R. Bhaskar's recent work in the philosophy of science where
the above-mentioned distinction is one of the pillars upon which his
theory is built. The thesis I want to submit is not that Bhaskar is
a systems theorist; rather, my thesis is that Bhaskar's adoption of
the closed/open system dichotomy as a central feature of his
theoretical construction cannot but lead him to conservative stands
and conclusions and that this conservative character stems from the
a-critical incorporation in his approach of that dichotomy, i.e. of
an essential element of an inherently conservative approach (systems
theory). What follows, therefore, does not aim at a review of all
aspects of Bhaskar's work, (60) some of which are, without any doubt,
important elements for the construction of a radical ontology and
epistemology. I am thinking, for example, of his distinction between
the transitive and the intransitive objects of knowledge (61) and of
his cogent critique of a number of philosophers and philosophical
currents (62) based upon that distinction. Rather, my aim is to
show my thesis by focusing the discussion on Bhaskar's treatment of
laws, both natural and social.

As already anticipated, Bhaskar's argument hinges upon the basic
difference between open and closed systems: the latter disrupt the
course of nature and produce through man's action a sequence of
events, constant conjunctions, which otherwise would not have taken
place. If this conjunction allows us to identify a law, then that
law, to be generally valid, must be valid also without experimental
conditions, in an open system, and thus does not imply necessarily
a constant conjunction of events. This shows that real structures,
generating mechanisms, do exist even though only their effects are
visible. (63) On the face of it, this is a very attractive strategy
which at one stroke dismisses empiricism and establishes, by the
pure strength of logic, the tendential nature of natural and social
laws. If we want to make intelligible experimental activity and
thus justify the existence of science, then the world must be made
up of generating mechanisms and their effects (the two often being
'out of phase') and science must be the study of those mechanisms.
On Bhaskar's view, the universality of a law is that it must continue
to act also in spite of other systems' influences, i.e. in an open
system, and thus without a constant conjunction of events. The
absence of such a conjunction is explained in terms of disturbances,
fetters to the working of the law. These fetters become then the

countertendencies which obstruct, from outside the system, what
would be the functioning of the system (mechanism) in a closure.

Now, it can be objected that the assumption that a law valid under
certain conditions (closed system) must continue to be valid also
under different conditions (open system), can hold only if there is
no radical modification of the system when the closure is opened.
To take only one example in the social world: if a pre-capitalist
system is opened to capitalist infiltration, the outcome can be a
radical change in the former's generating mechanism and laws rather
than the effect anticipated by Bhaskar. The problem with this
approach is the assumption, unwarranted in my opinion, of a world
of events basically generated by systems which are not only closed
but also essentially independent, i.e. the basically a-dialectical
distinction between closed and open systems. Even though, in Bhaskar's
approach, in the non-experimental world events are generated in open
systems, from a logical (and not chronological) point of view, i.e.
as far as the logic of the generating mechanism is concerned, events
are first generated by and in closed and independent systems and then
subjected to 'offsetting factors' when the system is ideally opened.
On this basis, it is difficult to imagine how a satisfactory way
(or any way at all) can be found of inquiring into what governs the
functioning of the mechanisms in an open world. This seems to be
too high a price to pay in order to be able to show - in a purely
logical way, and thus apart from the nasty need to prove a theory in
practice - the existence of non-empirical structures. The differences
between Bhaskar's approach and a dialectical one is that in the
former the external factors can only slow down, so to speak, the
generative activity of a certain system; (64) in the latter, on the
other hand, the determinant instance, or generative mechanism in
Bhaskar's terminology, has already in itself a multiplicity of
possible conditions of existence or supersession out of which only
some find concrete realization. In their turn, these latter, the
determined instances, react upon (overdetermine) the determinant
instance. It is this complex relationship of determination, rather
than simple addition of effects, which explains the possibility of
the non-realization of the consequent as well as (and this is perhaps
even more important) the non-constancy of the forms taken by it. In
a dialectical view, contradictory phenomena do not come from outside
the system: (65) both the determinant instance and the determined
ones are essential parts of the same system. Moreover, for Bhaskar,
open system events are generated by two or more mechanisms (the
economic, the physical, the natural, etc.) (66) 'so that because
we do not know ex-ante which mechanisms will actually be at work
(and perhaps have no knowledge of their mode of articulation) events
are not deductively predictable'. (67) In a dialectical view, the
generative mechanism, due to its inner contradictoriness, generates
a play of tendencies and countertendencies which make only perfectly
accurate predictions (at least in the social sciences (68))
impossible. Dialectics presupposes a view of the world in terms of
tendencies (normic statements, in Bhaskar's terminology) but the
reverse is not necessarily true, as Bhaskar's theory shows.

The basic weakness in Bhaskar's approach consists thus in his
concept of, and distinction between, closed and open systems. 'If
a system is closed then a tendency once set in motion must be fulfille

If a system is open this might not happen due to the presence of "offsetting factors" or "countervailing causes".... Once a tendency is set in motion it is fulfilled unless it is prevented'. (69) The closed system is not a dialectical one, not even a tendential one (since it does produce constant conjunctions of events), but is a machine-like generator of events. In systems theory the machine and the organism are the two major metaphors. No matter how important the differences between these two metaphors (and the approaches inspired by them) are, their common element is the impossibility for both of them to accommodate a dialectical view of reality, a view that explains movement and change in terms of internal contradictions and which accounts for the structure which generates those contradictions. Rather than going back to Durkheim's concept of organism, Bhaskar's concept of laws is heavily influenced by the Weberian metaphor of mechanism and by this author's conception of concrete phenomena as deviations from ideal types. (70) It is not by chance that for Bhaskar 'it is a mistake of the greatest magnitude to suppose that [theory] ... will tell us what to do' (71) and that he must therefore conclude that 'Marxist science is subversive in virtue of its cognitive power alone'. (72) On these fundamental issues Bhaskar shakes hands with Weber rather than with Marx. A theory which denies predictability and stresses only explanatory power is useless for a class engaged in a radical transformation of social reality. Bhaskar's laws are tendential but no predictions can be made about them. But it is precisely the analysis and prediction of tendencies (laws) and thus of the possible developments of the phenomena regulated by these laws which lends meaningfulness to social science. This all shows very clearly not only the conservative consequences of the acceptance of a fundamentally a-dialectical element of knowledge, i.e. the open system/closed system scheme, but also the social, i.e. class, determination of that element of knowledge. And this not only in terms of the functionality of this element of knowledge for class domination at the theoretical/ideological level, but also in terms of the origin of this element of knowledge. In fact, (73) the concept of closed system and thus of closure and of constant events applies to physics and chemistry, (74) the two sciences whose development is fundamental for the development of capitalism after the Second World War (late capitalism), but it is not applicable to other natural sciences (e.g. cosmology) and certainly not to the social sciences. Bhaskar extends this scheme to all sciences on the strength of the argument that if science must be possible then this scheme must apply. (75) What he achieves is thus not the proof of a certain ontological nature of the real concrete but only a further example of the non-neutrality of knowledge, in this particular case of the impossibility of building a Marxist ontology from a class-neutral point of view, in terms of 'pure' logic.

Given the a-dialectical separation between closed and open systems, it is not surprising that Bhaskar's theory founders when confronted with the basic question as to how events are generated in open systems, i.e. with the question of the relationship among systems in the open world, or if you want, of the nature of this system of systems. 'To completely account for an event', says Bhaskar, 'would be to describe all the different principles involved

in its generation.' (76) But what about the articulation of all
these different principles? Surely, a description of each one of
them is quite a different thing from an analysis of their reciprocal
interaction, of the nature of the interrelation which must be
postulated if we postulate the multiple, rather than the individual
generation of events. Yet, this question is simply not tackled by
Bhaskar. (77) Consequently, the failure to account for how a complex
system tends, because of its inner nature, to generate an event
generates the double and related failure to account, first, for how
there can be a multiple generation of conjunctures and, second, for
the articulation of this multiplicity of generating mechanisms.
Given this lack of a theory of a system of systems, Bhaskar's
transcendental realism cannot account for why there is this plurality,
i.e. it cannot account for it in sociological terms (which, correctly,
are the only ones acceptable to him). Thus, Bhaskar must resort,
first, to the individual scientist as the generator of new theories
and, second, to the 'creative employment of his [i.e. the scientist's]
imagination' (78) as the motor of the production of knowledge. True,
Bhaskar emphasizes, correctly, that 'man never creates, but only
changes his knowledge' (79) and that knowledge 'can never be seen as
a function of individual sense-experience' (80) so that the sociological dimension of knowledge is given by its being a non-individu-
alistic acquisition. Knowledge 'though it exists only in virtue of
human activity ... is irreducible to the acts of men' (81) and men
are active agents rather than passive sensors (which is the view of
the empirical realist). However, it is the individual rather than
the class which is still the unit of scientific production. Bhaskar's
theory might not be individualistic à la empirical realism but is
still individualistic. (82) On his account, individuals are not
atoms, they presuppose each other; they are carriers of social
relations, but they are not embodiments of aspects of class relations,
and, if they are, their being carriers of class relations is not
given any privileged (determinant) status. (83) On this fundamental
point, again, Bhaskar is much closer to Weber than to Marx.

More recent writings have shown concern for some of the issues
mentioned above. Even though my critique hinges upon Bhaskar's
incorporation of the closed/open system dichotomy in his thinking,
I shall comment briefly also on how Bhaskar elaborates on, and
amplifies, the fact/value distinction. My general point will be
that while (further) concern for these issues marks a welcome
development in Bhaskar's approach and might add much to his already
stimulating work, I am convinced neither that the direction in which
Bhaskar goes leads to the development of a Marxist dialectical view
nor that these new developments in his theory are consistent with
the bulk of his previous writing.

Concerning the closed/open system dichotomy, a distinction can be
made between the meaning that Bhaskar himself thinks should be
attached to this dichotomy and the way in which he deals with the
problem posed by the lack of theorization of a 'system of systems'.
Concerning the former point, the closed/open system dichotomy plays
a double role. On the one hand, this dichotomy is used by Bhaskar
to generate an imminent critique of empiricist ontology. To this
it must be replied that if one uses a certain concept to criticize
a certain view, then, having shown this concept's validity as a

critical tool, one will use the same concept as a building block of
his own view. This is exactly what Bhaskar does. Critique of
alternative views and construction of one's own view are two
inextricably connected aspects of the same theoretical process. My
contention is that, given this connection and the conservative
nature of this dichotomy, this concept should be discarded also as
a tool of theoretical criticism and that therefore empiricism should
be criticized on different grounds. On the other hand, Bhaskar's
intention is to use this concept to highlight the epistemological
difference between the social sciences and the 'classical' natural
sciences of physics and chemistry. Again, while it is correct to
point out that such a difference exists, it is incorrect - if one
aims at a dialectical view - to draw that distinction on the basis
of an inherently a-dialectical concept. Therefore, once more, that
border should be drawn but along different lines. To sum up, the
notion of closed and open systems does play a very important role
in Bhaskar's theory, perhaps even more important than that author
is willing to concede.

Even more important is the way in which Bhaskar tackles the
question of the interrelation between generative systems. In a
forthcoming article (84) Bhaskar considers, without further
elaborating on it, the case (case II) of the 'determination of
events within a "system" in an open system' where event E_0 is
determined by three interrelated mechanisms (M1, M2 and M3) and by
a fourth mechanism (M4) completely separated from the first three.
This, however, does not remove the above-mentioned objections for
the following three reasons. First, this case (case II) is a
'modification' of case I which is the 'determination of events in
an open system' where there is no relation at all between M1, M2
and M3. The relation between systems seems to be logically posterior.
Second, there is here no solution but only a shift of the problem.
In fact, how can an event be the outcome of two categories of
systems (one category being constituted by interrelated mechanisms
and the other by disjuncted mechanisms) if no relation is established
between these two types of mechanisms? And, third, the concept
that at least some systems generating an event might be interrelated
is neither given a theoretical elaboration (we only find a statement
to the effect that those systems or mechanisms which are interrelated
are tied by a relation of 'causal interdependence', itself a Weberian
rather than a Marxist concept) nor organically integrated in the body
of Bhaskar's theory. Something which, in my opinion, should be at
the centre of his theorization, is only mentioned in passing.

Lastly, a few comments on the fact/value distinction. Bhaskar's
latest position on this point seems to be that

   if we have a consistent set of theories T which (i) shows some
   belief P to be false, and (ii) explains why that belief is
   believed; then the inferences to (iii) a negative evaluation of
   the object S (e.g. system of social relations) accounting for the
   falsity of the belief (i.e. mismatch in reality between the belief
   P and what it is about O) and (iv) a positive evaluation of action
   rationally directed at removing (disconnecting or transforming)
   that object, i.e. the source(s) of false consciousness, appear
   mandatory CP. (85)
The crux of the matter is, of course, verification: how do we know

(actually, who - e.g. individuals, classes, etc. - knows and by means of which method) that a belief is false, i.e. that there is a mismatch (lack of correspondence) between that belief and its object? Since discussion of this aspect of Bhaskar's theory requires a discussion of verification, I will not go further into this topic. My only comment, therefore, will be similar to the previous ones. A positive evaluation of the action rationally aimed at removing the causes of false beliefs (consciousness) is not enough for me, if I want a theory which not only reassures me that I am morally justified in my action but which also tells me 'what to do'. Bhaskar's view, in earlier writings, that to expect this from a theory is a 'mistake of the greatest magnitude' is echoed again in his more recent article so that no change can be discerned on this point: 'Diagnosis is not therapy. We may know that something is causing a problem without knowing how to get rid or change it ... an explanatory critique of this type ... does not tell us what to do'. (86) It has been my thesis that the subscription to this (false) belief, the difficulty in theorizing an epistemology in which the principle role of knowledge is precisely to tell us what to do, is a consequence of the central role adjudicated to the open/closed systems distinction and consequently of the impossibility of reconciling this element with a dialectical view.

To conclude, Bhaskar's approach is yet another attempt to base philosophy on the prestige of a science which is supposed (at least implicitly) to be class neutral, of a science seen through the spectacles of a theoretical category (the closed/open system dichotomy) taken from a body of thought (systems thinking) which draws its prestige from ideological reasons as well as from its function- ality not for the solution of practical problems (contrary to the claims of systems thinking's supporters), but for an authoritarian management of society. The closed/open system scheme, and the notion of natural and social laws built upon it, cannot but be an obstacle for the development of Marxist dialectics.

Chapter 3

ON THE PROCESS OF MENTAL TRANSFORMATION

INTRODUCTION

The previous two chapters have argued for the class determination of
social phenomena and thus of knowledge as a social phenomenon. From
this point of view there is thus no separation between cognition and
class domination on the ideological level; nay, the former is
automatically at the same time a means of achieving the latter. The
question then arises: how do we produce these abstractions, how can
classes realize their theoretical vision/domination through an
individual process of mental production (alternatively, how can
individual mental producers produce a social phenomenon)? In the
present chapter we will examine the production of knowledge (in its
double character as vision/domination) in artificial isolation from
the production of other, alternative, knowledges. This is only a
didactical device, meant to facilitate the exposition in order to
focus, to begin with, on how the social determination of knowledge
realizes itself through the mental labour of individuals. We will
first of all examine the mechanisms of the appropriation in thought
of the real concrete on an individual level (the process of mental
production) in sections 1 and 2 of this chapter, and the mechanism
of the reaction of the concrete in thought on the real concrete,
once this knowledge has become a social phenomenon, in section 3.
Once this will have been done, the way will have been opened to an
analysis, to be carried out in the next chapter, of the contemporaneous production of alternative and competing knowledges and of the
specific mechanism through which they compete for ideological
supremacy, i.e. through which they become social phenomena. At
the end of the fourth chapter, therefore, we will have concluded
our analysis of the class determination of knowledge through a
theorization of (i) the potential class determined knowledges, or
potential conditions of class domination on the ideological level;
(ii) their fragmentation into a myriad of individual internalizations
(the individual processes of mental production); (iii) the recomposition of these fragmented knowledges into a few social phenomena;
and (iv) the reaction of these upon other social phenomena, both in
the real concrete and in the realm of knowledge. Then the task of
the present chapter is an analysis of steps (ii) and (iv) while

step (iii) will be left for the next chapter. Thus, the method of
presentation differs slightly from the method of inquiry. In turn,
this latter stresses the possibility of separating the four steps
logically, where the sequence is, of course, not accidental, and the
impossibility of separating them chronologically. Before we embark
on such an analysis, however, one more word on the relation between
concrete in thought and real concrete. In our view, neither do we
have a simple relation, (1) nor a non-simple one in the sense that
the real object is necessarily always more complex than its depiction
in thought; (2) but a complex relation of determination and thus a
multiple process of cognition of the same reality. To repeat our
analogy, each subject of cognition (class) looks at the same real
concrete through the same prism, and is bound to look only through
one (its own) facet. Let us then consider Marx's concrete-abstract-
concrete circle.

1   FROM REAL CONCRETE TO IMAGINED CONCRETE

Marx distinguishes between two types of abstraction, the imagined
concrete, i.e. 'a chaotic conception of the whole', which is the
outcome of the process of observation, and the concrete in thought,
a structured model, an analytical construction which at the highest
level of abstraction encompasses only the determinant elements of
our model ('the simplest determinations') and the relations between
them. As already said, the concrete in thought can be constructed
at different levels of abstraction, i.e. at different levels of
complexity, by developing the elements (contradictions) already
implicit in the 'simplest determinations' (given these latter's
nature as historical condensations), until we reach the 'rich
totality of many determinations and relations'. (3) There is no
doubt, then, that Marx attaches great importance to observation and
to its outcome, the imagined concrete. And this could not be
otherwise, since without observation the gap between the two orders
of phenomena (real concrete and mental products) would be unbridgable:
(4) sensory perception, the action of matter upon our sense organs,
(5) is the mechanism transforming one type of phenomena into another
thus making possible a materialist view of knowledge. At this point
there are three possibilities:
(a) observation is independent of social conditioning. This is a
physiological view which is often the pre-condition for the most
extreme form of 'reflection' theory.
(b) observation is totally determined by the social environment
(Althusser) so that the only difference between imagined concrete
and concrete in thought is one of degree. This is sociologism.
(c) observation is the product both of matter acting upon our sense
organs and of the social environment, or the filtering of the former
through the latter. This seems to us to be the only correct
approach, i.e. the only approach consistent with both a materialist
and a class determination view of the process of mental transformation (PMT).
The production of new knowledge involves always observation and
conception. (6) This, however, does not have to imply either that
there is no difference between these two types of abstraction (we

will argue that there is a qualitative difference), or that it is
impossible to discern them because of their chronological contemporaneity. Chronologically, it would be senseless to try and see when
observation stops and when conception begins. The fact that
observation and conception might take place at the same time in the
mental producer's head is a question which has to do with the
mechanism of the human brain, something hardly relevant for our
purposes. The distinction is relevant, however, for a logical
analysis of the PMT. For us, observation is sensory perception of
natural and social reality filtered through the individual's previous
knowledge and participation in the class struggle. The reason for
this is that sensory perception can never be neutral: rather it is
influenced by the knowledge already acquired by the individual and
by his/her social practice. (7) The social content of the individual's
observation is thus given by the socially (class) determined
character of the 'filter'. It is precisely this coming into contact
with social reality (participation in social practice) through sensory
perception which is the condition for the possibility for the
individual to perceive a tension, discrepancy, between previous
knowledge and the outcome of observation; and it is this tension
which starts a process of conception. This will be the topic of the
next section. Here we want to stress some points of clarification.
    First, the tension which starts a process of conception is not
between a physiological factor (sensory perception) and a social one
(knowledge). This would imply a logical separability between the two
factors and ultimately a concept of a neutral sensory perception.
The tension is rather between two social factors, between a sensory
perception socially filtered (by previous knowledge and by participation in social practice) and previous knowledge. Previous knowledge
is thus both an element of perception's social filter, an element
thus of the content of the imagined concrete, and the material which
must be transformed due to the tension arising between knowledge
itself and the imagined concrete. But this is possible only if this
latter is influenced by something else than previous knowledge, i.e.
by participation in social practice. Observation is thus not sensory
perception. Rather, the latter is the channel through which social
practice, which is never independent of existing knowledge, can
originate the need to change that knowledge. Second, given that we
have rejected an internalist view of the development of knowledge,
the perception of the above-mentioned tension, and of the need to
start a process of conception aimed at removing that tension, will
result in the starting of such a process when the scientific
community (defined as all those who engage in a process of conception,
and thus not necessarily as only those who are professionally engaged
in such an activity) will perceive the 'anomalous' character of some
imagined concretes; this in turn will happen when the development of
the real concrete as perceived through class struggle will force
upon classes the realization of the qualitatively 'new' character of
some imagined concretes. It is only on this condition that the
imagined concrete can be set against existing knowledge and be
perceived to be discrepant with it, i.e. that the theoretical problem
can be perceived as such. Third, as implied in what has just been
said, the raw material of the PMT are two, both the outcome of
previous conception and the outcome of new observations. We will see

in chapter 4 that the discrepancy between these two elements can originate either in a real change in the real concrete as perceived through observation or in the penetration of foreign elements into a class's existing knowledge. Finally, no confusion should be made, in a positivist and empiricist fashion, between the outcome of observation and 'facts'. As we have argued in the previous chapters and as we will argue again, observation does not constitute social facts. (8)

Having argued for the centrality of observation for a Marxist theory of knowledge, we can now identify the essential difference between it and conception. This difference is not only, and not primarily, one of degree, in the sense that the outcome of observation is chaotic and unstructured not in an absolute sense but in relation to the theoretical problem to be posed. The difference is first of all a qualitative one in the specific sense that it is the outcome of observation which allows the theoretical problem to be perceived as such and thus to be posed; which allows, in other words, for the possibility for the new developments in the real concrete to surface in the consciousness of the mental producer. Observation is not yet conception, it is only its preparatory stage, the process which allows the signalling of theoretical (i.e. within a certain theory) difficulties, the posing of theoretical problems. Conception is, and cannot but be, the transformation of mental products (existing knowledge and new imagined concrete): in it sensory perception (and thus participation in class struggle) can play a role only when crystallized in the imagined concrete, in a mental product. Logically, and not 'naturally' or 'psychologically', therefore, the difference between imagined concrete and concrete in thought is one between a mental product in which all types and forms of class struggle enter directly and a mental product in which they enter indirectly as crystallized in the imagined concrete. (9) In other words, it is not 'theories' which transform themselves, it is people who transform theories under the stimulus of class struggle, as perceived through a sensory perception filtered through previous knowledge. But this means that it is not people as individuals but individuals as carriers of social relations who carry out the PMT. And this is already visible at the level of observation, due to the social (class) nature of sensory perception's filter.

2   FROM IMAGINED CONCRETE TO CONCRETE IN THOUGHT

The second type of abstraction considered by Marx is conception, the production of the concrete in thought. Similarly to observation, conception has a social nature, and this in three different but inter-related ways. First of all, conception is an individual act, but it is also socially determined through the social (class) content of its raw materials, i.e. the imagined concrete and the existing knowledge. This is the first way in which the individual agent of mental production becomes a carrier of ideological class relations. Second, the class content of the raw materials is the basis of the class content of the outcome of conception. The latter's class content, however, is not strictly determined by the class content of the imagined concrete and existing knowledge because of what we will call in the next chapter the penetration/incorporation mechanism, i.e. the penetration of foreign elements of knowledge into an existing body of knowledge and the possibility for the former to change the class content of the latter. This is the second way in which the individual mental agent of production becomes a carrier of ideological class relations. Third, as we have seen in chapter 2, not all socially determined phenomena are social phenomena in the full sense of the definition. Only a few mental products become social phenomena (i.e. when certain conditions to be specified in the next chapter will be satisifed). In this case the agent of mental production becomes the personification of the concretization on the ideological level of a class's condition of domination.

It is useful to start our discussion of conception by distinguishing mental products (MPs) from mental operations (MOs). (10) The PMT as a whole starts from the real concrete, (11) which is neither an MP nor an MO. The agent of mental production, through the MO observation, produces the MP imagined concrete. If a tension arises between the two MPs imagined concrete and existing knowledge (the two types of the raw materials of the PMT), then a process of conception will be started. This tension originates at the level of the imagined concrete and sets this latter against the existing knowledge: it is thus not yet conception. This latter is the transformation of the raw materials of mental production (12) into a new MP, the new knowledge, or concrete in thought. That tension logically precedes this transformation. New knowledge arises basically from changes in the real concrete as perceived by a class in its class determined perspective through the channel of the individual agent of mental production. As implied in our approach and as dealt with in detail in the next chapter, however, new knowledge can arise from ideological class struggle even in the absence of changes in the real concrete. But given the primacy (determination) of this latter on mental production, there will always be a tendency for changes originating purely in the realm of the ideological to be superseded by other mental products. Ideologies must have a real substratum (which implies some sort of correspondence between the real concrete and the concrete in thought, as discussed in chapter 4), as the examples provided in chapter 1 show. The fact that different interpretations of the same real concrete are possible even for the same class and that the fight for supremacy among these interpretations might cause conceptions to integrate foreign elements of knowledge even to the point of undergoing radical transformation, create the (idealist) illusion that it is purely from the clash between different types of knowledge (theories) that new knowledge arises. This is, for instance, Althusser's position, which we will briefly criticize in section 4 of this chapter. (13)

Conception begins with the posing of the problem (MO), with the comparison of the two elements of the raw materials, therefore with the signalling of the difficulty, and thus with the theoretical expression of that difficulty. This first stage of conception, which ends with the problem unsolved (MP), is followed by a second stage, the solution of the problem (MO) which results in the completed transformation of the raw materials into new knowledge (MP). Conception is thus that (two-stage) process which sets and solves problems in the realm of knowledge and which thus produces new knowledge. The rationale for this can perhaps be best understood if we draw a comparison with the labour process producing material goods as analysed by Marx. This is the transformation of use values (raw

materials) into the new use values (the product) by the agent of
production through the expenditure of concrete labour and with the
help of the instruments of production (again, considered as use
values). (14) Conception, considered not in the context of class
struggle but as a mental labour process, the mental substratum of
the production of knowledge under any social system, and thus as the
production of mental use values is, first, the posing of the problem,
i.e. given the perception of a problem through observation, the
transformation of this perceived, not worked out, state into an
expression of the problem in terms of a theory by the agent of
mental transformation and with the help of the instruments of mental
transformation; and, second, the solution of the problem, i.e. the
transformation of the unsolved, yet theoretically expressed, problem
by the agent and with the help of the instruments of mental transformation, into a solved problem, i.e. into new knowledge. In short,
whenever on the basis of existing knowledge and observation, a
problem in the realm of knowledge – at whatever level of complexity –
is posed and solved through the application of concrete labour and
with the help of certain instruments of mental transformation, the
raw materials are combined and transformed into something new, a
knowledge which is new because it can be put to a different use,
because it allows the subject of knowledge to relate differently to
the real concrete and to satisfy new needs. The most radical example
of a production of new knowledge in the social sciences is the
transformation of an ideology into science and vice versa, or the
transformation of a knowledge functional for the domination of a
class into a knowledge functional for the domination of another
class. A mental use value can thus be defined as any product of the
transformation of existing knowledge and imagined concrete, i.e. of
a PMT, which because of this transformation can be used to satisfy
a new need.

Having said this, we must hasten to anticipate some results to be
proved in the subsequent chapters in order to avoid being misunderstood on a vital point. It is one of our theses that under specific
social conditions, i.e. under capitalism, the product of conception
is not necessarily a use value. As Marx said,

> In order to examine the connection between spiritual production
> and material production it is above all necessary to grasp the
> latter itself not as a general category but in *definite historical*
> form. Thus for example different kinds of spiritual production
> correspond to the capitalist mode of production and to the mode
> of production of the Middle Ages. If material production itself
> is not conceived in its *specific historical* form, it is
> impossible to understand what is specific in the spiritual
> production corresponding to it and the reciprocal influence of
> one on the other. (15)

The question, therefore, of whether and when the PMT, the transformation of knowledge, produces mental use values, cannot be answered
separately from an analysis of the capitalist production process and,
as we will see in chapter 5, of this process on the societal level.
There we will see that, to be productive of mental use values, the
PMT must not be part of an unproductive labour process, i.e. it must
not be condition for the formal transformation of material use
values on a societal scale. We will see also that, given the

specific nature of the capitalist production process, there are agents of mental production whose conception is a condition for the performance of the control over the producers (material and mental) and who, therefore, strictly speaking, cannot be considered as mental producers, (16) as producers of mental use values.

There is only one element to be briefly considered before we can round up our discussion of conception, i.e. the instruments of mental transformation. They can be either disembodied, as, for example, theories, techniques, etc., or incorporated in the material aids of mental production (from pencils, to books, to computers). In the material labour process, some of the outcomes of the previous process become raw materials of the new process, while other products become instruments of production. Similarly for the PMT: some products will become raw materials while others will become instruments of mental transformation. The difference between material and mental labour process, however, as we have seen, is that in the latter a mental product, in its role both as product, as raw material, and as instrument of transformation has the quality of having a social (class) content and, as far as the social sciences are concerned, of being either science or ideology. The following scheme summarizes, then, the process of conception where, for the sake of brevity, the following notation has been used:

K	= knowledge	Ko	= existing knowledge
K1	= new knowledge	IC	= imagined concrete
m.a.	= material aids to mental transformation	MP	= mental product
		MO	= mental operation
$\rightarrow$	= transformation	$\leftrightarrow$	= combination

Stage 1: the posing of the problem

$$\left\{ \begin{matrix} K_0 \ (MP) \\ IC \ (MP) \end{matrix} \right\} \begin{matrix} \text{raw material,} \\ \text{or objects} \\ \text{of labour} \end{matrix} + \begin{matrix} \text{instruments of} \\ \text{labour, or of} \\ \text{transformation} \end{matrix} \left\{ \begin{matrix} K_0 \ (MP) \\ m.a. \end{matrix} \right\} \begin{matrix} \text{posing} \\ \text{of the} \\ \text{problem} \end{matrix} \rightarrow \begin{matrix} \text{problem} \\ \text{unsolved} \\ (MP) \end{matrix}$$

Agent's application of concrete labour ——————(MO)

Stage 2: the solution of the problem

$$\left\{ \begin{matrix} \text{problem} \\ \text{unsolved} \\ (MP) \end{matrix} \right\} \begin{matrix} \text{raw} \\ \text{material} \end{matrix} + \begin{matrix} \text{instruments} \\ \text{of labour} \end{matrix} \left\{ \begin{matrix} K_0(MP) \\ m.a. \end{matrix} \right\} \begin{matrix} \text{solution} \\ \text{of the} \\ \text{problem} \end{matrix} \rightarrow \begin{matrix} K_1 \ (MP) \text{ or} \\ \text{concrete-in-} \\ \text{thought} \end{matrix}$$

Agent's application of concrete labour ——— (MO)

Figure 3.1 Conception (or PMT proper)

Since we are interested in conception rather than in observation, i.e. in the PMT proper rather than in the process of mental transformation as a whole, from now on we will refer to conception as the PMT, unless differently indicated. The PMT (conception) will then be schematized as follows:

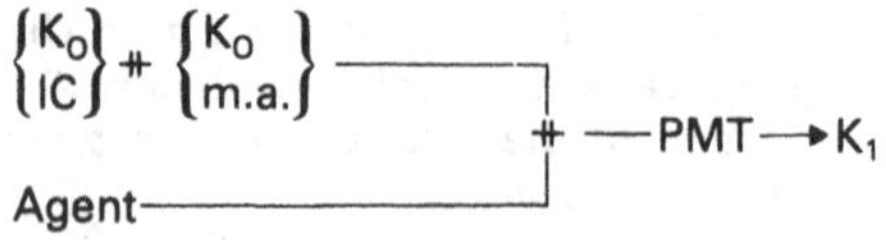

$$\left\{ {K_o \atop IC} \right\} + \left\{ {K_o \atop m.a.} \right\} \quad\underline{\qquad\qquad}$$

$$\text{Agent} \underline{\qquad\qquad\qquad} + \;\text{—PMT}\rightarrow K_1$$

Figure 3.2   The PMT

3   FROM CONCRETE IN THOUGHT TO REAL CONCRETE

Abstraction, in its double stage of observation and conception as analysed above, is thus the mechanism mediating (bridging) two radically different realms. However, 'the real subject retains its autonomous existence outside the head just as before; namely, as long as the head's conduct is merely speculative, merely theoretical'; (17) i.e. we might add, in the light of our discussion of social phenomena, as long as knowledge remains an individual abstraction, as long as it does not become a social phenomenon. The concrete in thought can never produce the real concrete (Hegel's idealism as criticized by Marx), but the former can act upon and modify the latter. There exists thus also a bridge from the concrete in thought back to the real concrete. In fact, the former is a form of class struggle, as we have seen, it is a condition of domination at the ideological level (a form of ideological class relations), and as such is functional either for the reproduction or for the super- session of the existing social relations. We have seen that this holds both for the social and for the natural sciences. The concrete in thought, by being an element of class struggle, reacts upon all other forms and types of class struggle and thus upon the real concrete. It follows that the real concrete is such, i.e. it exists before appropriation in thought, only in its existence as influenced, modified, by social practice, i.e. by class struggle, and thus also by knowledge. And this holds not only for social but also for natural reality.

Let us indicate the process of mental transformation by PMT; economic, ideological, and political relations by respectively ER, IR, and PR; let us also use the following notation concerning knowledge (symbolized as K):

$${}^1_2 K^3_4$$

where the symbols in position 4 indicate the time period during which knowledge is produced; in position 3, the DLI of K, the class for which that knowledge is a condition of domination; in position 2, the individual producer of that knowledge; and in position 1, given that there is a number of different knowledges all determined by the same class, the type of knowledge (among the knowledges produced by a certain class) referred to. Thus, for example,

$${}^2_n K^A_1$$

indicates the second type of knowledge, among all types determined in the last instance by class A, as produced by agent n during time

1. Finally, we will use a dash above the symbol K ($\bar{K}$) to indicate
that we refer to knowledge realized on the social level, to knowledge
as a social phenomenon, and not simply as an individual production.
Then, the social determination of the production of knowledge can be
schematized as follows, where by economic, political, and ideological
we mean respectively the ER and their forms, the PR and their forms,
and the IR and their forms; where the two symbols => and <--> indicate
respectively determination and reciprocal interaction; and where
←ODT— indicates overdetermination:

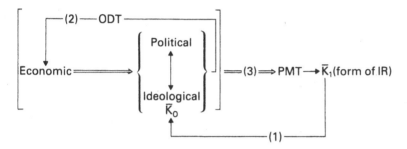

Figure 3.3   The social determination of new knowledge

The square brackets contain the real concrete as well as the concrete
in thought before the new PMT starts, i.e. before these objectively
existing concretes are transformed into new knowledge, $\bar{K}_1$.
Notice that (a) $\bar{K}_1$ becomes as soon as it becomes objective (independent of the will of the individuals and thus of the individual
producing knowledge) immediately part of the ideological (arrow 1
indicates the integration of the new into existing knowledge);
(b) $\bar{K}_1$ is determined not only by the real concrete but also by $\bar{K}_0$,
a previously existing form of ideological relations (arrow 3 indicates
this concrete realization); (c) $\bar{K}_1$, because of point (a) above, is
integrated into the real concrete (modifies it or prevents its
modification) through its interaction with the political and through
its overdetermination of the economic.
    Let us compare Figure 3.2 and 3.3 above. While Figure 3.3 depicts
the social determination of knowledge as a social phenomenon, as
realized social knowledge, Figure 3.2 depicts the social determination
of individual knowledge, i.e. of a knowledge which, even though
socially determined, has not yet realized itself on the social level.
(When Figure 3.2 is used, as it will be in the next chapter, to depict
the individual production of a knowledge which has become a social
phenomenon, then Figure 3.2 can be inserted in Figure 3.3.   The
result will be a global view, even though in its simplest expression,
of the social production of social knowledge.)   Figure 3.3 concerns
the structural level, Figure 3.2 the individual one.   Without
Figure 3.3 we cannot understand why Figure 3.2 depicts essentially
a social, rather than an individual, process or in other words why
the raw materials and the means of mental transformation used by
the individual agent in his PMT have a social content, have been
socially determined, so that his product has the possibility of
becoming a social phenomenon.   Without Figure 3.2, we cannot understand how the social determination of knowledge can realize itself,

i.e. through which concrete mechanism, through which concrete
activity of individual mental producers.

　　Figure 3.3 can now be made more comprehensive if we recall that,
in our view, there is a relation of DLI between the economic and the
concrete in thought, that the economic comes to life as a number of
classes identifiable in terms of production relations, and that each
class can create potentially more than one type of knowledge, i.e.
more than one type of theoretical domination over other classes.
This can all be represented as in Figure 3.4 where for the time being

economic (real concrete)	concrete in thought

class 1 $\Longrightarrow$ $\left\{ \begin{matrix} {}^1K^1 \\ \vdots \\ {}^nK^1 \end{matrix} \right\} \rightarrow \bar{K}^1$

class n $\Longrightarrow$ $\left\{ \begin{matrix} {}^1K^n \\ \vdots \\ {}^nK^n \end{matrix} \right\} \rightarrow \bar{K}^n$

Figure 3.4　DLI of a plurality of knowledges

we consider only one type of realized knowledge for each class.
These restrictions will be lifted in the next chapter. Now Figure
3.3 can become Figure 3.5 where the different PMTs are still

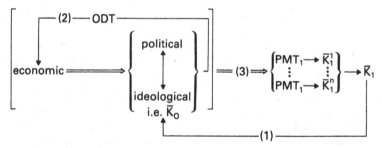

Figure 3.5　Concrete determination of a plurality of knowledges

considered as separated one from the other. This restriction too
will be lifted in the following chapter. This scheme shows the
internal structure of the new societal knowledge, $\bar{K}_1$, its being a
complex unity in determination of different knowledges. In the
following chapter we will examine the process of interaction among
all these different knowledges and thus the internal structure of
each of these different knowledges, i.e. the fact that each of these
$\bar{K}^1 \ldots \bar{K}^n$ is a complex unity in determination of several elements of
knowledge. It is this doubly structured $\bar{K}_1$ which will influence
social practice and thus become part of class struggle thus modifying
the real concrete.

4   AN EXAMPLE OF IDEALIST CONCEPTION: ALTHUSSER'S THEORETICAL
PRACTICE

This will not be an attempt to draw on all the literature on
Althusser's work (this would be out of proportion to its usefulness).
Rather, our aim is to consider Althusser's notion of PMT, or theoretical practice, as he calls it, in his work 'For Marx' (1970) in order
to bring out some basic differences with the present approach, thus
stressing some points fundamental for our discussion.   Theoretical
practice is, for Althusser, the process by which Generality I, the
raw materials, is transformed into Generality III, the mental product,
by Generality II, the means of production.   Let us consider the raw
materials of mental production first:
> Contrary to the ideological illusions ... of empiricism or
> sensualism, a science never works on an existence whose essence is
> pure immediacy and singularity.... At its moment of constitution ...
> a science always works on existing concepts.... It does not 'work'
> on a purely objective 'given', that of pure and absolute 'facts'.
> On the contrary, its particular labour consists of *elaborating its*
> *own scientific facts* through a critique of the *ideological* 'facts'
> elaborated by an earlier theoretical practice. (pp.183-4)

Althusser seems to us to be going too far.   In fact, while, on the
one hand, he denies (correctly) an 'existence whose essence is pure
immediacy', i.e. pure observation, on the other hand he conflates
observations influenced by previous knowledge, i.e. ideational
observations, and theory.   For him, an observation influenced by
existing knowledge is no longer an observation, it is conception.
Consequence of this unwarranted operation is the denial to the
researcher of the faculty of observing reality under the stimulus of
his social praxis, of observing changes in reality or discrepancies
between reality and existing products of conception.   Althusser's
research is thus condemned to move in a world of mental products
which have lost all contacts with the real concrete.   This latter
is neither taken as the starting point of the PMT (as Marx explicitly
does, for example in the 'Grundrisse'), nor is it considered as
modified by social practice and thus by those mental products.   As
Althusser clearly puts it: 'The work whereby Generality I becomes
Generality III ... *only* involves the process of theoretical practice,
that is *it all takes place within knowledge*' (p. 185, emphasis
added).   Here Althusser and Popper shake hands.   Both authors reject
observation in order to refute inductive empiricism, and both fall
into idealism. (18)
> Second, Generality II, i.e. the means of mental production:
> If we abstract from men in these means of production ... Generality
> II (is constituted by) the corpus of concepts whose more or less
> contradictory unity constitutes the 'theory' of the science at
> the (historical) moment under consideration, the 'theory' which
> defines the field in which all the problems of the science must
> necessarily be posed. (pp.184-5)

But men are not means of mental production, they are agents of mental
transformation. (19)   Just as in the material labour process the
agents of production are aided by the means of production which
incorporate a certain level and development of the productive forces,
in the process of mental transformation the agents are aided by

theories, methods, techniques, material facilities, etc., which
also reflect the level and development of the productive forces. (20)
But it is not the instruments which transform the raw materials into
the finished products (material or mental), it is the agents with
the help of the instruments of production. The fact that in the PMT
the means of transformation are inside rather than outside the
individuals does not warrant this logical confusion. Generality I is
transformed into Generality III by the agent with the help of
Generality II. A socialist system will develop the individuals not
as means of production: it will develop the means of mental production
within the individuals. Althusser is mistaken, but at least he is
consistent in his mistakes. Since there is no place in his scheme for
agents of mental transformation, there can be no place for observation
either and men are reduced to the status of means of production.

Finally, as far as Generality III is concerned, Althusser's
criticism of Hegel is correct. This latter fails to see the
'qualitative discontinuity' between the raw materials of mental
production and the mental product, i.e. fails to see that the knowledge
produced is qualitatively different from the knowledge used at the
beginning of the process. Hegel 'takes the universal concept that
figures at the beginning of the process of knowledge ... for the
essence and motor of the process, for the "self-engendering concept"'
(p.188). Althusser's process is discontinuous rather than continuous
in the sense that the product is qualitatively different from the raw
material. Yet Althusser goes to the extreme of considering this
qualitative difference only in terms of a transformation of ideology
into science (and, presumably, vice versa). This is, however, only
the most radical (and from the point of view of the ideological class
struggle the most important) instance of transformation taking place
within the process of mental transformation. In the mental labour
process, the use value of the raw material must not necessarily be
changed from the point of view of the class struggle for a real
transformation to take place. Such a transformation can also take
place within the realm of a science (or ideology) when the use value
of knowledge is changed through conception.

Most important for our purposes is the conclusion that Althusser's
concept of theoretical practice cannot but lead to his inability to
come to grips with the problem of verification in terms of correspondence with reality. We, on the other hand, have stressed the social
determination of the reconstruction in thought of reality and the
possibility for the former to react upon the latter. This has left
open the possibility of knowledge's verification against objective
reality. This is our thesis. It will have to be shown within the
theoretical space delimited in this and the previous chapters. This
will be the specific task of the following chapter.

Chapter 4

VERIFICATION, OR EPISTEMOLOGY AND THE FUNCTION OF CAPITAL

A theory, like the one submitted in the previous chapter, which roots knowledge in the real concrete (class structure) and which, at the same time, assigns to the former the role of leading the action aimed at acting upon the latter, is obviously faced with the problem of reconciliation of the principle of the social, class, determination of knowledge (i.e. the social relativity of knowledge) with the need to find objective criteria of correctness founded upon some kind of correspondence between the real concrete and its mental conception. Usually, the theories of truth to be encountered in philosophical treatises are of three kinds. (1) For the correspondence type the criterion of truth is the correspondence of facts with theory. That somehow our perception and conception of reality should be checked by (against) reality itself is a sound and indispensable criterion which, however, if not carefully stated, can lead to either the idealism of reducing our model of reality (provided the model is sufficiently detailed) to reality itself (2) or to the empiricist reduction of reality to neutral 'facts', thus overlooking that what is called 'facts' is our interpretation of reality and that therefore facts, or data, can never be neutral but are always theory-laden. The coherence type is based upon the criterion of the internal coherence among all propositions or parts of a certain theory. This approach is usually chosen by those who, faced with the difficulty of finding a 'word-world' relation, give up the attempt and seek the criterion of truth only in the internal relations among the several theoretical constituent parts. Again, a theory should be internally coherent and consistent, but this should not be the only requirement and should be based upon a success, and not a failure, in finding a mediating way of confronting two essentially heterogeneous concretes: reality and our appropriation in thought of it. It should hardly be necessary to mention that whenever the tie with the 'real concrete', as Marx calls it, is severed, the outcome cannot but be idealism. (3) Finally, we have the pragmatist type of theory for which only success in practice, i.e. successful results and successful predictions, can be the yardstick of truth. This, in a sense, could be considered as a sub-species of the correspondence type, since successful action implies that we have found somehow a way of comparing thought and reality. For anybody who believes in Marx's eleventh thesis on Feuerbach, (4) i.e. that our task (not only as philosophers, we would add, but also as scientists, social and natural) is not only to interpret the world but also to change it, the criterion of success in practice is an obvious requirement. Nevertheless, there is a great difference between this requirement and its bourgeois version, i.e. pragmatism, as we will see further down. The point is thus to recognize that all three types of approach express some legitimate requirements. But we should not fall into the temptation of artificially glueing together their 'positive' aspects and discard the 'negative' ones. The task is one of superseding these three types of theories with a new one, basically and qualitatively different from all three. (5) This supersession cannot be achieved by patching up the different elements of a neurotic split. The task is that of re-casting those elements into a theory of verification inherently dialectical and based upon the concept of social class, i.e. into the context of a theory of class determination of knowledge. Outside this context such a theory would loose its class, revolutionary character.

The previous chapters have provided the theoretical frame within which to carry out this task. Let us summarize some fundamental points:

1 Social systems are characterized by structures (social relations)
2 Structures exist only through people, through carriers of contradictory aspects of those relations, i.e. through agents, classes.
3 The contradictory nature of the structure manifests itself as the struggle of classes against each other.
4 Class struggle is thus structurally inherent and has as its aim the domination of one class over the others.
5 Classes achieve this aim by creating the conditions (forms) of domination (social phenomena) which are, at the same time: (a) the conditions of existence or of supersession of the structure; (b) perceived by classes as their own interests.
6 One of those conditions of domination is the production of knowledge, i.e. the need classes have to develop their own vision of the world (in order to act upon it, and basically in order to produce the material conditions of their own reproduction) cannot but have as a consequence a multiplicity of world-views, all of them struggling for domination, i.e. cannot but have as a consequence ideological class struggle.

Within this context our theory must be able to account for a number of phenomena apparently contradicting the principle of the class determination of knowledge, i.e. of the determination of knowledge in the last instance by the economic. More specifically, on the one hand, our theory must reconcile the existence of a variety of knowledges, all of them being the theoretical expression of different classes, with the following four interrelated order of problems: (i) the existence of a variety of knowledges, all of them being the expression at the theoretical level of the same class; (ii) the reciprocal penetration of all knowledges, i.e. the co-existence of elements of a knowledge into the context of another problematic; (iii) the possibility of a class's accepting a knowledge determined in the last instance by another class; and (iv) the possibility of one knowledge's being correct while being, just like all other knowledges, class determined. On the other hand, our theory must reconcile the existence of a variety of individual knowledges with their social dimension (determination) by starting from this latter without either denying the former or explaining the social conscious-ness in terms of a summation of the individual consciousness. In other words, the individual mental producers must be considered as social producers, social determination must be explained through (and thus necessarily by taking into consideration), but not starting from, the individual production of knowledge. Consequently, the theoretical space must be created to account for the relative autonomy of theory both at the individual level (the individual mental production vis-á-vis the class determined mental production) and at the social level (theory vis-á-vis social practice) within the context of a concept of dialectical determination of the concrete-in-thought by the real concrete and of the individual concrete-in-thought by the social concrete-in-thought.

1   VERIFICATION AS PRODUCTION OF KNOWLEDGE

(a)   Practical and theoretical knowledge

Humankind must transform the real concrete in order to reproduce itself. In order to do this, it must develop a knowledge of the real concrete, a knowledge which is first of all aimed at providing the solution of practical problems, of problems concerning the attainment of those ends whose common element is the transformation of the real concrete, both natural and social. Let us call practical knowledge the ensemble of practical problems, the theories within which these problems are posed, and the solutions they provide. But, given the complexity of reality, very rarely can a practical problem be immediately solved, i.e. can a knowledge be produced which allows the immediate realization of a practical end. Usually such a solution requires the posing and solution of a number of other problems (which in turn require the development of other theories) which are only indirectly (i.e. through the practical problems which have determined them) tied to the real concrete's transformation. Let us call this ensemble of problems, theories, and solutions, theoretical knowledge. The distinction (determination) between practical and theoretical knowledge is an important one as far as verification is concerned. Verification of practical knowledge is the process by which we inquire into whether the solution of a practical problem is consistent with the end aimed at and with the broader theory which has served to pose that problem. Let us call the former aspect practical verification and the latter aspect logical verification. Then it follows that while practical knowledge can be directly subjected to both practical and logical verification, theoretical knowledge can be subjected directly only to logical verification and only indirectly to practical verification, i.e. through the practical verification of the determining practical knowledge. Let us examine these cases in some detail.

(b)   Production of practical knowledge

The process starts when there is a change in the real concrete (in
this case a problem arises) which must be accounted for theoretically:
i.e. a problem must be solved. (6) We start then a PMT. As we have
seen a PMT is a transformation, by the agent of mental transformation,
of the raw materials of mental transformation, with the help of the
means of mental transformation, into new knowledge. This process
starts with the tension between the elements of the raw materials of
mental transformation as perceived by the agent. The raw materials
are the knowledge existing at the time the PMT is carried out and the
outcome of observation (or imagined concrete), of observed changes in
the real concrete, in this case of the problem which has arisen within
the real concrete. Since observation takes place (logically, not
chronologically) before the PMT starts, it is still filtered through
the previous knowledge. However, it is the observation of a changed
real concrete, i.e. the imagined concrete (IC) at time 1 is still
filtered through the knowledge of the previous time (K_o) and it is
thus indicated as $IC_{o,1}$. The agent, by using the means of mental
production T_o (a part of K_o, just as in material production the means
of production are previous products) and the material aids of mental
production produces a new knowledge, K_1, in this case the solution
to the practical problem. Let us refer to the PMT at times 1, 2 ... n
as PMT_1, PMT_2 ... PMT_n. Then

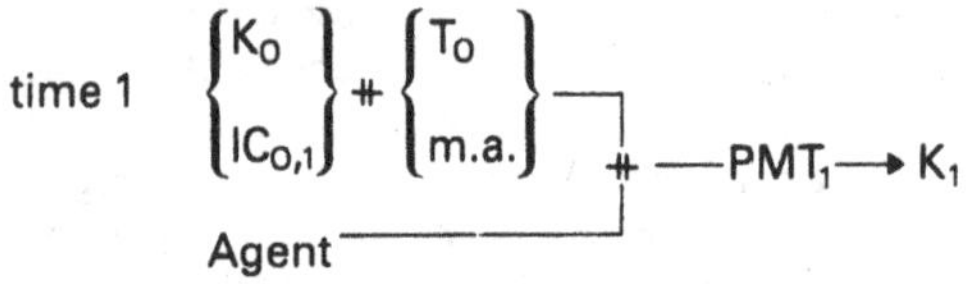

$$\text{time 1} \quad \begin{Bmatrix} K_o \\ IC_{o,1} \end{Bmatrix} + \begin{Bmatrix} T_o \\ m.a. \end{Bmatrix} \quad + \ \text{—} PMT_1 \longrightarrow K_1$$

Agent

Figure 4.1 The production of practical knowledge as PMT
Where the symbols ++ and → indicate respectively combination (rather
than simple addition) and transformation.

Verification of practical knowledge: practical verification

This solution (K_1) must now be verified. First of all, we examine
the question whether this solution allows us to achieve the aim
sought, i.e. we engage in practical verification. A mental product
is verified to be correct when it leads to successful action (the
pragmatic element), when it guides classes to successful action.
Practical verification means that theory must be able to solve the
problems of classes in struggle. But solutions (practice), even
though being part of social practice and thus outside theory, are
appropriated in thought, are an interpretation of the real concrete
and become mental products. Practical verification is thus always
the comparison between two mental products and never between the
real concrete and something essentially different from it (the
concrete in thought). Practical verification is thus based upon a
mental process. More specifically, problems are posed by the real
concrete, i.e. by class struggle, and perceived in terms of class

determined knowledge. The solution must lead to correct action,
i.e. correct in terms of the ends posed by the theory itself and
thus in terms of that class determined theory. Thus a theory provides
a socially determined view not only of the problems to be solved but
also of the ends which we should be able to achieve through the
solution of those problems. Practical verification is the comparison
between the former and the latter and even though it does not take
place completely within theory (because of the role played by the
real concrete) it is completely circumscribed within a theory. Let
us refer to that particular process of mental transformation which is
practical verification as PMT(P). Then the PMT(P) must solve the
problem: is the new knowledge K_1 consistent with the end sought?
The end is a part of the previous knowledge, i.e. K_o. Then Figure 4.2
results.

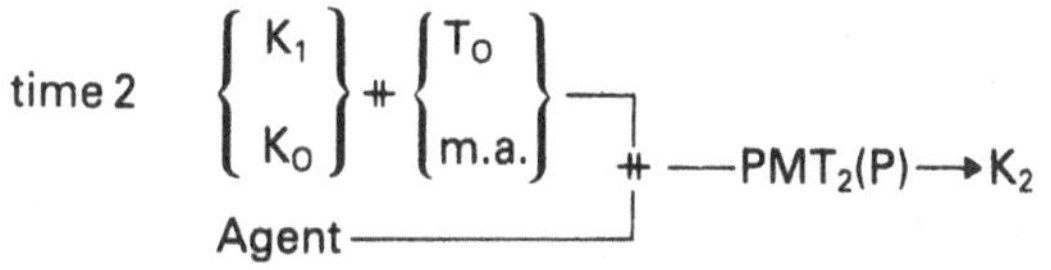

$$\text{time 2} \quad \left\{ \begin{array}{c} K_1 \\ K_0 \end{array} \right\} + \left\{ \begin{array}{c} T_0 \\ \text{m.a.} \end{array} \right\} + \text{PMT}_2(P) \rightarrow K_2$$
$$\text{Agent}$$

Figure 4.2   The PMT(P)

If K_2 shows consistency between K_1 and K_o then the solution to the
practical problem has been immediately verified and practical verification stops here. If K_2 shows inconsistency between K_1 and K_o then
we have three possibilities:
(a) we can look for a new aim, i.e. Figure 4.3

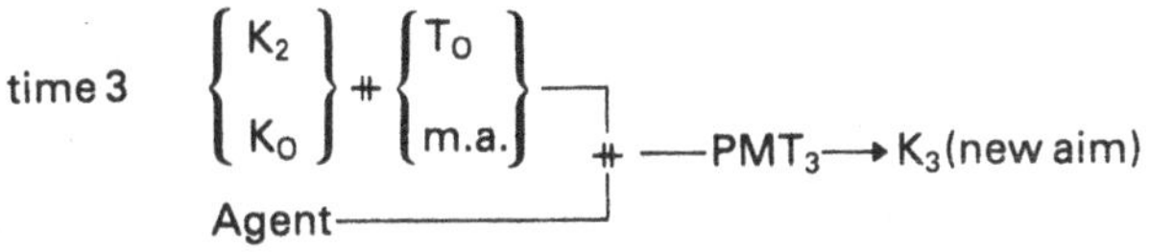

$$\text{time 3} \quad \left\{ \begin{array}{c} K_2 \\ K_0 \end{array} \right\} + \left\{ \begin{array}{c} T_0 \\ \text{m.a.} \end{array} \right\} + \text{PMT}_3 \rightarrow K_3 (\text{new aim})$$
$$\text{Agent}$$

Figure 4.3

(b) we can look for a new solution to achieve the same end, i.e.
Figure 4.4

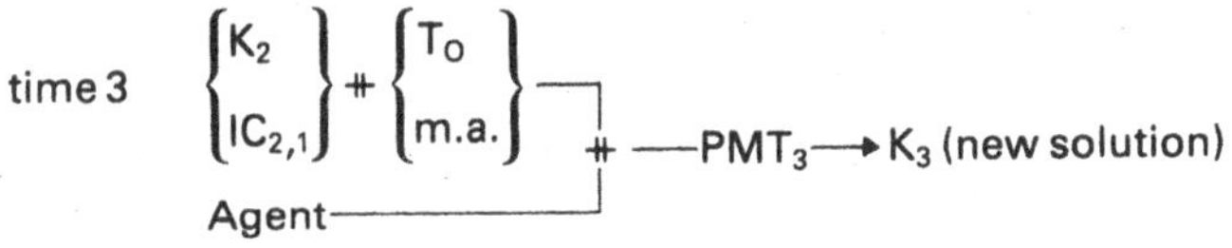

$$\text{time 3} \quad \left\{ \begin{array}{c} K_2 \\ IC_{2,1} \end{array} \right\} + \left\{ \begin{array}{c} T_0 \\ \text{m.a.} \end{array} \right\} + \text{PMT}_3 \rightarrow K_3 (\text{new solution})$$
$$\text{Agent}$$

Figure 4.4

(c) we can retain K_1 even if K_2 shows that this solution is
inconsistent with the end sought: this is the case of relative
autonomy of practical knowledge from practical verification which
will be examined further down (see subsection (e)).

Verification of practical knowledge: logical verification

We have assumed that in case the solution is inconsistent with the
aim (i.e. wrong in terms of the ends sought) a new solution (K_1) or
a new aim (K_0) and not a new theory (T_0) must be sought. The task
of logical verification is precisely that of examining whether the
new knowledge is consistent or not with the existing theory. More
specifically, the new elements of knowledge must now be incorporated
into the existing body of knowledge, i.e. checked for consistency
with the latter. This is logical verification, based upon a PMT
which we will refer to as PMT(L), the second stadium of this process
of verification. The new knowledge, K_1, will now be used by T_0 to
work upon itself. In other words, in the PMT(L) the raw materials
are a certain knowledge, K_1, and a theory (or complex of theories),
T_0, antecedent to it and which has served to form it. K_1 is new
vis-à-vis T_0 because of the incorporation in thought of the change
in the real concrete through the observation in the previous PMT_1.
These new aspects, elements of knowledge, account for the tension
which can arise between that knowledge and the existing theory
(and which sets in motion the PMT(L)) as well as for the possibility
to produce new knowledge and new theories (i.e. K_2 and T_2). The
agent uses the existing body of theory T_0 also as a means of mental
transformation (theory modifies itself) together with the material
aids to mental transformation. Schematically, this is shown in
Figure 4.5.

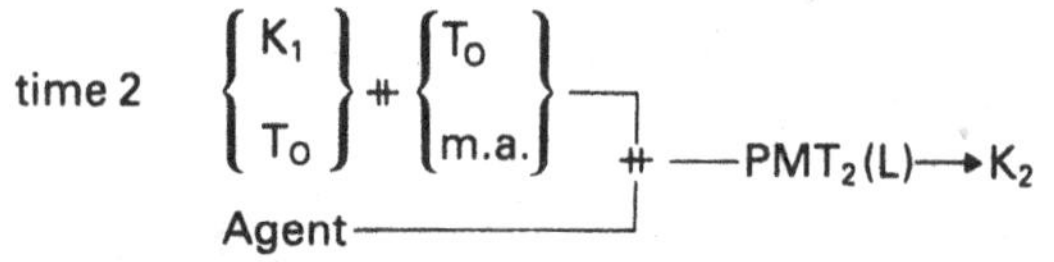

$$\text{time 2} \quad \left\{ \begin{array}{c} K_1 \\ T_0 \end{array} \right\} + \left\{ \begin{array}{c} T_0 \\ m.a. \end{array} \right\} \quad + \quad \text{---} PMT_2(L) \longrightarrow K_2$$

Agent

Figure 4.5   The PMT(L)

The aim of $PMT_2(L)$ is to ascertain whether K_1 can be accounted for
in terms of T_0. There are two cases. Case A: if the outcome K_2
is positive, then $PMT_2(L)$ will have tackled and answered the question
as to why the discrepancy between $IC_{0,1}$ and K_0 in Figure 4.1 can be
explained in terms of T_0, i.e. why T_0 can still explain social
reality, why it is possible to modify K_0 without having to modify T_0
or why it is possible to change parts of T_0 without having to change
T_0 as a whole, i.e. why there is no discrepancy between K_1 and T_0
as a whole. T_0 will have not to be changed, only adapted (in a way
to be seen in a moment, when we will discuss the three levels of a
theory's internal consistency) to the changed social concrete. Then
the discrepancy between K_0 and $IC_{0,1}$ can be eliminated (disregarding
the case of a mistaken application or of a mistaken observation and
assuming that there has been no change in the real concrete between
time 1 and time 3) in the next PMT. Schematically, this is shown
in Figure 4.6
   If there is no further change in the real concrete, K_3 will
explain the change in the real concrete and every 're-run' of PMT(P)
will always turn out a knowledge consistent with the imagined concrete.

$$\text{time 3} \quad \left\{ \begin{matrix} K_2 \\ IC_{2,1} \end{matrix} \right\} + \left\{ \begin{matrix} T_0 \\ m.a. \end{matrix} \right\} \!\!\!- \! + \!\!-\!\!PMT_3 \longrightarrow K_3$$

$$\text{Agent} \!\!-\!\!\!-\!\!\!-\!\!\!-\!\!\!-\!\!\!-\!\!\!-\!\!\!-\!\!\!-\!\!\!-$$

Figure 4.6   The PMT adjusting T_0 to the new real concrete

If there is a change in the real concrete, the process starts again. Case B: in this case K_1 cannot be explained in terms of T_0. If K_1 has been practically substantiated, T_0 must be changed. $PMT_2(L)$ will have tackled and answered the question as to why the discrepancy between $IC_{0,1}$ and K_0 cannot be explained in terms of T_0, i.e. why T_0 cannot explain social reality any longer and what must be changed in order to transform T_0, i.e. why it is not possible to change parts of T_0 without changing the whole of it; why there is an irreconcilable discrepancy between K_1 and T_0. Then this new knowledge will be used to produce a new theory (the scheme according to which this takes place is in Figure 4.6 above, where instead of K_3 we have a new theory, T_3, as the mental product) which will then be subjected to practical and logical verification.

We have seen, in discussing Case A, that a theory can be verified in its totality but not in some of its parts. We should be more specific. We can distinguish three levels of logical verification in which a theory can be verified as a whole but not in some of its parts, based upon three levels of a theory's internal consistency (the coherence element). A theory must be consistent in the sense that (a) its several component parts are consistent with each other (according to the principle of consistency which - as we have seen - is by no means equal for all types of theory and which is itself one of the elements of the theory); (b) the problems to be solved must be framed in terms of that theory; (c) the solutions (data) produced must be consistent with the theory (and thus not with the alternative, competing theories) but not necessarily with the problems which have arisen within the framework of that theory nor with the single parts of that theory. Then, a theory T_0 can be verified in terms of components consistency, problems consistency, and data consistency, i.e. some of its components can be changed, some new problems posed and solved, and some new contradicting data produced without T_0 having to be changed as a whole. We will see in the following subsection when this is possible. Here we want to stress that, first, a knowledge can be verified in its totality and yet not be the same after verification because of the role played by the new imagined concrete in the production of practical knowledge or by the new knowledge K_1 in the PMT(L), when components are changed, problems posed and solved, and data produced. The fact that a knowledge does not change as a whole, and yet the outcome of the process of verification is new knowledge, is of fundamental importance for an analysis of the conditions under which mental labour can be productive of surplus value, an analysis which will be undertaken in the following chapter. Second, no postulate of an ordered real concrete is necessary in order to legitimate the possibility of a structured, internally consistent, concrete-in-thought (and even less do we have to postulate reflection of the former into the latter or a structure

common to both of them). For us, logical verification, though
necessary, is a condition of existence of, i.e. determined by,
practical verification. It is enough to refer to the universal need
which humankind (a class) has to act upon the real concrete by using,
by being led by, knowledge to understand that no successful action
on the real concrete is possible on the basis of an internally
inconsistent theory. (7) In fact, in this case contradictory indications will be drawn from different components; problems posed by the
real concrete will not be framed within that theory and solved; and
the data produced will not be consistent with that theory.

(c) Production of theoretical knowledge

This type of knowledge cannot be directly subjected to practical
verification but only to logical verification. We start from a PMT
similar to the one in Figure 4.1 in which, however, the problem solved
is a theoretical and not a practical one.   Thus, in Figure 4.7 where

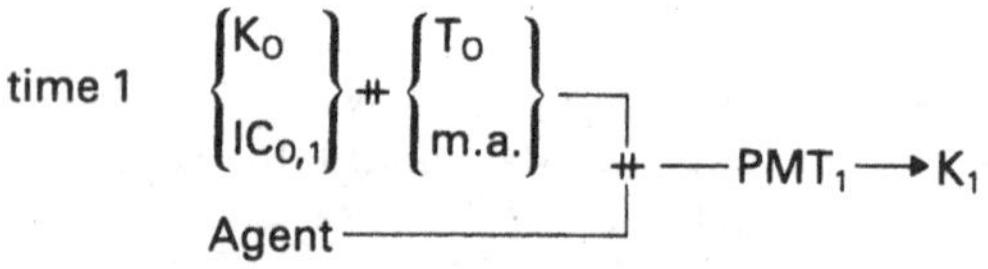

$$\text{time 1} \quad \begin{Bmatrix} K_0 \\ IC_{0,1} \end{Bmatrix} + \begin{Bmatrix} T_0 \\ m.a. \end{Bmatrix} + - PMT_1 \rightarrow K_1$$

Agent

Figure 4.7 The production of theoretical knowledge

K_1 is the solution of a problem whose solution is a precondition for
the solution of a practical problem. For example, the search for a
social law (K_1) is based upon the observation of regularities, $IC_{0,1}$,
where the subscript 1 denotes either a changed (new) real concrete,
e.g. the emergence of new regularities, or, as we will see in section
2 below, the new perspective adopted by the observer under the thrust
of class struggle.

Verification of theoretical knowledge

K_1 is now subjected to logical verification as in Figure 4.5 above.
The outcome, K_2, can show that K_1 can be explained or not in terms
of, is consistent or not with, T_0. If there is consistency, i.e. if
T_0 does not have to be changed, K_1 can be used for the solution of
the practical problems, becomes a raw material, the other being the
imagined concrete at time 3 perceived through T_0 and thus through K_1.
Thus in Figure 4.8, K_3, practical knowledge, is now subjected to practi-

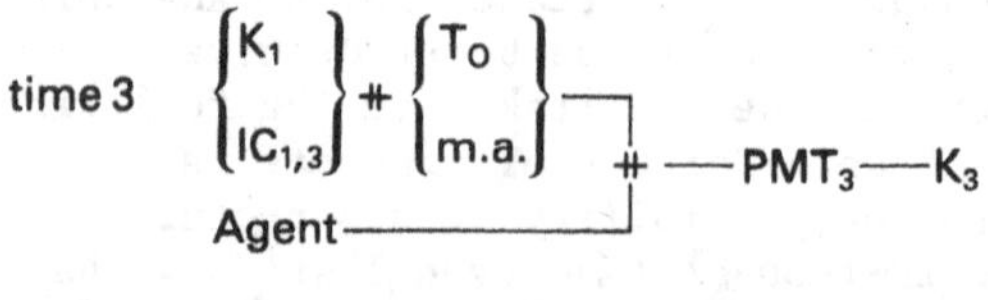

$$\text{time 3} \quad \begin{Bmatrix} K_1 \\ IC_{1,3} \end{Bmatrix} + \begin{Bmatrix} T_0 \\ m.a. \end{Bmatrix} + - PMT_3 - K_3$$

Agent

Figure 4.8 The production of practical knowledge

and logical verification, as above (where only the subscripts must be adapted). If K_2 shows that K_1 cannot be accounted for in terms of T_o, then T_o must be changed.

(d)   The individual aspects of the production of knowledge

There is no danger in our approach of individualism, i.e. of reducing the production of knowledge to the individual sphere. Even though this process can be carried out individually, the process the producer engages in is basically a social one. And this is so not only because, as we have said, the real test is social practice, something outside the individual sphere, so that the producer adapts his mental product to that test on the basis of indications emerging from the struggle itself. The social character of the process by which the individual theorist produces knowledge derives from the social, i.e. objective character of both 'his' raw materials and 'his' means of mental transformation (i.e. of 'his' knowledge) (8) as well as from the social impact that theoretical production has, once it acquires an objective existence, on the real concrete. It is through the social nature of the raw materials and the means of mental transformation that the individual agent (i) turns out a mental product which, in spite of the individual characteristics, has the feature of being class determined, functional for class domination, and (ii) can, but not necessarily does, turn out a mental product capable of having a social impact (we will see in section 2 when this happens). The individual characteristics cannot explain the social character of the individual knowledges (either by summation or by any other process starting from those individual features), but they are necessary for an account of that character because they account for the variety of possible interpretations, all class determined, of the real concrete. As we will see in section 2, it is from these possibilities, already social in nature, because socially determined and thus carrying a social potential, that one or more interpretations will realize that potential on a social scale, become social phenomena. Thus, if it is the individual characteristics of the PMT which allow the agent to 'choose', as it were, one of the many possible interpretations of reality on behalf of the class whose interests he represents in the last instance, it is through the social character of the PMT that all these possible interpretations are expressions of class interests and can become channels through which those interests are represented on a social level. In this context, then, the individual features of a mental product are considered as necessary only in their quality of being forms through which the social content of knowledge can realize itself. They provide a variety of possible forms through which the social content of knowledge realizes itself, (9) i.e. they provide the possibility of knowledge's relative autonomy. Bourgeois epistemology makes an error similar to that of bourgeois economics. This latter is in the last analysis a rationalization of the behaviour and mentality (socially determined, as Marx has shown) of the individual capitalist and is therefore unable (cannot) transcend this level in order to study the social laws of society's development. In an analogous way, the bourgeois epistemologists reduce the relevant question 'What are the objective, i.e. social, conditions which

determine the production, nature, and acceptance of new knowledge?'
to the one-dimensional and misleading: 'How does the (individual)
scientist produce and logically examine new knowledge?' Here, as
there, a social problematic is reduced to an individual one. And
this mistake is made by neo-positivists and Popperians (left or
right) alike. These latter deny that the production of knowledge
can be subjected to logical analysis, thus producing a theory of
knowledge in which the essential part - the production of knowledge -
becomes an exogenous variable, something which Popper calls
'elimination of psychologism'. True, Popper might be right in
asserting that there is no logical method which gives the scientists
the key for the production of new ideas, discoveries. Of course,
a method is not a machine in which you feed old knowledge and which
automatically produces a new one. This triviality is used by Popper
to deny that there is a logic within the process of mental transformation, a logic which explains why ideas arise and are accepted
by a certain community at a certain historical moment.

(e) Verification, pragmatism, and relative autonomy

It should be clear by now that, even if we have retained the pragmatic
element, the method outlined above is to pragmatism as the devil is
to holy water. This is so basically because of the relationship of
dialectical determination existing between real concrete and mental
products. (10) Certainly, the Marxist classics have not always been
clear on this point, but a good deal of confusion derives simply
from mis-reading. Take Engels's 'the proof of the pudding is in the
eating'. (11) This often quoted recipe, at which Althusser hurls
himself vigorously with ill-omened results, should in fact be seen in
the light of the context within which Engels used it, i.e. of his
critique of agnosticism, and not as a fully worked out concept (even
less theory) of verification. Only by forgetting this essential
element can Engels be accused of pragmatism. (12) To the agnostic
who asks 'how do we know that our senses give us correct representations of the objects we perceive through [senses]?' Engels's answer
is that we can test whether our perception of reality agrees with
reality outside ourselves by turning those objects to our own use.
(13) If the aim is accomplished as shown by verification there is
a correspondence between our perception of reality and reality
itself, i.e. the pudding tastes good. If we fail, then either our
perceptions are 'incomplete and superficial' or the combinations of
our perceptions and the results of other perceptions (knowledge) is
faulty. Now, this is not enough. We still do not know when the
observation of a failure vitiates our theory. Not by chance, there
seems to be a feeling of uneasiness in Lenin when he warns us not
to

> forget that the criterion of practice can never, in the nature of
> things, either confirm or refute any human idea *completely*. This
> criterion too is sufficiently 'indefinite' not to allow human
> knowledge to become 'absolute', but at the same time it is
> sufficiently definite to wage a ruthless fight on all varieties
> of idealism and agnosticism. (14)

This is not surprising given that Lenin relies heavily upon Engels

for his theory of truth. And similar remarks apply just as well to
Mao Tse-Tung. For him too, social practice 'alone' is the criterion
of truth, (15) but, 'in social struggle, the forces representing the
advanced class sometimes suffer defeat not because their ideas are
incorrect but because, in the balance of forces engaged in struggle,
they are not as powerful for the time being as the forces of reaction'
so that 'often, a correct idea can be arrived at only after many
repetitions of the process leading from matter to consciousness and
then back to matter, that is, leading from practice to knowledge and
then back to practice'. (16) This is certainly so. Yet, in Mao, as
in Lenin and Engels before him, no clear answer can be found to the
question 'how many repetitions?' (17) This is not by chance, since
the whole dimension of the relative autonomy of knowledge is only
marginally present (due, as we have seen in chapter 1, to the
insufficient theorization of the distinction and diversity between
simple and complex contradictory unities).

Now, if the question of relative autonomy is framed basically in
terms of a time limit, as it is usually framed, no meaningful answer
can be found. One of the two. Either we establish a priori a time
limit, an obviously absurd approach. Or we are entitled to continue
testing ad infinitum, or at least until when - after no matter how
many failures - we establish the 'truth' of a theory which 'we knew'
in advance to be true. Obviously then, the relative autonomy of
theory from practice must be first of all a logical question. It is
Lukács who, somewhat obscurely, points the way. In his 'polemic'
against Engels he points out that

> the task that Engels imposes here on *immediate* praxis of putting
> an end to the Kantian theory of the 'intangible thing in itself'
> is far from being solved.... If praxis is to fulfil the function
> Engels rightly assigned to it, it must go beyond this immediacy
> [i.e. the production of an object as the immediately correct
> verification of an assumption, a theory] while remaining praxis
> and developing into a *comprehensive* praxis. (18)

We believe that this passage can provide the key if interpreted along
the lines suggested by E. Craib, who stresses the point of view of
the totality in Lukács and points out that 'Marxism is able to raise
itself in a consistent rather than an arbitrary or piecemeal way'. (19)
In short, we believe that the relative autonomy of theory from practice
must be understood in the specific sense that practical verification
can prove that a solution to a problem fails to achieve the end aimed
at and yet that solution can be retained when, through an analysis
of that failure, we can show that a component of the theory tested,
or the way the problem has been posed, or some data, are inconsistent
with that theory without vitiating it as a whole, i.e. when the theory
itself can be used to explain that failure. If, by vitiating a part,
we do not, thanks to the logical aspect of verification, vitiate the
whole, then we have a whole which is able to explain, account for,
its own failures. It is thus only when practical verification shows
the whole of the theory to be incorrect by vitiating it as a whole,
i.e. by vitiating its own dominant elements, that this theory must
be abandoned. This concept of relative autonomy can be expanded in
the following five short points. First, the incorrectness of a part
of a theory (practical failure) does not necessarily vitiate the
whole of the theory: it can very well be that it is only that part

that is incorrect. Actually, and this is the second point, what is
dangerous for a theory is not the incorrectness of a part of it, but
the impossibility of explaining that failure in terms of the theory
itself. It is through this impossibility that the vitiating character
of the part extends itself to the whole. In fact, and this is the
third point, when such an explanation is possible, failure will serve
to enrich rather than to undermine a theory. (20) Fourth, and this
is the necessary converse of the previous point, if failure is not
necessarily an indictment, success does not necessarily imply
correctness. Finally, we maintain that essential for a theory to be
a correct interpretation of reality is the possibility for its parts
(not for the whole) to become incorrect. Reality changes continuously
and its appropriation in thought must take into account these changes.
A theory must be able 'to revise those statements as soon as they
become inappropriate without creating destructive internal contradictions'. (21) A theory which would always be verified in all its
parts would thus have no (or loose its) explanatory power because
it would be unable to perceive at the theoretical level the changed
real concrete. (22) Thus relative autonomy is first of all such in
logical, consistency terms, i.e. in terms of components, problems,
and data.

(f) Verification and the objective possibility of correct knowledge

The criteria we just gave concern the possibility for any theory to
be proved correct or to be vitiated. However, Marxism claims to
provide the framework for a correct interpretation of reality. How
can Marxism's claim be reconciled with the claim to be socially, i.e.
class determined and thus with the thesis of the incommensurability
of theories and thus of the data produced within the framework of
those theories? Marxist epistemology is based upon the principle
that it is the real world which determines the world of ideas and
that therefore only those who deal with reality (by transforming
it, in order to produce their means of reproduction) can produce
an independent knowledge of it. (23) In class divided societies,
the transformation of reality is carried out not by individuals but
by groups of people which thus enter into relations with each other
in the very act of production, i.e. into production relations. It
follows thus that the unit of social life (and thus of cognition) is
the social class, and not the individual, and that only those
classes which are identifiable in terms of production relations
specific to them can produce an independent knowledge. There is
thus no reflection but at least as many possible independent types
of knowledge as there are social classes. This point will be further
developed in section 2 below where we will see that each of these
types can (and usually does) take on a plurality of realized, co-
existing and struggling, forms and that the way these types and
forms of knowledge struggle is by attempting reciprocal penetration
and incorporation. The point, however, that there are different,
objectively determined views of reality and not a simple reflection
of reality in consciousness, should not be used to argue for a
plurality of possible correct knowledges of the same real concrete.
Marxism's point of view is that the proletariat has the objectively

determined possibility not only to know reality but also to know it correctly, not because this class is the exploited class, but because it is the class which carries out the societal labour process, the class which deals with use values, with reality, and thus, by transforming it, can know it. (24) The proletariat can be the depository of correct knowledge because it is the (collective) labourer, because of its position in the capitalist production process seen from the point of view of the labour process and not from the point of view of the surplus value producing process. (25) The bourgeoisie, on the other hand, participates in the production process only from the point of view of the work of control and surveillance. This class is necessary for, but does not participate in, the transformation of use values, and therefore is structurally unable to participate in the process of transformation of reality and cannot thus systematically acquire a correct knowledge of it. (26) This conclusion is of the utmost importance and consistent with the materialist nature of Marxism and with the centrality in it of the process of production, of the transformation of reality. It justifies the claim that the proletariat both needs and is able to achieve correct knowledge.

But this basic epistemological principle (only those who deal with reality by transforming it can know it correctly), when restricted first to class societies in general (only classes identifiable in terms of production relations can have a correct knowledge of reality) and then to capitalism (only the proletariat has this privileged epistemological role since this is the class which carries out the societal labour process), must be further qualified by distinguishing the knowledge of the social and that of the natural world, i.e. the social and the natural sciences.

As far as the latter are concerned, the principle according to which they can be developed by those who transform natural reality (use values), i.e. by the proletariat, must be immediately qualified in the light of the fact that this class does not own the means through which this transformation is carried out. It is the bourgeoisie which owns the means of material production so that the producers transform reality on behalf of the non-producers. This means that the proletariat gains a knowledge of the natural world on behalf of the bourgeoisie in the sense that (i) this knowledge (natural sciences) has a practical value (it solves problems posed by production) and a theoretical value (it solves problems whose solution is necessary for the solution of practical problems) but also, and at the same time, (iii) that this knowledge has been gained by mental producers in a situation in which not only they do not own the material aids to mental production but also, and most importantly, must solve problems defined as such by the bourgeoisie, framed within the optic (class determined view) of the bourgeoisie, and solved for the benefit of the bourgeoisie. In slightly different words, the fact that the collective labourer is made to deal with reality implies that he can produce a knowledge of it. But the fact that he does not own the means of mental transformation implies that he can solve practical problems (and thus engage also in theoretical knowledge) only on behalf of the bourgeoisie. And by this we mean that the content itself of natural sciences, and not only their application, is bourgeois in the sense that they are functional for bourgeois domination. In short, since the bourgeoisie owns the means of material production, it owns also the means of mental production so that only one type (even though in several forms) of natural science, the one functional for bourgeois domination, is possible. (27)

It is this practical aspect which lends a strong ideological appeal to the natural sciences as a legitimating factor of capitalism. But this is not all. It is not only the practical value of the natural sciences but also the socially determined possibility for only one class to produce natural sciences and to impose them upon other classes (which thus cannot relate themselves to nature in a way functional for their own domination over other classes), it is the impossibility under capitalism of producing alternative natural sciences that accounts for the myth of the neutrality of the natural sciences and for the power of this myth. And the functionality for natural sciences as developed under capitalism for the reproduction of this system is strictly correlated with their incapacity to understand the natural world without at the same time destroying it, as shown by the exploiting and destructive nature of the relation the former have with the latter. Not by chance does nature thus become antagonistic to the bourgeoisie (as deemly perceived by the 'limits of growth' theorists) and consequently to humankind in general. A science born from a class which owes its existence to a relation of existential interdependence with other classes, where the essence of this interdependence is exploitation and destruction, as well as to an internal relation of competition, cannot relate to nature in the same way as it would be possible if men could relate to each other on the basis of co-operation. Bourgeois natural sciences can solve practical problems and produce a corresponding body of theory but its objectively (class) determined understanding of the natural real concrete cannot but lead to an antagonistic and ultimately destructive relationship with nature.

Things are different as far as the knowledge of the social world is concerned. The fact that the proletariat transforms reality (even though on behalf of the bourgeoisie) and does this in all basic spheres of society, means that it participates in all aspects of social life, that it deals with all aspects of social reality, and that it acquires the possibility to know it. Participation in the transformation, and thus the understanding, of social reality does not presuppose the ownership of the means of material production. The proletariat can develop its own means of mental production, its own view of reality, its own means of theoretical domination over the bourgeoisie and other classes, simply because it participates in the process of transformation of social reality, in class struggle. The same holds for the bourgeoisie (and other classes). Both classes can thus produce their own vision of the social world. However, the bourgeoisie is structurally unable to gain a correct view of the social world, just as in the case of the natural sciences, but for a different reason. In that case, it did not deal with natural reality. Here, it does deal with social reality but, since it is structurally, and thus objectively, the bearer of the tendency the system has to reproduce itself, it cannot look into the fundamental contradictions, those which indicate to us the transitoriness of the system. This is much more than a simple lack of interest. It is a structurally determined lack of interest. Therefore, the bourgeoisie cannot know the essence of the system,

cannot reach a correct view of social reality. Again, bourgeois
social sciences can have at most a practical value. And, again,
just as for the natural sciences, these social sciences are bourgeois
in nature because functional for bourgeois domination.

That these sciences are functional for bourgeois domination is
something which scarcely needs to be argued. Less visible, perhaps,
is the fact that they have only a practical value, i.e. that they
can offer at most a partial, temporary solution to problems which
then reappear elsewhere or after some time, under a new form.
Bourgeois economics, for example, does have a practical value (for
the bourgeoisie), it makes possible the management of the enterprise,
it solves immediate problems, but is unable to understand their real
nature and thus is impotent to offer real, definitive solutions.
This knowledge is not capable, as shown by verification, of providing
permanent solutions to the problems the bourgeoisie itself defines
as such (wars, revolutions, inflation, unemployment, famine, etc.).
Yet it is precisely this practical usefulness, even though a limited
one, this ability to solve problems for one class as if the solutions
were to the advantage of 'everybody', which lends legitimation to
this type of knowledge. As S. Clegg and D. Dunkerley say, concerning
another branch of bourgeois social sciences, organization theory,
'The most effective forms of subjection in the organization are not
only ideological but also practical: they are ideological practices,
such as Taylorism, human relations, or dimensional re-design of
organization structures. At their most subtle these practices will
be at their most opaque, as in the literature of "industrial
democracy"'. (28)

The proletariat, on the other hand, is the carrier of the
tendency which the system has to supersede itself, is antagonistic
to the system and thus to itself as part of the system. For the
proletariat, to create the conditions of supersession of the
capitalist system, i.e. the conditions of its domination over the
bourgeoisie, does not mean to create the conditions of its own
reproduction as proletariat (since this would perpetuate the system)
but to introduce new social (and to begin with, production)
relations, i.e. to transform radically the very essence of capitalism.
For this reason the proletariat has to know the fundamental contradictions of the capitalist system. Differently from the bourgeoisie,
which has to attempt to maintain and reproduce, through non-
essential transformations, the capitalist system and which is
consequently only interested in solving local contradictions, the
proletariat must, because of the contradictory nature of the system,
attempt its supersession and thus has the structurally determined
need and possibility to know social reality completely and correctly.
To sum up, the proletariat cannot work out its own natural sciences
because it has to work with alien means of material and thus mental
production. It can, however, work out its own correct social
sciences. But this is only a possibility. In other words, the
proletariat might not be able to prevent the transformation of its
own knowledge of society by other classes. It is to this type of
transformation that we now turn.

2 VERIFICATION AND PRODUCTION OF KNOWLEDGE IN THE CONTEXT OF CLASS STRUGGLE

(A) Verification and ideological class struggle. First aspect: the penetration/incorporation mechanism

The tension between the two elements of the PMT's raw materials has been considered in the previous section as basically caused by a change in the real concrete and thus in our perception of it. But a PMT can be started also due to a change in our perception of the real concrete without having to assume a change in this latter, a real change. It is from this latter point of view that the PMT and thus verification will be looked at in the present section. We can put this point also in the form of a question. We have integrated in the previous section in an organic whole the class relativity of knowledge and the objective possibility for one class to produce a knowledge which is both class determined and correct in terms of correspondence with (but not reflection of) the real concrete. But if this is so, why can the proletariat make 'mistakes', produce incorrect knowledge? The only answer consonant with our approach is that these 'mistakes' are the acceptance, incorporation, by the proletariat of foreign elements of knowledge, determined by other classes and thus functional for other classes' domination over the proletariat itself. The theoretical justification of this answer will constitute the major thrust of this section. To this end, we will need to go further than the analysis of the process of mental transformation, as given in the previous section. There we analysed the production of a knowledge in (artificial) isolation from the production of other knowledges, i.e. in isolation from the process of ideological class struggle. We need now to go into the question of the specificity of the simultaneous production of alternative knowledges.(29)
    Knowledge has been argued to be a condition of domination, thus a form of ideological class struggle. How will each subject of knowledge (class) produce its own vision of the world, which is also necessarily, a means of its domination over other classes? Or, how can a class accept elements of knowledge determined in the last instance by other classes, i.e. how can knowledge, e.g. ideology, be shared by more than one class and yet be class determined? This thesis requires that we postulate that each subject of knowledge will engage in theoretical production at the same time incorporating elements of other knowledges (either as instruments or as raw materials of mental transformation) and penetrating other knowledges (by introducing elements of its knowledge into the theoretical production of other subjects of knowledge). In other words, the realization of alternative and competing knowledges presupposes a penetration incorporation mechanism (P/I-M) which is the mechanism specific to the joint production of knowledges, to the concrete and contemporaneous realization of several knowledges, and thus to ideological class struggle. This being so, how can we justify theoretically the postulated P/I-M as a mechanism capable of expressing the condition of supersession (as well as of reproduction) of the system? Let us premise right away that this theoretical task would be impossible within the limits of the reflection postulate

since in this case a class could generate only knowledges reflecting
its economic structure and interests. This is clearly not the case.
But our task would be equally impossible within an Althusserian
structuralist framework where it is the structure which creates the
conditions of its own existence. Within this framework classes can
express only the ideological conditions of existence of that structure
and thus of themselves as carriers of contradictory aspects of that
structure, and not the ideological conditions of supersession of that
structure and thus of themselves as well. Ironically, therefore, in
spite of the importance openly assigned to it by Althusser, ideological
class struggle becomes, in fact, unimportant as a motor of radical
change. (30)

What we need here is a shift of emphasis, a radical one, from the
structure as the hidden subject, to social classes: it is classes
which tend to create their conditions of domination over other classes
and thus tend to create the conditions of reproduction or of supersession of the structure. Even though classes are carriers of
structures, it is the former and not the latter who make history.
This fundamental shift of emphasis (in our opinion a return to Marx's
own view) means, for instance, that an ideology of a certain class,
A, can incorporate elements of another class, B, because B has
managed to impose those elements upon A as an aspect of B's attempt
to dominate (ideologically) A and thus as an aspect of the attempt
to reproduce, or supersede, the relation between A and B (structure).
But this does not mean that the 'foreign' elements in A's ideology
are not class, economically, determined. These elements too are
class determined, not only because they are determined by the class
attempting ideological penetration, but also because - as we will
see - their incorporation is at the same time transformation by the
incorporating class. An ideology (or elements of it) generated by
a certain class and functional for domination of that class, can be
imposed upon another class just because of this functionality, just
because of its being a condition of domination (and thus of reproduction
or of supersession), just because of the determination in the last
instance by the economic. Consequently, a class's knowledge can have
elements determined in the last instance by that class, i.e. elements
which are conditions of domination of that class over another class;
and elements which are determined in the last instance by another
class and which are thus conditions of domination of this latter over
the former. A class's knowledge becomes thus an internally structured
and contradictory unity in which some elements will be dominant over
the others and will thus characterize the class nature of that
knowledge, i.e. will carry the social significance of the 'discourse'.
We will refer, therefore, to a knowledge (and thus ideology) as a
mental unity in domination. Verification, therefore, or elimination
of 'mistakes' at the level of theory, implies first of all on the part
of the proletariat the identification of foreign sources of knowledge.
But this is only the first step which must be followed by a PMT, the
aim of which is the depuration of these foreign aspects from the means
of mental transformation. Since this will be a process opposite to
the way in which foreign elements penetrate a certain knowledge, we
have first of all to turn to some specific features of the P/I-M,
i.e. the transfiguration of the elements incorporated and the retaining,
or not, of their class character in this transfiguration.

Ideological penetration/incorporation does not mean mechanical
addition (in a structuralist fashion) of foreign elements. If this
were so, the task of social analysis and ideological class struggle
could be greatly simplified. Ideological penetration/incorporation
means the transformation of a mental product due to its coming into
contact with the class character of another mental product. Both
elements tend to reverberate, to spread their class character throughout each other and throughout the whole of the mental unity in
domination of which they are part. If an analogy with the process of
production producing material objects is allowed, the P/I-M is not
similar to the assembling of different elements, rather it resembles
a chemical reaction in which two elements fuse into another one. The outcome, however, retains, as its social concreteness, the class nature
of either one or the other of the two original elements. This has
the following seven important consequences. First, given that a
knowledge is a unity in domination of different elements, the
incorporation of a foreign element will have a different impact on
the different elements of the whole and only in this way can it have
an impact on the whole itself. Second, knowledges (or elements of
them) are not necessarily immediately recognizable as being conditions
of domination of a certain class. Determination in the last instance
is not transparent and the foreign class character of an element of
a certain mental unity in domination (when immersed in that unity,
i.e. when it is articulated in an organic unity with the dominant
elements of that knowledge) is not necessarily immediately recognizable
as representing the interests of a class. For example, the progressive
bourgeois ideologists of the seventeenth century did not advocate
private ownership and class domination (which would be a transparent
way to advocate capitalism), but on the contrary, given that they
were fighting on behalf of (i.e. given that their ideological fight
was a structural expression, the condition of domination by) the
bourgeoisie against feudalism, they stressed that in a natural
situation, as Spinoza put it, 'alles gehört allen'. (31)   Third, the
P/I-M is a continuous rather than a discrete process so that depuration
is by no means a simple subtraction of elements, as it would be if a
knowledge or its elements were simple reflections of the interests of
a class. Fourth, at any given moment the characteristic feature of
a certain knowledge is given by the class nature of the dominant
element, i.e. of the fundamental element for the existence of that
ideology as a condition of domination of a class and/or of supersession
of the previous, antagonistic ideology. It is not the nature of the
articulation which lends the class character to its (neutral) elements
but it is the class nature of the dominant element which constitutes
that articulation. For example: elements of an anti-capitalist
ideology can be found in the ideology of National Socialism in a
contradictory unity with other elements. (32) This, however, does not
imply that anti-capitalism is a neutral ideological element which can
be combined, articulated within either a conservative or a revolutionary ideology. The anti-capitalism of those who want to abolish
capital, and thus labour, is not the same as the anti-capitalism of
those who believe it is possible to occupy a neutral position between
capital and labour. Fifth, there are limits to penetration/incorpora-
tion beyond which the class nature of the incorporating knowledge,
and thus of the dominant elements, change. In that case the foreign

elements will have become dominant, fundamental for the domination of the class whose interests they express over the class which has incorporated them and which therefore is now ideologically dominated. For example, bourgeois ideology becomes reformism when the dominant elements of the working class's knowledge have a bourgeois character (e.g. class collaboration instead of class struggle). Consequently, when those limits have been reached and trespassed, no depuration is possible any more and that knowledge must be rejected tout court and replaced with a completely different one. Sixth, not all elements of a foreign knowledge can be incorporated and their class nature changed into the class nature of the receiving mental unity in domination. These will be the elements expressing antagonistic contradictions. Elements which express non-antagonistic contradictions can be transformed in contradictory conditions of existence or reproduction of the incorporating body of knowledge. Thus, not all elements of proletarian knowledge can be 'articulated' to bourgeois ideology (and vice versa). This is why a demand for reforms can be functionally incorporated (and thus transformed, thus loosing its class, proletarian character), (33) while a demand for co-operation (rather than competition) among economic production units cannot. (34) Finally, there is nothing spontaneous in the production of knowledge, e.g. in the acceptance of trade unionism by the proletariat. This class's production in the realm of knowledge is revolutionary or reformist (i.e. is its condition of domination over or by the bourgeoisie) only as the outcome of a process of class struggle.

(b) Verification and ideological class struggle. Second aspect: the debunking mechanism

We have submitted in the previous section that knowledge (i) does not simply reflect the interests of the class which determines it, (ii) and yet it is determined in the last instance by the economic, i.e. it is class determined. This means that from a genetic point of view a class must be formed in its essential economic characteristics (i.e. identifiable in terms of production relations) before it can produce systematically its own vision of the world. (35) Logically, this knowledge, already in its original formulation, will be on a continuum (because continuously subjected to modifications - penetration and incorporation - due to class struggle in the ideological sphere) on which it will lose its class nature only in as much as it acquires another class nature. But class determination of knowledge implies also incommensurability, i.e. the impossibility of comparing different knowledges in neutral terms. However, class determination of knowledge does not exclude the comparison of alternative theories in their own terms. This is the second major mode of operation of ideological class struggle which, as we will see, is strictly related to the P/I-M. Let us consider this second mechanism in some detail.
Let us call two conflicting social theories T_1 and T_2 and let us use the notations A_1 and A_2 to indicate the data constituted within each of these theories. Because of their incommensurability, A_1 cannot be used to verify T_2 and, vice versa, A_2 cannot be used to verify T_1. (36) What we can do in examining an alternative theory, e.g. T_2, is (a) use A_2 to provide negative evidence for T_2, i.e. we

can try to weaken T_2's claim to component- problem- and data-consistency and (b) use T_1 to produce A_1 through a reworking of A_2 in order to provide evidence for T_1. These are two ways, which we call the direct and the indirect debunking, to provide evidence for a theory, to verify it in its own terms. These ways do not verify alternative theories. Particularly important is the status of quantitative data (i.e. data in the social sciences obtained by using mathematical and statistical techniques). The application of such techniques is neither the production of neutral data nor verification. It is not the former because at each stage of this production the producer must solve the problem as to (1) which techniques (and thus which theory) to choose and (2) how to adapt those techniques to and for the production of data. To provide only one example, the value judgments implicit at each stage of cost benefit analysis are such that numbers produced on the basis of such a method are nothing more than numbers drawn out of the air. (37) But the application of quantitative techniques is not verification either. Verification (more precisely, logical verification) is rather the solution of the problem of whether these data (K_1) are accountable in terms of the theory tested (T_0). This is the case depicted in Figure 4.5. Moreover, the application of quantitative data to the social sciences is subjected to two further qualifications. First, obviously, only quantifiable hypotheses can be quantified and thus subjected to this type of verification. Second, and strictly related to the former point, the use of quantitative techniques as the essential method (i.e. when this method becomes the essence of the model of society) for the study of social phenomena results in the restriction of the field of social analysis to only those phenomena which are liable to quantitative analysis. (38) This has important ideological consequences since, given that mathematics or statistics cannot build a model of contradiction, a dialectical model which accounts for qualitative changes, the picture of reality which will derive will be one excluding the inner contradictoriness of social phenomena and stressing their evolutionary mode of development and their inner equilibrium. (39) Finally, the debunking aspect of ideological class struggle is meaningful only because alternative theories claim to solve the same problems, i.e. because they analyse the same social reality. It is this objective existence of social reality, forcing itself through a class determined perception, which lends meaningfulness to the comparison between different theories. The criterion of correctness is the ability to solve real and thus common problems in terms of one's own problematic and thus the criterion for preferring one theory to another is, as D. Bloor puts it, the ability to maintain its internal coherence 'over a wider range of theoretically interpreted experiments and experiences'. (40)

(c) Knowledge's relative autonomy in the context of class struggle

If we pause for a moment to consider what we have done so far, we can see that the P/I-M allows us to understand how and why a certain knowledge, determined in the last instance by a certain class definable in terms of production relations, i.e. economically determined, can be common to more than one class, i.e. can be integrated (subjected to

the process of transformation as depicted above) by classes other
than the class of which that knowledge is a condition of ideological
domination. But this necessary first step is not sufficient for our
purposes. Our approach must allow us to explain also how a class
might express more than one knowledge, all of them expressions of
that class's interests, and all of them attempting to become dominant.
We do not refer here to different fractions of a class, as, for
example, industrial, commercial, or agricultural capitalists, all of
them having different interests and potentially able to express
different variations of a certain knowledge. We refer to the
possibility for one class to express its own knowledge in a plurality
of ways, forms. And, related to this problem, we must also be able
to explain how members of a class (i.e. belonging to that class in
terms of production relations) can subscribe to different types of
a knowledge determined by that class or even by another class. To
begin with the latter question. If members of a class are exposed
to different and competing knowledges as well as to different
individual experiences (participation in the class struggle in all
its types and forms), the knowledge determined by the class to which
those agents belong can be internalized by them in a variety of ways.
All these variations will be functional for the domination of one or
another class, i.e. class determined, even though different at the
individual level. This is the relative autonomy of the individual
consciousness, which is the consequence of the relative autonomy of
knowledge and not its precondition. There is no need to slip into
psychologism or biologism to explain either relative autonomy, why
certain agents belonging to a certain class become carriers of other
classes' ideologies (and ideological relations), or, more generally,
the relative autonomy of the individuals. While a theory of
personality should consider social relations only as determinant in
the last instance and concentrate on the mechanisms mediating the
social and the personal in order to account for the variety of the
individual personalities, (41) a theory of knowledge should focus
on the specific features of these individual personalities in their
quality of being socially determined as well as in their capacity
to (and on the conditions under which they can) act on a social level.

   All these different internalizations, or forms of consciousness,
express in their individual differences the multitude of possible
forms which a class's knowledge can take and they can express this
because they are class determined. However, the fact that they are
functional for the domination of a certain class is necessary but not
sufficient to qualify them as social phenomena. To be such, these
different forms of knowledge, consciosness, must acquire the
characteristic of being also social determinants, of being able to
influence, react upon, social phenomena (or they will not be able to
act as a condition of class domination). The question is then, given
that a class determines a certain knowledge and given that that
knowledge is internalized at the individual level in a variety of
ways, when will one or more of these knowledges leave the realm of
the individual to become a social phenomenon? Obviously, a knowledge
is socially useless if it is not accepted by, spread among, individual
agents. A knowledge realizes itself, thus, not so much when it is
produced, formulated by the individual theorists on behalf of a class,
but when it is consumed, accepted, internalized by a number of people,

even though in a great number of variations. These variations are
important at the individual level (and thus as the object of a theory
of personality) but not significant at the social level as long as
they share the dominant elements of that knowledge. Under these
conditions, it is clear that a knowledge realizes itself as a social
phenomenon not necessarily in its original formulation nor as the
'sum ... [or] the average of what is thought and felt by the single
individuals who make up a class', (42) but when it takes one or more
forms whose dominant elements have been accepted by a number of
individuals sufficient to make of it a social phenomenon, able to
influence other social phenomena. And, the struggle among different
forms of individual knowledges, all determined in the last instance
by the same class, will obviously be connected with all other forms
of ideological class struggle and with all other forms and types of
class struggle.

But a class can (and usually has to) express more than one type
of knowledge as a social phenomenon (just think of the different types
of bourgeois economic theories). Again, the concrete realization of
one or more types of a class's knowledge is by no means an affair
internal to that class. The struggle between all these different
realized forms of a class's knowledge (all of them social phenomena)
will result in one of them becoming dominant when it will have become
the fundamental one for that class's domination over other classes
or for the domination of another class over that class. (43)   The
process of knowledge formation is thus a double one of fragmentation
and recomposition. Each class's knowledge emerges at the individual
level in a fragmented way, in a variety of individual internalizations
which are determined in the last instance by the production relations
to which the individual agents belong and which are modified by the
P/I-M. These are all socially, class, determined, as it can be seen
from their functionality for class domination. These different
internalizations then regroup themselves in a number of socially
determinant knowledges in which the individual conceptions share the
dominant elements. All these socially realized knowledges engage
into (are part of) class struggle in order to achieve ideological
supremacy, thus realizing on the ideological level the determination
in the last instance by the economic. (44) Let us provide an example
in a schematic fashion. We will depict the case of three knowledges
(i.e. ideologies) realized on the social level and fighting for
domination through the P/I-M. Two of them are conditions of domination
of class A (i.e. $^1\overline{K}^A$ and $^2\overline{K}^A$) and the third one is a condition of
domination of class B ($^1\overline{K}^B$). Each of these knowledges is the aggregation of a certain number of similar (because sharing some dominant
elements) individual knowledges. For example, $^1\overline{K}^A$ is the aggregation
of a certain number of individual knowledges, as exemplified by the
two knowledges produced by agents n and m (i.e. $_nK^A$ and $_mK^A$) in which
the former production penetrates the latter. Notice that $_nK^A$ and
$_mK^A$ are not yet socially realized, something which is indicated by
not using the dash above the symbol K yet. Schematically, then, this
is shown in Figure 4.9.

In this scheme the area on the left of the individual/social (IS)
diagonal line represents the realm of the individual where the social
determination of individual knowledges (in this case $_nK$ and $_mK$) is
given by the social content of the K (and thus T) and IC used by

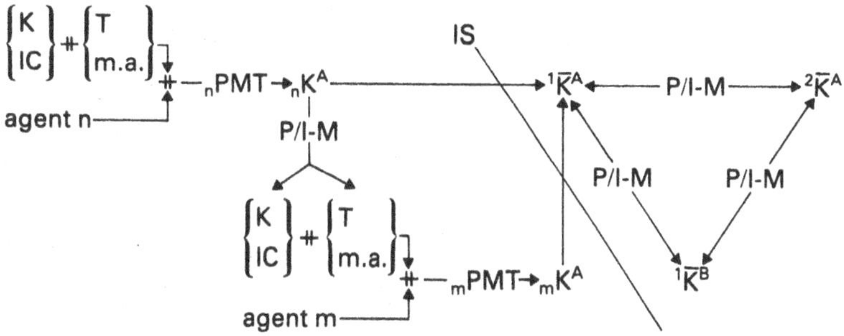

$$\begin{Bmatrix} K \\ IC \end{Bmatrix} + \begin{Bmatrix} T \\ m.a. \end{Bmatrix} \# -_nPMT \rightarrow {}_nK^A \longrightarrow {}^1\bar{K}^A \longleftarrow P/I\text{-}M \longrightarrow {}^2\bar{K}^A$$

agent n

$P/I\text{-}M$ IS

$$\begin{Bmatrix} K \\ IC \end{Bmatrix} + \begin{Bmatrix} T \\ m.a. \end{Bmatrix} \# -_mPMT \rightarrow {}_mK^A$$

agent m

$P/I\text{-}M$ $P/I\text{-}M$ ${}^1\bar{K}^B$

Figure 4.9

agents n and m as raw materials and instruments of mental production.
These K and IC are here assumed to be conditions of ideological
domination of the class definable in terms of production relations
to which agents n and m belong so that, no matter what the individual
characteristics of (or differences between) n and m, and thus of ${}_nK$
and ${}_mK$, both knowledges are K^A (functional for A's domination) and
both belong to the same type because they share some dominant element
(e.g. they believe in predestination) first at the level of K and
IC and then at the level of ${}^1\bar{K}^A$. The area on the right of the IS
line represents the social where the individual knowledges, all
fighting to achieve supremacy and thus to realize their determination
in the last instance, aggregate into a number of realized knowledges
($\bar{K}$s). It is in this area that the various knowledges become
socially significant, social phenomena. The realm of the individual
is thus the realm of the possible social knowledges, the realm of
the social is the realm of the realized social knowledges. But if
the realized knowledges can ascend to the status of realized
conditions of domination only by being accepted by a number of
individual agents, they can ascend to the status of dominant
knowledge vis-à-vis knowledges determined by other classes only by
being accepted (in various ways) by agents belonging to other
classes. Individuals belonging objectively to a class can become
carriers of ideologies determined in the last instance by other
classes. For example, agent n could become carrier of foreign
ideological elements determined by class B. In this case we should
add in the scheme above, an arrow connecting, through a P/I-M, ${}^1\bar{K}^B$
and the K and IC of ${}_nPMT$. Assuming that ${}_nPMT$ turns out a K in which
the dominant elements are now functional for B's domination, agent n
will now produce ${}_nK^B$, a potential condition of domination of B over
A which, if accepted by a sufficient number of agents belonging to
class A, e.g. if accepted by m so that ${}_mK$ is now ${}_mK^B$, will become a
realized condition of B's domination over A, e.g. ${}^2\bar{K}^B$. The arrow
connecting, through a P/I-M, ${}^1\bar{K}^B$ to ${}^1\bar{K}^A$ and going from the former
to the latter, then, only summarizes at the social level the
penetration of ${}^1\bar{K}^B$ into ${}^1\bar{K}^A$, the transformation of ${}^1\bar{K}^A$ into ${}^2\bar{K}^B$.
In Figure 4.9, then, ${}^1\bar{K}^A$ would have to be replaced by ${}^2\bar{K}^B$. The
arrow connecting them, then, would be a short-cut replacing a complex
graphic depiction of how ${}^1\bar{K}^B$ influences all PMT's of agents belonging
to n's and m's category and the aggregation of all these knowledges

into $2\overline{K}B$. The formation of class determined knowledge is a
simultaneous and continuing process of fragmentation, recomposition,
and penetration/incorporation. (45)

To recapitulate some important points, it is quite clear that to
be determined in the last instance, i.e. to be a condition of
domination and thus condition of reproduction or supersession of the
determinant instance, does not exclude but actually calls for, as
necessary integrating elements of the explanatory model, first the
plurality of possible types of a certain determined instance
(knowledge) as different expressions of different aspects or of the
same aspect of the production relations. While the possibility of
the plurality of different knowledges as expressions of different
classes is explained in terms of these knowledges being conditions
of class domination at the level of mental production, the possibility
of plurality of different types of knowledges as expressions of the
same class is explained in terms of the different internalizations of
a certain class determined knowledge. We call this the plurality of
possibilities aspect. Second, there is the plurality of realized
knowledges, some of them determined by different classes and some
by the same class, i.e. the regrouping of the different individual
internalizations into several types, each type being characterized
by some dominant elements common to all the individual knowledges
grouped in that type. These socially realized knowledges are
constantly engaged in a struggle for supremacy as the way the
determination in the last instance by the economic realizes itself
concretely. We call this the plurality of concretizations problem.
And third, there is also the plurality of elements of different
knowledges within a certain knowledge, as sketched through the
P/I-M. This is the plurality within concretizations. These are
the three aspects of knowledge's relative autonomy. There is, then,
no contradiction, but complementarity, between determination in the
last instance by the economic and the relative autonomy of social
(as well as individual) forms of consciousness.

(d)   Summary and concluding remarks

In discussing the determination of politics and culture by the
economic with particular reference to Lukács's imputed consciousness,
A. Cutler et al. confront us with the following argument:
    either consciousness is ultimately reducible to class position
    at the end of a long process of development (it must then be
    irreducible to class position at all other points), *or* conscious-
    ness is irreducible to class position: class consciousness may
    develop but there is no necessity for it to do so. Forms of
    politics and culture that do not express class interests and that
    are irreducible to class determination are therefore a real
    possibility. (46)
The reader might be well advised to pay no attention to these authors'
ridiculous conception of determination in the last instance in
chronological rather than in logical terms. Let us rather examine
what kind of 'logic' these authors use to inflate their theoretical
bellows. A superficial acquaintance with the history of philosophy
reveals that this logic is at least as old as one of Zeno's ways of

refuting motion, as told by Hegel and as quoted by Lenin in his
'Philosophical Notebooks':

> If we speak of motion in general, we say that the body is at one
> place and then it goes to another; because it moves it is no
> longer in the first, but yet not in the second; were it in either
> it would be at rest. If we say that it is between both this is
> to say nothing at all, for were in between both, it would be in
> a place, and this presents the same difficulty. (47)

to which Hegel objects: 'But movement means to be in this place and
not to be in it; this is the continuity of space and time – and it
is this which first makes motion possible', (48) so that Lenin can
add (and his commentary is appropriate also for our 'Marxist' authors'
rejection of determination in the last instance) that this refutation
of motion (of determination in the last instance) is incorrect because:
'(1) it describes the *result* of motion, but not motion *itself*; (2) it
does not show, it does not contain in itself the *possibility* of
motion; (3) it depicts motion as a sum, as a concatenation of states
at *rest*, that is to say, the (dialectical) contradiction is not
removed by it, but only concealed, shifted, screened, covered over'.
(49)

This would be enough to dispose of A. Cutler et al. who re-discover
the well seasoned procedure of setting up a caricature of Marxism
in order to hurl themselves (safely) at it. But we do not limit
ourselves to point out that their claim, i.e. that consciousness is
irreducible to class position, is unwarranted logically, i.e. from
the point of view of dialectics. We submit also that from the point
of view of the proletariat all forms of knowledge are class determined,
or determined in the last instance by the economic since the classes
which can produce an independent vision of the world are those which
can be identified in economic terms, in terms of production relations.
These different world-views are conditions of class domination and
thus conditions of reproduction or supersession of the existing
economic structure (the unity in determination of the different types
of economic relations and to begin with of production relations).
These forms of knowledge, or of class consciousness, can come into
existence only through individuals, i.e. through individual consciousnesses, through a process of internalization by individuals who can
express these types of knowledge to begin with because they are
carriers of production relations, of those production relations which
create their conditions of domination on the ideological level. We
have, therefore, first of all a process of fragmentation of class
consciousness among all individuals belonging objectively, i.e. in
terms of production relations, to that class. It is in this sense
that the individual consciousnesses are determined in the last
instance by the economic because they all are, in spite of their
individual differences, potential conditions of domination of a
certain class. They can be conditions of domination of a class
because of their social origin (they are expressions on an individual
level of a condition of domination of certain class), but they are
not yet such, not yet socially realized, because this social origin
has, as yet, found only an individual expression.

But first, only few of these individual expressions of a social
consciousness rise again to the role of social phenomena, become
concrete realizations of those conditions of class domination by

imposing themselves on other individual knowledges. This takes place
through the P/I-M so that only those knowledges which will penetrate
a number of other knowledges (will make acceptable to the latter
their own dominant elements, if not all elements) sufficient to
influence other social phenomena, will realize themselves socially,
at the same time realizing a certain class's forms of domination
over other classes. We have therefore a process of recomposition of
individual consciousness into (one or) a few social consciousnesses,
all expressions of the interests of the same class and all sharing
the same dominant elements.   The superindividual objectivity
expresses itself through the double process of fragmentation/
internalization and of recomposition/realization. Individuals are
thus neither simple (functionalist) carriers of social relations nor
social monads. The study of personifications does not exclude but
actually presupposes the recognition of the role played by persons,
by concrete and specific individuals and by their specific mental
productions. (50) Persons are important here both because of their
subjectivity and as moments of objectivity; i.e. their subjectivity
is important as potential social realization, their specific
individual features are not disregarded (within a view only stressing
the study of personifications) but are given an intermediate and
mediating role in the formation of personifications. While the
process of fragmentations/internalization falls within the scope of
a theory of personality formation (and thus outside our scope), the
process of recomposition/realization, through the P/I-M, must become
an area of major interest in a theory of class determined knowledge.
It is within this frame that the role of the intellectuals, as those
mental producers whose specific function is that of producing
suitable candidates (i.e. mental products) for the role of social
(hegemonic) phenomena, can be analysed.

Second, recomposition through the P/I-M, i.e. the fight for
domination on the ideological level, is a process involving not only
those knowledges determined by a certain class, but also knowledges
determined by other classes, since it is ultimately by showing its
strength against 'inimical' knowledges that a form of consciousness
can impose itself within its own class. The selecting principle for
the recomposition of individual consciousnesses into social ones is
thus the ability a knowledge has to dominate (be a condition of
domination of one class vis-à-vis) other classes, an ability which
is forged not only in the realm of the ideological but also in all
other types of class struggle. It is thus perfectly consistent with
our approach to accept the existence of a plurality of realized
knowledges even within a certain class as well as the existence of
elements of knowledges being incorporated into problematics with a
different determination in the last instance. The power a knowledge
has to penetrate/incorporate other knowledges without losing its own
class character, i.e. the power a class has to impose a knowledge
functional for its domination upon other classes, is thus dependent
upon class struggle in all its types and forms in their conjunctural
combination. This does not contradict the emphasis placed upon the
power a theory has to solve problems as shown by practical verification. The solution of problems is in itself an aspect of class
domination: problems are not solved for the benefit of all classes
but only of one (or some) of them. This is obvious in the social

sciences but it is a thesis that we have defended also in the natural sciences. Therefore, the greater the power a theory will have to solve problems (as shown by practical and thus logical verification), the greater its debunking power and the greater its possibility of penetrating/incorporating other knowledges. But how? Again, we will have to see how individuals become carriers (agents) of social forces.

Let us examine first of all the relationship between the two aspects of the ideological class struggle. Such a relationship exists both on an objective and on an individual level: on an objective level, because both the P/I-M and the debunking aspect are parts of the PMT in general and because indirect debunking is also an example of incorporation of foreign elements of knowledge; on a personal level, because the P/I-M, even when it is a social phenomenon, is carried out by individuals who must be motivated to introduce foreign elements of knowledge into other knowledges; to transform a knowledge from a condition of domination of one class into the condition of domination of another class; to be the agents who concretely realize the determination in the last instance of knowledge. The motivation to carry out the P/I-M derives for the individual agent of mental production from the ability a theory has (through his agents of mental production) to debunk alternative theories or to resist debunking. Thus, if, for example, T_1, by directly debunking T_2, provides negative evidence for the latter (but no positive evidence for itself), it provides also at the same time a powerful incentive for individual agents to initiate a series of P/I-Ms and thus possibly the trans- formation of T_2 as a social phenomenon. Just as the need capital has to accumulate is felt by the individual capitalists as the need to produce for profit, the need classes have to dominate ideologically (through the P/I-M) is felt by the individuals as the need to provide negative evidence for alternative theories and positive evidence for their own theory. In short, debunking is the way the structure motivates the individuals to realize its own conditions of existence or supersession at the level of theory, the way it motivates them to realize the determination in the last instance of theory by the economic. The same can be repeated as far as the relationship between verification and the P/I-M is concerned. A knowledge (both science and ideology) must have some degree of pragmatic value and internal consistency in order to be able to appeal to the individual mental producer. Therefore the individual is motivated to carry out the P/I-M inasmuch as a theory (knowledge) has both a verification and debunking power. The process of what has been called the 'cognitive negotiation', i.e. the fact that even 'research scientists often employ persuasive tactics which are directly analogous to those used in ordinary political life', (51) or that 'a small group of scientists ... manipulate the flow of *acceptable* information and therefore control the supply of *legitimate* perceptions within a profession', (52) becomes perfectly intelligible from a social, i.e. class, point of view. And also the Mertonian emphasis on rewards can now be seen in a different perspective. Rewards, in their functionalist interpretation, (53) apply only to a small number of mental producers, i.e. more or less to those who make mental production their own profession. But the great majority of the population engages in the process of mental transformation, forms a certain type of consciousness, without any material or otherwise reward, aside from the inner one which derives from a better understanding of the world in the process of dealing with it. For all these people (agents), the need to understand the world in order to act upon it realizes itself through ideological class struggle, i.e. through the double and interrelated process of debunking and P/I-M. And the same applies to scientists, who make of this activity their profession (whether they are aware of it or not) and for whom rewards would not be operative if they were not convinced of the validity of their theories. It is this structural, i.e. class, dimension that allows the system of rewards to function. And it is our contention that the analysis of this dimension can most fruitfully be carried out within the framework of class analysis.

3 AN EXAMPLE: DOMESTIC LABOUR

In this last section we shall apply the scheme outlined above to the analysis of (i) a phenomenon frequently mentioned by those who submit that class determination, or determination in the last instance by the economic, is too reductionist: the nuclear family and the position of women within it; and (ii) of the different, class determined, types of knowledge through which this phenomenon is perceived by all those who are its personification. From the point of view of an a-historical, structuralist explanation, it is quite obvious that this cluster of social relations is not determined in the last instance by the capitalist economic structure (relations), since it is common to a variety of classes identifiable in quite different, even opposite, economic terms. (54) But, this is not our view. By applying our theory we can submit that the nuclear family is determined in the last instance by economics, i.e. is a condition of domination of one class over other classes, and thus it takes on a specific, historical character (form) because of its being determined by capitalist social relations. Thus, the determination in the last instance of family relations does not exhaust our analysis. We must inquire also into the realized (and the possible future) forms of the nuclear family as well as into the mechanism through which these forms take shape while at the same time being determined in the last instance by the economic.

Let us begin with the study of how the nuclear family is a condition of reproduction of the capitalist social relations. This can be seen at the economic level, not so much because it reproduces, together with other instances, principally the state, future labour power (this task is not specific of the family, even if the family plays of course a very important role in it), but because of a series of other, specific, functions of domestic labour. To mention only a few: first, domestic labour, as concrete labour, by making the family's unproductive consumption possible, is necessary for the formation of future labour power, the regeneration of existing labour power, and the maintenance of this latter during periods of inactivity, thus for the transfer of the value of these socially necessary commodities to the value of labour power; (55) second, the family makes possible the payment of wages lower than the value of women's labour power. In fact this is possible for workers who are easily dispensable and can be discriminated against on ideo-

logical grounds. Women can be easily discriminated against because
of sexist ideologies and can be dispensed with because they can
conveniently disappear from the labour force, when not needed any
longer, by returning into the family. There is here a striking
parallel with migrant workers who are also discriminated against on
basis of racist ideologies and can also conveniently disappear, under
late capitalism, when they become redundant, thanks to the new,
active role taken up by the state as importing-repatriating agency
of foreign labour power. (56) The payment of a value lower than the
value of women's labour power should not be confused with the fact
that women are mostly employed in low-paid jobs, something which
derives from their (also socially determined) being unskilled workers,
with relatively low production costs of their labour power, and from
the necessary (for capitalism) tendential correspondence between the
value of the agents' labour power and the value required by the
occupied position. (57) Third, the nuclear family, by acting as a
warehouse of potential labour power, makes possible the introduction
of women on the labour market at times of high economic conjuncture
thus making possible also a compression of wages and a rise in the
rate of surplus value. And fourth, the nuclear family, by imposing
upon women the double role of performing not only wage labour but
also domestic labour, is essential for the formation of a labour
power particularly willing to take part-time jobs, thus contributing
to the provision of an elastic labour force. Or, another example of
determination in the last instance of family relations by capitalist
social relations in the realm of the ideological is the well-known
importance of the nuclear family for the socialization of children,
especially before school age.
    But, as mentioned above, we should look not only into the deter-
mination in the last instance but also into the form family relations
take through the mechanism of realization, the form they take because
they reproduce within the family the capitalist social relations
(these forms being variable rather than unique). This reproduction
is the way family relations are concretely determined by capitalist
social relations, the way family relations become forms of domination
at the social level. To mention only a few examples: the capitalist
economic relations are reproduced within the family - similarly to
capitalist control over labour power - in the form of male's control
over female's domestic labour, so that men perform within the family
the equivalent of the work of control and surveillance - or function
of capital - within the capitalist production process. Since this
labour includes also the procreative activity, male control must
include also control of female fertility and ultimately of sexuality
and of physical development. Or, again, the capitalist division of
labour is reproduced in the form of men-roles/women-roles which,
through the way wealth is acquired and distributed within the family,
ensures men's domination over women in the form of appropriation
(enjoyment) of the outcome of women's labour (similarly to exploitation on a social scale). The political relations typical of
capitalism are reproduced within the family as men's greater rights
(as, for example, the limited or total exclusion of women from
ownership rights, the right men have to give their name to the
family and to the children, etc.). The ideological capitalist
relations are reproduced, for example, in the form of ideologies

stressing the biological, rather than social, basis of sex-specific
jobs. These ideologies, in turn, reinforce the sexual division of
labour within the family and in society at large. Marxist methodology
requires an abstraction which does not eliminate but concentrates on
these historically specific functions and forms as well as 'an examination of the shifting weights of the various components that secure
women's subordination in any specific instance'. (58)   In short, the
determination of the nuclear family by capitalist production (and
thus social relations) indicates the function the nuclear family
performs for the maintenance of the capitalist system in all its
realms, the forms the nuclear family relations take concretely, among
a variety of possible forms, and the contradictory way in which these
forms perform those functions.

The study of this determination shows us a system of relations of
domination (the family) by the bourgeoisie over all other classes, a
system in which women of all classes experience, are subjected to, a
similar condition of domination. Yet women cannot be considered as
a class, or a fraction of a class, since they cannot be identified
in terms of production relations. This statement might cause
surprise since, on the face of it, there is in the household a labour
process, a transformation of use values, and thus there should be
production. We, on the other hand, submit that there is no production
and that, even if there were production within the family, it could
not be a social production, a production based upon social relations.
Our strategy will be to show that, if there were production, it would
have to be individual production. But since women are carriers of
social relations, they must be carriers of other than social production relations. They cannot thus be identifiable in these terms, and
cannot be considered as a class. It should be clear, however, that
in the light of the approach submitted so far, this conclusion cannot
be used to minimize the political importance of women's struggle as
a possible condition of supersession of the capitalist production
relations. Within our concept of determination, the abolition of
domestic labour becomes a necessary condition for the abolition of
the capitalist system.

Consider the nuclear family as an economic unit. The product of
domestic labour's transformation (e.g. cooking) lacks the property
of being exchanged on the market so that if this were production,
it would have to be production for internal consumption. In the
household, transformation and consumption of use values are immediately circumscribed within its boundaries so that the 'product' cannot
be part of social 'production'. Production is social when it breaks
up into a number of branches (social division of labour) and, within
these branches, of production units which produce for exchange (of
course, not necessarily through money) and not for own consumption.
The socialization of production, i.e. the existence of a social
production process, implies thus a fragmentation of this latter into
separate production processes, tied to each other through the
exchange of their respective outputs for further transformation (as
inputs). (59)   In a society in which each person produced for his/her
own immediate consumption (productive and unproductive) the producers
would be independent of each other and there would be no socialization of labour, no social production process and product, and
ultimately no social life, no society, even though there would be

production of use values and thus independent labour (and production) processes. The producers would not constitute a social class but only an aggregate, a summation of individuals. Classes, on the other hand, are social because they participate in the production of the social product, of the product of society. Domestic labour, in spite of its usefulness, and in spite of the fact that it is performed under conditions of subordination resulting from the determination of the family relations by the capitalist social relations, results in a product which does not enter the social product. This transformation thus cannot be part of social production and these relations cannot be social production relations.

Yet, these relations are obviously social phenomena, they have the characteristic of being independent of the will of the individuals. (60) Our thesis is that we have here social consumption. The general point to be made is that even though production is necessarily transformation of use values, not every transformation of use values is necessarily a production process. Consumption is also such a transformation while, on the other hand, production involves also consumption of both the means of production and the labour power employed. Where are the boundaries, then, between a production process and a consumption process? The answer presupposes a distinction first between immediate and mediated consumption and then between productive and unproductive consumption. By immediate consumption we do not refer to the aim nor to the length of the process of transformation, nor to the length of the period during which the transformed use values are consumed. 'Immediate' refers to 'own' consumption of what has been transformed, and 'mediated' refers to the product of transformation being consumed, through exchange, by other than the transforming agent. Moreover, consumption can be either productive, if the outcome of the labour process is employed (consumed) in the next labour process, or unproductive. This is shown schematically in Figure 4.10.

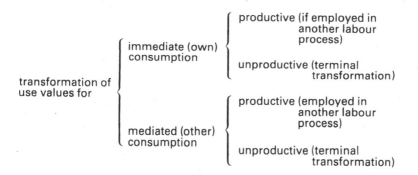

Figure 4.10   Production and consumption

What is usually referred to, in common parlance, as production is transformation both for immediate productive and for mediated consumption, while the exact meaning of what is usually referred to as consumption is transformation of use values for immediate unproductive consumption. The relevant comparison will be between mediated consumption and immediate, unproductive consumption, (61) bearing in mind that a labour process can very well be a combination of immediate and mediated consumption in which one of the two is dominant. Thus in a typical capitalist production process the labour process is a process of transformation of use values for mediated consumption, i.e. the product is typically consumed by other than the transforming (production) unit, i.e. it enters another labour process, either for productive or unproductive consumption. Domestic labour, on the other hand, is a process of transformation of use values for immediate (within the domestic unit) and unproductive consumption, i.e. as a labour process it is a process of consumption rather than of production. Thus, production is transformation of use values, i.e. a labour process, the product of which enters another labour process, while the outcome of a process of consumption (also a labour process) does not enter a subsequent labour process. The illusion that domestic labour is a production process derives from the fact that there is a labour process and that women's labour is part of a division of labour within the consumption process through which some agents (usually women) are allowed to participate in a process of consumption only by performing a transformation of use values also for other agents (usually men) to whom the former agents are therefore subordinated, tied in a relation of subordination. All transformations within the nuclear family, whether carried out by women, by men, or by children have as their aim the immediate (in terms of the house- hold) unproductive consumption of the transformed use values so that all labour performed within the household (from acquiring the use values, to transforming them to moving the jaws in order to consume them) is part of a consumption process either by the dominant consumer or by any other agent who performs aspects of that labour as the dominated consumer. To sum up. Domestic labour is based upon a labour process and on social relations. What is transformed is immediately consumed for unproductive purposes. There are thus no production relations but social consumption relations which, because of their determination by capitalist social relations, are at the same time relations of domination. Women and men cannot be economi- cally (i.e. in terms of production relations) identifiable classes: at the economic level they must be considered as carriers of social relations of consumption, as dominated and dominant consumers.

Women are carriers of social relations of consumption (domination) which are determined by the capitalist production relations and which, just because of this determination, cut across social classes. Now these social relations, by not being identifiable as class relations, by not being based upon autonomous production relations, cannot generate an autonomous knowledge, consciousness. It is not by chance that a generalized (social) consciousness of these common forms, conditions, of domination (through the feminist movement) becomes possible only when women enter the labour market, become directly part of the proletariat. (62) And it is also not by chance that it is only in times of acute social struggle and keen class consciousness, when all the capitalist social relations are challenged and new social relations are created within the still basically capitalist society as conditions of birth and enlarged reproduction of the new, socialist society, that the family - a condition of existence of the capitalist system and thus of the capitalist

production relations - loses its appeal and significance among a large
strata of the population. The feminist movement, the awareness it
brings with it of these generalized conditions of domination, becomes
a condition of proletarian domination, becomes knowledge functional
for the supersession of the capitalist system and whose possible
acceptance by all women finds its rationale in their common condition
as carriers of specific social relations of domination. But this
consciousness is class determined for two interrelated reasons, i.e.
not only because it is a condition of class (proletarian) domination
but also because the way some women will experience this common
reality of domination, their knowledge of it, will be different from
the knowledge other women will have of it, these different ways being
class determined. In fact, women as carriers of family relations do
not belong to any specific social class, but as carriers of those
relations with a man who is both at the dominating end of the family
relation and himself a carrier of class relations (63) belong
indirectly but objectively to that same class. (64). In short,
women as carriers of family relations experience the same reality
of domination but as (indirect) members of a certain class experience
a specific reality (65) so that the perception of the former becomes
modified through the perception of the latter. The outcome is the
concrete realization of all these forms of knowledge in their
interrelation. Therefore women are class heterogeneous only in terms
of individual women's class affiliation, i.e. only in terms of a
common condition of domination, but are class homogeneous in the
double sense that that common situation of oppression is class
determined (a condition of domination of a class over all other
classes) and takes on different connotations according to the class
to which women indirectly but objectively belong. The homogeneity
of women - the common element apparently unrelated to class determination - can thus in fact be accounted for only in terms of a class
explanatory model. This model becomes thus a pre-requisite for the
necessary inquiry into the specific function and forms of women's
oppression. And, the same model can explain not only the variety of
these forms of oppression but also the several forms taken by the
knowledge of this same common situation of domination as well as,
through the mechanism of ideological class struggle, the possible
transformation of this knowledge, its becoming a condition of
bourgeois domination instead of a condition of proletarian domination.
(66) Exclusive emphasis only on this common condition of oppression,
usually separated from an analysis of its determination in the last
instance, or class determination, is just one such example. On the
other hand, the recognition of the functionality of these forms of
domination for the capitalist system and thus for the bourgeoisie
requires also, from the point of view of the struggle for socialism,
the analysis of these forms in their specificity and thus the
engagement in the struggle for their abolition as an integral part
of the struggle for socialism. But this latter can be correctly led
only upon realization that the sharing of common, intra-class forms
of domination neither collapses women into one class nor disproves
class determination.

MATERIAL AND MENTAL TRANSFORMATION, THE FUNCTION OF CAPITAL, AND CAPITALIST PRODUCTION

1 REAL TRANSFORMATION: MATERIAL AND MENTAL

The previous chapters have attempted a reconstruction of the epistemological foundations of some of Marx's most important economic categories. It is now time to start building the latter upon the former. We can now examine the economic aspect of the question concerning what happens when the process of mental transformation (PMT) is immersed in a capitalist production process (CPP). This theoretical step will allow us to define in a clear and non-circular way both when and how conception is productive of surplus value and the general conditions for labour to be productive in a capitalist sense. It is in fact one of the contentions of this book that Marxist analyses on this issue have fluctuated between a de facto or even open restriction of the production of surplus value to material production and more or less elaborated re-statements of well-known and correct classic studies (among which by far the most important still are Marx's own) which, however, should be elaborated and extended in order to understand capitalism's new developments. To do this, we will need a general view of the labour process, both material and mental. This is then what we will do in this section, before we pass on to the topic more specific to this chapter.

As we have seen in chapter 2, for Marx the labour process is the process which 'forms new use-values by useful labour with use-values'. (1) Let us indicate the use value of a commodity as C_u. Then the labour process referred to by Marx is a $C_u \rightarrow C_u^{\neq}$ transformation where the symbol $\neq$ indicates a different, new use value. However, this is a specific type of labour process, based upon a real transformation, a transformation of use values. Essential for this transformation is first of all the application of concrete labour, i.e. the expenditure of human energy (always of a 'mental' and of a 'physical' type) of a certain, particular type; the expenditure of human energy, i.e. considered from the point of view of its peculiar characteristics. But this is not enough. This concrete, useful (2) labour must be incorporated, and it is precisely this incorporation which makes possible the $C_u \rightarrow C_u^{\neq}$ transformation. But what has been transformed? If we recall our definition of the means of transformation as being made up of objects

of labour and instruments of labour, then a real transformation is
the transformation of the use value of the objects of labour due to
the incorporation in them of the agent's concrete labour. Since
this incorporation takes place with the aid of the instruments of
labour, and since these latter's use value disappears progressively
during the labour process, the instruments of labour's use value
too will be transformed and incorporated into the new use value,
the product. Let us call a labour process based upon a real
transformation a transformative labour process, or TLP_r.

But there is also the possibility that concrete labour might be
applied to, but not incorporated into, the objects of labour's use
values. This is still a labour process, but of a particular kind.
The labour employed in it does deal with use values, is expenditure
of human energy of a particular kind, and yet, by not being incorporated into those use values does not change them and thus cannot
perform a real transformation. C_u remains C_u. Such a labour process
is based upon a 'formal' transformation of the money-commodity or
of the commodity-money type (or related to it) in which the use
value of the commodity dealt with does not change. We will call
this type of labour process, based upon a formal transformation, a
non-transformative labour process, or non-TLP_r.

But a transformation can also be either material or mental,
according to whether it is a transformation of material objects of
labour or it is conception (which has been discussed in chapter 3).
Notice that if it is impossible, both analytically and in practice,
to separate the expenditure of physical from the expenditure of
mental human energy, it is possible on both a theoretical and a
practical level to operate a distinction and separation between the
actual transformation of material objects and the conception needed
for such a transformation. In fact, this separation is a characteristic feature of the capitalist production process. One important
difference should be underlined here between material and mental
transformation. In the former there is a logical as well as a
chronological separation between transformation and consumption (both
for unproductive and for productive purposes). In the latter there
is only a logical separation between the two processes (the producer
and the consumer can be two different persons, engaged in two
different processes, as, for instance, the teacher and the pupil, in
which the former is engaged in a conception the outcome of which is
consumed by the latter: or they can be united in the same person
who, however, is both producer and consumer). However, these two
processes must be chronologically contemporaneous. The consumer
acquires education, enjoys entertainment, etc.,while the mental
producer provides education, entertainment etc.; or, the former
consumes the new use value while it is produced by the latter. This
does not hold any longer when the mental product is materialized in,
say, a video-tape. Then the possibility arises for production and
consumption to be chronologically separated but this is due, of
course, to the material form in which the mental product has been
incorporated. Now, since both a real and a formal transformation
can be both material and mental, we have the following four types
of transformation:

	real	formal
material	RM_aT	FM_aT
mental	RM_eT	FM_eT

where RM_aT = real material transformation
$\qquad RM_eT$ = real mental transformation
$\qquad FM_aT$ = formal material transformation
$\qquad FM_eT$ = formal mental transformation

Figure 5.1   Types of transformation

Let us consider again a material transformation, this time split into
its two types, in some more detail. An RM_aT is the transformation
of the physical characteristics of the objects of labour, through
the application of concrete labour. It is the change in the physical
characteristics which makes objectively possible a different use,
the satisfaction of an objectively different need in those who will
use the product. But the satisfaction of a need, the possibility
of using an object, is not possible unless that object is brought
to the user. Therefore, an RM_aT encompasses not only the actual
physical change of those characteristics but also the delivery of a
use value to a certain spatial/temporal point where that object can
be put to use. Without such a delivery the object could not realize
its usefulness. This is why storage, maintenance, transportation,
etc., are aspects of the RM_aT of use values while commerce, specula-
tion, etc., are elements of FM_aT. These latter do not change the
physical characteristics of the object nor do they complete that
transformation in a temporal or geographical dimension. The object
(product) is already essentially able to satisfy a new need: it
does not have to be sold, speculated upon, etc., in order to realize
its use value. Once the object has reached the geographical point,
or it has been preserved up to the moment, in which it can be
consumed, any further labour will not affect its use value any
longer. Advertising might 'create' a 'new' need but since the
objective features of the commodity will have not changed, there is
no real transformation. (Advertising is an example of FM_eT to be
discussed below). (3)

At this point we should discuss the mental transformation both
in its real and in its formal type. However, reasons of exposition
force us to discuss first the labour process in order to be able to
understand what an FM_eT is. This will allow us to draw a rigorous
distinction between mental and material labour and to reject the
theoretically shaky categories of manual/mental labour or blue
collar/white collar work. As R. Crompton and J. Gubbay rightly
stress: 'recent technical developments have made it even more
difficult (if it was every easy) to distinguish between white collar
and manual employment'. (4) On the other hand, the distinction
mental/material labour can be solidly founded upon a Marxist analysis
of the labour process. Since the expenditure of human energy is
always both physical and mental (even the work at the conveyer belt
implies a minimum of thinking and even the purest of the intellectuals
consumes pencils and paper), the material or mental nature of labour
must depend upon the nature of the labour process (whether it is based

upon a real or a formal transformation is irrelevant at this juncture)
in which labour is expended. At first sight, the nature of the labour
process could be thought to be identifiable by looking at the nature
(whether material or mental) of its raw materials. But this would be
an empiricist mistake because a labour process in its totality is
always a transformation of material and mental objects of labour, is
always an M_aT and an M_eT. Confusion arises from the fact that the
societal labour process, in which the M_aT is always determinant, has
split due to the social division of labour into a number of labour
processes of basically two types. In the first the M_aT is still
determinant, while in the second it is the M_eT which is determinant.
The question, then, when analysing a certain labour process, revolves
around which aspect of the total transformation determines the other.
In symbols the question is whether

$$M_aT => M_eT \quad \text{or} \quad M_eT => M_aT$$

where => indicates determination. Or, if we use the symbol $\overset{\text{⊥⊥}}{<=>}$ to
indicate a combination of two different aspects of the same process in
which either one can be determinant and if we use the symbol LP_r for
the labour process, then

$$LP_r = M_aT \overset{\text{⊹⊹}}{<=>} M_eT. \quad (5)$$

In other words, a labour process is always a unity in determination of
material and mental transformation; the nature (material or mental) of
the labour process will be given by which type of transformation
(material or mental) is determinant in it; and the determinant aspect
of the labour process (its nature) will determine the determinant
aspect (material or mental) of the labour (concrete) employed in it.
But this is not all. Given the necessarily 'double' nature of both
the labour process and (thus) of the concrete labour needed for it,
the nature of the product will also always be both material and mental.
However, the product will appear as either material in nature or as
conception, i.e. only one aspect (usually but not necessarily the
determinant) will be empirically given. Therefore, if we distinguish
the two levels of real transformation and of empirical appearance,
the result is Figure 5.2.

Level of transformation		empirical level
objects of labour (material+mental) $+$ instruments of labour (material+mental) $\rfloor$	$+-(M_aT \overset{\pm}{\leftrightharpoons} M_eT) \rightarrow$ product	⎰material ⎱nature
agent's concrete labour _____↑ (material+mental)		or ⎰mental ⎱nature

Figure 5.2   The double nature of the labour process

Now, the labour process under capitalism is subjected to the technical
division of labour. One aspect of this is the fragmentation of the
labour process in a number of positions which (if we disregard for
the time being the fact that the CPF is also a production of surplus
value and thus that each position has a social content, it is the
performance of either the function of capital or of the function of

labour) (6) are either (a part of) M_aT or (a part of) M_eT. The production of cars, for example, is a labour process of the $M_aT \Rightarrow M_eT$ type but within this labour process there will be agents (positions) performing only M_aT (no conception – as defined in chapter 3 – is required) and others only M_eT. The former type of agent will perform material labour, the latter mental labour (even though both will expend, let us repeat it, both mental and physical energy). Thus, while it is correct to say that a position's technical content requires either material labour (if concrete labour is applied to carry out an M_aT) or mental labour (if concrete labour is applied to carry out an M_eT), at the level of an individual labour process as a whole (where there must be always both M_aT and M_eT but where either one can be determinant), we can say that that labour process is material or mental (and thus that the concrete labour applied is material or mental) only as a short-cut. It is the level of the empirical appearance of the product which usually allows us to recognize the determinant aspect of the labour process. Moreover, given the determination of the concrete in thought by the real concrete, both on a societal level and on the level of the individual transformation units in which the material aspect is determinant, this determination ($M_aT \Rightarrow M_eT$) will result not only in the usually empirically observable nature of the product but also in the nature of the problems to be posed and solved. Conversely, in a labour process of the $M_eT \Rightarrow M_aT$ type, it will be conception which will determine the nature of the product as well as the nature of the material aids of production.

Against this background we can now discuss M_eT in its real and formal type. We have defined above a TLP_r as a labour process based upon a real transformation and a non-TLP_r as one based upon a formal transformation, one in which concrete labour deals with but does not change the objects of labour's use values. Since each individual labour process is based upon a unity in determination of M_aT and M_eT and since we call, for sake of conveniency, a material labour process one in which M_aT is determinant and a mental labour process one in which it is conception which is determinant, it follows that there are the four types of labour process shown in Figure 5.3

	Transformative	Non-transformative
M_aT determinant	Material TLP_r	Material non-TLP_r
M_eT determinant	Mental TLP_r	Mental non-TLP_r

Figure 5.3 Types of labour processes

A TLP_r is thus always either material, if $M_aT \Rightarrow M_eT$ or mental, in the contrary sense. The same holds for a non-TLP_r. Let us take first a material non-TLP_r, e.g. a commercial enterprise. Here it is the dealing with material objects of labour which is determinant vis-à-vis the necessary process of conception. We have therefore an FM_aT which determines not only a certain type of conception (of M_eT) but also its nature. Since the M_aT is formal, does not create new material use values, the type of M_eT determined by it cannot create new mental use values. There is, at the level of M_eT, production of new knowledge (the result of conception) but this new knowledge, by being a part of a process which does not transform material use values cannot be a new mental use value. Consequently, at the level of M_eT, a process of conception does not necessarily create new mental use values. Marx considered the branching off of the commercial activity from the CPP into a separate branch of the economy and concluded that there can be no production of surplus value in it, since the social division of labour does not introduce an essential difference in the nature of the labour process which remains a non-TLP_r. The same applies when, due to a further step in the social division of labour, the conception needed for commercial activities, or more generally for non-TLP_rs, becomes a separate area of activity (e.g. advertising). In this new type of labour process, the M_eT will be determinant and M_aT determined but the formal character of the M_eT will not change. We still have FM_eT. Therefore, to sum up, while in principle an RM_eT can be any kind of conception, an FM_eT is a conception which is (or has been) part of (determined by) a material non-TLP_r.

We have now all the elements necessary for a rigorous definition of production. We have seen in chapter 4 that production strictly speaking is transformation for immediate productive or mediated consumption. We can now be more precise and apply this definition to both M_aT and to M_eT. Production in general is a TLP_r, either material or mental, for immediate productive or mediated consumption. The distinction between immediate productive and immediate un-productive consumption is analytically unproblematic in case of RM_aT, i.e. of a material TLP_r, but much more difficult to draw in case of RM_eT. However, it is still possible to hold that a product of an agent's conception for own's consumtion can become part, either in isolation or in a wider body of acquired knowledge, in a logically separable process, of the objects or instruments of mental labour in a further M_eT. In any case this is not an essential point for us because we are interested not in production in general but in capitalist production, i.e. in the context of the present discussion, in the labour process forming the real substratum of a capitalist production process. In fact, under capitalism, production is never a TLP_r for immediate, but always for mediated, consumption since the product is made in order to be sold to the consumer.

We can now understand why an entertainer, for example, is engaged not only in a mental TLP_r, but also in a type of labour process which can serve as a substratum for capitalist production. On the basis of his knowledge (and skills) and of his perception of a certain type of problem (need in the spectator), he expends concrete labour and transforms those two elements of the objects of labour thus producing a mental product (entertainment) whose use value is new (because product of conception) and thus, because of this, can satisfy a different need in, can be put to a different use by, the spectator (consumer). The entertainer not only produces a new use value (since he is engaged in a mental TLP_r), he produces it for mediated consumption. This labour process is thus suitable for incorporation within a capitalist production process, a production of surplus value. Similarly for the teacher. The knowledge he imparts to the pupils might not be new for him but is new for the pupils and it is

on the basis of the teacher's perception (imagined concrete) of the
pupils' needs that the teacher will transform, through the application
of concrete labour, that knowledge, give it a new form accessible to
the pupils.

2 REAL TRANSFORMATION AND CAPITALIST PRODUCTION: PRODUCTIVE AND UNPRODUCTIVE LABOUR

We have seen that under capitalism production is restricted to a
transformative labour process for mediated consumption. This is the
characteristic of a capitalist production process when its real
substratum, the labour process, is considered. However, the essential
feature of a capitalist production process (CPP) is that the labour
process becomes a channel for the self-expansion of capital, for the
production of surplus value. The CPP becomes the unity in determination of the transformative labour process (TLP_r) for mediated
consumption and of the surplus value producing process (sPP). If
we use the symbol => to indicate determination (where the direction
of determination goes in the direction of the arrow) then

$$CPP = sPP => \text{TLP}_r. \quad (7)$$

This is the CPP proper, whose essence is the production of surplus
value. In it, the labour process is the qualitative aspect while the
surplus value producing process is the quantitative aspect. This
latter, as Marx has shown, is the outcome of the process of utilization
of the commodity labour power, i.e. is made possible because of the use
value of labour power. The CPP as a whole, however, is an $M \to M'$
transformation, the transformation of a certain amount of money (M)
into a bigger amount (M'). Marx summarizes this transformation as in
Figure 5.4. (8)

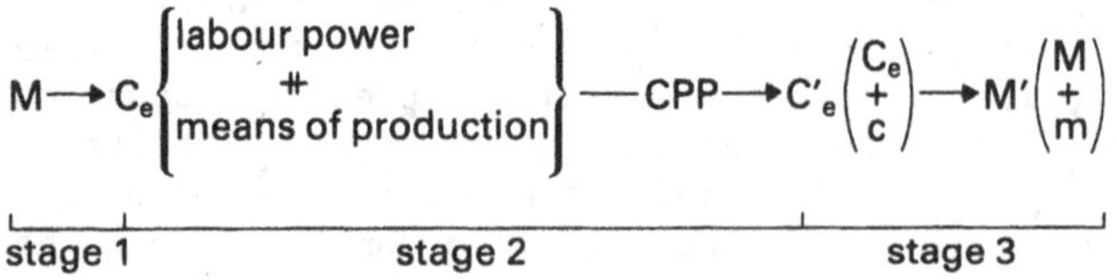

$$M \to C_e \begin{Bmatrix} \text{labour power} \\ + \\ \text{means of production} \end{Bmatrix} - CPP \to C'_e \begin{pmatrix} C_e \\ + \\ c \end{pmatrix} \to M' \begin{pmatrix} M \\ + \\ m \end{pmatrix}$$

stage 1   stage 2   stage 3

Figure 5.4 The CPP as a whole

Here $\to$ indicates formal transformation in stages 1 and 3 and real
transformation in stage 2, and C_e refers to the commodity as an
exchange value. What this scheme depicts is the investment of a
certain amount of money (M) by the capitalist in order to buy
commodities (C_e). These are basically of two types, i.e. labour
power and means of production (both raw materials and instruments
of labour). The combination of these two types of commodity, i.e.
the capitalist production process, produces the product (C'_e) which
in terms of exchange value is greater than the initial commodity
by c (i.e. $C'_e = C_e + c$) and which, therefore, upon sale on the
market, brings in an amount of money (M') greater than the initially
invested amount by m (i.e. $M' = M + m$).

   In this process there will be a creation of value, i.e. C will
have been transformed into C' and thus M into M', for two reasons.

First, there is an expropriation of surplus labour, i.e. the labourers are made to work for a time longer than the time socially deemed necessary to reproduce their labour power. But this is not enough. A further condition is that this CPP is based upon a material or mental TLP_r. There must be a transformation of the type $C_u \rightarrow C_u{}^{\neq}$, a real transformation of the objects of labour's use value. More specifically, productive labour under capitalism is the labour employed in a material and mental TLP_r for mediated consumption when this TLP_r is carried out for profit. There are then three conditions. The first is that the LP_r is now carried out for profit. We express this condition as follows: $M \rightarrow M'$. The second condition is that the LP_r is part of the social labour process; i.e. is part of the dealing with (real or formal transformation) of use values for mediated consumption. Since the social labour process is articulated upon the social division of labour, i.e. the specialization of society's labour process in branches which exchange their products, we can express the second condition as $LP_r \ \epsilon \ SDL$, where SDL means social division of labour and ϵ indicates membership in a set. Thirdly, the LP_r must be a transformative one, or $LP_r = C_u \rightarrow C_u{}^{\neq}$ where $C_u \rightarrow C_u{}^{\neq} = (RM_a \ T \overset{u}{\rightleftharpoons} RM_e \ T)$. To sum up:
Conditions for labour to be productive under capitalism
(1) $M \rightarrow M'$
(2) $LP_r \ \epsilon \ SDL$
(3) $LP_r = (C_u \rightarrow C_u{}^{\neq})$
There is no circularity in this definition of surplus value. Moreover, the explicit statement of these three conditions allows us to distinguish the case of capitalist production (in which all three conditions apply) from that of simple commodity production (in which only (2) and (3) apply), from that of domestic labour (in which only (3) applies), from that of the unproductive capitalist enterprise (in which only (1) and (2) apply) and from that of an enterprise in which only the function of capital is carried out (in which only (1) applies). These latter two cases will be examined in detail later on.

   We can now make two considerations. First, value is a social substance, it must be produced within definite social relations. It is abstract labour congealed in the product of concrete labour when employed in a TLP_r for mediated consumption under conditions of non-ownership of the means of production. (9) It would thus be wrong to think of surplus value as the money form of surplus labour (or at least insufficient). Also, condition (2) implies that the value produced must be realized through exchange, i.e. exchange value is the element which lends a historically specific rationality to the way in which labour manifests its social nature through a specific division of labour. (10)

   Second, surplus value can be created on the basis of an $M_e T$. As we have seen above, $M_e T$ produces mental use values unless it is a part of (determined by) a material non-TLP_r (or has been before its branching out into a separate activity): if this restriction does not apply, the $M_e T$ can then be the basis of a CPP proper, of the creation of surplus value, of real wealth. There is no need, therefore, to restrict the production of surplus value to material production, against the spirit and the explicit statements of Marx's theory of value. According to E. Mandel, for example

the frontier between productive capital and circulating capital
thus runs between wage labour which increases, changes, or
preserves a use value, or is indispensable for its realization –
and wage labour which makes no difference to a use-value, i.e.
to the *bodily form* of a commodity, but merely arises from the
specific needs involved, i.e. altering (as opposed to *creating)*
the form of an exchange value. (11)

This formulation does not deal with M_eT and thus cannot explain why,
for instance, a privately owned school can be a productive (in the
capitalist sense) enterprise. Moreover, wage labour which makes no
difference to a use value can be both unproductive labour (if employed
in a labour process of an unproductive enterprise) and non-labour
(if employed in order to perform the function of capital). These
differences will be worked out in detail later on in this chapter.
Even more explicit is N. Poulantzas:

On dira ainsi qu'est travail productif, dans le mode de
production capitaliste, celui qui produit de la plus-value *en*
reproduisant directement les *éléments matériels* qui servent de
substrat au rapport d'exploitation: *celui donc qui intervient
directement dans la production matérielle en produisant des
valeurs d'usage qui augmentent les richesses matérielles.* (12)

This is, as E.O. Wright correctly remarks, an 'arbitrary assumption'.
(13) However, the problem is not solved by pointing out that 'If
use values take the form of services, and if those services are
produced for the market, then there is no reason why surplus value
cannot be generated in non-material production as well as production
of physical commodities'. In fact, the category of 'services' just
as those of 'white collar' and 'manual labour' should be relegated
to the museum of the social sciences. A janitor produces a 'service'
but can be productive (irrespectively of whether he works in a
productive or in an unproductive enterprise) because he is engaged
in a real M_aT for mediated consumption. A teacher produces a
'service' too, but he can be productive because he is engaged in a
real M_eT also for mediated consumption. But a bank employee
produces also a 'service' and yet can under no conditions be a
productive labourer (irrespective of whether he deals with material
use values or is engaged in conception) because his activity is part
of a non-TLP_r.

At this juncture we must make explicit a point essential for our
argument, a point already implicit in the previous discussion. The
point of view which must be taken in inquiring whether the combination
$M_aT \Longleftrightarrow M_eT$ is a real or formal transformation of use values and
whether it is a material or a mental transformation, must be that of
the societal labour process and not that of the individual labour
process nor of its constituent elements; while the point of view
which must be taken in inquiring why a labour process has a certain
nature must be that of the surplus value producing process. It
follows that, in deciding upon the nature of a position in terms of
the transformation required by it (i.e. whether real or formal,
mental or material), we might want, to facilitate our task, to
collocate first that position within the labour process of which it
is a part, and then that labour process within the societal labour
process. But the final decision rests always with the societal
labour process. It is for this reason that a teacher or an enter-

tainer, when employed by a capitalist, are productive mental labourers given that their conceptions are not part, on a societal level, of a formal transformation. (14) It is also for this reason that a janitor is always a material productive labourer, if employed by capital, since he is always engaged in the maintenance of material use values, no matter whether he works in a productive or in an unproductive enterprise. And it is also for the same reason that an advertising agent or an economist doing market research for a capitalist are unproductive mental labourers, again irrespective of the transformative or non-transformative nature of the economic unit in which they are employed.

Notice that these are all examples in which the material or mental content of the positions is easily detectable and explicit reference to the societal labour process is made in order to detect the real or formal nature of the transformation (i.e. whether the agents are productive or unproductive labourers) thus skipping the first step (the individual labour process). This, however, might sometimes be difficult or not possible. Further down we will consider the example of a draftsman concerning whom the decision whether he performs material or mental labour is facilitated by considering that position first within the labour process as a whole. And a typist might perform alternatively productive and unproductive labour, even within the same day and even if the technical content of her position does not change, if she types first for the R and D department and then for the sales department of the same enterprise. In this case reference to the individual labour process is a necessary previous step before collocating that position definitively within the wider, societal labour process.

On the basis of these considerations let us now consider a commercial enterprise (and what follows applies to all $M \rightarrow M'$ processes based upon a non-TLP_r, upon a formal transformation). In this case it is incorrect to speak of a capitalist production process. If there is no TLP_r, there can be no production and thus no production of surplus value. We will refer then to this kind of enterprise as the unproductive capitalist process (UCP) in order to distinguish it from the CPP proper. (15) The question now arises: how can a UCP satisfy the first condition (see p. 133 above) without satisfying the third one? Marx submits in the second volume of 'Capital' that a UCP can transform M into M' only by participating in the redistribution of surplus value produced in the productive spheres of the economy through the expropriation of the surplus labour of the unproductive labourers. As we have mentioned elsewhere, it might be useful to speak of exploitation for the productive labourer and of economic oppression for the unproductive one. (16) Then, when there is a non-TLP_r, there can be no productive labour and no real self-expansion of capital on a societal level. There is only self-expansion of some capitals to the detriment of other capitals, redistribution of already produced surplus value thanks to economic oppression. If, as Marx holds, the economic oppression of the unproductive labourers (the fact that they are paid the value of their labour power but are made to work for a time longer than the time necessary to produce their socially deemed necessary means of subsistence) is the mechanism through which this redistribution takes place, how is then

this redistribution tied to that economic oppression? Why and how
is the expropriation of surplus labour (which we will call the
surplus labour producing process, or s1PP) tied to the specific
non-TLP$_r$ of the commercial enterprise? And, second, to what extent
must the unproductive labourer be economically oppressed? Or, how
much surplus value must be appropriated through his surplus labour
in order for the capitalist to be engaged in an enterprise of average
profitability?

Let us consider first the latter question and let us start from
the first volume of 'Capital', from the basic elements of Marx's
analysis of the CPP proper. There, Marx shows that concrete labour
has a double function vis-à-vis the means of production (i.e. the
objects and the instruments of labour). On the one hand, it
transforms the use value of dead labour (means of production) into
the new use value of the product. On the other hand, just because
this transformation takes place, there is a transfer of the means
of production's exchange value into the exchange value of the
product. Or, a part of the exchange value of the product, a part
equal to the value of the means of production needed to produce it,
has been transferred to it through concrete labour. As Marx puts
it, 'Value exists only in articles of utility.... If therefore an
article loses its utility, it also loses its value. The reason why
the means of production do not lose their value, is this: they
lose in the labour process the original form of their use value,
only to assume in the product the form of a new use value'. (17)
But labour is always both concrete and abstract. Thus, each moment
of labour not only transfers to the product a fraction of the
exchange value of the means of production, as concrete labour, but
also creates new exchange value, as abstract labour. When the new
exchange value created will be equal to the exchange value of the
labour power used, the process of creation of surplus value will
begin to take place: this will be value produced by the labourer
but appropriated by the capitalist.

Let us now go back to the UCP, and specifically to the commercial
enterprise. Here too we have instruments of labour (buildings,
furniture, stationery, computers, etc.) and objects of labour (the
commodities bought and sold). As we have seen, here we have the
application of concrete labour (the labour needed to sell airplanes
is different from that needed to sell household articles), yet this
labour does not enter the objects of labour, does not transform
them into something different. There is no combination of concrete
labour and means of production (which we can better call in this
case means of transformation, given that this latter can be both
real and formal), but simple application of the former to the
latter. However, while the raw materials do not change, the
instruments of labour do lose their use value in the course of time,
in the course of the non-TLP$_r$. Since, however, there is no transformation of the objects of labour (the commodity bought and sold
remains the same) we cannot possibly assume that the use value of
the instruments of labour is transformed into the use value of the
commodity bought and sold and thus we cannot assume that the exchange
value of instruments of labour is transferred to those commodities.
Unproductive labour not only cannot produce exchange value as
abstract labour: it cannot transfer old exchange value either, as

concrete labour. Yet the capitalist cannot simply watch the
exchange value of the instruments of labour fade away without
claiming an equal value at the end of the labour process. And, he
cannot pay the value of his unproductive labourers' labour power
without claiming not only an equal value but also surplus value.
Therefore, the surplus value transferred from the productive sphere
of the economy must serve not only to pay the wages and salaries of
the unproductive labourers but also to repay the value of the
instruments of labour consumed in the course of the non-TLP_r and to
gratify the capitalist with an adequate amount of surplus value as
his profit. As far as this latter element is concerned, his profit
must be such that, if

c_1 = the constant capital needed to buy the commodity
c_2 = the constant capital needed to repay the depreciation of the
  instruments of labour in the course of the purchase and sale
  of the commodity
w_u = wages and salaries of the unproductive labourers
m = the capitalist's profit
p = the capitalist's rate of profit
$\bar{p}$ = the average rate of profit

then m must be such that $m/(c_1 + c_2 + w_u) = p = \bar{p}$.   This simply
means that the commercial capitalist, given that he anticipates
(invests) capital equal to $c_1 + c_2 + w_u$, must be able to appropriate
through the economic oppression of his labourers enough surplus
value not only to recover the anticipated capital but also a profit
(m) such that his rate of profit is equal to the average rate of
profit. The ration m/w_u then will indicate the 'normal' extent
to which the unproductive labourer is economically oppressed. We
call this ratio the rate of economic oppression, to be abbreviated
as REO.

 Given, then, a 'normal' extent of economic oppression and given
that there is no production (but appropriation from other areas of
the economy) of surplus value, how does this redistribution take
place and how is it related to economic oppression? Redistribution
means unequal exchange, it means appropriation of surplus value
from the productive sphere of the economy through the workings of
the price mechanism, it means, in short, that, if the commodity
must be sold at its value (the whole of Marxian economics is based
upon this principle), then it must be bought from the producing
unit at a value lower than its own value so that it can be sold
to the consumer by the commercial capitalist at its value. Therefore,
the unproductive labourer is the channel through which the capitalist
appropriates surplus value (under conditions of average efficiency,
in the quantity specified above) in the specific sense that it is
through the unproductive labourer that the capitalist can buy a
commodity at less than its value and sell it at its value, thus
appropriating the difference. This particular non-TLP_r can be
represented in Figure 5.5 where we use the symbol + instead of ++
to indicate that there is no combination but simple addition of
concrete labour and thus of the instruments of labour. How, then,
is this non-TLP_r tied to the expropriation of surplus labour, a
process we call surplus labour producing process (slPP)? That is,
why does the capitalist let his unproductive labourers carry out
this non-TLP_r through a constant attempt to increase the REO? The

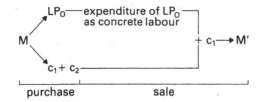

Figure 5.5   The non-TLP$_r$ of a commercial enterprise

answer is that first without economic oppression there is no profit
and second that the commercial capitalist, as all capitalists, is
not content with the average rate of profit. As shown by Marx,
the nature of the system is such that he must constantly attempt to
increase his rate of profit and we submit that he can do that
basically through an increase in the REO. To illustrate this point,
let us provide a simple example. Suppose that the capitalist
invests
40 to buy the commodity
 5 to buy the instruments of labour (we assume complete depreciation)
 5 to buy the labour power.
Suppose further that
the value of C_e is 50
the average time to buy and sell C_e is 4 hours
the average rate of profit ($\bar{p}$) is 10 per cent.
If, then, the unproductive labourer works only four hours he can
buy C_e at 40 and sell it at 50 for the capitalist. The difference,
10, goes in equal parts to pay for labour power and for depreciation.
It could be argued that this hypothetical case is simply a numerical
example of what we want to show and that thus it cannot prove our
point. But in fact we could not find, theoretically speaking, room
for surplus value by buying the means of production or labour power
'more cheaply' or by selling the commodity at a value higher than
its own. Since commodities are bought and sold at their value, we
must assume that C_e must be sold at 50, that labour power is bought
at 5 and that the instruments of labour (consumed at an average
degree of intensity) are also bought at 5. And we cannot find room
for profit in buying the commodity C_e at less than 40 because
competition will ensure an equalization of the price of C_e at a
level lower than its value but not at an arbitrary level. It will
be the level which will allow the commercial capitalist of average
efficiency to realize an average rate of profit, thus 40. In fact,
average efficiency means average use of the instruments of labour
and of labour power. This latter needs then the average time (four
hours) to sell and buy C_e and is made to work for the average length
of the working day, i.e. eight hours. Now, if the labourer is made
to work for four hours, the difference, ten, will go in equal parts
for depreciation and for wages and salaries and there will be no
economic oppression but also no profit. If the labourer is made to
work for the average, i.e. for eight hours, the additional difference
of 10 will now be subdivided in equal parts between depreciation and
profit and p = 5/(40 + 5 + 5) = 10 per cent. To assume an average
level lower than 40 would mean in fact to assume a higher average

rate of profit and again we could not find here a mechanism for
making profit. And, since competition constantly forces the
capitalist to increase his p above $\bar{p}$, it follows that there will be
a constant attempt on the part of the capitalist to increase the
REO. If the capitalist, for example, could force the labourers to
work twelve instead of eight hours, the additional profit of 5 would
raise p to 20 per cent and the REO would go from 100 per cent to
200 percent. This can all be generalized to all UCPs and summarized
as follows: UCP = s1PP => non-TLP$_r$.

Having considered which conditions must be satisfied for a mental
and material labour process (but of particular theoretical interest
is the mental LP$_r$) to be the real substratum of the sPP, let us now
conclude this section by examining some important ways in which the
sPP brings about modifications in the LP$_r$ and particularly in the
mental one. We have already seen that the cause of the independent
existence of a mental LP$_r$ is the combined and interrelated effect
of the technical and social capitalist division of labour. The
former subdivides the LP$_r$, which is always a combination of material
and mental transformation, into a number of different positions
which require either an M$_a$T or an M$_e$T (even though in both cases
there is expenditure of both physical and mental energy). The
latter separates an aspect of the M$_e$T from the original LP$_r$ and
makes of it a separate branch of activity, a separate LP$_r$ (e.g. R and
D enterprises) in which M$_e$T is determinant. Now, as soon as this
mental LP$_r$ comes into independent life, the laws of capitalist
production begin to act upon it too. This means, for our purposes,
essentially three things. We will consider the first two here and
the third one at the beginning of the next section.

First, the technical division of labour emerges again. Conception
becomes the task of the collective labourer, positions (tasks) are
subjected to fragmentation and dequalification, the labour power
of the agents of mental transformation is devalued. This means the
emergence of a dequalified mental producer who fills positions the
technical content of which has been so depauperized that, from their
individual point of view, they could hardly be described as engaged
in mental labour. But, as argued above, we must take the point of
view of the societal labour process and not be led astray by what
seem to be the characteristics of that 'job' taken in isolation.
Let us take the example of an architect's office planning, say, the
building of a block of houses for a capitalist. At the lowest layer
of this office's organization of the labour process we find the
draughtsman. His work is part of a process of conception carried
out collectively and which requires also the graphic posing and
solution of certain problems, even if it could be simply a problem
of graphically depicting the solution of a certain problem. The
draughtsman performs thus mental labour, even though of an extremely
dequalified type. And this is so not because he is part of an
enterprise based upon a mental LP$_r$ (the janitor of that office is
not a mental labourer), nor because he does not do 'manual' labour
or expends basically 'nervous' rather than 'physical' energy, but
because, from the point of view of the societal LP$_r$, his labour is
part of a process of M$_e$T. In fact, the mental nature of his labour
would remain the same if he had to perform the same labour within
a material LP$_r$, for example if the capitalist had his own planning

department engaging both architects and draughtsmen. And, by the
way, it is again the societal level which decides whether the
draughtsman's mental labour is productive (transformative in a real
sense) or not, according to whether, for example, he works for an
architect's office or for an advertising agency. Just as working at
the conveyor belt requires practically no material skills (i.e.
skills necessary for the performance of material transformations),
the draughtsman's work in the above-given example requires also
practically no mental skills. Yet the former is (dequalified)
material labour just as the latter is dequalified mental labour.
Similarly to M_aT, mental use values are now produced by a number of
mental labourers only some of whom can still be considered as
skilled. Thus, if 'all men are intellectuals', only some are
engaged in mental transformation and are thus mental labourers, and
still fewer are qualified, skilled mental labourers or, to say it
with Gramsci, 'have the function of intellectuals'. (18)
    Second, submission to capitalist rule means the introduction of
the work of control and surveillance (the function of capital, FC)
within the mental LP_r. The planning of new production processes,
the expansion of existing ones, etc., are nowadays a collective
effort and not the task of the individual capitalist any longer
(who, by the way, when engaged in that planning was acting as a
labourer and not as a capitalist) which implies a collective process
of mental transformation subject to a global process of control and
surveillance. Or, to take an example of a separate mental LP_r, a
firm producing software, i.e. mental use values in the form of
writing programmes and designing software systems, subjects its
mental labourers not only to fragmentation of positions, dequalification of labour and devaluation of labour power, but also to a
specific form of control for the maximum extraction of surplus
value. (19) Not only this, but the technical division of labour
applies also to this work of control and surveillance and again, at
a certain point, the social division of labour causes a separation
of aspects of the work of control and surveillance into separate
capitalist processes (the consulting agency producing advice for
the capitalists on, say, labour relations or new systems of control
and surveillance of the labourers).   These last two topics, however,
will be dealt with in section 4 where we will examine the economic
significance of the agents performing the work of control and
surveillance, and in section 5 where we will analyse the economic
nature of separate capitalist processes (to be called FC-PP or
function of capital producing processes) which conceive new forms or
applications of control and surveillance.

3 VARIETIES OF LABOUR PROCESSES AS CAPITALIST PROCESSES

In the light of the previous discussion, and especially of our
analysis of M_eT and of its interpenetration with M_aT within a
capitalist context, we can now submit a typology of several labour
processes in order to examine of which kind of capitalist processes
they are the substratum and how the former and the latter influence
each other. Of these processes only one (yet the most important,
the determinant) has been studied extensively by Marx, i.e. the

labour process producing material goods and being the basis of the
CPP proper. We accept Marx's analysis as still valid, but we need
to go further, we need to inquire into other types of labour
processes and capitalist processes. This is the task of this section.
A satisfactory completion of this task, however, is dependent upon
the introduction of one more element, namely upon our recalling
another important feature of the M_eT in class divided societies - as
analysed in chapter 4 - i.e. the fact that, as far as the knowledge
of the social world is concerned, the outcome of this process of
M_eT is either science or ideology. This has the all-important effect,
at the level of the labour process, that the difference between the
material labour process (studied by Marx) and that mental LP_r whose
outcome is the knowledge of the social world (i.e. based upon the
social sciences), is that the latter, besides having a use and an
exchange value, has also the characteristic of spreading either
science or ideology. This is the third effect of the subjugation of
M_eT to capitalist rule (the other two being the separation of material
from mental labour and the introduction of the work of control and
surveillance, the FC, within the process of M_eT, as discussed at the
end of the previous section). This has the consequence, at the
level of the individual agent of mental transformation, that this
agent, especially the one who has 'the function of the intellectual',
the surviving craftsman of conception, is already on the locus of
production a carrier of both economic and ideological relations, it
participates already in the production site automatically both in
the production of surplus value (if engaged in a TLP_r) and in the
ideological class struggle.
   We now have all elements to proceed to a taxonomy of some
capitalist processes (20) which we present in Table 5.1.

Table 5.1   Varieties of labour processes as capitalist processes

	TLP_r		Non-TLP_r
	Based on natural sciences	Based on social sciences	
Material LP_r	1	-	4
Mental LP_r	2	3	5

Before we proceed to a discussion of these five types of processes,
let us make two points of clarification. First of all, there are no
processes of real transformation of material use values based on the
social sciences for the reason that material reality is changed on
the basis of the knowledge of the material (physical) world. Second,
Table 5.1 above concerns itself with labour processes as various
substrata of production for profit and with how this latter
determines the characteristics specific to each of those LP_rs. The
two characteristics mentioned at the end of section 2 and concerning
the effects of the submission of the mental labour process to the
production for profit, namely the fragmentation of positions and
the introduction of the FC, are valid for all LP_rs and thus will not
be repeated in what follows. For reasons of exposition, we have to

postpone an analysis of the surplus value producing process, i.e. of the FC both in its economic significance and as a separate type of capitalist process, to the next sections. Having said this, we can now proceed to compare the five processes contained in Table 5.1. We will do this, in order to facilitate our exposition, under three headings: (a) characteristics of the process; (b) characteristics of the commodity; and (c) component parts of the value of the commodity.

Process no. 1

Examples of this process are industry, mining, etc.

(a)   Characteristics of the process

This LP_r is a real transformation of material use values (to repeat, of material and mental use values in which the M_aT is determinant, as it can be seen in this case from the material nature of the product) and cannot but be based upon the natural sciences. Because of this nature, this LP_r is the basis of the production of wealth in a capitalist form, i.e. as surplus value. The sPP determines a variety of LP_rs of this type (industry, etc.) which, however, in the last instance, all have the common feature of being the condition of production of surplus value and of reproduction of the surplus value producing process. Being immersed in a capitalist context (production of surplus value), this TLP_r must be transformation for mediated consumption. In symbols, this labour process is part of a CPP proper = sPP => TLP_r. This labour process is the fundamental one in all societies and thus also under capitalism because it provides the material basis of society and encompasses, at the societal level, also the (determined) knowledge necessary for that material transformation. It is because it is the fundamental labour process that the CPP based upon it is the CPP proper.

(b)   Characteristics of the commodity

It is material (in the sense that its dominant aspect is material). It is a unit in determination of exchange value and of use value (in the sense that the latter is a condition of existence of the former). It is a product and a commodity in the proper sense of the words, i.e. it is the outcome of a real transformation and it is produced for sale, it has both a use value and an exchange value. It has no direct ideological content. Only indirectly, and under favourable economic conditions can this product have an ideological effect if it serves to legitimate the capitalist system.

(c)   Component parts of the value of the commodity

We have three components. First, a part has been transferred from the means of transformation (means of production) to it through the concrete labour of the labourers. Second, a part has been created ex novo by abstract labour and this is the value equal to the value

of the labourer's labour power. Third, there is the value which
has been created again ex novo by the labourer and which exceeds the
value of the labourer's labour power. This last component is the
surplus value. Both old and new values are incorporated in the new
form of the material use value.

Process no. 2

As an example of this process we can mention a research and development enterprise.

(a)   Characteristics of the process

We have here, as far as the labour process is concerned, a real
transformation of mental use values which is based upon the natural
sciences. Given that this conception is also production of new
(mental) use values, this process can be the basis for production
of new wealth in the form of surplus value. Again, the sPP determines
a variety of TLP_rs which all have one thing in common, that of being
conditions of production of surplus value (or of reproduction of the
sPP). Again, this real, mental transformation must be carried out
for mediated consumption. It can be symbolized as the determined
aspect of the CPP proper as in process no.1. Here, however, because
of the mental nature of the transformation, we cannot generalize this
labour process to the societal level.

(b)   Characteristics of the commodity

It is mental, yet in spite of its non-materiality it has a use (it
is a new use value) and thus an exchange value: it is a unity in
determination of exchange and use value. The exchange value is
partly old and partly new due to the fact that this commodity is
the result of a real transformation. The R and D enterprise produces
new use values (inventions) and sells them on the market. Inventions
become a capitalist business, a capitalist commodity. (21) This
commodity has no direct ideological content but, perhaps even more
than the material commodity of process no. 1, lends itself to an
indirect ideological function of legitimation of the capitalist
system. Moreover, as submitted in chapter 1, it is a type of
science (an element of the capitalist productive forces) functional
for the contradictory development of capitalism.

(c)   Component parts of the value of the commodity

What was said above concerning the exchange value of the product of
process no. 1 can be repeated here with only one modification. The
mental means of transformation have no exchange value unless they
have become a capitalist commodity, either material (i.e. incorporated
in a material form) or mental (e.g. patents). Therefore, only the
exchange value of these latter means of production is transferred
to the value of the mental product through concrete labour. Notice

that here the material form of the material aids to mental production is transformed, through concrete labour, into a mental form, a mental use value. Or, the material form of these aids disappears, but their use value re-emerges in the non-material product (and thus their exchange value as well).

Process no. 3

An example can be found in a private institute teaching social sciences or a privately owned business administration school. Most of what has been said concerning process no. 2 applies here as well and need not be repeated. The only difference is that now the LP_r is based upon the transformation of knowledge concerning the social world and that this transformation, while being the substratum for the production of surplus value, is also immediately an element of ideological class struggle. What, on the other hand, needs more careful attention is a special case of process no. 3, i.e. the mental TLP_r which needs (determines) a specific type of material form in order to realize its use value. We have mentioned above in passing the example of a video-tape. Here we want to consider in some detail the example of a newspaper.

One of the most important results of Marx's analysis of the CPP is that use values are produced as a means for the production of exchange values and thus of profit. We have defined this concept as a unity in determination of the sPP and of the TLP_r, in which the former determines the latter. We have also considered a labour process as either a real or a formal transformation, each one of them being a unity in determination of M_aT and M_eT. Here, however, the direction of determination can go two ways. It follows that the sPP determines not only the real or formal nature of the labour process, it determines also which of the two aspects (the material or the mental) determines the other by determining which one of them is dominant, i.e. by determining which one of them is the most important for the production of surplus value. Consider the production of the newspaper. Here we have both an M_aT (paper must be printed, etc., up to the delivery of the product) and an M_eT (a knowledge of the social world must be produced). Of these two aspects of the labour process it is the mental transformation which is dominant, essential for the production of surplus value: the sales figures will depend in the last analysis upon the content of the newspaper. Thus, the sPP calls into existence a certain LP_r, without which there could be no production of surplus value, and also assigns to the M_eT aspect of this LP_r the dominant role. But the sale of the outcome of this M_eT in its turn necessitates a certain material form (printed paper) and thus an M_aT. This latter is determined by M_eT because this, in its turn, is dominant for the ultimately determinant element of the CPP, the production of surplus value (sPP). The difference between this labour process and the ones considered so far is that here the double nature of the commodity (both material and mental) emerges at the empirical level so that confusion could arise as to the material or mental nature of the newspaper. In fact here the empirical level deceives because it could be easily thought that this commodity is an

essentially material one. But a newspaper is in essence, at the
level of transformation, a mental commodity even though empirically
it has a material form. In it the transformation/production of the
knowledge (of a knowledge) of the social world is dominant (it is
the essential element for the production of surplus value) and thus
determinant of the material transformation needed for that knowledge
to reach the consumer, for the use value of the commodity to realize
itself. Here it is the determined aspect of the transformation, and
not the determinant one, which becomes visible. And since that M_aT
in its turn needs as a condition of its existence a certain type of
mental transformation based upon the natural sciences (the technical,
engineering, etc., aspects of the making of a newspaper), the
production of knowledge of the social world determines not only the
needed M_aT within this particular CPP but also the needed M_eT based
upon the natural sciences.

What has been said so far about the newspaper, however, is not
yet specific of a mental TLP_r based upon the social sciences and
producing a commodity which needs a certain material form to realize
its use value. The same is valid also for a similar LP_r based upon
the natural sciences (e.g. the making of a video-tape for didactical
use in technical schools or the production of an invention which
needs a certain material form). A further specific characteristic
of the LP_r under discussion has to do with the ideological content
of the mental transformation. Because of this commodity's peculiar
characteristic of being a direct means of ideological class struggle
and because this characteristic is inextricably tied to the M_eT
and thus to its dominant role, it is possible for an ideologically
important newspaper to be run on a deficit, at least under
particular circumstances. For example, a newspaper running on a
deficit can be taken over by a large corporation perhaps not with
the aim of making a profitable investment (even though attempts
will certainly be made in this direction) but because of the
possibility of influencing public opinion and government decisions
offered by a newspaper with a large, perhaps nationwide, circulation.
At the level of the individual production unit, the ideological is
not a condition of production of surplus value, (22) yet it remains
so at the level of the corporation and in the long run. The point
is even clearer if one considers those newspapers which are organs
of political parties.

Process no. 4

A typical example of this process is the commercial enterprise.

(a) Characteristics of the process

As we have seen, this process is capitalist (there is an M → M'
transformation) but is not productive (of surplus value) because
there is only a formal transformation. Thus the use value of the
instruments of labour is consumed but cannot be incorporated in the
object of labour: it simply disappears, and with it the exchange
value. This labour process is a non-TLP_r in which the material
nature is determinant. Agents are expropriated of surplus labour

which, however, cannot take the form of surplus value (and thus of wealth) because of the non-transformative nature of the LP_r. Surplus value is appropriated from the productive spheres of the economy through the price mechanism and in proportion to the REO of the unproductive labourers.

(b)   Characteristics of the commodity

It is material and a unit in determination of exchange and use values. There is no new exchange value added to it. It is not a product because it is the outcome of a non-TLP_r.

(c)   Component parts of the value of the commodity

If the commodity is sold at its value, then it has been shown in section 2 that the value appropriated must cover the value anticipated to buy the commodity (c_1), the consumed instruments of labour (c_2), and the labour power (w_u), plus an extra amount (m) such that $m/(c_1 + c_2 + w_u) = p = \bar{p}$, the average rate of profit. Alternatively, the capitalist must buy the commodity at $c_1 = C_e - c_2 - w_u - m$.

Process no. 5

This process can be exemplified by an advertising agency. What was said about process no. 4 can be repeated here, with the only difference that this is a mental, instead of being a material, non-TLP_r. For reasons explained above, this conception cannot be considered to be transformative of mental use values. Notice that the conception needed for the sale of the commodities (which is determinant in process no. 5 and determined in process no. 4) is always a production of a knowledge of the social world and as such it has also a direct ideological content. (23)

4   THE ECONOMIC SIGNIFICANCE OF THE FUNCTION OF CAPITAL

There is no capitalist process, productive or unproductive, without expropriation of surplus value or surplus labour, i.e. without a process of expropriation within capitalist production itself. This means that already within the capitalist process there are agents whose function has the common feature of being extraction of surplus value or of surplus labour from other agents. The latter produce surplus value or labour, the former extract it either for themselves or on behalf of someone else. Both are necessary for the production or appropriation (through redistribution) of wealth under capitalism. Those who extract surplus value or surplus labour do that through a specific type of work, the work of control and surveillance, and are referred to by Marx as being non-labourers. In short, in the capitalist process two types of agents participate, those who deal with use values (the labourers, both material and mental, i.e. those who perform the function of labour) and those who do not deal with either material or mental use values, whose work is that of controlling other agents and who are thus the non-labourers (i.e. those who perform the function of capital). The function of labour (FL) and the function of capital (FC) have been analysed extensively in a previous work (24) to which the reader is referred. Here we only want to stress that the distinction between labourers and non-labourers is not necessarily one between the working class and the bourgeoisie, not even at the level of production relations. For the purposes of our discussion the distinction between labourers and non-labourers is important because only after this distinction has been made can we draw a dividing line between productive and un-productive labourers. Usually, unproductive labourers and non-labourers are conflated into one category. It will be our contention in what follows that there is an economic difference between these two categories and that, from the point of view of the production relation, to conflate these two categories means to conflate two irreducibly antithetical elements. (25)

What, then, is non-labour? It is the actual expenditure of physical and mental human energy, the use of labour power (just as labour), in order to coerce others to labour, i.e. to deal with use values. Are there objective criteria for the definition of material and mental, of concrete and abstract non-labour? We think there are. Let us begin with the material/mental dichotomy. Again, we should reject any demarcation line based upon the 'mental/manual' expenditure of human energy. Non-labour, as well as labour, is always both. Just as we have found an objective distinction between material and mental labour in the nature of the transformation in which labour is employed, in a similar way we can find a distinction between material and mental non-labour in the nature of the trans-formation for which the work of control and surveillance is needed. Therefore, the material or mental nature of non-labour depends upon the material or mental nature of the labour supervised. See further down in this section for a more precise formulation of this general principle. For example, not only the scientist's supervisor but also the draughtsman's supervisor, inasmuch as these supervisors perform the work of control and surveillance, the FC, and do not co-ordinate the labour process, are mental non-labourers. The foreman controlling workers at the conveyor belt, on the other hand, supervises an aspect of M_aT and thus is a material non-labourer. Both types of non-labour can be said to be expenditures of basically nervous human energy and this is so because under capitalism the work of control and surveillance is expenditure of basically nervous rather than physical human energy (contrary to what happens, for example, in a slave system). (26) Yet this is no reason to conceive all supervisors in a capitalist system as being mental non-labourers.

But it is one thing to supervise a team of highly specialized engineers working on a prototype in an R and D enterprise, another to supervise workers at the conveyor belt, and yet another to control the work of bank employees. The work of control and surveillance takes different forms, for which different levels of qualification are needed, according to the nature of the labour supervised. Just as each labour process is characterized by the transformation aimed at and is fragmented under capitalism into a number of different positions, each one of them having its specificity in terms of its participation in the transformation, or simply in the dealing with, use values; in a similar way the work of control and surveillance has to be adapted to, has to take a different form according to, the nature of the labour process supervised and of its different constituent parts (positions), and must be fragmented into a number of different positions. The former category of positions is characterized, in terms of production relations, by the fact that its social content is that of performing the FL. In terms of the production process, each one of these positions has a technical content given by the nature of the concrete labour required by each position (and which differentiates one position from the other). Similarly, the latter category of positions, those whose common feature in terms of production relations is that of performing the FC, is characterized by the fact that each one of them has a technical content which is the form non-labour has to take in order to be able to control a certain type of concrete labour. It is this technical content of non-labour, of the FC, which we call concrete non-labour.

Implicit in what was just said is the extension of the technical division of labour not only to the labourers but also to the non-labourers. More specifically, with the advent of big industry first and then of monopoly capitalism, the FL, the transformation of (or dealing with) use values becomes the task of a number of labourers, all of them performing a different task (a different concrete labour), and all of them members of what Marx calls the collective labourer, because all of them participate in the making of the final product. We refer, therefore, to these agents as performing the function of collective labour (FCL). But the transformation of the labourer into the collective labourer requires also the transformation of the non-labourer for the latter to be able to control the former. The function of capital is fragmented into a number of different positions, each one with its specific technical content. All these positions, i.e. all these non-labourers performing conjointly the control of the collective labourer (of the whole of the labour process), do now in a much more specialized way what the individual capitalist used to do as a capitalist, i.e. they are members of what we call the global non-labourer, they perform the global function of capital (GFC). (27)

Non-labour, as labour power in action, is also abstract non-labour when we disregard the technical content of it. Certain agents' labour power is bought by the capitalist not because they can produce, or be the channel for the appropriation through redistribution of, surplus value, but to force that production or appropriation. From the point of view of the abstract expenditure of their energy, the non-labourers neither produce nor appropriate surplus value for the capitalist, yet they are employed by him in order to expend that energy. From the point of view of the individual capitalist there is no difference between abstract non-labour and abstract labour (both productive and not): both are wage 'labour' and both must thus be subjected to the same economic laws. This means that the technical division of labour, the law of devaluation of labour power and of the dequalification of positions (deskilling of labour), etc., make their way into the FC, transform it into the GFC. But this means also and first of all that there must be an economic significance in the subjugation of the non-labourer to capitalist rule (just as there is such a significance for the labourer), even though this is of a different nature from the labourer's exploitation or economic oppression. In other words, the capitalist employs labour power which, when activated as non-labour, is for him a necessary expenditure of human energy both of a certain type (concrete) and in general (abstract). This expenditure of energy is for the capitalist labour, while from the point of view of the societal labour process, this is non-labour. The capitalist pays that 'worker' a wage which, because of that agent's concrete task as non-labour, and thus because of the specifically required qualifications, is tendentially determined by the value of the non-labourer's labour power. (28) The capitalist, then, forces this agent to expend his labour power for a time longer than the time necessary to reconstitute that labour power, but for the purposes of control. And this is possible because that agent is not the owner of the means of production and thus is dependent upon the capitalist for his subsistence, just as the labourer is. We can thus say that this non-labourer (inasmuch as he is not the owner of the means of production) is also economically oppressed provided we keep in mind that he is at the same time the expropriator (oppressor) of other agents. What is, then, the specificity of the non-labourer's economic oppression?

First of all, clearly, the capitalist is interested in the agent performing the function of capital (GFC) because, without this agent, labourers (both productive and unproductive) could not be made to provide surplus value or labour. But, at the same time, the capitalist is interested also in making the non-labourer 'work' longer than the time necessary to produce the non-labourers' wage goods. The capitalist forces the non-labourer to provide surplus non-labour. To understand why, let us begin with an hypothetical numerical example. Let us introduce the following symbols:

s = surplus value $\simeq$ profit
sl = surplus labour
$sn\text{-}l$ = surplus non-labour
c = constant capital
w_p = wages of productive labourers $\simeq$ necessary labour time for productive labourers
w_u = wages of unproductive labourers $\simeq$ necessary labour time for unproductive labourers
w_n = wages of non-labourers $\simeq$ necessary labour time for non-labourers
Then
$s' = s/w_p$ = rate of exploitation
$REO_u = sl/w_u$ = rate of economic oppression of unproductive labourers
$REO_n = sn\text{-}l/w_n$ = rate of economic oppression of non-labourers
$\bar{s}' = s/(w_p + w_n)$
$p = s/(c + w_p + w_n)$
Let us now consider a CPP proper where, in its purest form, only productive labourers and non-labourers are employed by the capitalist. Suppose the initial situation is

$$200c + \begin{bmatrix} 100 \ w_p \\ 20 \ w_n \end{bmatrix} + 100s$$

where $s' = 100$ per cent; $REO_n = 100$ per cent; $\bar{s}' = 83$ per cent; $p = 31$ per cent; and where we assume a working day of eight hours, 100 productive labourers and 20 non-labourers.

In order to understand what the difference is between an increase in s' and in REO_n in economic terms, i.e. in terms of capital accumulation, i.e. why the capitalist is interested in the economic oppression of the non-labourers as well, let us suppose there is no change in the production function and let us compare two situations.

(a) The REO_n does not change while there is an increase in s'. This can take place because, for instance, there is an increase in absolute surplus value, say because the working day is increased from eight to twelve hours. If the REO_n must not change, then the capitalist must hire additional non-labourers (or let the already employed ones work longer and pay them more). Suppose he employs more supervisors. Then he will have to hire 10 more non-labourers (if 20 non-labourers can supervise 100 labourers working eight hours each, 10 non-labourers can supervise 100 labourers working four hours each). There will be an additional cost of $10w_n$. Thus,

$$200c + \begin{bmatrix} 100w_p \\ 30w_u \end{bmatrix} + 200s$$

so that $s' = 200$ per cent; $REO_n = 100$ per cent; $\bar{s}' = 154$ per cent; $p = 61$ per cent. Or, s' can be increased through an increase in relative surplus value if, say, the value of the productive labourer's labour power is halved. In this case no additional supervisors are needed and thus

$$200c + \begin{bmatrix} 50w_p \\ 20w_n \end{bmatrix} + 150s$$

so that $s' = 300$ per cent, $REO_n = 100$ per cent; $\bar{s}' = 214$ per cent; $p = 55$ per cent. In both cases, situation (a) is characterized by an increase both in the mass of surplus value and in the rate of profit.

(b) Now it is s' which does not change and REO_n which must increase. Such an increase can take place by letting the non-labourers work harder. But this can only mean an increase in the ratio of non-labourers/labourers, i.e. a reduction of the number of the non-labourers relative to the labourers. Suppose the 100 labourers are now to be supervised by 10 non-labourers. Now the ratio is 10 to 1, which corresponds to a situation in which one supervisor supervises five labourers in eight hours (the initial situation) and then five more labourers in the following eight hours. Thus

$$200c + \begin{bmatrix} 100w_p \\ 10w_n \end{bmatrix} + 100s$$

so that $s' = 100$ per cent; $REO_n = 300$ per cent; $\bar{s}' = 91$ per cent; $p = 32$ per cent. (Notice the increase in p from 31 per cent to 32 per cent if the REO_n increases from 100 per cent to 300 per cent as against an increase in p from 31 per cent to 55 per cent when it is s' to increase from 100 per cent to 300 per cent.) Or, an increase in the REO_n could be achieved by reducing w_n. If we assume that the non-labourer is paid for two hours instead of four and made to work for eight hours as before, the $REO_n = 300$ per cent and we get the same results as above. Thus situation (b) is characterized by an increase in p but not by an increase in the mass of the surplus value produced.

The same examples, applied to a UCP in which only unproductive labourers and non-labourers are employed, lead to similar results. But again, while an increase in REO_n does not increase the mass of surplus value produced, it increases the mass of surplus value appropriated by the commercial capitalist through redistribution thanks to the economic oppression of the non-labourers and thus his rate of profit. On the contrary, an increase in REO_n can only increase p but not the mass of surplus value appropriated.

If this is so, the restriction of the absence of change in the production function can be lifted without these results having to be modified. A choice between two different production functions will be made, if only economic considerations are made, in favour of the function implying a larger proportion of labour vis-à-vis non-labour. And this could not be otherwise because, given that non-labourers are neither a means of producing nor of appropriating surplus value, the higher the non-labourers/labourers ratio the less the surplus value produced or appropriated. W_p is productive of surplus value (this is the variable capital proper) and thus of wealth both for the individual production unit and for the economy as a whole. W_u is unproductive, a faux frais of production on the societal scale but productive, so to speak, for the individual capitalist (the more unproductive labourers he employs, the more surplus value he can appropriate, ceteris paribus). And finally W_n is 'unproductive', a faux frais also for the individual capitalist. The capitalist has an interest in employing as many labourers as possible (both productive and unproductive) but as few non-labourers as possible in the specific sense that he will try not only to reduce the percentage of capital invested in the acquisition of labour power in relation to constant capital (i.e. he is interested in an increase in productivity due to an increase in the organic composition of capital), but also to reduce, within this former percentage, w_n in relation to w_p and/or w_u. This is what explains the tendency under capitalism to reduce as much as possible agents who are nevertheless necessary for the capitalist production process. The way this happens is the social and technical dequalification of positions, basically the disappearance of positions within the GFC due to the technical dequalification of other positions within the FCL, as I explained elsewhere (1977). But, in the absence of technical changes or of major changes in the structure of positions making up the production process (technical revolution), or side by side with these changes, other ways can be tried by the capitalist (job rotation, job enlargement, etc.), which, however, while attempting to reduce the incidence of w_n on the costs of production and thus to achieve a higher rate of profit, still keep the worker in a position of complete subordination to the capitalist. In fact, the real importance of the schemes worked out by the industrial sociologists on behalf of the capitalist (or of the capitalist class) is often more ideological than directly economic.

Political and ideological considerations play here an important role, as important as the economic ones. The creation of false expectations (career making), the restructuring of work along lines which only serve to divide the workers, the giving of false feelings of 'responsibility' to increase motivation and thus productivity (i.e. exploitation), job enlargement, job rotation, etc., schemes, these and many others are all tasks of control and surveillance, all different aspects of the FC. The FC goes•from the thinking up of the various forms of the work of control and surveillance to the delegation of its performance to a whole series of intermediate layers of non-labourers, down to its actual carrying it out on the labourers. The FC can thus be performed directly, when the non-labourer forces directly (immediately) the labourers to provide either surplus value or surplus labour, i.e. when the relation between the non-labourer and the labourer is not mediated by other non-labourers; or indirectly, when the non-labourer forces labourers to provide surplus labour or surplus value in a mediated way so that he forces other non-labourers, in the lower echelons of the hierarchy, to provide surplus non-labour (with the economic effects discussed above). Conception, when applied to non-labour, is an indirect way to perform the FC. If we now combine what was just submitted with our definition of material and mental non-labour, we can draw two conclusions. The first is that, since the material or mental nature of non-labour depends upon the nature of the labour supervised, direct or indirect extraction of surplus value or of surplus labour can be either material or mental non-labour. Second, given that the FC is performed globally, there can be several layers of 'intermediate' non-labourers, of controllers who in their turn are controlled by higher-level managers. Following our line of reasoning, the only way to identify objectively this non-labour as material or mental is to look at the nature of the non-labour supervised. But this applies to the actual carrying out of the FC on other non-labourers, and not to the conception of the FC. This latter is always mental non-labour, transformation of knowledge which, given the capitalist characteristic of the societal labour and production process, cannot be considered as productive of mental use values. Figure 5.6 summarizes the various situations in which non-labour can be material or mental.

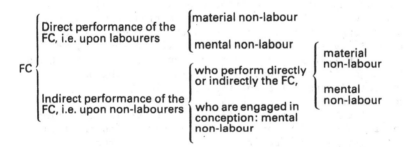

Figure 5.6 Material and mental non-labour

In the light of our discussion of conception in the previous sections, it should not strike us as odd that the conception connected with the performance of the FC is not productive of mental use values. At the level of the individual capitalist process or of the individual position it might look as if this conception is a trans-formation of use values. However, as we have shown in dealing with unproductive labour, not all conception is transformation of use

values. In order to be such from an economic point of view, from
the point of view of the creation of wealth and thus of surplus
value, certain conditions must be satisfied. As we have seen, these
conditions can be recognized only from the point of view of the
totality, of the societal labour process. Thus, if we took the
point of view of the individual firm, we would have to conclude that
an advertising agency, to choose only one example, is a productive
(of surplus value) activity since there is a process of conception
upon which a capitalist process is based. This is clearly against
Marx's own analysis of unproductive labour. (29) Or, we would have
to conclude that this firm is not productive because there is no
material transformation. But then the same would have to apply to
the capitalist school, to the theatre, etc., again a conclusion
contrary to Marx's theory of value. The same principles which allow
us to ground Marx's own examples concerning unproductive labour
into his own theory of value, can thus serve to determine the nature
of conception when it is an aspect of the FC. This mental activity
does transform knowledge but, from an economic point of view, not
only does it not transform, it does not even deal with mental use
values. Therefore, the conditions under which labour can be
productive, as given in section 2 of this chapter, undergo a further
qualification: not only the thinking up and carrying out of formal
transformations but also the conception and carrying out of the FC
cannot be considered as the substratum of the creation of wealth.

Thus, all conception can be a condition for the real transformation of the totality of material use values (even the remotest
conception from real M_aT can be shown to be a condition of real
M_aT on a societal scale), unless it is a type of conception which
is a condition either of the dealing with, without transforming,
material use values, or of that part of human activity which does
not deal with, even though it is necessary for, the transformation
(real or formal) of material use values. More specifically,
conception is sometimes directly and sometimes (very) indirectly a
condition of real material transformation. Some conception will
be necessary for the production of specific material use values
because it is applied to specific material labour processes. It
is thus a direct condition of material transformation. This type
of conception is applied either to a material TLP_r or to a material
non-TLP_r and, within each of these, either to think up forms of
the FL or of the FC. It is on this basis that we can decide when
conception creates or does not create mental use values. Some
other conception will be necessary for the production of material
use values in general, i.e. it is not applied to any specific
material LP_r and has to go through several intermediate stages and
processes before it finally becomes a condition for the production
of a specific material use value by a specific producer. This is
more visible for the capitalist school than for the (capitalistically
run) opera-house, yet the connection could be laid also in the
latter case. This conception is an indirect condition of material
transformation. It is thus a transformation of mental use values
and can be the substratum for the production of wealth (surplus
value). However, there are limits. These are given by that type
of conception which is the result of the branching off of a part
of a material LP_r. When conception is the determinant aspect, to

find out whether we have a mental TLP_r or a mental non-TLP_r or a
mental aspect of the FC, we must inquire into whether that conception
has been part of a material LP_r and of which type of material LP_r.
Whether we have transformation of use values or not, then, even under
the new social division of labour in which that particular mental
activity has become a separate branch of activity, is a question that
can be answered as in the case of knowledge being a direct condition
of material transformation. At the level of the individual capitalist
enterprise, then, we can say that all conception which is a direct
condition of material transformation (in the sense that it is applied
to a specific real process of transformation of the type $M_aT => M_eT$)
or an indirect condition of material transformation (because it is
applied in an $M_eT => M_aT$ process which, however, has not been part
of, and thus is not the condition of, either a material non-TLP_r or
of the performance of the FC) is the basis of the production of
surplus value when immersed in an $M \rightarrow M'$ context. It is only in
this sense that a connection can be established between M_aT and
production of surplus value. Not all production of surplus value
is based upon an M_aT at the level of the individual capitalist unit
but all production of surplus value is a direct or indirect condition
of the societal M_aT, of the transformation of the totality of the
material use values.

5   THE SPECIALIZED PERFORMANCE OF THE FUNCTION OF CAPITAL AS A CAPITALIST PROCESS

We have seen that the introduction of the technical division of
labour within the function of capital has created a hierarchical
and bureaucratic organization of non-labourers who globally perform
what previously used to be the task (function) of the capitalist as
capitalist (as not as the co-ordinator of the labour process). We
have referred to this organization as the global non-labourer, the
global controller of the collective labourer. But under capitalism,
we have seen this above, there is constant interplay between the
technical and the social division of labour. The global non-labourer
does not escape this law. A part of the task (function) of the
global non-labourer can detach itself and become a separate
capitalist process, enterprise. When this happens, we have a special
case of capitalist process, the task of which is the exclusive
performance of the function of capital as an article to be sold on
the market. As an example, we can mention a consulting office being
paid by a capitalist enterprise in order to devise 'better' ways
to control its labourers. This is a capitalist process, it aims at
the $M \rightarrow M'$ transformation, but of a very special kind. Let us call
this process the function of capital producing process, to be
abbreviated as FC-PP. Let us examine it in some detail.
    Originally, the FC which is now the object of the capitalist
process was thought up and performed within a CPP proper or a UCP.
The fact that the FC is now thought up by a separate organization
as its specific activity and not only for one but for many enterprises
does not alter the social nature of that activity, its being non-
labour. Therefore, and this might surprise at first, in this
enterprise there is no dealing with mental use values and thus there

cannot be a labour process specific to it. From the point of view
of society, which is the only correct one, those who 'work' in the
enterprise perform only the FC. We refer here, of course, to the
dominant utilization of the labour power employed. In this enterprise,
the janitor remains a productive labourer and the accountant an
unproductive one. But the essential utilization of labour power for
this kind of enterprise is as non-labour. The employees of the FC-PP
do not deal with mental use values. They are part of the societal
mechanism for the control and subjugation of labour even if they
perform this function in a most indirect way. Their control is now
mediated through the social division of labour. We must therefore
conclude that, in the absence of a labour process, there cannot be
creation of use values and thus of exchange values and that therefore
the 'commodity produced' within this enterprise has neither a use
value nor an exchange value. Yet this firm sells something which,
from the point of view of those who sell and buy it, has a use value
(or it would not be sold and bought) and an exchange value (or it
would not have a price). How can this apparent theoretical contradiction be solved? An easy way out could be to consider this firm
as engaged in a mental labour process. But this would mean assuming
that the social division of labour has the effect of changing the
social nature of this activity, of changing it from non-labour to
labour. But this would be contrary to Marx's methodology (as already
pointed out above), and would thus lead to the absurd conclusion
that those who supervise the creation of wealth (at the social
level) are also engaged at the same time in the creation of wealth
(at the level of the enterprise engaged in the FC-PP). One of the
basic distinctions between Marxian and bourgeois economics and
sociology would thus disappear. Moreover, the same method would
have to be applied to unproductive capital as a separate branch of
the economy, so that not only the boundary between labour and non-
labour, but also between productive and unproductive labour would
fade away.

This would be a mistake, an ideological mistake. It would be the
generalization to the social whole of the point of view of the
individual capitalist, it would be to fall prey to this ideological
illusion. Due to this illusion, it is impossible to see that the
capitalist mode of production is characterized by a determinant
capitalist process, the CPP proper, and by other capitalist processes
which, because determined by the former, function as if they were
productive of surplus value. Our whole discussion of the UCP has
been based upon this principle. In this enterprise the labourers
are unproductive, yet as far as the firm itself is concerned they
are as productive as industrial workers are for the industrial
capitalist. The same principle applies to our FC-PP, our consulting
office. The moment this aspect of the work of control and
surveillance detaches itself from the CPP, the moment it becomes a
separate branch of the capitalist economy, it becomes like all
other capitalist processes subordinated to the CPP proper and thus
it too begins to function as if it were a CPP, i.e. the unity in
determination of the surplus value producing process and of the
labour process. The 'commodity' must have a 'use value' and thus
an 'exchange value', the firm must make a profit, and thus the
'workers' must be somehow productive. (30) But in fact the

conception going on within this enterprise is not part of the
societal labour process. From the societal point of view it is not
even a condition for dealing with, let alone transforming, material
use values. In this enterprise there is no real labour process but
only, and this will be our thesis, expenditure of concrete and
abstract non-labour.

The problem is, then, how can this capitalist, the owner of the
consulting office, get hold of surplus value? For this to be
possible, after the social division of labour has taken place, the
non-labourers employed in the FC-PP must remain an indirect means
to expropriate surplus value (or surplus labour) on a societal scale
and they remain non-labourers within the FC-PP, but must become at
the same time a way for this type of capitalist to appropriate
surplus value from the productive spheres of society, just as if non-
labour were unproductive labour and, from the point of view of the
capitalist himself, just as if non-labour were productive labour.
Due to the determination of the FC-PP by the CPP proper, the outcome
of this process of conception behaves as if it were a capitalist
commodity, while it is not a commodity at all since it has no use
value and thus no exchange value on a societal level. It has only
a use and an exchange value for the individual capitalist. What
is the use value for the individual capitalist is in fact the
technical content of the function of capital on the social level.
As to the exchange value, this 'commodity' has no value, yet it is
sold for a price, which is the way the non-productive capitalist
participates in the redistribution of surplus value. The mechanism
through which he participates in this redistribution is the economic
oppression of his non-labourers. In fact, the capitalist must sell
the 'product' at a value such that not only constant and 'variable'
capital is repaid but also an extra surplus value is appropriated
so that the capitalist's rate of profit is equal to the average
rate of profit. Similarly to what was shown for unproductive
labour, the higher the REO_n, the higher the surplus value appropriated. The difference with the economic oppression of the non-
labourers employed in a CPP proper or in a UCP is that now the
economic oppression is a channel for increasing the mass of surplus
value appropriated. In fact, non-labour, by becoming the specific
activity of a branch of the economy, starts behaving as if it were
labour, so that concrete non-labour appears as if it were concrete
labour and abstract non-labour appears as if it were abstract
labour. Consequently, concrete non-labour appears as if it were
engaged in a (non-material) labour process and thus in the production
of a use value, while abstract non-labour appears as if it were
engaged in the production of value. But abstract non-labour does
not create value: it is only the way in which the non-productive
capitalist participates in the redistribution of surplus value
since he anticipates M and gets M' in return. And this is due to
the fact that the function of capital is now produced for sale, just
as if it were a commodity. To understand this we must recall how
value is distributed in a capitalist economy. Marx has shown that
value is distributed among all those units which not only are
engaged in capitalist production proper, but also among all those
units which, while not participating in this production, are necessary
for capitalist production as a whole. The most obvious example is

the commercial enterprise which, while not producing use and thus
exchange value, is necessary for the realization not of use value
but of exchange value. The labour of the unproductive labourers
gives the right to the unproductive capitalist to participate in the
redistribution of social wealth because that labour is necessary for
the realization of exchange value. Now, the FC-PP is also necessary
for capitalist production because what it produces is an aspect of
the expropriation of surplus value on the societal scale and therefore
a necessary aspect of production under capitalism. This enterprise,
our consulting firm, once it becomes a separate unit, must participate
in the redistribution of social wealth (or it will succumb) and it
will do this through the economic oppression of the non-labourers.
This capitalist process is an aspect of the societal surplus value
producing process. It employs non-labourers and thus cannot produce
value. Yet, since it is necessary for capitalist production, that
non-labour will become the channel for the appropriation of that
enterprise's share of profit. The social division of labour does
not bring about a change in the social nature of non-labour nor does
it change its economic function, significance. It only establishes
a claim on social wealth for the new branch of economic activity.

But, again, as soon as this specialized type of activity becomes
a separate process, due to the social division of labour, it becomes
subordinated to the laws of the capitalist mode of production. This
means, in the context of the present discussion, basically two
things. First, the technical division of labour reappears again.
It reappears in the form it takes in the other capitalist processes
so that also those employed in this enterprise will be subjected to
fragmentation of positions, dequalification, devaluation of their
labour power, etc. But even more important for our purposes, the
basic social division of labour under capitalism, the division
between labourers and non-labourers within the capitalist production
process, reappears within the FC-PP as if this latter, too, were the
combined outcome of both labourers' and non-labourers' efforts.
This means that within this enterprise, there will be those non-
labourers who will appear as labourers and those non-labourers who
will retain an appearance consonant with the real nature of their
activity, i.e. the performance of the function of capital within
the FC-PP. The former are for the non-productive capitalist what
the unproductive labourers are for the unproductive capitalist.
They provide the concrete form of the function of capital for other
capitalist processes, for sale, and thus become the channel for the
appropriation of wealth on behalf of the capitalist and thus are
subjected themselves to direct work of control and surveillance.
The latter are the agents who supervise the former, who make sure
on behalf of the capitalist that the function of capital to be sold
is 'produced' in a capitalistically efficient way. The former
agents are a faux frais of production on a societal level but not
any more so for the individual non-productive capitalist. Yet they
do remain, as their direct supervisors, non-labourers. The social
division of labour is the basis here of a powerful ideological
illusion.

To sum up, the social division of labour has the following effect
on the economic significance of the function of capital. If this
function is performed within a capitalist enterprise as an aspect

of commodity production, the work of control and surveillance is not
a channel for the appropriation through redistribution of surplus
value. As abstract non-labour, it is a faux frais both on the social
and on the individual level. If the provision of the function of
capital becomes a separate branch of the economy and the function
of capital itself becomes the content of what is sold and bought on
the market, then the work of those non-labourers who think up, either
individually or collectively, the concrete forms of the function of
capital for sale becomes the channel for the redistribution of surplus
value. In short, if the function of capital is directed towards the
agents working within a capitalist process, it is a faux frais also
at the level of that enterprise. If it becomes the aim of the
capitalist process, due to the social division of labour, then
inasmuch as it is production of that aim, it becomes a way to
appropriate surplus value through redistribution.

It might be useful, to conclude this section, to sum up briefly
the basic characteristics of the CPP proper, of the UCP, and of the
FC-PP in the light of our discussion of the economic (i.e. in terms
of capital accumulation) and social (i.e. in terms of the social
relations of production) significance of non-labour. In the CPP
proper the dominant type of labour is productive labour, even if, of
course, unproductive labourers will have to be employed in it (e.g.
accountants). Concrete labour transforms use values, as part of
the societal labour process, and thus transfers the value of the
means of transformation to the value of the commodity. Abstract
labour creates new value, first equal to the value of labour power
and then above that value. This is surplus value, for the production
of which non-labourers are necessary. They force the labourers to
work for a time longer than the time necessary to produce (in terms
of the societal labour process) their labour power; they extract
thus surplus value on behalf of the capitalist. But these non-
labourers are also subjected to extraction of, they must provide,
surplus non-labour, they must 'work', perform the function of
capital, for a time longer than the time necessary to produce their
labour power. This surplus non-labour, however, is not a way of
increasing the mass of surplus value produced, it is only a way of
producing the same with less wage costs, and thus to increase the
individual rate of profit.

In the UCP we have basically unproductive labourers and non-
labourers. The former deal with, but do not transform, the use
values of the objects of labour. Therefore, their concrete labour
cannot transfer the value of the instruments of labour to the
commodity, nor can their abstract labour create new value. The
capitalist can participate in the redistribution of the social
product because unproductive capital has become a separate branch
necessary for the societal production process. This redistribution
takes place through the economic oppression of the unproductive
labourers, since they are made to work for a time longer than the
necessary labour time. For the economic oppression of the unproductive labourers non-labourers are necessary. These latter extract
surplus labour and provide also surplus non-labour. They are a
faux frais of production both on a societal and on an individual
level, while the unproductive labourers are a faux frais only on the
societal level and not on the level of the enterprise.

Finally, the FC-PP employs basically (essentially) non-labourers. Since the function of capital has become the specific aim of a capitalist process, this latter must participate in the redistribution of society's wealth. This firm is necessary for capitalist production as a whole. Of the non-labourers employed in it, some work out the concrete forms of the function of capital to be sold to other firms. Their non-labour, because of its similarity with labour, becomes the channel through which this non-productive capital participates in the redistribution of the social product in proportion to the rate of economic oppression of this non-labour. Even though the social significance of their activity does not change (it remains non-labour), from the point of view of the individual firm's capital accumulation their non-labour is now a channel for the increase of the mass of the surplus value appropriated, as well as, of course, of the FC-PP's rate of profit. These non-labourers are subjected to the supervision of other non-labourers who thus perform the function of capital within the FC-PP. For these latter agents an increase in their rate of economic oppression can only result in a decrease in the costs of production.

To conclude, let us listen to Marx's own words.

If, then, capitalist management has two aspects by reason of the twofold nature of the process of production itself - which, on the one hand, is a social process for producing use-values, on the other, a process for creating surplus-value - in form it is despotic. *As co-operation extends its scale, this despotism assumes particular forms.* Just as, at first, the capitalist is relieved from manual labour, so soon as his capital has reached that minimum amount with which real capitalist production begins, so now, he hands over the work of direct and constant supervision of the individual workman, and groups of workmen, to a special kind of wage-labourer. An industrial army of workmen, under the command of a capitalist, requires, like a real army, officers (managers), and sergeants (foremen, overlookers) who exercise authority on behalf of the capitalist during the labour process. *The work of supervision becomes their established and exclusive function.* (31)

What we have tried to do in this chapter has only been an attempt to go further in the direction so clearly pointed out by Marx.

6   SUMMARY AND CONCLUSIONS

We have argued that mental labour can be the real basis for the production of wealth under capitalism and that this is perfectly consistent with Marx's analysis of productive and unproductive labour. A precondition for this is the definite rejection of categories like manual/mental, physical/nervous, hand/brain labour and the grounding of the material/mental category in the analysis of the labour process and of the capitalist production process. (32) This latter is, for Marx, both production of surplus value and for surplus value. The former aspect refers to the objective workings of the capitalist mode of production, the latter aspect to the need this system has to come to life and to act through people (agents) who thus have to internalize the objective needs of the system and

externalize these needs' satisfaction in the form of the agents'
own personal behaviour. The capitalist then begins the production
cycle (see Figure 5.4) because he wants to produce profit. At this
stage production is still production for profit. Our previous
discussion allows us to follow the process through which production
for profit becomes production of profit. In symbols:
Production for and of surplus value.

Given   (1) $M \to M'$ as production *for* profit (surplus value)
           (2) $LP_r \ \epsilon \ SDL$
           (3) $LP_r = (C_u \to C_u^{\ell})$

then   (4) $C_e \to C_e'$ production of surplus value
           (5) $C_e^{\ell} \to M'$ realization of surplus value

so that $M \to M'$ as production *of* profit (surplus value).

Condition (1) reveals to us the intention of the capitalist, who
invests M, to get M'. The capitalist has internalized capital's
inner drive to self-expansion. The third condition adds to the
first the requirement that the capitalist invests his money in a
TLP_r, either material or mental. Or, there must be a transformation
of use values, the creation of new, different use values. As far as
M_aT is concerned, there is a new use value, i.e. the possibility to
satisfy a new need, only when the physical characteristics of the
object of labour are changed. As far as M_eT is concerned, there
must be a transformation of knowledge and imagined concrete into
new knowledge (conception). This new knowledge can thus satisfy
new needs. However, conception is transformation of (mental)
use values and thus can be the basis of production of wealth only
if it is a condition for material transformation. There are certain
restrictions under which conception cannot be a condition for material
transformation. And there are also restrictions (as we have seen
in discussing domestic labour) under which material transformation
cannot be part of societal production. These restrictions emerge
once we take the point of view of the totality. (33) It is because
of this that we introduce condition (2). The combination of
conditions (2) and (3) tells us that, in order to be the basis of
the creation of surplus value, an individual LP_r must be either part
of the social real M_aT (if we have an $M_aT \Rightarrow M_eT$ process) or a
condition of social real M_aT (if we have an $M_eT \Rightarrow M_aT$ process),
i.e. it must be either part or condition of social production (or
production for mediated consumption). This means that all labour
(material and mental) becomes productive when employed by capital,
unless employed (1) for the UCP (like the commercial or advertising
enterprise); (2) for the destruction of use values; or (3) for
the performance of the function of capital (and in this case we
refer to non-labour): this means also that all labour employed in
(4) private, rather than social, production (like artisanal
production) and (5) in consumption (the case of domestic labour)
cannot be considered as productive in a capitalist sense. If these
restrictions (given by conditions 2 and 3) do not apply, then there
will be production of surplus value, i.e. the object of labour, now
considered as exchange value, will have been transformed in a
product with a value higher than the exchange value of the means of
transformation and of the labour power employed. C_e will have
become C_e'. Consequently, upon sale on the market, C_e' will bring

in the surplus value incorporated in it in money form. $C_e^!$ will
have become M'. At this point M will have been transformed into M'
on the basis of a real (material or mental) transformation. There
will have been a production of profit not only on the level of the
individual capital but also at the societal level. There will have
been a real increase in society's wealth.

What (partial) conclusions can be drawn concerning the nature of
productive labour and more generally concerning the organization of
labour under a communist system? One of Marx's fundamental teachings
is that capitalism can increase the productivity of labour only
through the fragmentation of the individual, the partial development
and ossification of his/her personality, the subjection of man to
man. Under communism, on the other hand, man 'does not reproduce
himself in one specificity, but produces his totality'. (34) Under
new, communist conditions of production, labour will be the means
for the full development of the producer, for the full growth of
all aspects of his personality. Productive labour will be then 'a
complex entity of production and reflection upon the social
conditions of production'. (35) What does this mean in terms of
the social and technical division of labour? According to Marx,
the reproduction of an individual's totality can be achieved because
'in a communist society, where nobody has an exclusive sphere of
activity but each can become accomplished in any branch he wishes,
society regulates the general production and thus makes it possible
for me to do one thing today and another tomorrow'. (36) This does
not imply that 'the self is an asocial "substance" distinct from
socially material roles'. (37) On the contrary. It is just because
men will be exposed to different practices that they will be able
to develop an all-round personality. The problem is not this.
The problem is: given that the division of labour cannot be done
away with under communism (unless one wants to go back to primitive
communism), what will have to be changed? The avoidance of the
'fixation of social activity' will not be enough. Concerning the
social division of labour, there will be a radical change which
will reflect both the change in the production relations (i.e. the
products will have lost the quality of being commodities and the
division between country and town, between industry and agriculture,
will have disappeared) and the resulting change in the allocation
of resources (i.e. different use values will be produced). Yet,
the changes undergone by the technical division of labour will be
even more radical. According to Marx, it is this latter, and not
the former, which is typical of capitalism. Does this mean that,
given a change in the social system, the technical division of
labour will fade away and then totally disappear? As long as one
is a 'hunter, fisherman, shepherd or critic', this is possible,
but these examples seem to be taken more from simple commodity
production than from a fully developed communist society. We
believe that the technical division of labour cannot be abolished
(in any case certainly not in the transition and in the socialist
period) but that what will have to disappear will be both those
aspects typical of capitalist domination (i.e. the control over
labour within the production process, through the work of control
and surveillance, or the function of capital) and those typical of
class domination in general as, for example, the division between
mental and material labour.

To understand this, let us recall that what we have attempted to
do is not only to inquire into the new forms taken by 'despotism'
within production (for example, the specialized performance of the
function of capital) and into its economic significance. We have, in
fact, also inquired into the way in which 'despotism' in production
causes the labour process to take particular, specific forms. Not
only is the societal labour process fragmented in a variety of types
and forms of labour processes as determined by the capitalist nature
of production. The internal structure itself of the labour process,
of co-operation, of the transformation of use values, is shaped by
the capitalist nature of production through the introduction of the
technical division of labour within it, one aspect of which being
the subdivision of the material and mental labour process and, again,
of the technical division of labour within these two broad categories
and the reproduction within them of the performance of material or
mental labour. The surplus value producing process changes thus
also the form of the mental transformation as well as of the material
transformation. In capitalist production, the surplus value
producing process is thus not simply superimposed upon the labour
process, upon the same labour process in all societies and modes of
production. The need to transform use values is a-historical, the
transformation of use values is not, the way use values are
transformed is historically and socially specific. The labour
process, and thus co-operation, is not external to the surplus value
producing process, (38) the labour process as such is capitalist in
nature. It is thus important to stress that the capitalist nature
objectifies itself, as M. Turchetto correctly points out, in a type
of machine which is functional for the fragmentation of positions
(tasks) and thus for the real subordination of labour to capital.
(39) But it is equally important to stress that no amount of
recomposition of positions can be functional for socialism unless
the function of capital has completely disappeared. Therefore, a
non-capitalist technical division of labour will have, first of all,
to eliminate the work of control and surveillance; second, it will
have not only to regroup positions in order to do away with their
alienating one-sidedness, but also to regroup them (in fact, remould
them) in such a way as to combine in each one of them not only both
material and mental labour but also skilled material and mental
(conception) labour, and thus both conception and execution. (40)
This, in turn, implies that the worker will have participated in
the planning (and thus will have general, even though not detailed,
knowledge) of the whole of the production process.

Moreover, such a radical change in the technical and social
content of positions and in the way in which they are articulated
cannot take place without a parallel change of the principle which
allocates the agents of production to these new positions. It will
be co-operation, rather than competition, which will guide production
and thus inform not only the social division of labour but also the
technical division of labour. For example, we can assume a socialist
technical division of labour in which all positions have roughly the
same degree of difficulty - in spite of their different technical
content - but we can assume this only as a tendency, if the
production process must be a dynamic one. Now, in order for these
temporary differentials not to become permanent ones, it will be the

less able agents who, with the help of the more qualified ones, will perform those more difficult tasks and, again, not on the basis of coercion but on the basis of mutual help and co-operation. Only then will vertical mobility have its full effect of enriching the experience and qualifications of the individuals. Production under communism undergoes therefore a double process of restriction/ extension. All activities associated with the function of capital disappear, but all activities associated with 'reflecting upon the social conditions of production', i.e. with the development of the individual producer in his/her totality, enter into it. There is thus no question of attempting to reproduce superseded modes of production in which there is no technical division of labour. The return to small-scale production in which there is no technical division of labour is basically an anarchist ideology. The point is rather the creation of a production process in which the technical division of labour does not separate mental from material labour and in which the means of transformation are dominated and directed by the producers rather than the latter being an extension of the former. An ideology of a return to a pre-industrial, 'manual labour', mode of production or to a 'small-scale' mode of production, is as objectively reactionary as is any ideology of the construction of socialism upon the existing technical division of labour.

These seem to us to be the conditions for a technical division of labour functional for the communist mode of production. Without these basic preconditions, rotation (mobility, either functional, geographic, or economic, as explained in the last chapter of this book, to put it better) will only expose the same agent to different alienating experiences, i.e. different agents to the same alienating experience. This is quite clear in the different job enlargement and job rotation schemes where, as a worker put it, 'you move from one dirty, boring, monotonous job to another dirty, boring, monotonous job'. (41) This is perhaps less evident, but equally true, of methods based upon the recomposition of the fragmented positions, as, for example, in the production process based upon a system of sub-assembly stations manned by 'natural units' or teams with a certain degree of autonomy as far as the internal subdivisions of tasks and the speed of the pieces to be assembled or produced in one day are concerned. Is this a true enrichment, a beginning of a supersession of the division between supervised and supervisor, between mental and material labour, between conception and execution? As B. Corjat's analysis shows, this is certainly not so. (42) These methods of production are born of the need to overcome the limits posed to capitalist accumulation by the traditional assembly line system.

These limits are not only ideological (they reflect a crisis of legitimation, an antagonism towards the existing production and distribution relations, perceived by bourgeois sociologists as 'dissatisfaction'), but also and first of all economic. As Corjat stresses, there are several technical economic limits to the assembly line system. First, fragmentation of positions increases their number and thus the time of transfer between them. This time of transfer is 'dead' time, during it there is no labour performed. Second, the resulting problem is that of 'equilibrating' the organization of labour, i.e. of respecting the constraint that some

jobs must be performed before other jobs, that the labour power
employed be minimized, and that the time during which the worker can
work be maximized (or that the 'dead' time be minimized). (43)
Third, this organization of labour exposes the whole of the conveyor
belt (factory) to localized stoppages for technical reasons since
the workers do not have the knowledge to cope with these difficulties.
(44) Fourth, this organization of labour is based upon individual
positions and on the principle that a certain supervisor must
supervise a certain individual worker. This creates a complex and
large hierarchy of supervisors who, as shown above, neither produce
value nor are the channel (contrary to the unproductive workers)
through which the value produced elsewhere is appropriated through
redistribution. These non-labourers are a 'faux frais' of production
for society and for the individual unit. This method of supervision
combines the work of control and surveillance (FC) with quality
control (FL) and this means that if a fault escapes the attention
of the labourer or of the supervisor, it will only be discovered
when it passes into the consumers' hand. (45) This, coupled with
the worker's lack of motivation, results in a high rate of defective
products.
     On the other hand, the system based upon 'islands' or 'modules'
of assembly or production still satisfies the triple condition to
the effect that they must allow (a) mass production, and (b) low
value of product per unit through (c) relatively low levels of
wages and salaries in order to satisfy the permanent need for a
large and cheap labour power. (46) They achieve this through (a) the
reduction of 'dead' time; (b) the reduction or abolition of the time
devoted to the work of control and surveillance; (c) the reduction
of the time devoted to quality control; and (d) the possibility of
producing 'alternative products', i.e. of producing different
products through the different assembly of elementary elements and
thus of a very rapid tuning of production to demand variations.
The final outcome is thus a great increase in productivity, i.e.
exploitation. At the same time, political and ideological domination
over the working class is increased as well. As A. Zimbalist
correctly remarks, it is not by chance that when these schemes
unleashed a degree of workers' enthusiasm capable of jeopardizing
the existing power relations, 'these experiments were quickly
terminated by management'. (47) These developments based upon the
recomposition of positions are certainly more than 'slight ameliora-
tions' of the capitalist production process, as H. Braverman holds
(1974, p.381), but they are not a new organization of production
either, in the sense that they do not mark an inversion in the
tendency towards the fragmentation of positions. It is also an open
question whether, as B. Corjat submits, (48) a production process
based upon 'modules' will replace the existing one based upon
Taylorism and Fordism. Two things seem, in any case, to be sure.
First, if, as Luperini submits, the 1970s have marked a wide-scale
and long-term restructuring of the capitalist economy under the
stimulus of electronics' gigantic stride forwards, if this latter
becomes the sector which conditions the development of the whole of
the economy, which fosters the spreading and application of
cybernetics and computer science, and the computerization of work
in the enterprise, (49) then new forms of combination, on the one

hand, of authoritarian centralization and, on the other, of decentralized management (or controlled decentralization), will become both conceivable and applicable. But, and this is our second point, these new types of organization of production are important counter-tendencies to the basic capitalist law of the fragmentation of positions, deskilling (dequalification) of labour, and devaluation of labour power. This recomposition of positions increases, rather than diminishes, class domination. It is only by abolishing the technical division of labour functional for class domination (both in its general and in its capitalist forms) that men and women can fully develop themselves and that their cultural and political consciousness can be raised. There is complete incompatibility (antagonistic contradiction) between the principle of coercion, or the function of capital in all its managerial forms, and the construction of socialism. It is an analysis along these lines which allows us to determine accurately what is specific to the capitalist mode of production and what must be revolutionized if a socialist system is to be built.

Chapter 6

ELEMENTS OF LATE CAPITALIST PRODUCTION RELATIONS

INTRODUCTION

We have examined in the last chapter the way capital spreads and deepens its domination upon labour. That analysis has been an entertwining of three themes. The first theme is the labour process and its capital nature. Emphasis has been placed upon the capitalist character of the social division of labour, of the technical division of labour, and of the interrelation between these two forms of division of labour. As far as the social division of labour is concerned, capitalist rule determines (a) the variety of the commodities produced and (b) the types of labour processes determined by the capitalist production process proper. As far as this deter- mination is concerned, we have seen that its specific significance in this case means that these labour processes are not the basis for the production of surplus value and yet (i) are necessary for the production of surplus value as a whole, (ii) behave as if they were the basis for such a production, and (iii) are based upon production relations which are similar to those in which the capitalist on the one hand and the productive labourers on the other engage. As far as the technical division of labour is concerned, we have stressed that (a) the nature itself of the labour process is capitalist due to a technical division of labour (and to a type of means of production needed by it) functional for the real subordina- tion of labour to capital; and (b) each of these types of labour processes will have its own particular internal structure, or special organization of a variety of fragmented positions. As far as the interrelation between social and technical division of labour is concerned, we have stressed that parts of the fragmented labour process can detach themselves and become separate branches of activity which will tend to reproduce within themselves the same technical division of labour.

The second theme concerns the surplus value producing process and the way it determines the capitalist production process and thus, as we have just seen, the labour process itself. Capital's despotism is present within production also in the form of the work of control and surveillance, in the work of those agents of production who perform the function of capital, of those agents, i.e. whose function

is to force other agents to perform a real or formal, a mental or
material, transformation for a time longer than the necessary labour
time because this is the way surplus value can be extracted from the
producers.   An agent, then, can either labour or force others to
labour but cannot do both at the same time.   The function of capital
is therefore intrinsic to the capitalist production process but
extrinsic to the labour process as shaped by capitalism. (1)   Since
the surplus value producing process denotes the capitalist nature of
production and since, as we have seen, this nature determines the
nature of the social and technical division of labour as well as of
their interrelation, we can say that the surplus value producing
process determines the form of intrinsic domination within the labour
process.   The third theme considers the inverse relationship between
labour process and surplus value producing process, i.e. the overdetermination of the latter by the former.   'As co-operation extends
its scale, this despotism assumes particular forms'.   Or, this
variety of labour process requires a variety of surplus value (or
labour) producing processes and thus a variety of forms taken by the
function of capital due both to the differences between these labour
processes to be supervised and to their internal structures.
Moreover, these varied forms taken by the function of capital tend
to reproduce within themselves both the technical division of labour
and the interplay between this and the social division of labour,
as analysed in the case of the labour process.   As we have seen,
this can go so far as to cause the branching off of aspects of the
function of capital as separate units of economic activity.

   In all this, the function of capital has been basically considered
from an economic point of view, i.e. from the point of view of the
production process and of capital accumulation.   However, perhaps
even more important is the social nature of the function of capital
and its importance in terms of social relations.   Our thesis is
that, in examining the relations among the agents of production, or
production relations, in contemporary capitalist countries, it is
not enough to consider whether or not these agents own the means of
production and whether they exploit or are exploited by other agents.
(2)   The social nature of the function performed must also be taken
into consideration since within the production process we have both
labourers (those who perform the function of labour) and non-labourers
(those who perform the function of capital).   The purpose of this
chapter is, then, to analyse the capitalist production relations in
their contemporary form.   We will especially stress the functional
element, since it is this element which has been traditionally
disregarded through its conflation with the exploitation element.
Our thesis, to be developed in what follows, is that while it was
perfectly justifiable to equate the exploiter with the non-labourer
and the exploited with the labourer in the period of capitalist
development analysed by Marx, it is equally justifiable to separate
and analyse separately these two elements in present day's capitalist
formations.   The section that follows will provide a cursory treatment of the three basic elements of production relations under
present-day capitalism.

1   THE PLACE OF THE FUNCTION OF CAPITAL WITHIN THE CAPITALIST PRODUCTION RELATIONS

We have seen that the labour process, considered as the basis of life, of all life, is the transformation of old into new use values. This trans-epochal element of human life, however, can be common to all epochs inasmuch as it does not belong to any of them in particular, i.e. as long as we do not consider its concrete essence, i.e. its social (and thus socially determined) form and structure. Or, an a-historical concept of labour process as transformation of use values cannot help us in the analysis of concrete, historically specific, societies. This task requires abstractions as historical condensations. Similar considerations can be made for the relations in which people engage when participating in the labour process, i.e. the relations of material (or mental) transformation. In particular, with regard to the process of production (a moment of social transformation) production relations can be defined as the relations in which people, i.e. agents of production, engage when taking part in the production process. (3)   But, again, this definition has lost all its concreteness (specifity) not because it is abstract or generally valid but because it is an a-historical abstraction. It thus cannot tell us anything about the form (nature) the relations among producers take under specific social systems, and in particular under capitalism.

As it will be clear from the preceeding remarks, we submit that contemporary capitalist production relations have three aspects: the ownership, the functional, and the exploitation aspect. We will examine in this section each of these aspects in the initial stage of capitalism, the formal subordination of labour to capital (where the carriers of the capitalist production relations are still the individual capitalist and the individual worker). Then we will consider briefly how the functional aspect changes from the stage of formal subordination to the stage of real subordination of labour to capital and then to monopoly capitalism. When this has been done, the way will have been opened to examine in the next sections some modifications undergone by the capitalist production relations in the stage of capitalist development beginning after the Second World War and which we will refer to as late capitalism.

The capitalist production relations are first of all relations of ownership, i.e. between the owner and the non-owner of the means of production. The agent who has the ownership of the means of production has both the legal and the real, or economic, ownership, i.e. the power to dispose of the means of production. This economic ownership gives him also the power to dispose of labour power and thus of the surplus value produced. Second, this economic ownership extends itself both on simple reproduction (the daily running of the capitalist production process) and on expanded and restricted reproduction (i.e. the power to start new production processes, to expand the existing ones through capital concentration and centrali-zation, to reduce the scale of existing capitalist production processes, or to close them down completely). Third, economic ownership gives the capitalist the right to divide the surplus value produced into productive and unproductive consumption. Therefore, economic ownership gives the capitalist the right to decide whether he must enlarge, decrease, or leave unchanged the scale of production. Legal ownership, on the other hand, gives him the right to consume unproductively a part of surplus value, once the capitalist as real owner has decided how much of the surplus value produced can be consumed unproductively. At the other side of the relation we have the non-owner, who in this stage has neither the legal nor the economic ownership of the means of production. Since we are interested in the relations of production, we will consider only the economic ownership, unless differently indicated.

The capitalist production relations are also functional relations, or relations between the non-labourer and the labourer. In the stage of capitalist development considered, both the labourer and the non-labourer are represented by individuals. The labourer is he who carries out the labour process (both in its material and in its mental aspects), i.e. who performs the function of labour. To do this he must have the possession of the means of production, i.e. the ability to set them in motion and to govern them. Since the labourer produces the whole of the product, he must have the necessary knowledge for it, the possession of the means of production. At the other pole we have the non-labourer, he who participates in the production process without participating in the labour process, i.e. he who forces other agents (the labourers) to carry out the trans-formation of use values, without participating in that transformation, by carrying out the work of control and surveillance, i.e. the function of capital. As we have seen in chapter 5, the non-labourer can perform the function of capital either directly, when he forces, in a non-mediated way, the labourers to work, or the function of capital can be performed indirectly. In this stage of capitalism, when the capitalist (non-labourer) is still a person who performs practically all aspects of the function of capital, the indirect way to perform the function of capital is to engage in its conception. From this point of view, the producer is the labourer and the non-producer is the non-labourer.

Finally, the capitalist production relations are relations of exploitation. Under capitalism, people cannot reproduce themselves (i.e. their means of subsistence and reproduction) without at the same time subjugating each other. From this point of view, the relation is one between the exploiter and the exploited. The concept of exploitation is a complex one. It is extraction and appropriation of surplus value as far as the exploiter is concerned, and production and expropriation of surplus value as far as the exploited is concerned. To exploit means not only to perform (directly and indirectly) the function of capital. It means to do this for a time longer than the labourer's necessary labour time, i.e. it means to force surplus value. But the exploiter extracts surplus value in order to appropriate it, i.e. in order to have the power to dispose of it. Conversely, to be exploited means not only to be subjected to the work of control and surveillance. It means to be subjected to it because one is made to work (controlled) for a time longer than the necessary labour time, it means to have to produce surplus value. And, to produce surplus value means at the same time to have it expropriated, to have no power to dispose of it. From this point of view, the producer is he who produces, and has expropriated from him, surplus value, i.e. the exploited; while the non-producer is the exploiter.

Table 6.1 The three aspects of contemporary production relations

Aspects of production relations	Agents of production	
	Non-owner	Owner
Functional (labour process point of view)	labourer (performance of the function of labour)	non-labourer (direct and indirect performance of the function of capital
Exploitation (surplus value producing process point of view)	exploited ⎡ production: i.e. subjugation to the function of capital for a time longer than the necessary labour time expropriation: i.e. no power to dispose of surplus value produced	exploiter ⎡ extraction: i.e. direct or indirect performance of the function of capital for time longer than labourer's necessary labour time appropriation: i.e. power to dispose of surplus value

If we now consider that (a) the functional aspect corresponds to the labour process aspect of the capitalist production process, to the fact that in this latter participate both agents who, and agents who do not, transform use values, and (b) the exploitation element corresponds to the surplus value producing process aspect of the capitalist production relations, to the fact that in this process participate agents who produce, and agents who appropriate, surplus value, we can summarize what was said above in Table 6.1.

Some important theoretical conclusions can be drawn from this table. First of all, we have here the production relations determining the capitalist production process proper, the process essentially producing surplus value, or the fundamental (determining) process in a capitalist society. Therefore, these aspects of the production relations can serve to provide an identification of the two funda- mental classes under capitalism. The working class can thus be identified as the non-owner/labourer/exploited and the capitalist class as the owner/non-labourer/exploiter. This, however, can be done on condition that there is a logic to the two combinations just mentioned. That logic is, of course, the logic of capitalist production and of the relation determining it. The owner (carrier of the principal aspect of the relation of ownership, as seen in chapter 1) must appropriate surplus value in order to reproduce (as a condition of reproduction of) the relation of ownership. To this end, surplus value must be produced, i.e. a production process must be carried out. The owner can appropriate surplus value because of the real ownership of the means of production, but this surplus value must first of all be produced, i.e. the owner must extract it and to this end he must perform the function of capital. The owner must thus be the exploiter, he must appropriate surplus value and thus extract it. Therefore he must be the non-labourer. The owner is thus also the non-labourer and the exploiter. Converseley, the non-owner is expropriated, because he loses the power to dispose of his product (surplus value) and to this end he must be made to produce that surplus value. That is, he must create its real sub- stratum (transformation of use values), he must be the labourer (perform the function of labour); and he must perform this function for a time longer than the necessary labour time, something which, in conjunction with its being expropriated, defines him as being exploited. The non-owner is thus also the labourer and the exploited.

Second, as already implicit in what was just said, these three aspects are not equally important in terms of our understanding of the capitalist production relations. One of them is determinant, while the other two are conditions of reproduction of the former. As mentioned in chapter 1, the adjudication of a role in a logical scheme, in this case the determinant role, must rest on a historical analysis. It is this analysis that reveals to us the characteristic feature of capitalist production relations, the fact that for the first time in history people must produce their means of reproduction with means of production which do not belong to them. It is not the existence of labourers and non-labourers, producers and non- producers, which is typical of capitalism. It is the separation of the labourer/producer from his means of production which is the characteristic element. And it is because of this factor that the labourer/exploited and the non-labourer/exploiter take on specific

features. Now, since the determinant element contains already in
itself the determined ones as conditions of its own reproduction,
or supersession, we need mention only the former as a short means
of referring to the latter as well. Or, at the highest level of
abstraction, we can refer to the two fundamental classes as the
owners and non-owners of the means of production, provided we know
that this is only a shortened formula. (4) But this does not mean
that the functional and exploitation aspects are made superfluous.
A full description of capitalist production relations is one which
encompasses all three elements (even though the two determined ones
can be derived from the determinant one) because these three aspects
of the capitalist production relations correspond to the three
essential moments of the capitalist production process. Let us
review them briefly.

Marx has shown that under capitalism:

(1) There is a separation of the means of production from the
producer. Some agents own the means of production, others do not.
This is the ownership element which is characteristic of the agents
of production when they enter the labour market. This separation
implies that labour power itself becomes a commodity, i.e. that the
agents, after they enter the labour market but before they leave it
in order to enter the production process, must sell their labour
power in order to gain the culturally determined subsistence goods.
If we now consider the situation after the agents leave the labour
market in order to enter into and participate in the capitalist
production process, we see that production under capitalism is
production both of use values (labour process) and of exchange
values (surplus value producing process). Now, if production must
be regarded from two points of view, the same applies to the agents
who take part in it, i.e. the producer (the non-owner) and the non-
producer (the owner of the means of production).

(2) Thus, from the labour process point of view,

(a) a producer is he who deals with use values, who thus is a
labourer, who performs the function of labour;

(b) a non-producer is he who does not deal with use values, who
thus is the non-labourer (and who consequently performs the function
of capital, i.e. the work of control and surveillance).

(3) From the surplus value producing process point of view,

(c) a producer is he who is exploited, he who produces (is
expropriated of) surplus value;

(d) a non-producer is he who is the exploiter, who obliges the
labourer to produce (who extracts directly or indirectly) surplus
value and who appropriates surplus value. (5)

Third, the three aspects of the capitalist production relations
are presented in Table 6.1 above as they appear in the phase of
formal subordination of labour to capital. These aspects undergo
modification as we move from one phase to the next one. (6)
Particularly important for our discussion is, first, the transformation of the individual labourer in the collective labourer, a
process Marx situates in the stage of real subordination of labour
to capital and which he analyses in full detail. Due to the
introduction of the technical division of labour within the
production process, the final outcome is now the result of the
combined and co-ordinated effort of a great number of labourers,

performing different tasks (or, better said, filling different positions with a specific technical and social content) and thus participating collectively in the transformation (labour) process. Marx calls this the collective labourer. (7) Thus, to perform the function of the collective labourer (FCL) means to take part in the complex, scientifically organized, labour process while performing only one part of it. But the labourer is not the only one to undergo modifications. The following phase, the phase of monopoly capitalism, is characterized by a fragmentation of the function of capital parallel to that within the function of labour. The non-labourer becomes a global non-labourer, (8) the work of control and surveillance is now performed by a complex of agents hierarchically and bureaucratically organized. Each one of them performs now the global function of capital. To perform the global function of capital (GFC) means to take part in the complex, scientifically organized and hierarchically and bureaucratically structured work of control and surveillance while performing only one part of it. It should be stressed that the rise of the global non-labourer is not simply a question of the increase in the production unit's size, i.e. a technical need. Rather, historically, as the number of labourers within that unit increases, so does their resistance to capitalist rules. But even more important, as the forms of co-operation (varieties of labour processes) differentiate themselves, so do the forms of resistance to capital. The transformation of the non-labourer into the global non-labourer corresponds to the need to break that resistance in order to increase exploitation. This cannot be done without an adequate controlling structure, the global non-labourer, whose rise and development and different forms is first and foremost an economic need.

Fourth, Table 6.1 above offers the possibility of identifying in economic terms not only the two fundamental classes but also the middle classes, both old and new. (9) These are those classes which combine contradictory elements of the capitalist production relations. The old middle class is identifiable as all those agents who are the owners of the means of production (for them the distinction between real and legal ownership is not relevant), who perform not only the function of capital but also the function of labour (or the function of the collective worker and in particular the work of co-ordination and unity of the labour process), and who are either the economic oppressors or the exploiters. The characteristic of this class is that, since they are the owners and yet perform partly the function of labour, take part in the labour process, they not only exploit other agents but, in a sense, also themselves because, by taking part in the labour process, they contribute to the creation of surplus value which they appropriate (as owners of the means of production) without having, of course, to perform the function of capital on themselves. It could be objected that the capitalist, when taking part in the labour process (e.g. when performing the work of co-ordination and unity of the labour process), automatically controls himself and thus performs also the function of capital (on himself). But what interests us here is not the self-control the capitalist exercises on himself when functioning as a labourer (this is a psychological question which goes beyond the limits of our problematic), but rather the fact that, from the point of view

of the capitalist production process, the capitalist performs the
function of the collective worker since he co-ordinates the labour
process. The relevant question here is in objective terms, i.e. is
this part of the working day devoted to dealing with use values or
not? This is the criterion which establishes which aspects of the
capitalist production relations are to be attributed to the capitalist
when performing this function. The capitalist, when performing the
function of the (collective) worker, is (as far as the functional
element is concerned) an extreme example of the (collective) labourer
who, having internalized the capitalist 'values', need not be
controlled any more and thus need not have any agents who perform
on him the function of capital. It is in this sense that we can say
that the old middle class 'exploit' themselves. Finally, to complete
the picture, the new middle class. They are those agents who do not
own (really) the means of production, who either perform only the
global function of capital or both the global function of capital
and the function of the collective worker. Inasmuch as they perform
the global function of capital, they extract surplus value (which
they do not appropriate since they are the non-owners) and/or surplus
non-labour, while having to provide (since they are the non-owners)
surplus non-labour. Inasmuch as they perform the function of the
collective worker they produce and have expropriated from them
surplus value. These agents thus must both provide themselves and
extract surplus non-labour and also both extract and produce themselves (and thus be expropriated of) surplus value. This is the
typical contradiction inherent in the production relations of which
they are the carriers. (10)

Finally, let us make explicitly a point already implicitly
contained in what has just been said. The conflation of the three
elements of the capitalist production relations in only one, the
determinant, is justifiable logically, as mentioned above, because
the determinant element contains in itself the determined one;
provided we are aware that the analysis is carried out at the highest
level of abstraction. But such a simplification finds its justification also in the historical process of development of these relations,
in the fact that in the stage of capitalist development analysed by
Marx, the owner was also the exploiter and the non-labourer (with
the exception of his performing an aspect of the function of labour,
the work of co-ordination and unity of the labour process) and that
the non-owner was also the labourer and the exploited. Nowadays,
however, such a simplified view of the relations of production is
no longer acceptable. The separation of legal from real ownership,
of this latter from the function of capital, of the direct from the
indirect function of capital, etc., makes imperative an analysis of
the relations of production in line with these developments. It is
only on the basis of the recognition of the independent existence
of the functional element in contemporary production relations that
such an analysis can be attempted.

In what follows we will be concerned with the present stage of
capitalist development, or late capitalism. By this we mean that
sub-stage of monopoly capitalism which begins with the end of the
Second World War and which, at the level of the capitalist productive
forces, is characterized by what E. Mandel calls the third technological revolution. More specifically, Mandel distinguishes two

phases of monopoly capitalism, i.e. classic imperialism and late
capitalism, a distinction which Mandel places within the context of
his theory of long waves. Each long wave is characterized by a
period of accelerated growth and one of decelerated growth (each of
about 20-25 years) and is characterized by the application, in its
ascending phase, of major technological innovations to the economic
system. What are these thorough-going technological revolutions?
Following Marx, Mandel distinguishes among motive machinery,
transmission machinery, and tool or labour machinery. It is the first
which embodies the decisively dynamic elements of the whole. These
machines are first produced by hand-craft and manufacture methods,
and then by machines.

> The fundamental revolutions in power technology - the technology
> of production of motive machines by machines - thus appears as
> the determinant moment in revolutions of technology as a whole.
> Machine production of steam-driven motors since 1848; machine
> production of electric and combustion motors since the '90's of
> the 19th century; machine production of electronic and nuclear
> power apparatuses since the 40's of the 20th century - these are
> the three general revolutions in technology engendered by the
> capitalist mode of production since the 'original' industrial
> revolution of the later 18th century. (11)

These are the decisive moments as far as the productive forces are
concerned. But what about the production relations? Before we make
a first and partial attempt to identify the characteristic features
of late capitalism in terms of production relations, we must first
dwell on the reasons for these relations' opaqueness and thus on
the socialization of production. In turn, this discussion will
highlight the mechanism through which the late capitalist production
relations acquire their characteristic features. This is the task
of the following section.

2   THE GLOBAL FUNCTION OF CAPITAL AND THE OPAQUENESS OF CONTEMPORARY
    PRODUCTION RELATIONS

While in the previous stages of capitalist development it was clear
who was the capitalist (he was the owner, both legal and real; the
expropriator and appropriator, thus the exploiter; and he who
performed the function of capital) and who was the worker (i.e. the
non-owner; the exploited; and the labourer who, moreover, was the
individual and 'manual' labourer), under monopoly capitalism and
even more so under late capitalism, the social content of positions
is not immediately visible any longer. The capitalist production
relations become opaque, the class collocation of an increasing
number of types of agents cannot be worked out any longer on the
basis of formulae worn out by new developments in the real concrete.
The new types of agents, the new positions and their social content,
can be analysed only by applying Marx's complex theoretical tools
and not by abandoning his method nor by simply repeating the outcome
of his analysis. With regard to conception it should be stressed
that the (mistaken, i.e. ideological) attribution of a capitalist
character to all conception within the capitalist technical division
of labour is not without an historical basis. From the very

beginning of the capitalist system, the individual capitalist
performs tasks falling within both categories of the functional
distinction. We have seen, for example, that he engages in the
function of capital and thus also in the conception, as well as in
the carrying out, of the function of capital. Both aspects of the
function of capital will be delegated in subsequent stages of
capitalist development to other agents. But we have seen that he
engages also in an aspect of the function of labour, the work of
co-ordination and unity of the labour process. This task too will
be delegated later on. Now, as we will see in more detail later in
this chapter, another aspect of the function of labour is that of the
planning of the production process, a type of conception which has
been for a long time (a) the prerogative of the capitalist (only the
owner of capital could dispose of the necessary knowledge, especially
after the introduction of the technical division of labour within
the production process) and (b) coupled with another type of
conception, the one concerning the control and surveillance of the
production agents (the two types of conception being analytically
separable but often difficult to recognize in practice). The former
type is an activity of the capitalist but not a capitalist activity
(since it is carried out by the capitalist as labourer, as part of
the collective labourer, just as in the case of the co-ordination of
the labour process). The mistake commonly made resides exactly
here, in considering all activities carried out by the capitalist
as capitalist activities (or function of capital). (12)   The
opaqueness of those and other agents' collocation in the class
structure in terms of production relations must be broken through.
What are the objective causes of this opaqueness? As far as the
role played by the function of capital is concerned, we can mention
three strictly interrelated reasons.

The first and fundamental reason for this opaqueness resides in
the interplay between a tendency and a countertendency. The tendency
is that to delegate all tasks (whether they are parts of the function
of capital or of the function of labour) previously performed by
the capitalist, and which are not essential for the appropriation of
surplus value, to other agents. It is from this angle that the
separate existence of the functional element can be accounted for.
Some elements of the function of capital previously performed by the
capitalist and now performed by wage earners can thus be mistaken
for labour and even for productive labour (e.g. the conception of
the work of control and surveillance). Some elements of the function
of labour, previously performed by the capitalists and now performed
by wage labourers, on the other hand, will cast upon these agents
(e.g. technicians and scientists) the erroneous characterization of
non-labourers simply because they now do what previously was the
prerogative of the capitalist (as labourer). This tendency and thus
the separation of the function of capital from the function of labour
is a specific instance of the more general capitalist tendency to
fragment positions. Only by placing these positions again within
the context of the social and technical division of labour can we
rediscover their social content. But this task is made more difficult
by the countertendency, usually connected with the introduction of
new techniques within the production process but also dependent upon
ideological and political causes, to regroup elements of the function

of capital and of the function of labour into a position or to create
new positions, spurious in terms of their social content.

Second, the delegation of the function of capital to wage earners,
i.e. the separation of the ownership from the functional element,
implies both the rise of the global non-labourer and the economic
oppression of the non-labourers/non-owners. Both elements introduce
great opaqueness into production relations. The former because within
the global non-labourer there will be, in a way similar to the relation
between non-labourers and labourers, those who will give orders and
those who will execute them. This, however, is irrelevant in terms
of the social nature of these agents' position. The hierarchical and
bureaucratic structure which is the global non-labourer can only
function on the basis of giving and carrying out orders, yet this is
no reason to classify those who execute orders as labourers necessarily. Also, the great majority of the agents performing the global
function of capital are economically oppressed. As we have seen in
chapter 5, there is a tendency to abolish those functions requiring
the performance of the function of capital, since they are a faux
frais not only on a societal but also on an individual level. This
tendency is in contradiction with the phenomenon described in chapter
5, the increase of the extent of the function of capital, due to the
increased resistance of the collective worker made possible by the
increase in the scale of the labour process, and the search for new
forms of control of labour due to the changes in the composition of
the societal labour process. This quantitative and qualitative
widening of the function of capital on the one hand, and the constant
attempt to reduce it, i.e. both to abolish non-labour and to
standardize forms of control across different types of labour
processes, on the other hand, is not a contradiction within the method
of inquiry, a methodological inconsistency. This widening/restriction
of the function of capital is an expression of a real contradiction
as appropriated by a method which explains contradictions as the
essence of the social real concrete. Two instances can be contradictory and yet perfectly consistent within a logical scheme (method)
if, as explained in chapter 2, both are conditions of existence
(reproduction) of an inherently contradictory determinant instance.
Capital accumulation determines both a quantitative and a qualitative
widening of the function of capital (basically due to the corresponding
widening of the labour process) and a restriction of that function.
Of these two instances the latter is the tendency since it re-appears
as soon as new forms of work of control have come to life. This
tendency takes place through the economic oppression of non-labour
(since the only way to oppress economically the non-labourers is to
reduce their number), i.e. by forcing non-labourers to extract
surplus value (or labour) for a time longer than their own necessary
labour time. Again, as shown in chapter 5, this creates a superficial
similarity with unproductive labourers and thus a further element of
opaqueness in the social nature of many positions and thus in the
class collocation of many agents.

Third, for these reasons, the contradiction between the socialization of production and the private appropriation takes on a new form,
which again contributes powerfully to the opaque nature of present-
day capitalist production relations. To understand this we must
point out that the socialization of production must be considered not

only at the level of the societal production process but also at the
level of the individual production process. At the former level,
socialization of production is more than the social division of
labour, the splitting of the societal production process into a
variety of processes, even when the capitalist nature of this social
division of labour is considered, i.e. even when we consider the
social division of labour (the nature of the use values produced)
due to the determination by the capitalist production relations
process and thus by the capitalist production. Socialization of
production means, as Lenin has pointed out, not only the increase
in the branches of production (social division of labour) but also,
and at the same time, the decrease in the number of the production
units within each branch. (13) While the social division of labour
strengthens the interdependence of the branches of production,
capitalist competition, which results in capital concentration and
centralization, both on a national and on an international level,
by decreasing within each branch the number of the production units,
increases the interdependence of the units operating in one branch
with the units operating in other branches.

Implicit in this form of socialization of production is private
appropriation: the societal production process is composed of
individual production processes whose outcome is privately appropriated. While production becomes more and more social, appropriation
remains private and actually the number of those who appropriate
the wealth socially produced keeps decreasing. Socialization in
capitalist production implies its private appropriation. An
increase in the former cannot take place separately from an increase
in the latter, i.e. from an increase in capital concentration and/or
centralization. As Mandel points out, typical of present-day
capitalism is international capital centralization. (14) This is
the way in which fewer and fewer capitalists acquire the real
ownership of the means of production in contemporary capitalism,
the way in which private ownership (and thus appropriation) extends
itself over larger and larger capitals.

But the socialization of production and its private appropriation
at the level of the societal production process is neither the only
way production is socialized nor the most important one for our
purposes, i.e. as far as the opaqueness of the production relations
is concerned. As least as important in this respect is the socialization and appropriation at the level of the individual process of
production. We have seen that Lenin correctly points out that the
socialization of production at the macro-societal level is not so
much the increased number of agents working under one roof, but
rather the increased number of branches of production coupled with
a decrease in the number of production units within each branch.
Similarly, we can say that the socialization of production at the
level of the enterprise is not given by the number of agents working
in a production unit but rather by the interdependence among the
agents of production. The production process becomes increasingly
complex and articulated, both as a labour process and as a surplus
value producing process, and is now performed by the collective
worker and by the global non-labourer. This increased complexity
is necessarily coupled with a process of fragmentation of the
production process in an increasing number of positions. Therefore,

the increased socialization of production at the level of the individual enterprise is the increased interdependence among the agents of production - among labourers, among non-labourers, and between labourers and non-labourers. Again, socialization of production cannot be disjuncted from private appropriation. Appropriation becomes more and more private not only because the number of appropriators keeps decreasing (and this not only at the national but also at the international level), but also because the appropriators divest themselves more and more of all those aspects which are not strictly necessary for them to retain the real ownership of the means of production and thus appropriation of surplus value. Consequently, the contradiction between the social nature of production (interdependence) and its private appropriation takes a specific form under monopoly capitalism at the level of the production unit. Due to the separation between extraction and appropriation of surplus value, the agents carrying out expropriation have contradictory interests vis-à-vis not only the expropriated but also the appropriators. This is thus another objective reason for the opaqueness of the capitalist production relations.

To sum up, production becomes more and more socialized. By this we mean that the process by which less and less agents retain the real ownership of the means of production is coupled with a process which on the macro-level sees an increase in the branches of production - and thus an increase in the interrelation, dependence, of the production units in the several branches - and on the micro-level an increase in the positions and thus in the interrelationship among the agents of production, some of whom take over aspects of the capitalist's position which, even though originally belonging to the capitalist, are not essential for the real ownership of capital and thus for the appropriation of surplus value. More and more tasks which used to be the capitalist's (either as capitalist or as a labourer), are now delegated to agents who are not the capitalists since they cannot dispose of the means of production and thus of the surplus value produced. The origin of the global non-labourer (the development in the real concrete which provides the justification for the separate theoretical treatment of the functional element) must thus be seen in this perspective, as an aspect of the increased socialization of production at the level of the enterprise.

Socialization of production is thus a phenomenon concerning both the macro (societal) level and the micro (individual production process) level. At the micro level, this socialization takes on a capitalist essence (not only a form) through a double and interrelated tendency. On the one hand, we have the tendency to fragment the production process in an ever-increasing number of positions (belonging either to the function of capital or to the function of labour), something which, as far as the original figure of the capitalist is concerned, means that an ever-increasing number of tasks are delegated by the owner to non-owners of the means of production. On the other hand, there is a tendency towards an ever-increasing internationalization of the production process as a whole, in all its aspects. This means that an increasing number of positions become internationalized, i.e. are performed by international labour power, something which implies the supervision of a labour process which becomes increasingly internationalized. Both tendencies are typical of capitalism in all its phases. However, the different stages of capitalism differentiate themselves because of the specific forms taken by these two tendencies, fragmentation of positions and their internationalization. Similarly, at the macro level, socialization of production in its capitalist essence means not only a further increase in the social division of labour but also a certain internal structure of the societal production process (and thus the nature of the use values produced) together with the decrease in the number of the production units within each branch. Again, this tendency is combined with the other one, the internationalization of the production process. At the macro level this means that the different parts of the individual production process are carried out across national boundaries, i.e. it means the internationalization of the individual production process. This double tendency, the fragmentation of the societal production process and its internationalization, is again valid for all stages of development of capitalism but takes on particular forms in the different stages.

A study of late capitalist production relations is thus an inquiry into the forms taken by the socialization of production in this particular stage of capitalist development. Unfortunately, in this essential area the development of the social real concrete has left Marxist analysis a good deal behind. The remainder of this chapter is thus devoted to a modest attempt to add something to the few contributions already made in this field. We will focus on the two characteristics of the late capitalist production relations, one concerning a new aspect of the fragmentation of positions and the other a new form of the internationalization of the production process. Thus in section 3 we will consider the dependent capitalist within the capitalist production relations and in section 4 we will consider the internationalization of the acquisition of labour power. It goes without saying that no attempt at comprehensiveness has been made and that the two following chapters are more an indication of the direction to be followed than a full analysis of the late capitalist production relations. Finally, while in section 3 it is still possible to abstract from other than economic relations, this is not possible any longer in section 4 where the role of the state must be taken into consideration. Again, we will consider only those elements of the political which are strictly necessary for our purposes.

3 THE DEPENDENT CAPITALIST AND THE CONTROL OF THE CORPORATION

The birth of the global non-labourer (going from the real owner, through several layers of management down to the last supervisor and foreman) poses the question of the correct identification of the capitalist under monopoly and late capitalism. The issue is not only one of theories of insider control versus theories of proprietary control. In these terms, the view to be expounded below could fall into the latter category of theories which seem to be supported by considerable empirical evidence. (15) The issue is also: what is the relation between proprietors, whom we will call dominant shareholders, and top managers, or executives? In our opinion, the

question as to who controls corporations can be satisfactorily
answered only by considering this latter aspect.

Let us consider again the capitalist production process, as
analysed in chapter 5. Let us reproduce, for the sake of convenience,
Figure 5.4 of that chapter:

$$M \longrightarrow C_e \begin{cases} \text{labour power} \\ +\!\!+ \\ \text{means of production} \end{cases} \longrightarrow CPP \longrightarrow C'_e\begin{pmatrix} C_e \\ + \\ c \end{pmatrix} \longrightarrow M'\begin{pmatrix} M \\ + \\ m \end{pmatrix}$$

| stage 1 | stage 2 | stage 3 |

Figure 6.1   The CPP as a whole

This is the implementation (or running) of the production process,
which starts with stage 1, or acquisition, continues with stage 2,
or production proper, and ends with stage 3, or realization. However,
the phase of implementation must be preceded by two other phases,
scarcely analysed by Marx. The first is the phase of the planning
of the production process, which includes also the planning of
alternative processes, of alternative production functions. The
second is the phase of the selection of that particular combination
of constant and variable capital (both in quantitative and qualitative terms) which will maximize the rate of profit. Schematically,
then, the cycle of production is made up of the following three
phases:
(1) Planning
(2) Selection
(3) Implementation
     acquisition (stage 1)
     production proper (stage 2)
     realization (stage 3)
The distinction between planning, selection, and implementation is
scarcely relevant in the context of individual capitalism but becomes
necessary, as we will see soon, under monopoly capitalism and even
more under late capitalism. Under individual capitalism the
planning of new production processes, or the expansion of existing
ones through concentration or centralization, or the modification of
already functioning production processes through the introduction
of new techniques (machines), etc., is a prerogative of the
capitalist. The same holds for selection. Yet, what is a prerogative of the capitalist need not be an aspect of the function of
capital. For example, when the individual capitalist is engaged in
the acquisition stage or in the realization stage, he is an unproductive labourer, he performs the function of labour (or of the
collective labourer) since he deals with use values, without
changing them. Planning, on the other hand, as an aspect or instance
of the process of conception, can be an aspect either of the
function of labour or of the function of capital. Under the section
'The labour process or the production of use values' Marx considers
'labour in a form that stamps it as exclusively human'. He says:
   A spider conducts operations that resemble those of a weaver,
   and a bee puts to shame many architects in the construction of

the cells. But what distinguishes the worst architect from the
best of the bees is this, that the architect raises his structure
in imagination before he erects it in reality. At the end of
every labour-process we get a result that already existed in the
imagination of the labourer at its commencement. (16)
Planning is the architecture of the labour process. The owner of
the means of production is a labourer when performing this particular
type of mental labour. He can do this because he has expropriated
from the individual labourer not only his means of production (stage
of formal subordination of labour to capital) but also his knowledge
(real subordination of labour to capital). When, under monopoly and
even more under late capitalism, he delegates planning to a complex
of agents under his control, he thus delegates a part of the labour
process to agents who, inasmuch as they engage collectively in the
planning of the labour process, are (mental) labourers.

But, as seen in the previous chapter, conception, and thus
planning, can also be a part (aspect) of the function of capital.
The individual capitalist does not only plan how, what, where, and
how many use values to produce: he plans also the work of control
and surveillance which goes with it, something which implies also
the choice among several types of the work of control for a certain
type of the labour processes (production function) aiming at the
production of a certain commodity. In this case the individual
capitalist is engaged in mental non-labour so that those agents to
whom this type of planning is delegated, in the stage of monopoly
and late capitalism, cannot but be non-labourers, performers of
the function of capital. Differently from selection, which is always
a part of the function of capital since the selection of a certain
combination of variable and constant capital is a part of that type
of activity aimed at the maximization of the rate of profit and thus
at the creation of surplus value, planning can thus be either
function of capital or (but not at the same time) function of labour.
Along these lines we have the possibility of identifying the social
nature of planning when this type of conception ceases to be an
individual activity and becomes a common task, when it becomes the
task of a department of an enterprise and when finally it detaches
itself from that enterprise to become a separate branch of capital.
Since similar points have been made in chapter 5 concerning the
different types of conception, we will not elaborate further on this
point. We will only point out a specific case which might not be
obvious at first sight, the case of agents engaged in the planning
of capital concentration and centralization. An agent engaged in
investment decisions in the form of capital concentration (expansion
of the production process) will be a labourer (but not necessarily
a member of the working class in terms of production relations),
either productive or unproductive, according to whether he plans
the expansion of a productive or an unproductive process. The same
agent engaged in investment decisions in the form of capital
centralization (take over of other production units), since, on a
societal scale, he deals with material use values without changing
them (even though from the point of view of his job he deals only
with non-material use values), is an unproductive labourer. Finally,
the same agent, when engaged in the re-organization of the work of
control following either concentration or centralization, is a non-
labourer. (17)

Therefore, the individual capitalist
(1) plans the capitalist production process (in its double aspect
    and thus performs both the function of labour and of capital);
(2) selects it (performance of the function of capital);
(3) implements (or runs) it by:
    (a) acquiring the means of production and labour power (function
    of labour) in stage 1;
    (b) performing both the function of labour (the co-ordination
    and unity of the labour process) and the function of capital
    (work of control and surveillance) during the production proper
    (stage 2);
    (c) realizing 'his' surplus value (again, a function of labour)
    in stage 3.
There is in this stage of capitalist development practically no
delegation of functions or of power by the capitalist to other agents.
This is not so any longer under monopoly and late capitalism. With
the advent of the global non-labourer, to which is delegated an
increasing, and increasingly fragmented, number of functions, not
only the direct performance but also parts of the indirect performance
of the function of capital are now carried out by a complex of agents
bureaucratically and hierarchically organized. However, the
capitalist still performs an aspect of the global function of capital,
the remotest from the labour process and yet the most vital for the
control of the surplus value producing process: he controls both
labourers and non-labourers alike indirectly by controlling the work
of the executives (who are responsible for the whole of the enterprise)
through a check of the rate of profit figures. The capitalist needs
neither to think about nor to carry out directly the global function
of capital: he only needs to perform that function indirectly, i.e.
by controlling the controllers and by engaging in that type of
conception which is selection. As far as the function of capital
goes, the capitalist has thus delegated to the global non-labourer
both the conception and those aspects of the performance of the
global function of capital which are not essential in order to retain
the real ownership of the means of production and thus of surplus
value. The dominant stockholder must retain the ultimate real
ownership, the ultimate power to dispose of the means of production
and of labour power (including that of the executives). He must
retain thus the right to select, to decide about simple, expanded,
or restricted reproduction. A direct exercise, in the forms of
initiation of decision and giving up orders to the executives or in
the form of approval beforehand of the policies submitted by the
executives, can be retained by the dominant capitalist but is not
essential for the retaining of the ultimate real ownership (apart
from exceptional circumstances). An indirect exercise of this power,
real ownership, i.e. the subjection of the decisions taken by the
executives, after they have been executed, to the criterion of
long-term profitability for the corporation as a whole is usually
sufficient. Since the executives have been delegated a part of the
real ownership, the dominant shareholder retains not only real
ownership on the executives' labour power but also ultimate real
ownership on the corporation through the indirect control of the
executives' action.
What about the rest of the global non-labourer? Are the agents

making it up the capitalists?   Since those who do not have the
real ownership of the means of production cannot be capitalists, the
answer is immediately negative for the greatest part of the non-
labourers concerned. Yet, the executives have been delegated a part
of the real ownership, the one inherent in implementation and planning,
phases which the dominant shareholder need not and sometimes cannot
perform himself any longer. The executives have been delegated the
implementation of the decisions taken by or on behalf (and subject to
the a posteriori approval) of the dominant shareholders, including
the running of the unchanged production process, e.g. the replacement
of worn-out machinery, the hiring and dismissing of labour power, the
buying of raw materials and the selling of the products, the
maintenance of the system of control, etc. They have thus a limited
ownership of both the means of production and of labour power, a
limited power to dispose of them. The executives are also delegated,
especially after the Second World War, the planning of the production
process (in its double social content) something which they may carry
out only partially since they can, in their turn, delegate aspects of
planning to other, subordinate, agents. This does not imply
delegation of a part of real ownership unless they were in a position
to carry out, in a relatively independent way, those plans, but
always subject to the ultimate test of profitability, to the approval
of the dominant stock holder, who has delegated all direct participation in control. (18)

But are the executives, then, capitalists? As far as the workers
are concerned, the top manager is the capitalist because he (i) has
real ownership (even though a limited, delegated one), a fact which
prevents him from having to provide surplus non-labour, (19)
(ii) performs the global function of capital, and (iii) extracts
surplus value or surplus labour. However, from the point of view
of capitalist production relations he is not the capitalist 'pure
sang' because he lacks the fundamental aspect of real ownership and
thus lacks the power to dispose of surplus value (he is not the
appropriator). He is not, thus, the exploiter in the full sense of
the word. The two elements of exploitation lead now a different
life. We have seen previously that there are agents who, without
having any real ownership of the means of production, perform the
global function of capital (either only this function or in combination with the function of the collective worker). We see now that
there are also agents who perform the global function of capital
having had delegated to them a part of the real ownership of the
means of production and of the labour power. Their class collocation
is thus difficult. On the one hand, it could be said that, strictly
from the point of view of production relations, they are not
capitalists because they lack the essential element of the real
ownership. Strictly speaking, they could be considered as a special
case of the new middle class. However, in daily life, in the daily
running of the capitalist production process, from the point of view
of the labourers, it is they who are the capitalists, and not those
agents who are detached, but not separated, from the daily running
of the capitalist production process, who do not have to participate
directly in this process in order to be carriers of the capitalist
production relations. (20)

Thus, one aspect of the capitalist production relations, the

ultimate real ownership, falls out of the daily running of the
capitalist production process but not of the capitalist production
relations. Those who retain this aspect and thus appropriate surplus
value do so without having any longer an immediate contact with the
capitalist production process (aside from selection), without having
to bother with the running and possible planning of this process.
None the less, they are still carriers of capitalist production
relations. They are the capitalists, the appropriators of surplus
value, even though they have delegated both a good deal of the work
of control and surveillance and real ownership as far as the planning
and implementation go.

Yet the executives are the capitalists as far as the non-owners
are concerned, thus, vis-à-vis the working class and the new middle
class. They perform indirectly the global function of capital and
have a partial, real ownership of the means of production, which is
the reason why they, in turn, do not have surplus non-labour
expropriated from them. But, to say that the top managers, those who
have a delegated partial real ownership, are not the capitalist
strictly from the point of view of the capitalist production relations
and yet are the capitalist in the daily running of the capitalist
production process (and thus the daily aspects of the capitalist
production relations); to say that, in other words, they are the
capitalists as far as the workers are concerned, can be acceptable
from a practical point of view, but is not theoretically satisfactory.
In fact, the top managers are the capitalists also from the point of
view of the capitalist production relations. In fact, given the
determinant role of the ownership element vis-à-vis the other
elements, even the partial ownership of the means of production is
enough to collocate these agents on the capitalist side. (21) Under
monopoly capitalism the figure of the capitalist has split into two
parts, both of them with real ownership. (22) It is as if there is
a division of tasks whereby one agent is the capitalist as far as
the daily running of the system is concerned, and thus is in the
forefront of the economic class struggle, while the other agent sits
in the back-room and retains for himself the most important aspect
of the capitalist production relations, i.e. the power to appropriate
surplus value. To do this, he must have the ultimate power to
dispose of the means of production and thus to control the labour
power. The executive runs the enterprise on his account. He is an
incomplete (because he is delegated only a part of the real ownership) and dependent (because this delegation makes him dependent
upon those who ultimately have the power to dispose of the means of
production and of the labour power) capitalist, but none the less
he is a capitalist. He lacks the ultimate ownership of the means
of production and thus the power to dispose of the surplus value
produced, but he has, as far as capitalist production relations are
concerned, only capitalist characteristics. He has been delegated
all the features of the capitalist, but not the essential one which
remains with the dominant stockholder.

It is important to notice that the delegation of economic ownership is not visible in the daily running of the capitalist production
process and that it becomes visible only under exceptional circumstances just because it is revoked only under exceptional circumstances, e.g. the closing down of a factory. In this case, both the

workers and the top managers will lose their jobs and will share their interests in retaining it. However, this is not enough to collocate both managers and workers in the same class, not even at the level of production relations. The social content (in terms of production relations) of the executive's position is quite different (opposite) to that of the worker's. (23) This is so because under monopoly capitalism the capitalist class is represented not any longer by one type of production agent but by two types, the ultimate real owner and the top manager, tied in a relation of dependency. It is this fact that has made the singling out of the class enemy a difficult task. The former type of agent does not appear on the battlefield, he leaves the running of the class struggle to the latter type of agent who, even though incompletely and dependently, belongs to the same class as that of the agent who has the ultimate real ownership. The owner/non-labourer/exploiter of individual capitalism has split into two figures, the ultimate owner/indirect non-labourer/ appropriator of surplus value, and the partial and dependent owner/ indirect non-labourer/extractor of surplus value. Even though there might be at times contrasts between these two segments of the capitalist class, these differences will always be less important than the contradictions between both of these two types of agents, on the one side, and the non-owner/labourer/exploited, on the other.

The hypothesis submitted and resting on the double feature of (i) the split of the original figure of the capitalist into two figures and (ii) the relationship of dependency of one of them upon the other, finds some empirical evidence when the question as to the determination of the executives' income is tackled. In chapter 5, as well as in a previous writing (1977), we inquire into the determination of the non-labourer's income (revenue, as opposed to the labourer's wage) and into the economic significance of his activity, of his non-labour. The results are that, first, the income of the non-labourers (revenue) is determined just as that of the labourer (wage), i.e. is determined by the value of the labour power, the only difference being that the ideological and political elements are a constant factor in the revenue's determination and not in that of the wage; second, revenue is a necessary cost for the extraction of surplus value or of surplus labour, but is a faux frais of production both on a macro and on a micro level. (24) This, however, holds for those non-labourers who are non-owners, who have neither an ultimate nor a dependent and partial ownership. How is the executive's revenue determined? Empirical evidence shows that the major determinant of top managers' 'compensations' is the corpora- tion's rate of profit. (25) Now, if profit is the compensation for owning capital, as Marx says, then this empirical evidence tends to prove the hypothesis submitted above about the capitalist nature of the executives. As capitalists, it is logical that their 'salary' be tied not to the value of their labour power but to the profita- bility of the enterprise run by them. As incomplete and thus dependent capitalists it is logical that the way their salary is tied to profits is ultimately decided upon by those who have the ultimate ownership, who have also the power to dismiss their own representatives, the executives. There is thus a fundamental difference in the revenue determination of these two types of non- labourers, those who are capitalists, even though in an incomplete and dependent manner, and those who do not belong to this class because they do not have any real ownership. For the former, it is the profitability of the enterprise; for the latter, it is the value of their labour power, which determines their income.

On the basis of the preceding discussion, we can now conclude this section by considering the question as to who controls the corporation. In a sense, M. Zeitlin is right in stressing that: 'the real owners do not have actually to *manage* the corporation, or even be formally represented on the board, to have their objectives realized - that is to exert control'. (26)   However, do the managers only behave as if they were capitalists, or are they capitalists? And, if they are capitalists, on the basis of which theoretical argument should they be considered as such?   In a way A. Sohr-Rethel is correct too in pointing out that

The firm belongs to the capitalist, but is run by the management on behalf and for the benefit of the capitalist. Capital is dependent on the management for running the business, but the management is dependent upon capital, for its position of ruler-ship over the workers. (27)

Again, there is a mutual dependence between capital and management, but is the latter a segment of the capitalist class or not?   And, what is the nature of this relation of dependence, i.e. are both poles dependent upon each other in the same way (mutual inter-dependence)?   The answer is already implicit in the theoretical argument submitted above.   Let us state it explicitly.

The modern corporation is controlled neither by one segment of the global non-labourer rather than another (e.g. by the dominant stockholder rather than by the executive, or vice versa); nor by the global non-labourers as a whole (thus by all its parts) in which however a simple relation of mutual functional dependence exists among the parts; but by a global non-labourer the constituent parts of which are articulated on the basis of a relation of dependence and domination.   Our approach reveals our concern about who controls the collective labourer.   The question as to whether, say, the shareholders dominate the executives or vice versa (absolutized as the question in the literature on this subject) is for us important and can be correctly tackled only within the context of how capitalists control the workers and thus also the great majority of other controllers.   We have identified four segments of the global non-labourer, all of them necessary for the control of the corpora-tion (and thus of the collective labourer), but not all on the same footing in terms of relations of domination.   The first two segments belong objectively, i.e. in terms of production relations, to the capitalist class.   They are:

(1) The dominant shareholder, or dominant capitalist, who retains at least

    (a) the power to select (changes in) the production process;
    (b) the ultimate real ownership (without having to plan and implement the production process);
    (c) the appropriation of the surplus value;

(2) The dependent capitalist (executive), who

    (a) has partial and dependent real ownership, i.e. concerning the planning and implementation of the production process;
    (b) is ultimately responsible to the dominant stockholder for the extraction of surplus value.

The other two segments of the global non-labourer, of the controller, belong objectively to the new middle class. They are:
(3)   The non-owner, who
   (a) performs only the global function of capital (directly or indirectly);
   (b) extracts surplus value (or surplus non-labour);
   (c) provides surplus non-labour;
(4)   The non-owner, who
   (a) performs both the global function of capital (directly or indirectly) and the function of the collective worker;
   (b) extracts surplus value or surplus non-labour inasmuch as he performs the former function while providing surplus non-labour;
   (c) produces surplus value inasmuch as he performs the latter function.
These are the four elements of the hierarchically and scientifically organized controlling body. Within it, the ultimate real owner dominates the other segments of the non-labourer, has the ultimate power to dispose of the means of production and of labour power and thus can dispose of the surplus value produced. He has delegated all the aspects of the function of capital necessary for the control of the collective labourer (and thus of the controller) but not necessary for retaining the ultimate real ownership and thus for the appropriation of surplus value. But it is he who is the ultimate controller. Of course, his control over the collective labourer is unchallenged while his real ownership, ultimate vis-à-vis the other parts of the controlling system as well as the collective worker, might be limited by other, external capitals. It is for this reason that we should not restrict our study to the production unit or even to the corporation but should consider, as Zeitlin puts it 'the actual coalescence of financial and industrial capital'. (28)
However, such a study should be put in the proper perspective. If we restricted our inquiry to the study of the relationship between the ultimate owner and the dependent capitalist within the corporation, we might not be able to see that

   even in corporations in which a substantial minority of the stock (or even majority) is held by an identifiable ownership interest, this may not assure control: if the corporation has a long term debt to a given bank or insurance company, has that institution's representatives on its board, and must receive prior approval of significant financial and investment decisions, then control of that corporation may be exerted from the 'outside'; and this may be accentuated if several related financial institutions have a similar interest in that corporation. (29)

This, however, does not mean that in such a case neither the top managers nor the dominant stockholder have the ultimate ownership, nor that real ownership does not necessarily pass through a partial legal ownership of the means of production. The study of the relationship between the ultimate owner and the dependent capitalist (top manager), even though closely connected, is not the same as the study of how a corporation ensures for itself the real ownership of another corporation. The case mentioned by Zeitlin depicts either a way to, or a transition stage in, the take-over (through centralization) of that corporation, as it becomes visible in an initial restriction of the dominant owner's real ownership by other, external capitals. The debt will either be repaid, and then the dominant owner will acquire his complete real ownership again. Or, the debt will not be repaid, and in this case the outcome will be a take-over by the bank or insurance company of that corporation through the acquisition of (usually partial) legal ownership. But then, ultimate real ownership, and thus control and the right to appropriate surplus value, will change hands and a new real owner, within the corporation, will appear. We should not conflate control and centralization of capital. The latter is a way to achieve the former, or, to put it better, a way to exercise control in order to gain ultimate real ownership.

4 THE INTERNATIONALIZATION OF THE ACQUISITION OF LABOUR POWER

The immigrant worker in Europe is the 'poor cousin' of the European working class. He is also, of all the characters animating the stage of political economy, one of the most disregarded and neglected. He is treated unjustly not only in reality but also in the realm of theory. As we will attempt to show, an analysis of his nature and function under late capitalism can illuminate an important new aspect of the capitalist state, an aspect determined by a new form of capital accumulation and determining in its turn new ways of disciplining the working class. We will be concerned with the present stage of imperialism which, following E. Mandel, we will call 'late capitalism' in order to distinguish it from the pre-Second World War stage of classic imperialism, (31) and with the West European scene. More specifically, the industrialized West European countries will be considered as the 'centre' vis-à-vis a 'periphery' made up basically of the Mediterranean, but also of more distant, countries.

Let us first consider again the scheme of the capitalist production process as a whole in its three phases of acquisition (M-C), production proper (C-C'), and realization (C'-M'). All three stages were already internationalized under classic imperialism where raw materials were acquired from abroad and products sold on foreign markets and where, due to capital export, there was also an internationalization of surplus value production. However, the internationalization of the acquisition phase was not yet complete because it had not yet reached one of the two basic inputs of the capitalist production process, i.e. labour power. We will thus focus our attention on the internationalization of the purchase of labour power, i.e. on the purchase of labour power on foreign markets for (temporary) use on domestic markets. This will be considered as one of the new elements of the capitalist production process under late capitalism and as an important element in the analysis of social classes.

Classic imperialism is characterized by international concentration (Lenin's export of capital), i.e. by the international transfer of both constant and variable capital. This capital movement, which goes characteristically from the centre to the periphery, does not result, however, in an international migration of labour power, aside from the limited flow of managerial and qualified technical personnel. Setting up an enterprise abroad, in the periphery, means buying foreign labour power in the periphery to be used there. Transfer of variable capital and of labour power do not correspond. At the same time, however, there is a massive migration from the less developed countries of the centre to the more developed countries also of the centre. This is the new type of migration to which Lenin refers. (30) Capitalists purchase foreign labour power on their own domestic labour markets; there is no internationalization of the acquisition of labour power because the migration takes place before the foreign labour power is purchased. This immigrant labour power in the countries of the centre has a definite and permanent character in the sense that, even though this labour power is not immune from the capitalist trade cycle, it usually finds in the countries to which it migrates a distinctive location in the division of labour because it meets a structural rather than a conjunctural need for labour power. This internationalization of the collective worker, therefore, is important in the production but not yet in the acquisition stage.

Under late capitalism, on the other hand, while the flow of capital goes characteristically from the more developed to the less developed countries of the centre (this stage is characterized by international centralization), the flow of labour power goes increasingly from the periphery to the centre, according to Mandel 'for the very reason that capital does *not* (or does not sufficiently) flow out of [the centre] into those marginal areas'. (33) Now the flow of labour power changes its nature; it changes increasingly (though certainly not completely) from a permanent to a temporary flow. This is a consequence of the fact that migration is now consciously used in an anti-cyclical function, that it is tied to the ups and downs of the cycle. But such an attraction and expulsion of the commodity labour power requires a co-ordinating and planning effort which in the last analysis, as we will see, must be carried out by the state. Now it is also the acquisition of labour power which is internationalized, in the sense that foreign labour power is brought into the countries of immigration by the state on behalf of the capitalists. It is the internationalization of the acquisition stage which makes possible the ebb and flow movement of foreign labour power, which gives it its new and temporary (cyclical) character and which in turn is determined, as we shall see, by the needs of a new form of capital accumulation. (34)

We have said that international migration is characteristically permanent under classic imperialism and temporary under late imperialism. The permanent character of migration corresponds to a structural lack of labour power in the 'host' country. This does not imply that the flow of 'permanent' labour power is not subject to the economic cycle. The foreign workers usually do not return to the country of origin, but even when, under the stress of a depression, some of them do return - e.g. in France, beginning in 1931, more than half a million foreign workers were dismissed or had to leave the country - we still have a type of migration which is basically determined by structural rather than by cyclical needs. On the other hand, the temporary character of migration under late capitalism does not imply that this earlier phenomenon is bound to disappear. On the contrary, foreign labour power has become a structural element of the economies of the centre. (35) However,

while the need for foreign labour power has become permanent, also
due to its function as part of the reserve army of the unemployed,
(36) the possibility has arisen of using foreign labour power as an
element of anti-cyclical economic policy by changing the character
of the workers' residence from basically permanent to basically
temporary. This is the double nature of migration under late
capitalism: foreign labour power cannot be dispensed with any more,
but the workers selling that labour power must be subjected to
rotation, and to very high rates of rotation indeed. Peter Kammerer
is thus right in stressing that: 'Migration in Europe is both
permanent, i.e. structurally ingrained in the development of European
capitalism, and *temporary*, in the sense that the migrant's work
contract is temporary and precarious'. (37)

But precarious conditions of work and residence are a condition
for the cyclical attraction and rejection of foreign labour power,
which is itself a condition for capital accumulation, as we will see
shortly. Now, this is important because it allows us to avoid two
opposite but equally dangerous mistakes. While the various 'host'
governments have always emphasized up to very recently the temporary
nature of the immigrant workers, critics of these policies tend to
make the opposite mistake and argue that migration has become
permanent in order to foster a change in the governments' policies.
(38) The exclusive focus on the temporary nature of migration is
functional to capital in the labour power-importing countries because,
on the one hand, it provides a justification for the lack of decent
services and of the recognition of equal rights, and, on the other
hand, it tends to prevent the critics of the capitalist system from
realizing that the state can and will devise ways of integrating
foreign labourers into the system of the receiving country. On the
other hand, an exclusive emphasis on the permanent character of
migrant labour misses some important new elements of capital
accumulation and state intervention in the present stage of capitalist
development. Correct political action can be planned only if it is
realized that migration is now both permanent and temporary, and that
this temporariness takes a cyclical form.

But this is not enough. The thesis of the double nature of
migration must be further qualified by adding that not all foreign
workers are subject to highly temporary conditions of work and
residence; that, in other words, there are two sectors making up the
foreign working population, one relatively permanent and another
subjected to very high rates of rotation. (39) Consequently, the
fluctuations in the size and composition of foreign labour power are
basically borne by the latter sector. Often these two sectors
coincide quite narrowly with ethnic boundaries, as data given below
on rotation by nationality will show. It is the high rotation sector
which is characterized either by temporary residence and work
licences, or by 'illegal' workers. (40)

Some data on migration in the Netherlands will serve to corrobor-
ate the thesis concerning the 'buffer' function of foreign workers,
as shown in Table 6.2.

The years 1967, 1972 and 1975 were years of recession in Europe.
The dramatic decrease in official recruitment as well as the no less
dramatic increase in the rate of unemployment in 1975 (we lack data
on the previous recession years) are sufficient evidence of the

Table 6.2   Foreign labour power in the Netherlands: selected years

Year	Official recruitment	Rate of unemployment	Work licences	
			Permanent (in force)	Temporary (issued during year)
1966	2744	-	-	-
1967	566	-	-	-
1971	16765	-	16914	66810
1972	3981	-	25082	62429
1974	5131	(Jan) 1.8%	36327	56831
1975	902	(Nov) 7.8%	38561	53942

Source: R. Penninx and L. van Velzen (1976) Tables I and III

'shock-absorbing' function performed by the immigrant workers. However, Penninx and van Velzen, in an effort to prove that migration was changing from temporary to permanent, point out that the total number of licences to work increased from 1971 (16,914 + 66,810 = 83,724), a year of boom, to 1975 (38,561 + 53,942 = 92,503) a year of recession. But it should be noticed first, that fewer licences were issued in 1975 than in 1974, and, second, and more importantly, that there was an increase in permanent licences and a decrease in temporary ones. This fact, which seems to contradict the thesis of the tendential transformation of migration from permanent to temporary, really only reflects a characteristic not only of the Netherlands but also of the whole of Europe where migration is a recent phenomenon and where a permanet sector is still in the process of being formed. But, aside from this structural development, it is in line with our thesis that the temporary licences should diminish in times of recession and increase in times of prosperity, since the cumulative increase in the number of permanent licences cannot easily be stopped, given the right of the foreign workers to a permanent licence after a certain period of time (usually five years). It is much easier to act on the temporary (one-year) licences. And, in fact, in the three years of recovery and prosperity, 1969 to 1971 (1969 is the first year for which we could find statistics), the number of temporary work licences issued rose from 50,663 to 66,810. In 1972, a year of recession, issues of temporary licences dropped to 62,429 and remained on that level also in 1973, a year of boom. They decreased in the recession year 1974 (56,831) and decreased even further in the crisis year 1975 (53,942). Thus, with the exception of 1973 in which temporary licences fail to increase, these data support our thesis. (41) Not only are there two sectors (and thus two types) of migration, it is the temporary sector which basically bears the brunt of the government's anti-cyclical policy. And, it is not its permanent character but its temporary nature which characterizes the international mobility of labour power under late capitalism.

If this is so, this feature of labour power mobility must now be given a theoretical basis, i.e. it must be tied to the mechanism of capital accumulation. Now, it is quite obvious that both capital

export and import of labour power are means capital has at its
disposal to try and counteract the tendency of the rate of profit
to fall. Labour power importation has the effect, of course, of
increasing the rate of exploitation in a variety of ways in the
country of immigration (by reducing the costs of production and
reproduction of labour power; by establishing fictitious differences
not only between indigenous and foreign workers but also among foreign
workers, divisions which have, among other things, the effect of
making a high rate of exploitation possible, etc.). (42) This is
common to both stages of imperialism. But there are also, as we have
seen, differences. To repeat briefly, and to focus only on the
movement of labour power, under classic imperialism labour power
flows from the less to the more developed countries of the centre
and has a permanent character, while under late capitalism labour
flows from the periphery to the centre and is characteristically of
a temporary nature. (43) What are the reasons for such changes in
the direction of the flow, and in the nature of labour power migration?
As far as the changed direction of the flow is concerned, let us first
provide some data to support this thesis. Table 6.3 shows a clear
pattern of shifting importance from the countries of the centre to
those of the periphery as reservoirs of labour power.

Table 6.3 Countries of recruitment: Germany and Holland

Year	West Germany	Holland
1955	Italy	–
1960	Spain and Greece	Italy
1961	Turkey	Spain
1963	Morocco	Portugal
1964	Portugal	Turkey
1965	Tunisia	–
1966	–	Greece
1968	Yugoslavia	–
1970	–	Yugoslavia and Tunisia

Source: Kammerer (1976) and Penninx and Van Velzen (1976, p.234).

Table 6.4 gives also a chronological view of the changed composition
of the foreign part of the proletariat in West Germany and provides
further evidence to our thesis.
     The reasons for such a shift are numerous and will not be dealt
with systematically here. Rather, we would like to point out that,
if it is true that there is an ample supply of labour power in the
periphery because capital does not flow sufficiently there, as Mandel
says, it is also true that there must be a demand for labour power
in the centre, i.e. that the centre must open its doors to the
surplus population of the periphery. In short, the point we wish to
make and to which we will return further down is that if it is the
mechanism of capital accumulation on a world scale which gives rise
to the shortage of labour power at the centre and the abundance at
the periphery, it is the conjunctural vicissitudes of the centre
and not those of the periphery which determine the size and composition of the foreign part of the European working class. Suffice it

Table 6.4 Percentage of foreign workers by nationality: West Germany

	1966	1967	1968	1969	1970	1971
Yugoslavia	7.4	9.5	9.8	16.5	21.7	21.4
Turkey	12.0	13.4	13.7	15.5	18.2	20.2
Italy	30.4	26.8	28.3	24.8	19.6	18.2
Greece	14.9	14.3	13.4	12.7	12.4	12.0
Spain	14.1	12.5	11.1	9.9	8.8	8.3
Portugal	1.5	1.8	1.9	1.9	2.3	2.6
Other	19.7	21.6	21.8	18.7	17.0	17.3
Total	100.0	100.0	100.0	100.0	100.0	100.0

Source: Bundesanstalt für Arbeit, quoted in B. Groppo, Sviluppo
        economico e ciclo dell'emigrazione in Germania Occidentale,
        in A. Serafini (ed.), 1974, p.178.

to mention that the capitalists' decision to recruit foreign labour
power in the periphery is dictated not only by purely economic
considerations (the lower cost of foreign labour power) but also by
political and ideological consideration such as a (hoped for) greater
docility and acceptance of capital's plans and exploitation. As
F. Cipriani correctly stresses, this has been the plan of European
capital from the very beginning of the post-Second World War period
and has also played an important role in the economic integration
of Europe:

> Economic integration was not only meant to defeat some sectors
> of the European working class; it was also part of a larger
> political project, pivoted upon downward-elastic wages, i.e.
> upon a broadening of the stratification of the labour force,
> together with the preservation and even the expansion of sectors
> aiming more at the mass of surplus value than at the rate of
> surplus value. This project implied the massive influx of
> contingents of a new and politically weak labour force; it thus
> implied the formation of a marginal market of a 'non-trade
> unionist' labour force, able to erode the strength of the unions.
> (44)

But, if it is correct to stress the multidimensional nature of
social phenomena, we believe it to be mistaken to reject the thesis
of the determination by the economic in the last instance. Even if
the political impact of foreign labour power is taken into consideration (to which nobody is likely to object), i.e. its supposed
weakening of the indigenous workers' organizations, it will still be
the mechanism of capital accumulation (i.e. the impact this weakening
has on the rate of exploitation) which will ultimately determine and
explain the pattern of migration. Thus, it is only apparently a
paradox that the Treaty of Rome, while establishing the right to
free circulation for workers from member countries, has in fact
become an obstacle to it (and this applies especially to Italian
workers), since that principle makes the foreign labour power of
other countries of the centre dearer.

We come now to the reason for the other characteristic of migration under late capitalism, its temporariness. But first some

evidence.   As Gani puts it, in 1972 in France, 'certain sectors of
manufacture, such as the metal, iron, chemical, etc. industries,
which employed permanent labour, tend to recruit temporary labour
without a labour contract or with a fixed-term contract (three or
six months).' (45)   In England, 'the Act of 1971 ... finally
established a system of importing workers when they were needed and
sending them back when they were not'. (46)   This act puts the black
West Indian immigrant

> on the same footing as the foreign workers; he could only come in
> on a permit to do a specific job in a specific place for an
> initial period of no longer than twelve months.   He could not
> change his job without the permission of the government – which
> meant that he was dependent on his employer for recommendation:
> he had to be a good little wage-slave. (47)

In Germany, when the average period of residence of the Yugoslav
immigrants is broken down by republic of origin, we find the highest
average to be 3.2 years and the lowest 1.4 years. (48)   From 1964 to
1972, Turkish immigration to Germany increased from 94,054 to
528,414 but this did not take place through simple yearly additions
of immigrants.   During the same period, while 696,912 Turks entered
the country, 210,615 left it, which gives a rate of rotation of
30.2 per cent.   If we look at Italian workers in Germany in the same
period, we see an increase from 245,526 to 409,448 with a rate of
rotation of 85.6 per cent! (49)   Moreover, the cyclical pattern is
well indicated by the data on Spaniards in Germany.   In 1967, a
year of recession, 7,785 Spaniards entered the country while
63,995 left it. (50)   In France, from 1962 to 1968, 775,000 foreign
workers entered the country but 320,000 left it, which gives a rate
of rotation of 41.3 per cent.   In the same period there were more
than 270,000 naturalizations, almost all Italians and Spaniards, a
phenomenon which reflects a persistence in that country of a
structural lack of labour power. (51)

But let us not fall into the opposite mistake of thinking that
this high rate of rotation applies to all foreign workers.   As
already indicated, there is in the foreign sector, and thus in all
the nationalities making it up, both a more permanent and a highly
volatile sector.   Thus, in 1972 in Germany there were 409,448
Italians, 25,145 more than in the preceding year, due to 154,184
arrivals and 129,039 departures, giving a rate of rotation for 1972
of 83.7 per cent.   But, in the same year almost a quarter of the
Italian immigrants had a 'seniority' of ten years or more and almost
half of them had stayed five years or more in Germany. (52)   This
means that alongside a stratum of 'old timers' who have resisted
the 'natural' rotation, there is a stratum of new immigrants who
are destined for an extremely short period of residence.   The size
of the two sectors as well as the rate of rotation varies for each
nationality of immigrants and for each labour power-importing country.
For example, in Germany in 1972 the permanent sector encompassed
about one half of the Italians but only one third of all foreign
workers and one quarter of the Turks.   But what is common to all
countries and to all nationalities of immigrants is the existence of
two sectors of which the temporary one is subjected to extremely high
rates of rotation.   What P. Kammerer says of West Germany is common
to all labour power-importing countries of the centre: 'A mass of

workers, subjected to a rapid "natural rotation", causing a
continuous renewal of entire strata of workers, co-exists with a
large sector of immigrant workers with "experience" and remarkable
capacities of social adjustment'. (53)

Capital will select, for each national group, a more permanent
sector, according to economic, ideological and political criteria.
(54) This process of selection will, of course, take some years, a
fact which creates the illusion of a transformation of migration
from temporary to permanent, whereas, if we compare migration before
and after the Second World War, the reverse is true. Thus, 'a
system has been established which keeps the migrants as a reserve
army continually in motion, dependent on the respective interests of
capital.... The foreign worker can be deported when the trade cycle
requires it'. (55)

But, on the basis of what has been said so far, a three-fold
qualification should be added to this conclusion. First, these are
obviously only general remarks about the form that is taken by this
economic law under late capitalism. Each particular country will
develop specific ways to transform the character of migration from
permanent to temporary. For example, in France it was only under
the Fourth Republic that the utilization of seasonal workers in
agriculture increased greatly. This form of temporary migration
is rooted in one of the peculiarities of France, i.e. the high
incidence of immigrant workers in agriculture. (56) But there are
also forms to which all governments tacitly resort in various
degrees such as closing an eye (or both of them) towards 'tourists'
and towards outright illegal workers. It is particularly instruc-
tive to observe how the state (police) is at times particularly
tolerant of illegal workers (in Holland, these constitute an
estimated 10 per cent of the foreign working population) and then
at other times suddenly rediscovers its lawful mission. Second,
if it is obvious that, in order to have migration, there must be a
supply of and demand for labour power; if it is certainly true that
the same capitalist system on a world scale creates demand here and
supply there; it is also worthwhile stressing that it is the needs
of capital accumulation of the centre which ultimately determine
the direction, size, and composition of the flow of labour power.
This becomes particularly evident in times of recession when
'redundant' workers are repatriated, whether this is in the interest
of the labour power-exporting countries or not. And, finally, the
temporary and cyclical nature of migration does not exclude at all
the formation of a more permanent group of immigrants who respond
to more structural economic needs, but who must also offer political
and ideological guarantees. But, none the less, it is the temporary
and cyclical aspects which characterize late capitalist international
movements of labour power.

The reason for such high rates of rotation are not difficult to
find. This is basically the new feature of capital accumulation
after the Second World War, i.e. the conscious and programmed use
of foreign labour power by the countries of the centre in an anti-
cyclical 'krisenpufferfuntion'. This is the new means which, in
addition to the older mobility of capital on an international level,
the economies of the centre have at their disposal in order to

counter the tendential fall of the rate of profit. This implies
temporariness and, as we have seen, the internationalization of the
acquisition of labour power. Thus, foreign labour power has become
subject to conjunctural rather than (or together with) structural
movements. In the words of B. Groppo:

> The employment of foreign workers is strictly tied to the cyclical
> development of the German economy and in particular to the course
> of exports (essentially investment goods and durable consumption
> goods, such as motor-vehicles). The phase of recovery, within
> each cycle, begins usually with an increase of foreign demand,
> which causes large investment in export-oriented sectors (which
> are after all the sectors where the foreign labour force is
> concentrated). All this determines a further demand for labour
> power, and it is here that the possibility of drawing on the
> Mediterranean labour force shows itself to be precious for German
> capital: in this phase immigration means essentially the
> possibility of starting the cycle again at a higher level, the
> possibility of an accelerated development. But the analysis of
> the buffer-function is applicable above all to the phase of
> depression. Immigrants work especially in sectors highly sensitive
> to the conjuncture. (57)

Therefore, ideally, foreign labour power must be available on the
market when needed and must disappear when superfluous; disappear,
that is, first from production and then from the labour market
altogether. This implies co-ordination and planning on a national
scale and must thus sooner or later become a function of the state.
(58) Therefore, the difference between the international mobility
of capital and of labour power is that it is the state which nowadays
in all industrialized Western European countries takes upon itself
the task of providing the right quantity and quality of foreign
labour power. Thus, the state takes on new tasks; first of all
economically, by regulating the ebb and flow of foreign labour power,
and then also politically, by finding and carrying out new means of
direct and indirect political oppression, and finally ideologically,
by trying to integrate, on a non-political basis, the immigrant
workers selected to stay. These new tasks are an instance of the
modifications undergone by the late capitalist state and which are
concisely summed up by L. Ferrajoli as follows:

> The state is no longer a simple external guarantor of the general
> laws of the market. It becomes both an element of internal,
> structural regulation of the process of capital accumulation and
> also an instrument of tutelage, organization and control of labour
> force. The function of the state is no longer only that of
> guaranteeing from outside the peaceful course of civil life and
> respect for the juridical form of the labour-capital exchange.
> To this ancient *political* and/or juridical function two more,
> specifically capitalist functions, are added: that of ensuring
> the system's survival and development by fostering directly the
> social valorization of capital, by preventing and solving crises,
> by rationalizing and disciplining the anarchical, conflicting
> tendencies which disunite the interests of the individual
> capitalist (*economic* functions or functions of capitalist
> valorization); and, on the other hand, that of neutralizing the
> antagonism of the working class by mediating its conflicts with

capital, by protecting it from the arbitrariness of the market, by organizing its political integration, by ensuring its social discipline (*social* functions or functions of social stabilization). (59)

The importation of foreign labour power takes place in all countries of the centre through government agencies which, after having reached bilateral agreements with the labour power-exporting countries, on the basis of the entrepreneurs' demands in the countries of immigration, provide for the selection of the required quantity and quality of this commodity through offices in the labour power exporting countries. (60) The forced expulsion of redundant foreign labour power takes place either economically, automatically, by simply not renewing the licences to work, or it can take place through the judiciary, by approving decrees and laws, some of which are bribes (e.g. the 5,000 DM law), which in the context of an adverse economic conjuncture and of a more or less open hostility at all levels of society, acquire the force of expulsion. (61) Or, it can take place by denying the immigrants normal bourgeois democratic rights, thus subjecting them completely to the power of the police. In West Germany, immigrants have no freedom of meeting, of association, of residence, or of choosing their own job. In almost no labour power importing country have the immigrants the right to vote and in all these countries the possibility of immigrant workers participating in political life is made void by the discretion of the police. Forced expulsion can also take place through action by the executive, especially through the special branches of the police. In all 'host' countries, immigrants can be expelled at the discretion of the police for reasons of public order, security, and health. It is through a skilful combination of all these instruments that the modern state can act as the regulator of the supply of foreign labour power. (62) In times of economic expansion an influx of (supposedly) docile labour power for a very short time helps keep wages at bay. When depression and crisis appear, the reduction of the reserve army, or the keeping of it within existing limits, by drastically acting on the foreign component of the proletariat, while not advantageous for some capitalists who are able to survive only thanks to the super-exploitation of immigrant workers, is, however, necessary for the capitalist class as a whole, due to the dangerous political threat and the heavy economic burden constituted by too high a rate of unemployment. Thus, 1974 was the year in which all countries of immigration introduced measures to stop or reduce the influx of labour power. However, the first attempts to reduce this flow date back to 1968 when the first signs of recession began to appear. From that year on we witness an increasing homogenization of the rules and laws governing the influx of immigrants, rules and laws which are basically similar in West Germany, Switzerland, France, Belgium, Sweden, Austria, Great Britain, and Holland. (63) This contemporaneity of repressive economic, political and social measures is hardly surprising given the contemporaneity of the economic cycle in the countries of the centre. This legislation reflects not only the difficulties, economic and political, which capital has in financing social overheads (schools, houses, etc.) for foreign workers, especially in periods of depression; it reflects also an awareness of the potential danger constituted by a too large reserve army of foreign workers. In many

instances, in the 1970s, the immigrant workers have not only participated in labour's struggle: they have led it. They have not only
participated in existing forms of struggle: they have invented new
ones. (64)

The foregoing analysis, even though attempting to discover the new
features of international labour power mobility under late capitalism,
remains within the logic of 'classical' Marxism and thus does not make
any concession to 'workerist' interpretations.

> The immigrant labour power [says Y. Moulier] has its own laws of
> movement, and internal history. Its ebbs and flows are not the
> consequence of capital movements but constitute, if not their
> presupposition, at least the permanent condition, one of the
> essential chapters of the history of capital from the working
> class's point of view, from the point of view of the most directly
> productive labour. (65)

And the same author, in commenting on the statement by L. Gani to the
effect that:

> The massive immigration of workers in France and in other European
> capitalist countries has been and is still one of the components
> of the internationalisation of production and exchange within the
> framework of the capitalist world economy: labour is exported and
> imported just as all other commodities, (66)

holds that: 'Our hypothesis is exactly the contrary ... it is the
peculiar character of the commodity labour power (not the fact that
it is a commodity) which commands the capitalist system'. (67)

On this view the temporariness of migration is not determined by
a new form of capital accumulation - as has been held above. On the
contrary, it is the subterranean struggle of the 'immigrant mass-
worker' (e.g. absenteeism) which causes the great increase in
temporary jobs. Or, as K. Heinz Roth submits, the great influx of
migrant workers in the 1960s in Germany was not determined by the
relative scarcity of labour power but by the resistance of the
indigenous 'mass worker' to the de-humanizing conditions of work,
i.e. by the struggle (even though conducted in a passive way) of
the mass worker. In short, the migrant worker is capital's weapon
against the insubordination of the indigenous workers or, as B. Groppo
says succinctly, 'we read [economic] development in terms of relations
of power'. (68) Now, if it is correct to stress that labour power
does not travel 'like a suitcase', that its movements are not
exclusively determined by capital movements, it is also necessary
to see these autonomous movements (or lack of them) as ultimately
determined by the laws of capital accumulation. To reject this
approach leads either to a sort of multiple determination in which
everything determines everything else, or to the primacy of the
political over the economic. (69) In the workerist version, the
political, from being relatively autonomous, has become completely
autonomous, if not determinant.

Let us therefore, before we proceed with our analysis, review
briefly Marx's position on the national and international mobility
of labour power. De Gaudemar is right in emphasizing that Marx,
even if occasionally relating migration to the level of wages,
explains the former in terms of capital accumulation, variations in
wages being in Marxist theory only an induced phenomenon. (70) De
Gaudemar summarizes Marx's theory on this point in two steps as
follows:

(a) The exchange value of labour power is given by the culturally determined subsistence minimum. In turn, this exchange value determines tendentially the price actually paid, i.e. the wage. The difference between the exchange value of labour power and its price (wage) is caused by variations in demand and supply (discrepancies between them) which in turn are caused by fluctuations in capital accumulation which again are caused by the unequal sectoral levels of the various rates of profit. Accelerated capital accumulation makes the supply of labour relatively insufficient and thus raises the level of wages. This will lead to labour power immigration. A deceleration of capital accumulation makes the supply of labour relatively abundant and lowers the level of wages thus leading to labour power emigration. De Gaudemar makes two correct points. First, it is not the absolute number of workers which determines the level of wages but their number relatively to the needs of capital accumulation. (71) Second, we are very far from the neo-classical thesis which establishes a unilinear and unmediated relation between wages and supply of labour and which deduces a theory of migration as a process of adjustment of this supply to the level of wages. (b) Up to now we have considered the general level of wages and the fluctuations of this level around the exchange value of labour power on a macro-economic level; i.e. so far we have seen that the general rate of wages expresses a relationship between the collective capital and the collective labour force. But this must not be confused with the laws which distribute labour power within the several branches of production. From what has been said above we can exclude right away an explanation in terms of wage differentials. The various branches of the economy have different rates of profit. Those branches with a rate of capital accumulation higher than the average will need additional labour power and, in order to get it, will have to raise the level of wages. From the point of view of the individual labourer - as De Gaudemar rightly emphasizes - the reason for migrating is the wage differential. (72) However, from a social, global point of view, wage differentials are induced phenomena. Once the privileged branches are saturated with labour power, wages will fall. Immigration will stop and eventually will make room for emigration to other branches. (73)

This 'classical' Marxist analysis of mobility and capital accumulation is considered, in some Marxist circles, to have become problematic, at least as far as the foreign component of a country's labour power is concerned. The point some authors insistently make is basically that the immigrant workers cannot act as a reserve army because of the (partial) lack of competition between foreign and indigenous workers. Thus, B. Groppo submits that:

> in reality the decisive argument against the thesis of the
> industrial reserve army is that the foreign and the German worker
> are only partly competing groups. In fact the immigrant worker
> is located almost exclusively at certain levels of the organization
> of labour, and it is only with the German workers at his own level
> that he competes, thus exercising a direct pressure on wages. (74)

But is it not true of the indigenous workers as well that a downward pressure on wages will be the result of competition among workers at the same level of the organization of the production process? Have unskilled workers ever exercised such a pressure directly on the

wages of skilled workers? The argument, however, could easily be
recast. On the basis of the obvious high concentration of immigrants
in 'undesirable', i.e. dirty, dangerous, under-paid, etc., jobs, we
could assume a tendential impermeability of the two sectors of the
labour market, i.e. the indigenous and the foreign one. In this case,
the argument would run, there could be no competition between the
two sectors. To this we could object that the concept of such a
rigid segmentation of the domestic labour market into two sub-markets
is largely the result of wrong conclusions drawn from the observation
of national labour markets under conditions of long-term economic
expansion in Europe in the 1950s and in the 1960s, i.e. under
conditions of tendential scarcity of labour power. The 'unavailability' of indigenous workers for certain dequalified, dangerous,
dirty, etc., jobs could just as well be the result rather than the
cause of the presence of foreign labourers. Or, in other words, this
'unavailability' could transform itself into its opposite under
conditions of long-term stagnation and structural surplus of labour
power. This criticism could be met by focusing the discussion only
on the period following the Second World War and up to the end of
the 1960s, i.e. on the period in which this segmentation had taken
place. But even such a doubly improved formulation concerning the
failure of the foreign workers to function as part of the reserve
army of the unemployed cannot be accepted, for the following reasons.
Suppose there is such a segmentation. In this case the foreign
workers would still be, and function as, an industrial reserve army,
they would still compress the level of wages, because in their
absence capital would try and attract workers to the 'undesired'
jobs through an increase in the level of wages (which would probably
generalize itself to the whole of the economy); or they would, as
P. Baratta rightly observes, try and activate unemployed women, old
people, etc., thus causing a virtual disappearance of the industrial
reserve army, with disruptive economic and social consequences on a
scale which it is easy to imagine. (75) Moreover, the presence of
foreign workers in the 'lower' sectors makes it possible for
indigenous workers to compete in the higher sectors.

Only by taking this perspective can we understand the role played
by foreign labour power in the capital accumulation of the centre
and so reject the various essentially bourgeois positions on
immigration, which go from the moralistic acceptance of the immigrants
on grounds of human solidarity to their reactionary rejection because
they would 'steal' jobs from indigenous workers. The truth is that
the presence of foreign labour power is a condition for the full
employment of the indigenous labour power in times of high conjuncture
and of reduced unemployment in times of low conjuncture. Without
the foreign workers, in the former case the swiftly sailing ship of
the economy would run on to the rocks of the rapidly increasing level
of wages. In the latter case, if all foreign workers were subjected
to forced repatriation, the reduced supply of labour power would
further increase the economic difficulties (producing among other
things, an increase in wages and a decrease in profits) and thus
increase unemployment. (76) This is why Castells is essentially
correct in stating that 'in the short term, for each year, there is
a correspondence between the increase in unemployment and the decline
in immigration. But in the long term, there is a tendency for both

phenomena to increase together', (77) provided this is placed within
the context of a long wave of expansion.

So far we have reproduced Marx's analysis of the migration of
labour power, its ebbs and flows, within a country. But what applies
to the national level does not necessarily apply to the international
one. In the case of migration, there are differences between international and intranational migration which, if overlooked, can lead
to errors. For example, on a national level labour power follows the
stream of capital and is attracted by those geographical areas or
economic branches which have a high rate of capital accumulation. On
an international level we can have substantial flows of capital from
one country to another not followed by any substantial flow of labour
power. Generally speaking, it is the local labour power which will
be recruited in the country which imports capital. In considering
Marx's relative surplus population, and especially the latent part
of it, de Gaudemar says that it is that 'part of the male population
which is sent away by big industry when it (big industry) reaches its
maturity, and is forced to emigrate following the emigration of
capital'. (78) But, aside from the fact that this description fits
Marx's concept of floating rather than that of latent surplus
population, (79)
(1) capital export is characteristic of monopoly capitalism and not
of big industry,
(2) capital export, as we have seen, does not necessarily mean export
of labour power even if it is export of variable capital,
(3) international migration from the developed to the less developed
countries is basically tied to colonization (Lenin's 'old' migration),
to the export of part of the relative surplus population, rather
than to the export of capital.

Now, both capital movements and movements of labour power are
ultimately determined by (and determinants of) unequal development.
However, an important difference between these two forms of movement
on an international scale is the much lesser mobility of labour power.
This is an important point which has sometimes not been given due
consideration even by first-rate Marxist theoreticians. In reviewing
O. Bauer's and R. Luxemburg's positions, and their dispute, about the
nature of migratory movements, de Gaudemar points out that according
to the former author the flow goes from the colonies to the metropolis while for the latter author it goes in the opposite direction
since labour follows capital exports. (80) To these positions we
can add those of P.-P. Rey, according to whom, 'the two phenomena
alluded to - migration towards the colonies plus migration towards
the metropolis - are nothing but the successive effects of the same
process of extension of capitalism articulating itself with other
modes of production' (81) and of de Gaudemar who submits that both
theses are partial, i.e. both are aspects of the same theory of
imperialism since both forms of migration are typical of imperialism:
'immigration of labour power towards the metropolis, as a process
feeding relative surplus population, emigration towards the colonies
in the wake of capital migration ... imperialism is accompanied by
this double migratory phenomenon'. (82) In fact it is neither a
matter of choosing between two forms of migration nor of obliterating
their differences with arguments of the 'two sides of the same coin'
type. It is rather, we believe, a matter of singling out which is

the dominant form of labour power movement in each stage of capitalist development. We have submitted above that under classic imperialism there is migration both from the centre to the periphery (mainly of skilled, technical, and managerial personnel following capital export) (83) and the recruiting of (unskilled) labour power in the colonies, i.e. an internal migration in the colonies. But these are not the dominant forms of migration. What becomes the dominant form is rather the massive migration from the less to the more developed countries of the centre and it is, as we have seen, of a permanent character. This form of migration provided an important stimulus to capital accumulation in the centre. (84) Thus Bauer seems to have come closer to reality than Luxemburg. The movements of labour power following capital movements, on which Luxemburg focuses her attention, are important within, but much less between, countries. Under late capitalism labour power flows from the periphery to the centre and is of an ebb and flow type. (85) This flow depends basically on the cycle in the centre and is for this reason of a cyclical nature. It presupposes international and multinational firms, i.e. the firm with an international outlook as far as the acquisition not only of the raw materials but also of labour power is concerned. But it also presupposes that the internationalization of the acquisition of labour power becomes a task of the state. The state sets out to achieve a new economic task: all barriers to labour power mobility (or, better, to the capitalist use of it, as we will see in a moment) which had been done away with in the previous stages of capitalist development within a country, must now disappear also on an international level.

This need which capital has to abolish all barriers to the mobility of labour power both within and between countries raises the important question of the proletariat's strategy concerning mobility. We know that, in a capitalist system, labour power must be 'free' from the means of production and thus free to change job, enterprise, location, etc. at the entrepreneurs' command. But how can we then explain the recurrent capitalist attempts (not only under Fascism but also under social democracy, at least as far as the foreign workers are concerned) to bind the production agents to certain positions, locations, etc.? (86) The answer is that both mobility and immobility can be ways through which capital attempts to increase the rate of exploitation and reinforces its rule over labour. The mobility 'enjoyed' by labour power transforms itself into its opposite when labour power transforms itself into labour, i.e. when it leaves the labour market and enters the production process. (87) But, on the other hand, both immobility of labour power on the labour market (e.g. in order to keep an abundant supply of labour power in certain branches or areas) and mobility within the production process (dismissals, dequalifications, promotions of 'responsible' workers, etc.) can be, and usually are, necessary to achieve capital's aims. Therefore, no general formulae can be given for the desirability of mobility or of immobility. The decision about whether to oppose mobility or not must be taken exclusively in the light of the struggle to reduce capital's control over labour and thus exploitation. Thus, the conjunctural use of international migration is nothing more than an extension to the international level of the principle of the capitalist use of labour power's mobility.

It might now be useful, in conclusion, to attempt the location of the characteristic elements of labour power mobility (in its several dimensions) under late capitalism. Let us begin by distinguishing among several types of mobility.

(a) Geographical mobility, i.e. migration. This can take place either within a country (intranational migration) or between countries (international migration).

(b) Economic mobility, i.e. from one type of production process to another. We can distinguish again between two sub-cases, i.e. from a non-capitalist to a capitalist production process and from one type to another type of capitalist production process.

(c) Positional mobility, i.e. from one position to another within the capitalist type of production process. An analysis of the concept of position has been provided elsewhere. (88)   It is, however, important to stress that while in our discussion of positions, we focused on the positions and not on the agents, we now reverse the approach and assume (for the purpose of discussion) that the positions do not change and focus on the agents' mobility. We distinguish again between two orders of sub-cases, social and technical mobility (since positions have both a social and a technical content), and vertical and horizontal mobility. Social mobility refers to the social content, i.e. to the content of a position in terms of capitalist production relations. Technical mobility refers to the technical content of a position, i.e. to bourgeois sociology's 'job description'. Vertical mobility can then refer either to social mobility (if, for instance, an agent leaves a worker's position to become a foreman), or to technical mobility (if the change in the 'job' implies a change in the value labour power must have in order to fill the new position: i.e. if there is a change in the value required). Horizontal mobility implies no change in the position's value required or in the position's social content. Thus, social vertical mobility always implies technical mobility (either vertical or horizontal), i.e. a change in 'job', in the technical content of the position. And, social horizontal mobility (no change in terms of the social content, in terms of production relations) must imply technical mobility, must be coupled with a change in the technical nature of the position, or there will be no positional mobility. Vertical mobility can be upward or downward. Upward social mobility means to rise to positions closer to the capitalist's. Vice versa, downward social mobility means to descend to positions closer to the worker's. Upward technical mobility means a change from one job to another with a higher value required, and vice versa for downward technical mobility. (89) Schematically, then, mobility can be as shown in Figure 6.2.

It goes without saying that labour power mobility is often a mixture of these three types of mobility. The typical immigrant from the periphery is a worker who is usually employed for the first time in a capitalist production process. In this case we have geographical (international) and economic mobility but no positional mobility. Or take the case of an Italian industrial worker who, because of unemployment, migrates and accepts a dequalified position. Here we have geographical and positional mobility, but not necessarily economic (it will be so only if he is re-employed in a different production process). Or, the same worker might be subjected to

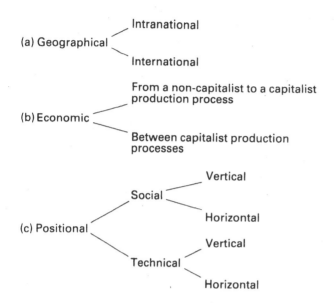

Figure 6.2

positional and economic mobility but not necessarily to geographical mobility. And, of course, a worker can be subjected to all three types of mobility at the same time.

We can now attempt a characterization of mobility of labour power under late capitalism. We have attempted to show elsewhere that, as far as positional mobility is concerned, what characterizes late capitalism is what has been called devaluation through dequalification, i.e. the devaluation of the agent's labour power, his occupying inferior and lower-paid positions, due to the dequalification (both social and technical) of the position he occupies. (90) As far as geographical mobility is concerned, we have attempted to show in the present chapter that typical of late capitalism is temporary migration coming from the periphery and subject to the cyclical fluctuations of capital accumulation in the centre. As far as economic mobility is concerned, what characterizes late capitalism is the attraction, for the first time, into the maelstrom of the capitalist labour market and production process of large masses of new workers (and this includes not only foreign workers but also the massive influx of women into the labour market, the commodification of services and of state activities, etc.). As far as foreign labour power is concerned, we should stress that the types of geographical and positional mobility described above are strictly connected. In fact, the massive introduction of foreign labour power is both cause and consequence of the massive dequalification of positions in order to make possible the employment of thoroughly unskilled labour power. As B. Groppo remarks, without the process of 'rationalization' and the concomitant influx of millions of foreign workers in the 1950s, the German economic 'miracle' would certainly not have been possible. (91) This massive dequalification of positions and use of unskilled labour power should be seen in the light of the conjunctural use of a relevant part of this unskilled labour power (the foreign part), as required by the big concerns' new mode of capital accumulation, and as made possible by the intervention of the state at all levels.

Appendix: migration and the rate of profit

As mentioned above, we skipped the discussion of the advantages and disadvantages of migration in order to focus on the new economic aspects of labour power mobility and on the consequent new functions of the capitalist state. Analyses of the economic effects of migration in both the sending and the receiving countries have already been carried out by other authors. If we were to embark on such an analysis, we would have to distinguish between temporary and permanent migration, in line with the general arguments of this section. It follows from the foregoing arguments that both types of migration act on the general level of wages by increasing the supply of labour power – thus also affecting the general rate of profit – but also that for the temporary sector the emphasis is more on the buffer function than on the super-exploitation of immigrant labour power, while the opposite holds for the more permanent sector. In this appendix we will not deal with these questions but will attempt to specify briefly in what way it can be said that foreign labour power is super-exploited, since this question seems to be the cause of frequent confusion.

Let us subdivide that part of the social product going to the working class into
(a) commodities (socially) necessary for the formation of new labour power which will replace existing labour power in the future (as, for example, education and training of the workers' children). Let us call the value of these commodities F;
(b) commodities (socially) necessary for the regeneration of current reproduction of the existing labour power when actively employed, i.e. when participating in the production process as a whole. Let us call the value of these commodities R;
(c) commodities (socially) necessary for the maintenance of the existing labour power during periods of inactivity (e.g. unemployment, sickness, retirement, etc.), the provision of which is thus postponed to that eventuality. Let us call the value of these commodities M.

At any given period n, then,

$$V_n = F_n + R_n + M_n \qquad\qquad\qquad (i)$$

where V_n is the value of labour power at time n.
Confusion often arises concerning F since this component is considered to be at the same time both the determinant of the value of labour power and a part of the value paid to the worker for the sale of his labour power. To clarify what we mean, let us recall that the exchange value of the commodity labour power is given by the culturally determined subsistence minimum, i.e. is equal to the exchange value of those commodities culturally deemed necessary for the formation of new labour power and for the regeneration and maintenance of the already existing labour power. (92) This is equation (i) above. This equation, however, only tells us how a certain quantity (V) is subdivided into three component parts, i.e.

it tells us that V is equal to F + R + M, but does not tell us how
that quantity (the value of labour power) is determined. Needless
to say, if we were to read equation (i) as a relation of determination,
we would only shift the problem from V to its component parts. We
know that the value of labour power is socially determined. What we
want to know is how the costs of formation of labour power relate to
the value of the formed labour power. Insight in this relationship
will allow us to avoid the confusion mentioned above.

Let us start, for the sake of convenience, from the reduction of
complex to simple labour. (93) We know that qualified, skilled labour
power has a higher value than (a value which is a multiple of the
value of) unskilled labour power because it has cost more time and
labour to produce it. In this case F refers to the value of those
material and non-material commodities (such as education, training,
etc.) which have been necessary in the past periods to produce the
more qualified labour power. Since its value is higher, its price
(wage) will be higher too. More generally, given that n years are
necessary for the production of a certain type of labour power, the
value of labour power at time n (V_n) will be determined by the
exchange value of the use values which are socially considered as
necessary over the years 1, 2, ... n-1 to produce that particular
type of labour power.

For example, $\sum_{i=1}^{n-1} F_i \rightarrow V_n$ (ii)

and substituting (i) into (ii) $\sum_{i=1}^{n-1} F_i \rightarrow F_n + R_n + M_n$ (iii)

It can now easily be seen that the confusion which we referred to
above is between the sum of the value F_i over the first n-1 years
and the value F_n. The quantity F_n refers to the formation cost of
future labour power, to the exchange value of those use values which
society considers necessary for the future reproduction of the
existing labour power. Thus, F_n is not a determinant of the value
of the already existing and formed labour power since this value is
determined by the formation costs in previous periods. Logically,
it is only after V_n has been determined (as shown in (ii) above)
that an equivalent value will be paid, a part of which (F_n) will be
devoted to the reproduction of the existing labour power, i.e. to
the formation of future labour power.

When we say that the worker is paid a value equivalent to the
value of his labour power we are only using a convenient shorthand
for saying that the worker is paid use values which are socially
deemed necessary for his regeneration, maintenance and future
reproduction and whose exchange value is equal to that of other use
values which have been considered as necessary for the formation in
previous periods of his labour power. In short, we refer to (iii)
above. Marx is clear on the fact that what has been called F_n above
refers to the value of those means of subsistence (and thus also to
education and training), necessary to produce future labour power
(and thus entering the determination of the value of future labour
power) and not to the value of those (past) means of subsistence
needed to produce the already existing labour power (and which

therefore cannot determine the value of the existing labour power):

> The owner of the labour power is mortal. If then his appearance
> in the market is to be continuous ... the seller of labour power
> must perpetuate himself.... Hence the sum of the means of
> subsistence necessary for the production of labour power must
> include the means necessary for the labourer's substitutes, i.e.
> his children.... The expenses of this education (excessively small
> in the case of ordinary labour power) enter pro tanto into the
> total value spent in its production. (94)

If this is so, the widespread belief that migration affects the
general rate of profit of the receiving country through the non-
payment of the formation expenses of the immigrant worker must be
deemed to be incorrect. For example, according to Cinanni:

> Of the three component parts of the labour force's costs, capital
> does not pay precisely those expenses needed for the formation of
> the labour force ... thus, thanks to this saving, paying the
> labour force less than its cost and obtaining, by employing it,
> a considerably higher rate of profit. (95)

And, according to Castells:

> one of the essential effects of immigration is to enable
> considerable savings to be made in the costs of social reproduction
> of the labour force as a whole, thereby raising correspondingly
> the overall average rate of profit. This occurs by means of three
> basic mechanisms: 1) First, because by recruiting immigrants
> primarily from among the young and productive ... it is possible
> to avoid paying the costs of 'rearing' the worker, and the
> maintenance costs after his/her working life has ended. (96)

The formation expenditures of previous periods enter the value
of the labour power of the present period and thus determine it.
This labour power emigrates. In the country of immigration the
immigrant worker is exploited just like the indigenous worker when
he is paid the equivalent of the value of his labour power, and is
super-exploited when, as is commonly the case, he is paid less than
that value (recalling that for emigrated labour power the relevant
sum F_i to F_{n-1} is that of the 'host', not the emigration country).
But the reason for his (super) exploitation is not the avoidance of
the payment of his formation costs, and a rise in the general rate
of profit does not depend upon the avoidance of those payments. No
worker, immigrant or indegenous, is exploited because the expenses
of his formation are not paid back, to him or anybody else. Workers
are exploited because the value they produce is more than the value
they receive, which is tendentially equivalent to the value of their
labour power (i.e. what it costs over the past years to form this
labour power), and not because they or the country of emigration
are not refunded these costs. Therefore, super-exploitation can
be achieved by diminishing either F_n, R_n or M_n, e.g. by 'saving' on
the education expenses for children of immigrants, by providing poor
housing and health services, by avoiding paying unemployment benefits
(since the unemployed immigrant will be liable to expatriation),
etc. It is in this way, by reducing F_n, R_n and/or M_n and not by
avoiding paying the formation costs of the value of labour power
that the rate of profit is increased.

NOTES

FOREWORD

1　See R. Luperini, Capitale e movimento operaio: ipotesi di una periodizzazione del novecento, in Geymonat (1980), p.10.
2　Marx (1967a), p.509.
3　Popper (1963), p.332.
4　Careful reading of A. Baracca's Appendix will reveal some theoretical differences with the theses put forward in the present book. These differences, however, can be considered as non-significant in the context of the present discussion.

1　DIALECTICAL DETERMINATION, KNOWLEDGE, AND TRANSITION TO SOCIALISM

1　See S. Clegg and D. Dunkerley's (1980, ch.3) discussion of the incompatibility between the neutrality of technology myth and the movement of the workers' councils.
2　See G. Planty-Bonjour (1968).
3　See A. Cutler et al. (1977, vol.I) and the critical articles by A. Collier (1978) and T. Skillen (1978). A. Cutler et al., in fact, simply 'rediscover' M. Weber's mutual interdependence. See M. Weber (1949).
4　We refer to the 'workerist' tradition started by Tronti (1966), criticized, for example, in A. Mangano (1978) and Various Authors (1978), and forming the theoretical substance, when applied to the analysis of the international migration of labour power, of works such as Serafini (1974). For a critique, see chapter 6, section 4 of this book.
5　An exponent of which is E. Laclau. See (1977) and (1979). For a critique of Laclau, see further below in this chapter.
6　See L. Althusser (1970), E. Balibar (1974) and L. Althusser and E. Balibar (1970).
7　We disregard here the whole range of ever-fashionable a-dialectical interpretation of Marxism. For a recent example, see C. Helberger (1974).
8　E. Balibar (1974, p.76) stresses correctly the difference between being determined and being pre-determined.

9 Therefore, a separation between determination and overdetermination
   is justifiable only for reasons of presentation.
10 R. Sorg (1976, p.74). R. Edgley (1976, p.30) points out that
   this distinction becomes the theoretical humus of reformist
   conceptions.
11 G. Carchedi (1977, chs 1 and 4). See also chapters 5 and 6 of
   this book.
12 N. Poulantzas (1974a, p.16) stresses the primacy of class struggle
   in the historical process. However, what is lacking in this
   author is a theory of the articulation of these two levels of
   analysis, i.e. the level of DLI and of realized determination.
   Statements to the effect that 'Lenin and Mao have many times
   stressed the fact that, while economics plays the determining
   role in the last instance (the fundamental contradiction), it is
   the *class struggle* (i.e. in the end *politics* and the *political
   class struggle*) which has *primacy* in the historical process'
   (ibid., p.40) do not fill the theoretical gap.
13 For an example of how different histories influence different
   forms of Marxism, see H.H. Holz (1972). See also P. Anderson
   (1976).
14 This thesis is of fundamental political importance not only
   because it stresses the significance of the struggle in the
   superstructure for a qualitative change in the economic basis
   (the struggle in the former is a necessary condition for a
   change in the latter), but also because, as will become clear
   as our argument develops, the functionality of the determined
   instance for the reproduction or supersession of the determinant
   one opens the possibility for phenomena common to more than one
   class (e.g. women's, ecological, students' movements; a certain
   type of ideology; etc.) to be analysed as determined in the
   last instance by the economic, i.e. as determined by a certain
   class identifiable in terms of production relations. A concept
   of DLI which leads to a 'one-to-one correspondence between a
   belief, or a set of beliefs, and a particular type of social
   class or interest group' would have to account for too great
   an amount of 'pathology' (Barnes, 1974, p.116). In this
   chapter we will justify theoretically our claim that DLI by the
   economic, or class determination, is not incompatible with a
   certain determined instance (an element of knowledge) being
   'shared' by more than one class. In chapter 4 we will focus
   on the social mechanism specific to the production of knowledge
   and on the role of individuals in it, both as such and as
   carriers of social relations.
15 Each order of instances is dependent upon the other, and on
   this we disagree with D.-H. Ruben (1977, p.127). But this
   relation is much more than simple interrelation or reciprocal
   causality because of the built-in asymmetry. The centre of
   gravity of this concept is contradiction rather than interdependence. See A. Badiou (1975, p.31). The determination in
   the last instance can be recognized through the fact that the
   basic features of the determinant instance are found in the
   determined one but 'translated', as it were, into the latter's
   language; as if seen in a transforming mirror. P. Petta, for
   example, has rightly stressed the parallel between the discussion

in parliamentarism and competition in capitalism (Various
Authors, 1978, pp.192-3). L. Ferrajoli draws a parallel between
the oligopolistic form of competition and the mechanism of
competition among parties in contemporary capitalism by stressing
the limits imposed respectively upon production and voting and
between the system of delegation and the joint stock company
(ibid., pp.204-5). Similarly, Darwin's theory reveals the marks
of the capitalist social environment because it 'esprime ... la
piena maturità dei meccanismi concorrenziali capitalistici'
(A. Baracca and R. Livi, 1976, p.32), and the development of
calculus reveals the same marks but in a different way (P. Raymond,
1978, pp.120-2). These are all examples of how the determination
in the last instance can be retraced in the determined one.
They indicate, in different ways, functional relations; they
do not explain those relations, nor do they explain concrete
realizations. The analogy between the two levels of social
reality functions as a 'spy', but is not a proof of determination.
Thus, the similarity between parliamentary democracy and
capitalist competition can only indicate a path of research but
does not prove yet that the former is compatible with bourgeois
rule and thus with capitalism and incompatible with socialism
which, as only the numerous historical experiences can show and
as only logical analysis can reveal, requires direct forms of
democracy.

16 K. Marx (1973, p.102).

17 R. Sbardello, in Various Authors (1978, p.33).

18 But the simplest determinations, those from which an increasingly
rich model of society can be unfolded, are not necessarily the
most suitable ones from which to start a presentation of that
model. Thus, M. Neuman (1976, p.35) is correct in stressing
that 'Capital' starts with an analysis of the commodity not
because of reasons of inquiry but because of reasons of
presentation. As far as logic is concerned, to postulate inner
contradictoriness means to postulate that a thing is itself
and is also not itself: $A = A$ and $A \neq A$. As it will become
clear further down, the real reason for choosing this point of
view (an objectively determined choice) is a class determined
reason just as the metaphysical, static, point of view ($A = A$)
is functional for bourgeois domination (it is a static point of
view, inherently unable to explain development and change). As
Sayers rightly says: 'By this account, a thing which remains
identical does not change, and a thing which changes thereby
loses its identity.... This account renders all *change* and
development incomprehensible: if a thing changes in any respect,
then it can no longer be the same thing' (R. Norman and S. Sayers,
1980, p.74). Sayers is also right in pointing out that 'Everything has self-identity, being-in-itself, but the matter does
not end there; for nothing is *merely* self-identical and self-
contained, except what is abstract, isolated, static and
unchanging. All real, concrete things are part of the world of
interaction, motion and change; and for them we must recognize
that things are not merely self-subsistent, but exist essentially
in relation to other things [and, we might add, in constant
change]' (p.3). However, contrary to Sayers's opinion, for us

contradictions exist first of all epistemologically, in the sense explained in the previous section. For us, to conceive of things as contradictory is to subscribe to the proletariat's point of view, a point of view which, as we will see further down in detail, cannot be made its own by other classes and especially not by the bourgeoisie. Thus, on this point, it is Norman who is correct when he points out that 'one cannot *appeal to* the scientific examples to *vindicate* the dialectical interpretation' (p.150), at least as long as these examples are considered to belong to a class neutral body of knowledge. And it is the emphasis placed upon the class determination of knowledge which differentiates our approach from both Sayers's and Norman's.

19 A. Martynow (1930).

20 This is the charge moved to us by T. Johnson (1977).

21 H. Lefebvre (1968, p.88).

22 A standpoint different from della Volpe's (1969) historicism in which contradictions are real because historically determined. Althusser is, of course, a critic of this standpoint but falls into absolute relativism, a position hardly useful for the proletariat. For an example of such an approach, see K. Tribe (1973).

23 See K. Williams (1975, p.331).

24 See G. Ciccotti et al. (1976, p.87).

25 See F. Engels (1970, p.32). On the other hand, for G.P. Frantsov, 'scientific communism is the supreme achievement in social thinking' (1975, p.12).

26 For a different position, see R. Norman (1976). L. Colletti (1975) submits that Marxism is a tool to understand only capitalist reality. For a critique, see Sayers (1976), and for a defence, see P. Dews (1977). A related position on the non-idealist concept of knowledge is taken by D. Lecourt (1975), but we share T. Counihan's (1976) critique of Lecourt.

27 See V.I. Lenin, no.38. For a critique concerning Lenin's reflection theory see H. Brinkmann (1978). D. Lecourt's position (1977, p.106) seems to us to conceal the complexity of the problem.

28 The theoretical argument, within a materialist context, is given in chapter 2. Here suffice it to note that to be the mode of existence is something quite different from being the condition of existence. Between class struggle and contradictory structures there is no relation of determination: such a relation exists only between structures and other social phenomena, i.e. among types and forms of class struggle.

29 Mao Tse-Tung (1967, p.333).

30 This argument can be easily extended to more than two classes.

31 As mentioned above, here we do not apply this scheme specifically to the production of knowledge and thus we disregard ideological class struggle. In other words, we deal here with the possibility of the existence of objectively determined interests and of their perception by agents; we do not deal here with the mechanism through which these interests manifest themselves in the consciousness of the agents.

32 And not, as R. Sorg (1976, p.23) submits, the mediating category

between basis and superstructure. It is for this reason that interests are felt by individuals as 'external coercive laws', as Marx says. Quoted in J. Mepham (1973).

33 See M. Weber (1949).

34 For a discussion of how this problematic made its way into Marxism between 1904 and 1930 and of the various attempted answers (from which the one submitted here differs radically) see L. Goldman (1972). See also R. Edgley (1976).

35 P. Binns (1973). See also N. Poulantzas's discussion (1974a) of the difference between the origin and the beginning of Fascism's growth.

36 In fact, if this mutual interaction left the determinant instance unchanged, i.e. if the determined instance did not affect the determinant one, no explanation could be offered of the change undergone by the latter instance apart from an explanation purely in terms of that instance's internal dynamics. But in this case not only the problem of the determined instance's relative autonomy would lose any practical and thus theoretical relevance (what is the use of studying change in the superstructure if it is irrelevant for the modification of the basis?) but also the very concept of being determined as being a condition of reproduction or supersession would become meaningless. That reproduction or supersession would depend only upon the determinant instance. In a sense, therefore, E. Laclau is right in emphasizing that 'no historical transformation can be explained exclusively by unfolding the internal logic of a determinate mode of production' (1977, p.42). Unfortunately, however, the conclusion he draws from it is that the concept of DLI must be abandoned.

37 We say 'basically' because at this stage of the exposition we do not consider yet the reciprocal influence of the determined instances and thus their being, in fact, an expression of more than one element of the determinant instance.

38 It is in reciprocal action that 'reflection usually takes shelter when the conviction grows that things can no longer be studied satisfactorily from a causal point of view' (G.W.F. Hegel, 1975, p.218).

39 R. Keat and J. Urry, for instance, doubt whether DLI can be reconciled with 'reciprocal and functional interdependence' (1975, p.102).

40 Even trusts and banks, though inevitable in all capitalist countries, 'differ in their concrete aspects from country to country' (V.I. Lenin, no.23, p.69). See also N. Abercrombie (1980, p.89).

41 See R. Miliband (1977, p.8) for an explanation of relative autonomy in terms of the role played by empirical factors.

42 A. Gramsci (1971, p.438).

43 Concerning the proletarian revolution, see Marxistische Aufbauorganisation (1973, p.155). For a similar point, see M. Zeitlin (1980, p.20).

44 See 1976, p.241. Engels's approach reflects a position widely held within the German labour movement of his time. Typical of this view are J. Dietzgen's writings. For a short selection, see I. Fetscher (1976). For a short introduction to Dietzgen,

see A. Buick (1975). For a critique, see H. Brinkmann (1978, pp.31-3).

45 This position (together with its epistemological basis of the reflection postulate) has become the official one (see, for example, H. Korch, 1980) and has been theorized by authors such as Lenin (no.14) and Lukàcs (1971). It is our contention, however, that this is alien to the spirit of Marx's thought. On Lukàcs's position, see G. Ciccotti et al. (1976, p.228), H. Brinkmann (1978, p.133), and I. Craib (1977).

46 This is the reason, to agree with K. Liebknecht, of the Bible's 'incomparable influence' and not, as that author holds, its being a (perhaps misused) source of wisdom and moral force. See 1976, pp.276-7. The fact that religion will disappear only when its social causes will disappear, is clearly seen also by Durkheim (A. Giddens, 1972, p.221).

47 In chapter 4 we provide an analysis of why and how a certain social phenomenon, the nuclear family, is class determined, i.e. condition of domination of one class over the others, even though, and actually just because, it is imposed upon all classes.

48 See, for example, Engels's account of mathematics' social determination (1970, pp.45-7) and D. Bloor's convincing argument that mathematics is grounded in experience (1976, ch.6). This shows the incorrectness of the position of P. Raymond, for whom mathematics cannot be a science since it is not based upon observation (1978). However, Engels is concerned here not only with the social, instead of class, determination of mathematics but, as we have seen, he recognizes this determination only as far as its origin is concerned. A standard work on the social (economic) determination of science is J. Bernal (1976) which is, however, written from the standpoint of the neutrality of science (and productive forces). As M. Cini says (in G. Ciccotti et al., 1976, p.16), this is understandable if one considers the conditions of theoretical backwardness of the workers' movement in the post-Second World War period. This standpoint leads obviously to a search for alternative uses of a 'neutral' science rather than for an alternative science. It is M. Weber, rather than Marx, who subscribes to the neutrality of mathematics thesis. In 'The Protestant Ethic and the Spirit of Capitalism' (1958) he holds that the 'origin of mathematics and mechanics [was not] determined by capitalist interests. But the *technical* utilization of scientific knowledge ... was certainly encouraged by economic considerations, which were extremely favourable to it in the Occident' (pp.24-5). Even Maxwell's theory can be shown to be socially, class, determined. See A. Baracca and A. Rossi (1976, p.119), and C. de Marzo (1978).

49 This is T. Kuhn's mistake (1970), as correctly criticized by Starnberger Studien 1 (1978, pp.198-9). These authors' emphasis on the 'bleibende' elements of knowledge, however, is cast within the framework of the 'Finalisierung' theory which (a) examines only the conscious introduction of external purposes in the development of science through the working out of special, aim-oriented theories (E. Mendelsohn et al., 1977, p.220); (b) considers the orientation of science according to the

purposes of an undifferentiated society, rather than of groups
(classes) within it (Starnberger Studien 1, 1978, p.238); and
(c) restricts the influence of external factors only on the
post-paradigmatic phase. For a study inspired by this approach,
see H. Mehrtens and S. Richter (1980).

50 For an example in linguistics, see C. Luporini (1975, p.210).
J. Krige stresses the appearance of continuity in revolutionary
changes (1979, p.12). Notice that, for us, supersession is far
from being della Volpe's 'negation of the negative' and 'the
retaining of the positive' (1969, p.305).

51 Examples of historical researchs can be found in the works
mentioned in the footnote above. Examples closer to the present
approach because stressing the class determination of the
natural sciences are given by G. Ciccotti et al. (1976);
A. Baracca and A. Rossi (1976); A. Baracca and R. Livi (1976);
A. Baracca, A. Russo and S. Ruffo (1979); C. De Marzo (1978).
For a useful summary - in English - of some of these authors'
basic themes of research, see Baracca et al. (1980). See also
A. Baracca's Appendix to this book.

52 K. Marx and F. Engels (1970b, p.104). See also K. Marx (1967a,
p.79). Even though Engels and Marx offer deeper insights into
the DLI of Calvinism than M. Weber (1958), Gramsci follows the
latter rather than the former (1975b, p.1389 and p.1086) as
also C. Boggs notices (1976, p.43).

53 The specificity of the present approach is not the emphasis
placed upon the impossibility to perceive 'facts' outside of a
theoretical frame. Rather, we stress, first of all, the class
determination of the theoretical frame. Thus, if we chose a
simple fact, e.g. that water can be transformed into ice, it
is insufficient and ultimately incorrect to point out that
this 'fact' acquires a different meaning for a chemist than for
an ice-skater (W. van Dooren, 1977, p.7). Once more it is the
individual rather than the social class which is chosen as the
subject of knowledge.

54 The account that follows of the change in the interpretation
of 'one' relies basically on D. Bloor (1976, ch.6). Bloor's
account is based upon J. Klein (1968), which is difficult but
rewarding reading.

55 (1968, pp.46-8, emphasis removed.)

56 Bloor, 1976, p.106.

57 (1968, p.140, emphasis removed.)

58 For example, 'the number ten was related to health and cosmic
order'. See D. Bloor (1976, p.107).

59 J. Klein (1968, pp.64-7).

60 D. Bloor (1976, p.107).

61 Ibid., p.104.

62 J. Klein (1968, p.151).

63 Ibid., p.175.

64 See B. Hessen in N.I. Bucharin et al. (1971, pp.149-212).

65 See not 15 above.

66 As we will see in the next section.

67 J.S. Ackerman (1949, p.86).

68 See G. Böhme et al., in Starnberger Studien 1 (1978, p.342).

69 J.S. Ackerman (1949, p.105).

70 Ibid., p.104.
71 For another example see P. Forman (1979). On the different possible interpretations of 'facts' in economics, see G. Green and P. Nore (1979).
72 In turn, as we argue in this work, natural sciences' models are socially, class, determined. Let us make one more example: systems theory. Its social determination is clearly visible in its founding philosophical stone: the concept (as made explicit by Laszlo) that hierarchy is a universal principle 'operating in all realms: inorganic nature, organic life, social life, and the cosmos'. See R. Lilienfeld (1978, p.164). Because of the constant interplay of all the forms of knowledge (something which is dealt with in the following chapters), both natural and social sciences can 'borrow' interpretative schemes from each other.
73 This procedure is exactly the opposite of what is advocated here as being the only one consistent with Marxist methodology. Consider, for example, the capitalist economic structure. There exist only concrete realized types of the capitalist economic structure. We appropriate in thought these forms, these real concretes, and then, by abstracting from these concretes in thought the specific features of the stage of capitalist development to which they belong, we get another abstraction, still historically pregnant, valid for all stages of capitalism, thus too general for an analysis of any specific stage but containing in itself the basic, historically specific, contradictions, from the development of which the different concrete forms can be reconstructed in thought.
74 For a review of the several variations on this structural theme, see M. Glucksman (1974). See also N. Smith (1980) and H. Lefebvre (1971).
75 'Dialectics, the so-called *objective* dialectics, prevails through nature, and so-called subjective dialectics, dialectical thought, is only the reflection of the notion through opposites which assert itself everywhere in nature, and which by the continual conflict of the opposites and their final passage into another, or into higher forms, determines the life of nature' (1976, p.211).
76 Which is the view expounded by Various Authors (1979, p.71).
77 D. Lecourt (1977, p.142).
78 See no.18, pp.594-5 and no.20, pp.152-4.
79 See no.27, pp.235-77 and no.42, pp.68-84.
80 Concerning the superimposition of conjunctural elements (e.g. the need to increase production due to the danger of imperialist war) on the theoretical inadequacy of not only Lenin but the whole of the Bolschevik Party, see Marxistische Aufbauorganisation (1973, p.29).
81 R. Guastini, in Various Authors (1977, p.34).
82 A. Gramsci (1975a).
83 A. Gramsci (1971, p.301)
84 Different interpretations of Gramsci, of course, teem. See, for instance, G. Barletta (1978) and F. Fistetti (1977). According to T. Perlini (1974), Gramsci develops a neutralist conception of the forces of production only in the 'Prison

Notebooks'. But the glorification of 'modernization' is a
constant not only of Gramsci's thought but also of the development
of Marxism. For a recent example of this view, see S. Sayers
(1980). For a careful study of the acceptance of Taylorism by
Lenin and Gramsci, see R. Whitaker (1979). Whitaker's difference
with our treatment is one of emphasis, since we stress much more
the role played by the diffuse belief in the neutrality of science
and technology as a powerful factor explaining that acceptance.

85 It is perfectly possible to theorize this overdetermination and
deny at the same time the social determination of science. For
M. Weber, for example, natural sciences, and especially mathematics have an intrinsic and a-historical rationality. Western
capitalism's superiority as a social system is due to the
systematic application of these sciences for the calculability
of the most important technical factors. This application is
'encouraged' by the social structure of Western capitalism whose
essence therefore is rationality (1958, pp.24-5).

86 Here we will mention only those aspects necessary for our
argument and will disregard both the many positive aspects of
Sohn-Rethel's work and its criticizable points such as his
notions of exchange and social synthesis. Let us only mention
a few points. C. Knee (1979) is right in stressing (1) the
similarity between Durkheim's collective representations and
Sohn-Rethel's social synthesis (both of them are a-historical,
given objects of investigation) and, related to this, (2) the
peculiar type of reflection theory implied in Sohn-Rethel's
approach (the one-to-one correspondence between social synthesis
and forms of thought). To this we can add (1) that knowledge
is anchored in exchange rather than in production and (2) that
Sohn-Rethel's social synthesis is, in fact, a functionalist
concept strongly reminiscent of Durkheim's division of labour.
There is no room in Sohn-Rethel's account for a dialectical
relation between real concrete and concrete in thought, including
the possibility of contradiction between them. For a sympathetic,
yet critical review from a different angle, see M. Reinfelder
and P. Slater (1978).

87 At this level of abstraction this dichotomy coincides with the
owner/non-owner and the exploiter/exploited ones. This means
that at this level of abstraction the essential capitalist
dichotomy is the one between the non-owner of the means of
production, who thus has to labour (transform use values) for
the owners of the means of production, and these latter who are
non-labourers because they only control and supervise that
transformation (and thus the labourers) and appropriate the
fruits of it. See chapter 6, for a more detailed discussion.

88 In chapter 5 we stress the radical difference between the mental/
manual dichotomy, which is irreconcilable with Marxism, and the
material/mental dichotomy which is a part of it.

89 In chapter 4 we elaborate on the possibility of the labourer's
producing his own view of social reality, in opposition to the
view developed by the non-labourer.

90 As we will see in chapter 5, the nature of non-labour, its being
material or mental derives from the nature of the labour
supervised. Today, the production of knowledge is organized along

lines similar to material transformation, i.e. with the necessary presence of supervisors.

91 Of course, in the present stage of capitalist development it is the computer which is the protagonist for the introduction of the capitalist division of labour also as far as mental labour is concerned. See on this point M. Cooley, (1981).

92 M. Cooley (1981, p.45).

93 Sohn-Rethel (1978, p.183).

94 N. Kapferer, in Slater (1980), p.93.

95 P.92. Kapferer refers here to Taylorism, but we think that this is an excellent description of the way (capitalist) technology fosters the domination of capital over labour.

96 On this point, see M. Reinfelder's Introduction to P. Slater (ed.), (1980).

97 In P. Slater (ed.) (1980, p.54).

98 As R. Coombs notes, the capitalist relations of production impose a certain 'pattern' on the capitalist productive forces. See 1978, p.94.

99 See G. Lukàcs (1971, p.36).

100 Thus accepting, as H. Brinkmann points out, the Widerspiegelungstheorie. See 1978, p.133.

101 G. Ciccotti et al. (1979, p.228).

102 N. Poulantzas stresses a similar and related point in his criticism of Fascism's characterization as 'retrograde' and of the technicist and economicist view of the capitalist productive forces in the Third International. See 1974a, pp.98-100.

103 As L. Maitan correctly reminds us. See 1977, p.47.

104 August-September, 1977. For a variation on this theme, see G.A. Cohen, 'Karl Marx's Theory of History: a Defence', as correctly criticized by E.O. Wright and A. Levine, 1980.

105 This is in broad lines the view which prevails among the intellectuals who gravitate around the Italian Communist Party and which is, in fact, functional for this Party's reformist political practice. See A. Gioannini (1978, p.18 and p.20).

106 An obviously class determined definition of rationality.

107 Concrete utopias are not whims of imagination nor do they simply express the needs of groups or classes. These needs are expressions of objectively determined, class determined contradictions. It is the elaboration of this last point which has been attempted in this chapter and which lacks in otherwise stimulating writings such as Various Authors (1980).

APPENDIX - ON THE DEVELOPMENT OF PHYSICS AND CHEMISTRY AT THE TURN OF THE NINETEENTH CENTURY: EXAMPLES OF A HISTORICAL MATERIALIST ANALYSIS

* The author is indebted to Dr Karl Figlio for useful comments and to him and Miss Caroline Meehan for help in the revision of the English form of the manuscript: nevertheless they do not share any responsibility for its content.

1 The distinction between social and natural sciences would merit a deeper consideration. We shall not analyse this problem here, but shall take the distinction as given in an intuitive way. For

a treatment of this problem, see chapter 2 of the present book.

2 It is not my aim here to analyse more carefully how science has been considered by all the Marxist currents: I consider basically correct the judgment that the problem of the natural sciences has been disregarded in the Marxist thought and that the possibility of a deeper influence of social events, which we shall instead consider here, has been substantially excluded.

3 For a critical evaluation from our point of view of the modern trends in the epistemological analyses see Ciccotti and Jona Lasinio (1973); Rossi (1975 and 1977a).

4 The quantity of motion is the product of mass and velocity. The vis viva is instead the product of mass and the square of velocity (the double of modern kinetic energy $T = \frac{1}{2}mv^2$). Now it turns out that what is linked to the execution of mechanical work – the product of the force acting on the system and the displacement produced (scalar product) – is just the kinetic energy: the increase of kinetic energy is equal to the work done (the exact relation introduces the factor $\frac{1}{2}$ which was absent from the abstract definition of the vis viva).

5 Power is the work (see note 4) done in the unit of time. It characterizes most properly the productivity of a machine.

6 Since in the example there is no moving force, there is clearly no work done in the above sense and that of note 4. The concept disregarded such energy processes, conforming to the aim of treating rigorously only those energy processes which could produce and, consequently, involve a moving force.

7 In modern terms the first process is interpreted as transformation of potential energy into mechanical work, while the second one is at first the transformation of potential energy into kinetic energy in the free fall of water and then the transformation of kinetic energy into mechanical work in the shock of water on the paddles: the last transformation could be complete only if the shock were completely elastic.

8 Temperature is simply a state index, whose change is caused by the exchange of a quantity of heat, which is instead a physical quantity. The same quantity of heat causes different temperature changes in different bodies: specific heat is the quantity of heat necessary to raise the temperature of a unit mass of a substance by one degree centigrade. In changes of state, temperature remains constant: the transferred heat is spent in the change of state, and the latent heat is defined as the quantity of heat exchanged by the unit mass.

9 This formulation is that every heat engine needs at least two heat supplies at different temperatures; it absorbs heat from the hotter one, it transforms into work a part of it and gives back the remaining part to the colder one. In the old Newcomen engine both the expansion and the condensation of vapour took place in the same container. Watt saw that, in order to reduce the waste of vapour, the container should have been hot during the expansion and cold during condensation: he thus posed the necessity of having two separate containers, one hot for expansion (the engine cylinder) and the other cold for condensation (the separate condenser, his invention). He thus recognized explicitly the necessity of two heat supplies.

10 These two processes need not, in principle, be related. The first is analogous to the free fall of water, the second one to water descending slowly while accompanying the paddles and thus producing work: in the case of water, the connection is established by the principle of mechanical energy conservation. For heat, the connection is made explicit by Watt's procedure and finally established by the two laws of thermodynamics.

11 Thermodynamical work, in the simplified case of a change ΔV in volume at constant pressure P, is defined as $L = P \cdot \Delta V$. Its formal equivalence with the concept of mechanical work as the product of the force F and the displacement d may be seen if one remembers that pressure is the force divided by the area, $P = F/A$, and the change in volume is the area times the displacement, $\Delta V = A \cdot d$, so that the thermodynamical work becomes $L = F \cdot A \cdot d/A = F \cdot d$.

12 The second law of thermodynamics establishes the expression for the efficiency of a perfect (Carnot) engine and the fact that every real heat engine working between the given temperatures has a lower efficiency. A mathematical development of this conclusion allows the introduction of a state function, called entropy, whose value grows in every irreversible process (this is a consequence of the abovementioned difference in efficiency between real engines – using irreversible transformations – and perfect engines – using instead reversible transformations), while it remains constant in reversible ideal processes.

13 Not every reaction between molecules A and B, leading to molecules C and D proceeds, in fixed thermodynamic conditions (values of temperature and pressure), until the exhaustion of the initial substances A and B. In fact, the final molecules C and D react among themselves and give back the initial molecules. The rates of the two opposite processes depend on the concentrations of the molecular species. When the velocities of the two processes become equal, the reaction clearly does not proceed further from a macroscopic point of view. One says that chemical equilibrium has been reached in the reaction indicated as:

$$A + B \rightleftharpoons C + D.$$

Guldberg and Waage's approach was based on the evaluation of the velocities of the two opposed processes on the basis of the frequency of the collisions between the reacting molecules: such rates clearly had to be proportional to the concentrations of the molecular species.

14 This led to the introduction of the state functions called Helmholtz's and Gibbs's free energy functions – respectively $F = U - TS$ and $G = U - TS + PV$. These functions were called also 'thermodynamical potentials', a name that betrayed the still dominant mechanistic attitude.

15 For example, the probability of a macroscopic system (composed of N molecules at temperature T in a container of volume V) having a given value $E(g, p)$ of total energy (that depends obviously by the canonical co-ordinates q and p of its constituent molecules) is given by the so-called canonical ensemble

$$\exp \left\{ \frac{F(N, V, T) - E(g, p)}{kT} \right\}$$

and the normalization function F is the free energy $F = U - TS$ of the system.

16 Such a body is defined as one which completely absorbs the electromagnetic radiation falling on its surface. The frequency spectrum of the radiation it has to emit for thermodynamic equilibrium cannot be determined on thermodynamic or electromagnetic grounds alone. Planck made first a definite hypothesis on the expression of the entropy of the system, and then tried to justify the result with the quantum hypothesis.

2   SOCIAL PHENOMENA AND SOCIAL LAWS

1 Or non-reflective materialism. For the reason why and conditions under which these two terms can be used interchangeably, see my Class Analysis and the Study of Social Forms, in G. Morgan (ed.), 'Beyond Method: A Study of Social Research Strategies', forthcoming. See also further on in this section.
2 K. Popper (1965, p.74).
3 As R. Bhaskar cogently remarks, on this view no real differences can be discerned between the activities of scientists and of 'bigamists, bimentallists and people whose surname begins with "P"' (1979, p.4).
4 B. Magee (1973, p.9).
5 Popper thus reduces epistemology to one of its aspects, the testing of hypotheses, which moreover is reduced to falsifiability. As B. Barnes says, 'all the interesting epistemological questions are pushed out of sight' (1974, p.25).
6 K. Popper (1972, p.55).
7 As G. Lukács says, 'the objective forms of all social phenomena change constantly in the course of their ceaseless dialectical interaction with each other' (1971, p.13).
8 Contrary to R. Keat and J. Urry, we do not think the reconciliation of 'reciprocal interaction and functional interdependence on the one hand, and the dominance of the economic on the other' to be problematic (1975, p.103).
9 G. Lukács (1971, p.13).
10 A point stressed also by M. Zeitlin (1980, p.2). However, this author collapses logical into historical analysis (p.3).
11 J.P. Cot and J.P. Monnier (1974, p.26). The authors, however, use the term 'social facts', strongly reminiscent of E. Durkheim's concept and thus of its idealist and empiricist context. See, for example (1966, ch.1). For a critique, see E. Hahn and F. Haug (1971, ch.1).
12 Notice that the notion of social determination here is used in quite a different way than in chapter 1. There, social determination was set off against class determination and referred to the determination of phenomena (knowledge) by a society conceived of as non-class-divided. Here, and in the rest of this book, social determination is used as a short-cut to refer to the determination of phenomena within a context of complex dialectical determination in which contradictory structures and thus classes are the founding, determining elements.
13 We are thus miles away from the identification of objectivity in

science with correct reflection of the real concrete, a view
which implies that subjectivity becomes a source of mistake!
See G. Assmann et al. (1978, pp.461-2).

14 See M.H. Dowidar (1974, p.5).

15 1970, p.38.

16 Each society has not only the basic, i.e. determinant, production,
etc. relations and their forms but also other types of economic
relations. See C. Meillassoux (1972, p.98). In capitalist
societies all types of social relations are determined by the
capitalist economic ones, i.e. are conditions of the latter's
reproduction or supersession. This holds also for previous types
of social (and thus also economic) relations: they either
disappear or survive but modified because conditions of existence
of the determinant social relations. Therefore the capitalist
economic structure is given not only by the capitalist economic
relations, but also by all other types of economic relations
determined by the former in their reciprocal relation of
determination. For an example of how Lenin analysed the economic
structure of the Soviet Union in 1921, see 'Collected Works',
no.32, pp.295-6.

17 The example of production relations is discussed later on.

18 However, the same problem arises; once we introduce the difference
between 'materie' and 'Stoff'. There is no philosophical
definition of 'Stoff' in Korsch's work.

19 The distinction between laws of development (Entwicklungsgesetzen)
and structural laws (Strukturgesetzen) reproduces within Marxism
the artificial separation between laws of statics and laws of
dynamics. M. Neumann's attempt to salvage this distinction is
not convincing. See M. Neumann (1976, pp.25-7).

20 Some such laws mentioned by Marx are: the law of the fall of
the rate of profit, the law of capital concentration and centralization, the law of the reduction of complex to simple labour,
the law of the devaluation of labour power, of the production
for profit, etc.

21 As Hans-Holger Paul remarks: 'Unter "naturgesetzen" sind hier
nicht fälschlicherweise die Resultate der Naturwissenschaften
zu begreifen, sondern die Gesetze der Kapitalistischen Produktion,
die sich hinter dem Rücken der Privatproduzenten durchsetzen'
(1978, p.192).

22 K. Marx, Results of the immediate process of production, in
A. Dragstedt (1976, p.83).

23 K. Marx to L. Kugelmann in Hanover, 11 July 1868, in K. Marx
and F. Engels (1969b, pp.418-19).

24 Thus we can agree with R. Keat and J. Urry that for Marx there
are no 'natural economic laws which are applicable to all
societies' only if by natural economic laws we understand their
(inevitable) social translation due to the nature of a certain,
socially and historically determined, system. See 1975, p.99.

25 We can thus say that the capitalist production process can be
regarded as a labour process, when the production of use values
is considered; and as a surplus value producing process, when
the production of exchange values and thus of surplus value is
considered. It is in this sense that the capitalist production
process can be defined as the unity in determination of the labour

process and of the surplus value producing process. See K. Marx, 1967a, and A. Dragstedt (1976).

26 K. Marx, to L. Kugelmann in Hanover in Marx and Engels (1969, p.419).

27 Loc. cit.

28 The 'mode of appearance' of the natural law has changed but the natural law continues to operate. It is therefore quite mistaken to hold that 'Capital cannot accept this reference to another text, to the Critique [of the Gotha Programme]'. A. Cutler et al. (1977, p.33). The two texts are part of the same theoretically consistent system.

29 1969, p.273.

30 K. Marx to L. Kugelmann in Hanover, in Marx and Engels (1969, p.419).

31 The reason for this will be given in the next section.

32 K. Marx (1967a, p.632).

33 Ibid., p.633.

34 Ibid., p.630.

35 Ibid., p.633.

36 Loc. cit.

37 Ibid., p.637.

38 1977, p.158.

39 L. Althusser and E. Balibar (1970, p.287).

40 1973, p.11.

41 If, as Althusser holds in 'Reading Capital', something exists only in its effects, if it is 'nothing outside its effects' (1970, p.189), can we still adjudicate separate existence to that which exists only in its effects? One would be inclined to consider this distinction as completely artificial. On the other hand, if such separate existence must be maintained (failure to maintain this separation opens the doors to empiricism), knowledge of the effects is not obviously knowledge of their cause. (Knowledge of the former is, however, very important in order to be able to infer 'the existence of causal agents' R. Bhaskar (1978, p.180).) Electricity cannot be seen, its effects can. But knowledge of the latter is not yet knowledge of the former. Similarly, we cannot see social structure, but we can see its effects. For example, for Balibar, 'L'analyse historique des classes sociales n'est rien d'autre que l'analyse des luttes de classes et de leurs effets' (1974, p.47). Yet, along this way, we will not be able to discover the social structure itself. Thus, J. Rancière is correct in stressing that 'the analysis of Althusser and Poulantzas ultimately result in a truism: the structure is defined by no more than its own opacity, manifested in its effects. In a work, it is the opacity of the structure which renders the structure opaque' (1974, p.13).

42 1964, p.29. For a discussion of this point of Weber's theory, see, for instance, A. Weights (1978, pp.56-73).

43 1964, pp.107-108.

44 1974, p.179.

45 Loc. cit.

46 It is in this sense that we can say that science is both descriptive (in the sense of analysis) and constructive of

reality and not in a phenomenological sense. This holds not only for social but also for natural reality since nature too is changed by human praxis. However, natural laws are not changed.

47 Thus, R. Bhaskar is correct in stressing that 'conjunctions of events [are] social products' and that 'for the transcendental realist laws, though not our knowledge of them, are categorically independent of men' (1978, p.57 and p.59). But, this applies only to the natural world. In the social world, laws are dependent upon men as classes. And it is precisely this, the class vantage point, that draws the fundamental demarcation line between R. Bhaskar's transcendental realism and a Marxist account of science. A detailed comparison between these two approaches follows in the next section.

48 Our discussion of the specificity of social phenomena justifies that 'puzzling' feature of Marxist methodology which H.V. McLachlan calls 'ontological pluralism' and which he would like to see 'eradicated' (1980, pp.66-77), probably in order to replace it with a view of Marxism based on formal logic.

49 This is an example of non-antagonistic contradiction as discussed in the last section of chapter 1.

50 This mistaken view can be found also in chapter 2 of my 'On the Economic Identification of Social Classes' (1977).

51 Another example: the tendency to dequalify (and thus to devalue) labour power and the countertendential creation of new qualified positions (jobs) as a result of the introduction of new technologies within the production process. See G. Carchedi (1977, chapters 1 and 4) and chapter 5 of this book.

52 See, for an analysis of these different forms, E. Mandel (1975).

53 R. Panzieri, Surplus Value and Planning: notes on the reading of 'Capital', "Various Authors" (1976, p.21).

54 Ibid.

55 Ibid.

56 'Science', vol.III (1950, pp.23-9), reprinted in F.E. Emery (1981), vol.1, pp.82-9.

57 Emery (1981, p.69).

58 For a critical discussion of the adoption of systems thinking by other disciplines, see R. Lilienfeld (1978).

59 Op. cit., p.83.

60 For two such attempts, see the reviews by P. Halfpenny (1980), and H. Radder (1980).

61 Similar, in fact, to Marx's concrete-in-thought and real concrete. See, for instance 'Grundrisse' (1973).

62 See, for instance, R. Bhaskar (1975).

63 1978, ch.1; Radder (1980).

64 'Law like statements ... make a claim about the activity of a tendency, i.e. about the operation of the generative mechanism that would, if undisturbed, result in the tendency's manifestation' (1978, p.98).

65 Contrary to Bhaskar's opinion. See (1978, p.231).

66 1978, p.119.

67 The arbitrariness of the distinction between different systems is clear. On the other hand, on a dialectical view rooted in the concept of social class the different areas of social phenomena (and thus the different social sciences, or sub-systems,

if you want) can be discerned because they are different types of class domination.

68 Moreover, as T. Benton (1981) correctly stresses, it is doubtful 'whether decisive tests of theory are possible in the natural sciences either' (1981, p.18).

69 Bhaskar (1978, p.98).

70 However, Bhaskar's closed systems are not ideal constructs but are real concretes.

71 1979, p.82.

72 P.90. It is the theoricism inherent in this position that R. Albury, G. Payne and W. Suchting rightly criticize (1981).

73 As Bhaskar himself mentions, without, however, drawing the same conclusions. See (1978), pp.104-5.

74 Not by chance in von Bertalanffy's article appear 'Physics' and 'Biology' in the title.

75 Let me stress that Bhaskar does not conflate the social and the natural sciences. He uses the open/closed system device to argue for the existence of generating mechanisms in both the natural and the social world (and it is in this sense that he extends a scheme derived from the natural sciences, from a certain type of natural science, to all science) as well as for an inquiry in the differences between these two basic types of science. In fact, Bhaskar recognizes that social phenomena cannot be studied under conditions of closed systems and actually this is for him one of the essential differences between social and natural sciences. However, he concludes from this the non-predictability in the former sciences (as opposed to the possibility of complete predictions in the latter sciences). See above and also: On the Possibility of Social Scientific Knowledge and the Limits of Naturalism', J. Mepham and D.-H. Ruben (1979, pp.127 and ff). My conclusion, on the other hand, is that, if you extend a scheme developed (for specific, historically determined and, to begin with, economic reasons) in certain branches of the natural sciences to the social sciences, then you not only implicitly assign a secondary status to the latter (where by definition closures are not possible) but in fact subordinate your conception (definition) of social science to a conception of natural science based upon an inherently a-dialectical and implicitly conservative hinge. These features will then re-emerge in your theorization of the social sciences.

76 1978, p.111.

77 It might be worth mentioning that in systems theory the often hidden connection among the different systems is of a hierarchical nature. See R. Lilienfeld (1978, p.164). It is at such theoretical junctures that the conservative nature of systems theory comes to the fore.

78 1978, p.166. Therefore, the application of a theory rather than another to explain the latent structure of nature becomes a matter of individual preferences. See On the Possibility of Social Scientific Knowledge and the Limits of Naturalism, in Mepham and Ruben (1979).

79 1978, p.148.

80 Ibid.

81 Ibid.
82 A conclusion strongly denied by Bhaskar but reached also by T.Benton
    (1981, p.17) even though along a different line of critique.
83 'Sociology is ... concerned ... with the persistent *relations*
    between individuals (and groups) and with the relations between
    these relations. Relations such as between capitalist and worker,
    MP and constituent, student and teacher, husband and wife' (in
    Mepham and Ruben, 1979, p.113). If we cannot abstract things
    from the relations in which they stand with each other (metaphysics),
    we cannot abstract relations from the things they relate either.
    If society studies, to begin with, the relations between
    individuals, it is these latter (and not classes as groups of
    individuals essentially different from the individuals themselves)
    who, in Bhaskar's view, are the basic unit of social life and
    thus of social analysis.
84 (1982).
85 1980, p.23.
86 1978, p.24.

3 ON THE PROCESS OF MENTAL TRANSFORMATION

1 Which seems to be Althusser's position as criticized by R. Keat
   and J. Urry (1975, p.135).
2 Which is R. Keat and J. Urry's (1975) position.
3 K. Marx, 1973, pp.100-1.
4 Those who deny this simple truth, as Althusser and all those
   who follow his epistemology, cannot thus but fall into idealism.
   See also I. Lakato's statement to the effect that 'there is no
   natural (i.e. psychological) demarcation between observational
   and theoretical propositions' (I. Lakatos and A. Mustrave, 1970,
   p.99).
5 V.I. Lenin, no.14, p.55.
6 P. Feyerabend (1975), p.168.
7 Only those who make of theoretical activity their only activity
   can forget the role participation in class struggle plays in
   influencing observation and thus mental production. Lenin, on
   the other hand, always stressed the importance of keeping in
   touch with the masses. See, for example, no.33, p.39.
8 In spite of the obvious differences with positivists, 'old' and
   'modern' alike, Popper (1959, pp.34-5) shares with them the
   belief that facts exist outside theory, that the task of the
   latter is to discover the former, and that the former are the
   test of the latter (p.27). But both the inductive positivist
   and the deductive Popperian are idealists.
9 This approach emphasizes the importance for conception of the
   mental producers' participation in all forms and types of class
   struggle and not only in the ideological class struggle.
10 For an example of the difficulties implied in the failure to
   make this distinction, in the specific case of Althusser, see
   P. Patton, 1978, pp.8-18.
11 The real concrete is always overdetermined by previous mental
   products through class struggle, as we will see in the next
   section.

12 Thus the question 'Which comes first, the hypothesis (H) or the observation (O)' which, according to Popper must be answered as 'an earlier kind of hypothesis' (1965, p.47) is a wrong question. New knowledge arises from both hypotheses and observations.

13 The stress on the role of observation for the production of new knowledge might appear to cause serious difficulties at least in the case of mathematics. P. Raymond (1978, pp.59 and ff.) attempts an answer by splitting 'le texte mathématique' into the 'mathématique', i.e. theory, and the 'mathématisé', i.e. reality. However, this latter is, for Raymond, the 'réalité symbolique et non purement sensible', i.e. for this author symbols become reality. But since no decree will ever change a mental abstraction into the reality which is its substratum, the 'mathématisé' remains a concrete in thought, just as the 'mathématique'. We submit that in mathematics the imagined concrete, and thus the need felt to develop mathematics in a certain, socially determined, direction is provided by other sciences, e.g. physics, etc., or even economics. It is because of this that mathematics lacks 'materiality', but it is also because of this that its conception can be used by, and embodied in, other sciences. Thus mathematics is neither the method, nor the language of science. This hypothesis is consistent with our theory, to be discussed in chapter 4, that in every science it is possible to distinguish between practical and theoretical knowledge and that while the former can be subjected to practical and logical verification, the latter can be subjected only to logical verification. In our opinion, mathematics is an exception, it is the only science lacking practical knowledge and is thus subjectable only to logical verification. Mathematics is subjected to practical verification only indirectly, through the verification of the sciences which must tackle practical problems, for the solution of which they need new developments in mathematics. When new developments in the real concrete, and especially in the economic, impose a radical turn to the more 'practical' sciences, then new developments will follow in mathematics as well. It is these sciences' imagined concrete which enter mathematics as incorporated in the 'practical' sciences' theoretical problems. Section 5 of chapter 1 has provided an example. To provide one more example: Colman considers $\text{Lim} \ (1 + \frac{1}{n})^n = 2.71828$ 'which arose from historical requirements of overseas trade, from the need to create, for practical calculations, the most suitable logarithmic tables. Therefore the answer to the question why this limit e and no other is dealt with, is given not by mathematics, but by history'. See N.I. Bucharin et al. (1971).

14 See chapter 2 and chapter 5 of this book.

15 K. Marx (1969c, p.285).

16 H. Brinkmann errs thus in defining use value everything which serves to reach a certain aim and not only objects which serve for immediate material consumption (1978, p.122). The extension of the concept of use value to non-material, i.e. mental, use values is correct, but it goes too far because, as it is usually the case in works on Marxist philosophy, philosophical questions are completely separated from social analysis. This, however, is not Marx's legacy.

17 K Marx (1973, p.101).
18 Notice that more or less contemporaneous with Popper's theory
of knowledge without a knowing subject is Althusser's theory of
history without a subject, an equally absurd conclusion. For a
similar opinion, see P. Patton (1978, p.10). For the revisionist
background and implications of the concept of 'progress without
a subject', see A. Badiou (1975, pp.54-61). For a critique of
Althusser complementary to the present one, see P. Binns (1973,
pp. 3-9 and 1974, pp. 30-3).
19 A. Sohn-Rethel falls into the same mistake, strongly reminiscent
of the bourgois theory of investment in human capital: '... these
means of production, both material and men' (1978, p. 129). For
Marx, the consumption by the worker of his means of subsistence
is unproductive since it takes place outside of the production
process, since it is the reproduction of his labour power. If
men were means of production, the consumption of their means of
subsistence would become productive. In Althusser's basically
structuralist universe, the roles are reversed: the agents of
mental production become means of mental production and vice
versa.
20 We use the expression 'level and development of the productive
forces' instead of 'level of development of the productive
forces' to emphasize the quantitative (level of productivity of
labour) and the qualitative (social nature, i.e. class determination) aspect of the productive forces.

4 VERIFICATION, OR EPISTEMOLOGY AND THE FUNCTION OF CAPITAL

1 See, for example, D.W. Hamlyn (1970, pp.117 and ff.).
2 On this point, see K. Marx (1973): 'In this way Hegel fell into
the illusion of conceiving the real as product of thought' (p.101).
3 The great revival of idealism takes the form in England, among
other things, of the denial of epistemology, of which Hindess,
and co-thinkers (Cutler et al., 1977) are a telling example. A
sharp and convincing critique of their position can be found in
T. Skillen (1978, pp.3-8). Apart from the many well-taken
points, we cannot but agree that 'it is handy ... to think that,
outside one's own system, no justification need to be sought for
one's beliefs and one's practices'. See also in the same issue,
A. Collier (1978, pp.8-21).
4 1969a, p.15.
5 Hamlyn too rejects all these alternatives. For him, the
criterion of truth is 'intersubjective agreement'. That is, 'if
people agree on a matter it is to be expected [why?] that what
they say will normally be true' (1970, p.142). Without clarity
on who 'people' are (the totality? the majority? a group? a
class? etc.), Hamlyn's criterion is at best useless. It is
often, and correctly, pointed out that social scientists lack
the necessary philosophical basis. Hamlyn is an example of a
philosopher whom an elementary training in the social sciences
could spare some unnecessary blunders.
6 Given that such a change is perceived through observation and
given that this latter is sensory perception filtered through

previous knowledge and participation in the class struggle, such
a change need not be a real change but can also be the changed
observation of the same real concrete due to the fact that
developments in the class struggle can impose upon us a changed
perspective. This will be the vantage point of the next section.

7   The existence of a structured real concrete is a consequence of
the position put forward here which implies that each class
definable in terms of production relations produces an independent
view (which, as we will see soon, is not, however, separated from
other classes' view) of the real concrete and that (something to
be shown shortly) only one class has the objective possibility
to know that reality (i.e. all of it) correctly. We have here
neither empirical realism (because of the role of knowledge not
reducible to pure experience) nor transcendental idealism
(since the real concrete is not a construction of human mind).
But we do not have here transcendental realism either because –
as we have seen in chapter 2 – there is no theorization in this
latter of what R. Bhaskar calls the open system and which we call
the unity in determination of the several instances of society
in which the economic has the determinant role in the last
instance.

8   Kuhn's opinion that 'the very idea of scientific knowledge as a
private product presents the same intrinsic problems as the
notion of a private language' (in Lakatos and Musgrave (eds),
1970, p.253) echoes Marx's opinion on the social nature of
language and thus of knowledge. As Bucharin has put it
'epistemological Robinson Crusoes are just as much out of place
as Robinson Crusoes were in the "atomistic" social science of
the eighteenth century'. See, for a position similar to the
one expounded here, R. Bhaskar (1978, p.147).

9   Quite clearly, then, our concept of verification has nothing
to do with M. Weber's 'Verification of subjective interpretation
by comparison with the concrete course of events' (1968, vol.1,
pp.9–11).

10 Ciccotti et al. see the difference between the Marxist concept
of practice as the test of theory and pragmatism in that the
former refers to the 'social individual' while the latter refers
to the isolated individual (see 1976, p.107). That it is
classes which decide the correctness of a theory is indeed a
fundamental tenet of Marxism. But this principle is not enough
to depurate Marxism of pragmatism since, taken in itself, it
cannot account for the fact that even the test performed by
'social man' can fail and that this failure does not necessarily
condemn that theory.

11 K. Marx and F. Engels (1970b, p.101).

12 But the bundle is far from being easily disentangled, given the
presence in Engels of elements of the reflection theory.

13 Here we meet again B. Hindess, P. Hirst, etc., still spinning
the old (this time Kantian) yarn. According to these gentlemen,
there is no way we can demonstrate that objects are appropriable
in discourse (see A. Cutler et al., 1977, p.216). Strange
Marxists, these gentlemen, who do not see that Engels's answer
makes agnostic doubts redundant. But, again, this is not the
only point of their work which is redundant.

14 'Collected Works', no.14, pp.142-3.

15 J. Ree is correct in stressing the social determination of Mao's emphasis on the criterion that correct ideas come from social practice. In fact, Mao's essays are the expression of the need the Chinese Communist Party had for greater freedom to learn from its own practice (to solve its own peculiar problems) rather than from the philosophical dogmas of the Soviet school. This is why they rely on Lenin, because they want to stress the peculiarity of particular contradictions (i.e. the Chinese Revolution) (1976). We do not agree, however, with Ree's degradation of Mao's essays practically to exercises in political propaganda. Mao's emphasis on the particularity of contradictions is brought to the fore also by M. Castells and E. de Epola (1970, pp.111-44). However, these authors are unclear about the difference between Mao's concept of practice and pragmatism even though, or perhaps because, they use the former to fight the latter.

16 1966, pp.135-6.

17 Similarly, L. Geymonat's point that Marxist practice is not pragmatism because the former is only a 'criterion of confirmation' of truth is, of course, correct but insufficient for practical purposes. For Geymonat, the two fundamental elements of a theory are coherence and correspondence (practice being only a criterion of confirmation), where the former seems to be the most important (1973, pp.178-94). Is this not as far from Lenin's epistemology (in spite of Geymonat's intentions) as idealism is from materialism?

18 1971, p.XIX. The point of view of the totality is not the exclusive appanage of Marxism. For a lucid and penetrating comparison between Marxist and functionalist holism, see A.G. Frank (1969, pp.95-107). However, we do not agree with that author that 'in Marxist theory change [is] the source of the social structure'. For us, the opposite is true, provided class struggle is organically integrated in the explanatory scheme.

19 1977, p.31.

20 D. Lecourt's claim that Lenin granted 'an undoubted *privilege* то *failure* over success' seems to us to go too far. Moreover, when one attempts an explanation of the relative autonomy of theory from practice by 'thinking them as a *process* in which the time of verification plays an essential part' thus disengaging them 'from the arbitrary immediacy which can sanctify any imposture', one has in fact not moved any further than the vagueness typical of much philosophy (1977, p.107).

21 I. Craib (1977).

22 Something which, needless to say, has nothing in common with Popperian falsificationism, whether sophisticated or not.

23 'Durch die Arbeit konstituiert das Subject die Welt seiner Erfahrungen und zugleich sich selbst als Subject dieser Erfarungen' (U. Volmerg, Zum Verhältnis von Produktion und Sozialisation am Beispiel industrieller Lohnarbeit, in T. Leithäuser and W.R. Heinz, 1976, p.107).

24 U. Cerroni rightly criticizes Althusser's 'peculiar conclusion' to the effect that Marxism is not false consciousness but scientific ideology simply because it is the ideology of a 'progressive and not-exploiting class' (1978, pp. 107 and ff.).

As Althusser puts it, 'it is only from the point of view of class exploitation that it is possible to *see* and analyse the mechanism of a class society and therefore to produce knowledge of it' ('Lenin and Philosophy', quoted in M. Gluckmann, 1974, p.125). There is no reason why the exploited class should be, because exploited, the depository of true, correct knowledge.

25 For an analysis of the capitalist production process, see Carchedi (1977) and chapter 5 of this book. Cerroni, however, is as silent as Althusser on the question as to why should the proletariat be structurally able to produce correct knowledge. And this silence is not accidental, because of the theoretical limits imposed by the myths (accepted by Cerroni) of the neutrality of science, i.e. because of the blindness to the fact that knowledge is class-determined and that therefore bourgeois knowledge (culture) is such because rooted into the interests of the bourgeoisie. For Cerroni, 'the working class ... ripens a completely new and "rich" classism which is able to take advantage of the universalism inherent in *any* cultural and scientific product' (1978, p.141, emphasis added). As to his charge that to deny the neutrality of science leads to individualism, sociology of knowledge, and social psychology (pp.114–16), this book's aim is to show that these are the consequences of precisely the opposite position.

26 Thus it is not 'reality' which deceives the subject, as Godelier submits and as R. Bhaskar approvingly repeats (1979, p.88), but the subject, the class, which is structurally either able or not to know reality. If reality (structures) secretes ideology, who (and why, and how) can tear its veil? Who can transform ideology into science? Structuralist Marxism cannot answer this question because of its failure to integrate organically the Marxist tenet that it is classes which perform the transformation. Here Bhaskar treads in the Althusserian footsteps.

27 Independent peasants and artisans own their means of production but their position of subordination vis-à-vis the capitalist mode of production and thus the bourgeoisie does not allow them to develop their own vision of the natural world.

28 1980, p.465.

29 Let us emphasize that what follows is not a discussion of ideology. Rather, its aim is to found an epistemology and thus a methodology of social inquiry on the concept of class. What follows therefore neither reviews past and present discussion on ideology nor submits a theory of its content, characteristics, and formation even though these topics will be touched upon from time to time. Our aim is to show the relevance of class for an analysis of social phenomena, even of those phenomena which would seem not to be class determined, as, for example, the nuclear family. In a sense, therefore, our attempt runs parallel to works such as E.O. Wright (1979), where the relevance of class for an analysis of income determination is shown. For our difference with Wright's approach, see our review in 'Science and Society', Fall, 1981.

30 Common to all structuralists is their inability to account for the supersession of the determinant instance (this is so also for Foucault (see 1969) something which H. Lefebvre has aptly called

'system fetishism' (1971, p.107). Typical of their approach is also what the same author has called a 'future without history' (p.16) where only different combinations of the same elements are allowed. Lefebvre points out also, correctly, that in structuralism one can detect the hidden model of a cybernetic system. For us, on the other hand, complex determination is not a cybernetic model because, even though there is action and reaction (determination and overdetermination) among different elements, our model is not based upon reciprocal interaction among history-less, already existing, elements but on the epistemological calling into existence of some elements by other elements as a consequence of the fact that classes tend to create the conditions of their domination.

31 Various Authors, 1979, p.20.

32 See on this point U. Troitzsch, Technikgeschichte in der Forschung und in der Sachbuchliteratur während des Nationasozialismus, in H. Mehrtens and S. Richter (1980, p.216).

33 Thus, as C.J. Cuneo argues, the introduction of the unemployment insurance in Canada (in 1941, along the lines of the Act of 1935), a demand of the working class, was accepted and transformed by the state into a condition of the reproduction of the capitalist system, not only by favouring a contributory unemployment insurance (according to Cuneo the demand for a non-contributory unemployment insurance could have had in the Depression, revolutionary consequences) but also by protecting in fact the employees against future unemployment rather than the chronically unemployed, thus completely isolating the latter (potentially, then, the most revolutionary part of the working class). In this way the most conservative sector of the working class was separated from the most revolutionary one and won to the support of the system (1980, pp.37-65). Another example: the way in which the US Department of Labour, a response to the American working class's demand, was 'carefully stripped of any radical content'. N. DiTomaso, Class Politics and Public Bureaucracy: The U.S. Department of Labour, in M. Zeitlin (ed.) (1980, pp. 135-52).

34 Thus the two conditions for the incorporation of elements of another knowledge into a receiving body of knowledge, if the class character of the latter must be retained, are that the foreign elements are not in antagonistic contradiction (they are not expressions of antagonistic contradiction in the real concrete at the structural level) and that they are depurated of their foreign class character. Thus, knowledge can 'be accepted and remain the same'. But I. Craib is correct in stressing that 'the examination of this problem will reveal a major theoretical gap in Marxism' (1977, p.32).

35 This thesis is not in contradiction with Marx and Engels's view, as expressed in the 'German Ideology', that the means of mental production are owned by the ruling class. Since the time of the 'German Ideology' the proletariat has shown a tremendous growth in its capacity to produce its own independent knowledge and thus to develop its own means of mental production. Marxism's task is that of accounting theoretically for this development within its own framework, i.e. in terms of class

struggle, rather than stressing one-sidedly the undoubted advantage the ruling class has in ideological class struggle. The study of J. Wrigley of the 'bitter conflict over control, funding and curriculum of the public schools' in Chicago from the beginning of the century to the Second World War provides a relevant example. This author points out how the American working class, which developed and formed itself in the period between the Civil War and the First World War, was able to stage fights over educational policy and how these fights 'are particularly striking because they reveal the ability of the labour movement to generate an independent educational perspective' (Class Politics and School Reform in Chicago, in M. Zeitlin (ed.) 1980, pp.153-71). We are quite far, therefore, from M. Neumann's tying the possibility of a scientific science of society to a certain degree of socialization of all areas of society (1976, pp.94-5) so that the science of society becomes 'der Prozess der Verwissenschaftlichung des Denkens der Gesellschaft über sich selbst' instead of the expression of the domination of a class on the theoretical level.

36 It is because of this class determination that a class can never be convinced by verification or by ideological class struggle that another class's theory is a better interpretation of reality, something which, of course, does not exclude that individuals can be gained to other ideologies or that classes adapt (through the P/I-M) other knowledges. This is why the bourgeoisie cannot adopt Marxism but only adapt it, transform it into an ideology.

37 M. Ball, Cost Benefit Analysis: A Critique, in F. Green and P. Nore (eds) (1979, p.78).

38 See Dowidar's statement to the effect that economic reasoning should not be replaced by another type of reasoning, the mathematical (1974, p.45).

39 We have here an example of an ideological shift due to the introduction of a foreign methodology. Two more examples of such an ideological shift. First, the application of the psychological method to the social sciences in the work of M. Weber. In this author's 'Interpretative sociology', as H.H. Gerth and C.W. Mills put it 'man can "understand" his own intentions through introspection, and he may interpret the motive of other men's conduct in terms of their professed or ascribed intentions' (1977, p.56). In Durkheim this ideological shift is achieved by the double movement of introducing an analogy (between the social and the biological organism) and of reducing the study of the former terms of this analogy to that of the latter (see, 1964). Since society is first equated and then reduced to a biological organism, equilibrium becomes the state of health of society, the normal state of affairs. Therefore, to take only one example, economic crises, which from the point of view of dialectics are necessary, destructive, and yet regenerating of capital, are reduced in Durkheim's conception to pathological phenomena.

40 D. Bloor (1976, p.34).

41 For such an attempt, see T. Leithäuser and W.R. Heinz (eds) (1976).

42 G. Lukács (1971, p.51).

43 Even though we are here basically concerned with the social
    sciences, we would like to mention that the same holds in our
    opinion also for the natural sciences. Quantum mechanics, for
    instance, which nowadays is made to imply the non-individuality
    and non-causality of atomic processes as well as an unintuitive
    and unpictorial description of these processes, was considered,
    in the Republic of Weimar, as implying exactly the opposit. On
    this point see P. Forman (1979). Forman's interesting and well
    documented argument, however, is cast into a theoretical frame-
    work different from the one submitted above.

44 In fact, just as the competing capitalists, carriers of capitalist
    production relations, must engage in competition, i.e. in an
    attempt to become dominant in order not to be pushed out of the
    market, the carriers of ideological relations, of different
    knowledges, must engage in a struggle for domination because
    this is the way these knowledges can remain competitive, i.e.
    not pushed out of the arena of ideological class struggle.

45 The consequences of this approach for a theory of personality –
    which we cannot develop here – are important because the conditions
    are created to account theoretically for the possibility that an
    individual consciousness be not a coherent, homogeneous whole but
    a unity of several contradictory elements articulated by one (or
    some) dominant element(s).

46 1977, p.195.

47 G.W.F. Hegel, 'The History of Philosophy', vol.I, quoted in
    V.I. Lenin, no.38, p.259.

48 Ibid.

49 Ibid. A. Collier criticizes A. Cutler et al. along similar
    lines: 'What these gentlemen lack is dialectic. The only
    concept of a totality of which they seem capable of conceiving,
    is of one which excludes dysfunctional aspects which, in short,
    cannot generate contradictions. Either teleology is in its
    heaven and all's well with the economy, or there can be no
    self-regulating mechanisms, and every crisis is terminal (1978,
    p.11).

50 The mistake made by Laclau and the other authors rejecting 'class
    reductionism' is precisely that of wanting to read in Marx's
    social analysis and in his elements of a theory of ideology
    (1) a theory of person (consciousness) formation (2) supposedly
    placed by Marx within a framework collapsing the determination
    of individual consciousnesses into their being specific only to
    a certain class. This is a deformed view of Marx's theory, one
    which is indeed widely accepted even nowadays and which should
    be severely criticized. Unfortunately, Marxism has provided
    only elements of a theory of personification and to a much
    lesser degree elements of a theory of personality formation.
    However, Laclau's attempt to explain why a certain worker (or
    a sector of the working class) acquires, say, a racist ideology
    or votes for conservative parties, leads him to reject the
    principle of the class determination of ideology and thus to the
    impossibility of explaining why the capitalists, both as
    individuals and as a class, consistently do not acquire a
    revolutionary ideology and consciousness.

51 M. Mulkay (1980, p.94).
52 M. Blisset, Politics and Science, quoted in M. Mulkay (1980).
53 The Mertonian emphasis on rewards, and its legitimating function
    for a system based on inequality, presupposes an internalization
    of certain values but is unable to account for the obvious class
    determination of those values.
54 For a critique of the Parsonian explanation of the apparent
    universality of the nuclear family, see V. Beechey, Critical
    Analysis of Some Ideological Theories of Women's Work, in A. Kuhn
    and A. Wolpe (1978, pp.155-97).
55 On this point see P. Smith, Domestic Labour and Marx's Theory
    of Value, in A. Kuhn and A. Wolpe (1978, pp.198-219).
56 See the last section of chapter 6 of this book.
57 On this last point, see G. Carchedi (1977, ch.4). Measures of
    income differentials (e.g. hourly earnings) between social groups
    (e.g. men/women, immigrant/autochthonous workers, etc.) usually
    conflate these two different components. Concerning immigrant
    workers, the view that they can be paid a wage lower than the
    value of their labour power because some of the costs of its
    formation are borne by the country of immigration (see S.J. Lord,
    Neoclassical Theories of Discrimination: a Critique, in F. Green
    and P. Nore, 1979, p.228) is criticized in chapter 6. As far
    as women are concerned, the distinction is important because it
    shows that equal pay, training, and opportunities for women are
    not sufficient to eliminate their discrimination, once women
    have already been formed as largely unskilled labour power. See
    S. Clegg and D. Dunkerley (1980, ch.2).
58 R. McDonough and R. Harrison, Patriarchy and Relations of
    Production, in A. Kuhn and A. Wolep (1978, p.39).
59 Therefore, it is not 'Because ... domestic labour does not
    constitute a branch of social production ... [that is] is not
    expressed as abstract labour, it does not enter into society's
    labour-totality', as P. Smith puts it (see Kuhn and Wolpe, 1978,
    p.210). It is because domestic labour is not part of the
    social labour process that it does not constitute a branch of
    social 'production' and thus cannot be considered as abstract
    (only as concrete labour).
60 The objection that women constitute a class since they produce
    future labour power, a commodity, is not only wrong - since
    labour power is not produced for exchange (sale, under capitalism) -
    but also self-destroying. In the production of future labour
    power participate also men; the state with its schools and health
    services, etc.; the Church; youth organizations, etc. and there
    is no way to show that women are more necessary than any other
    of the above-mentioned persons or institutions. Since every
    aspect of society participates in this 'production', the concept
    of class loses all meaning. Even worse is to consider women as
    productive labourers in their roles as 'producers' of future
    labour power.
61 The case of immediate productive consumption, for example, an
    independent farmer building his own means of production, is not
    relevant here. Notice that investments in state, unproductive,
    activities (e.g. infrastructures) belong to the category of
    production rather than consumption not because, as A. Emmanuel

(1972, p.172) submits, they are indirectly productive, but because they are a transformation (consumption) of use values for mediated consumption.

62 Not necessarily in the classic form of wage workers. In Italy, for example, a great amount of women's work is home (not in the sense of domestic) work and constitutes a part of what has been called the 'submerged' economy.

63 I.e. as the carriers of the dominated aspects of the relations of a family belonging – because of the class affiliation of the carriers of the dominant aspects of those relations – to a certain class.

64 'A wife inhabits her husband's class position, but not the equivalent relation to the means of production' (R. McDonogh and R. Harrison, in Kuhn and Wolpe, 1978, p.36). Notice that we are dealing here with the class collocation of women through their domination by carriers of production relations and not with the theoretically simple question of their collocation when they themselves become carriers of production relations.

65 Ibid., p.37.

66 The variety of ideological positions within the feminist movement is explained thus not only by the different, indirect class , affiliation of women, but also by their direct affiliation as carriers of relations when they leave the realm of domestic labour, as well as by the reciprocal incorporation and penetration (modification) of all these knowledges produced by women as (direct and indirect) carriers of production relations.

5 MATERIAL AND MENTAL TRANSFORMATION, THE FUNCTION OF CAPITAL, AND CAPITALIST PRODUCTION

1 K. Marx, Results of the immediate production process, in A. Dragstedt (1976, p.83).

2 Marx uses the term 'useful' labour to indicate labour which produces use values and not in the sense that this labour produces 'useful' instead of 'useless' things in a moral sense.

3 It follows therefore (and keeping in mind what was said in chapter 2) that a real transformation is not necessarily a transformation of the real concrete (it can be a transformation in the realm of the mental products) and that a non-material transformation is not necessarily a transformation of mental products (it can be also a transformation of the non-material real concrete, e.g. social relations).

4 1977, p.24.

5 In case of real transformation we have

$$RM_a T \xrightarrow{\text{ }} RM_e T = C_u \rightarrow C_u \neq .$$

6 For a discussion of the technical and social content of positions, see Carchedi (1977), especially ch.4.

7 The production of surplus value, and more specifically the maximization of the rate of profit, remains the basic principle moving a capitalist enterprise in all stages of development of capitalism. As capital centralization proceeds, however, and especially under monopoly and late capitalism, when the corpora-

tion becomes the dominant economic unit due to capital concentration and centralization's gigantic strides forward, the $M \rightarrow M'$ principle, or the principle of the maximization of the profit rate, applies not necessarily to the individual production unit any longer but to the corporation as a whole. It is thus even possible for a corporation to own (or control) two or more competitors producing the same commodity (e.g. detergents) as a way of maximizing its rate of profit, even though the general policy of the corporation might not be favourable to some individual units. On this point, see M. Zeitlin (1974).

8 K. Marx (1967b, ch. 1). The notation has been slightly modified for reasons of consistency.

9 A. Cutler et al. disagree with Marx's examples of 'cooks, actors, musicians, prostitutes, whose labour may be productive or unproductive depending on the nature of the economic relations in which it is performed' (1977, pp.292-3). Their rejection of this point is part of their rejection of Marx's distinction between productive and unproductive labour and ultimately of his theory of value. Thus, for example, they hold that 'Marx draws two distinct but interrelated types of distinction between productive and unproductive labour which are distinct and incompatible. One depends on the argument that certain functional tasks are essentially unproductive whether they are performed by capitalists or their employees while the other is clearly hegemonized by the theory of value' (pp.291-2). We have not two incompatible principles but one general principle, production of wealth, as it takes form under definite production relations.

10 We do not agree, therefore, with G. La Grassa, for whom exchange value is the 'specific capitalist form of social connexion'. See G. La Grassa's otherwise lucid article, Il valore come connessione sociale, in L. Geymonat (ed.) (1981).

11 E. Mandel (1975, pp.405-6).

12 N. Poulantzas (1974b, p.231).

13 E.O. Wright (1978, p.46).

14 Notice that it is the teacher (and the same applies to the entertainer, etc.) who produces use values and who therefore, within a $M \rightarrow M'$ context, is a productive labourer. The pupil consumes unproductively those new use values and is thus engaged in consumption proper (immediate unproductive). There is no productive labour in his act of consumption just as there is no productive consumption but only immediate unproductive consumption when the worker consumes his means of subsistence. There is a total irreconcilability between Marxist analysis on the one hand and theories of investment in human capital on the other.

15 Elsewhere we have referred to this type of capitalist enterprise as unproductive - CPP (see G. Carchedi, 1977, ch.1). To avoid confusion, we will drop the term 'production' in the case of the processes under consideration.

16 See G. Carchedi (1977, ch.1).

17 K. Marx (1967a, p.202).

18 A. Gramsci (1971, p.9). This famous quotation is seen here in a different light from Gramsci's own. This is hardly surprising

given our emphasis on what is conspicuous by its absence in Gramsci's work, i.e. the analysis of the LP_r and of the capitalist production process.

19   See P. Kraft, The industrialization of computer programming, in A. Zimbalist (ed.) (1979). There are even indications that in the USA different categories of computer technicians (from research specialist to the least-skilled technicians) not only are trained at different categories of institutions (from elite institutions to junior and community colleges) but also differ in their class of origin. It is thus not only insufficient, but also a sign of a-dialectical thinking, to submit that the law of value 'pousse à la déqualification maximale la proportion maximale de travailleurs manuels, [and] elle qualifie au maximum la proportion la plus petite possible de travailleurs intellec-tuelles' (Y. Maignien, 1975, p.67). Moreover, this author disregards completely the difference between different types of 'intellectual labour', i.e. the difference between the conception functional for the function of capital and the conception functional for the function of labour, and – as so many other Marxist works in this field – is marred by the implicit acceptance of the bourgeois categories 'intellectual' and 'manual' labour.

20   What follows is by no means exhaustive. For example, we will not deal here with an anomalous 'production' process, i.e. the purposive physical destruction of use values under conditions of monopoly as a means to increase appropriation of surplus value, or the planning (M_eT) of the reduction of a process' scale of production.

21   There is no need to invent a non-Marxist category as 'indirectly productive' for this type of enterprise. J.R. Ravetz speaks, correctly, of industrialized science (1971).

22   Notice that the ideological content does not become determinant. This would be the case of a newspaper not working for profit and yet dependent upon sales for its survival, e.g. a revolu-tionary newspaper. In it, it is the production and realization of a certain amount of value which is the condition for the reproduction of a certain ideological content (relations).

23   As R. Miliband (1969) points out, advertising sells not only commodities but also a way of life.

24   See G. Carchedi (1977) especially chs 1 and 4.

25   Even worse is to conflate productive labour and non-labour. For example, G. de Gaudemar merges the work of co-ordination of the labour process with the work of control and surveillance (1976, pp.133–4).

26   This does not exclude the use of basically physical energy (brute violence) to subdue especially material labour, as, for example, the beating of 'assembly workers for such transgressions of plant rules as talking to one another on the line' in Ford's factories in 1933. See M. Davies (1980, p.46).

27   It is essential to anchor these concepts to production (trans-formation of use values) and to ownership (control over this transformation). Once the materialist tie is severed as, for instance, in J.D. Stephen's definition of the global function of capital and of the function of the collective worker, the way is open to a 'gradualist conception of the transition to

socialism'. See 'The Transition From Capitalism to Socialism', Macmillan, 1979, p.25.

28 It is for this reason that we believe that any study attempting the determination of the non-labourers' income should start first of all from the value of these agents' labour power. This implies an analysis of the concrete aspects of non-labour, of the skill, education etc., needed to perform specific tasks of control and surveillance. Since to control usually requires knowledge of what is controlled, it is the difference between the value of the non-labourers' labour power and the value paid to them in the form of real wages which is explainable in terms of control over labour. As Corjat says concerning the 'tâcheronat', 'il s'agit d'utiliser le metier contre lui-même en employant le travail des autres' (1979, p.40). We believe that the adoption of such a standpoint would improve the already important empirical inquiry by E.O. Wright (1979) into income distribution.

29 Those Marxist authors who think that the sales effort is a productive (of surplus value) activity have fallen prey to this ideological illusion due to the choice of the point of view of the individual firm (which is a typical characteristic of bourgeois economics). The by now classic argument based on this erroneous vantage point can be found in P. Baran and P. Sweezy (1966).

30 This is the mistake T. Johnson thinks I make in my 'On the economic identification of social classes' (1977). 'Carchedi's logic', holds this author, 'then forces him into the untenable position that, while the labour process in the capitalist enterprise is reproduced according to the requirements of the expansionary dynamics of capital, at the same time it gives rise to an autonomous labour process which generates its own structure of unity and co-ordination - capitalist bureaucracy is exploitative and non-exploitative at the same time' (1977, p.205). On the contrary, the logical conclusion stemming from my argument is that there cannot be a labour process within this type of capitalist enterprise, something which becomes perfectly intelligible if we take the point of view of the totality.

31 K. Marx, 'Capital', vol.1, quoted in Bottomore (1956, pp.149-50).

32 Other attempts have been made to ground the concept of mental labour in a Marxist texture. We mention here N. Poulantzas's definition of mental labour as 'every form of work which takes the form of knowledge from which the direct producers are excluded' ('Classes in Contemporary Capitalism', quoted in E.O. Wright (1978, p.38). This type of approach could be criticized on a number of grounds.

33 Thus, the statement that 'Marxism is plagued by a "philosophy of labour" in which the (manual) labourer is conceived as the agent of transformation of raw materials as the sole creator of value' (A. Cutler, et al., 1977, pp.224-5) can be made only by forgetting not only what Marx said explicitly about the productivity of intellectual labourers but also his point of view of the totality.

34 K. Marx (1973, p.448).

35 Various Authors (1980, p.81).
36 K. Marx and F. Engels (1970a, p.53).
37 D. Murray (1979, p.24).
38 So that M. Turchetto is perfectly right in stressing the
    capitalist character of co-operation, see L. Geymonat (ed.)
    (1981, p.33). Turchetto's contribution is a valid critique of
    the 'trontian', or 'workerist', or 'autonomist' theorization of
    the 'mass worker' and thus implicitly of the (mistaken) choice
    of the strategy of the 'refusal of labour' instead of the
    (supposedly meaningless and outdated) fight for workers' control.
    Workers' control is still the strategy of labour provided the
    labour process is rid of capitalist rule not only in the form
    of the work of control and surveillance but also in the
    structure of the labour process itself. It is not by chance
    that Marx refers to the introduction of the technical division
    of labour and thus of the machines functional for this fragmenta-
    tion of the labour process as the real subordination of labour
    to capital.
39 Ibid., p.35.
40 Notice that we are trying here to provide some general concepts
    concerning epochal changes. During a transition period it
    might be perfectly justifiable to fight for the abolition of
    the conception/execution dichotomy rather than of the mental/
    material one.
41 A. Zimbalist (ed.), 1979, p.XVIII.
42 B. Corjat, 1979.
43 Ibid., p.205.
44 Ibid., p.213.
45 Ibid., p.212.
46 Ibid., pp.232-3.
47 Ibid., p.XXI.
48 Ibid., pp.239 and ff.
49 R. Luporini, in L. Geymonat (ed.) (1980, p.10).

6 ELEMENTS OF LATE CAPITALIST PRODUCTION RELATIONS

1 Yet, let us stress this again, both aspects are intrinsic to
   production under capitalism. Thus, a socialist mode of
   production would have to eliminate both aspects of the domination
   of capital over labour.
2 Or are economically oppressed, in case of unproductive labour.
3 Althusser is correct in stressing the objective character of
   the production relations (1970, p.180). Similarly, E. Hann
   rightly observes that social relations in Marx are objective
   (verhouding in Dutch, or Verhältnis in German) and not intersubjective (betrekking in Dutch, or Beziehung in German).
   However, the accent on the objective character of the production
   relations should not lead us to consider these latter as, for
   example, 'specific forms of combination of agents of production
   and means of production' (Poulantzas, 1973, p.66). This is
   a form of reification from which A. Cutler et al. do not escape
   either (1977; see, for instance, p.267). M.H. Dowidar speaks
   of relations among 'members of society' (and not classes)

'through the intermediary of material goods and services', and not, as he should, of the means of production (1974, p.27). Production relations could thus be defined as relations in which the agents of production engage when taking part in the production process through the intermediary of the means of production. However, the last part of the definition seems to us to be redundant given that participation in the production process must necessarily be mediated through the means of production.

4 The identification of expropriator/labourer and appropriator / non-labourer is justifiable only at the highest level of abstraction, if only the two fundamental classes are considered. But this limitation must be clearly spelled out in order to avoid theoretical confusion. This is T. Cutler's limit (1978).

5 E.O. Wright, in assessing my work (1977) sees the 'relations of expropriation' as 'redundant' since 'the expropriation element perfectly coincides with the functional element' (1980a). Strictly speaking this is not so, since the present distinction between extraction and appropriation as elements of exploitation and, as we will see, the possibility for different agents to appropriate and to extract, points at the non-coincidence of the functional and the exploitation elements. It could be held, however, that the redundancy of the exploitation element is due to the fact that, once we know the ownership and the functional element of an agent's position, we know also the exploitation aspect of it. To this we can object that, since we have introduced the distinction between the direct and indirect performance of the function of capital (extraction), the exploitation element cannot be fully known, once we know the ownership and functional element, since this does not tell us whether an agent performs the function of capital directly or indirectly. The real reason for retaining all three elements of the production relations, however, is another one. The question here is not one of formal logic in which, once two variables are known, the third follows logically and thus becomes, in a sense, redundant. Even if the exploitation element could be fully known on the basis of the other two elements, we would still have to consider all three elements since the functional and the exploitation elements correspond to the two aspects of the capitalist production process, respectively the labour process and the surplus value producing process and are thus integral to Marx's analysis of the production process under capitalism. Traditionally, Marxist analysis has focused on the ownership and the exploitation elements. Yet, as we hope to show, once the functional element too is given proper emphasis, a whole new area of research opens up. Equally, exclusive emphasis on the ownership and functional elements would lead to disregarding fundamental insights in Marx's analysis of the production process. For the difference between my theory and E.O. Wright's theory, see Wright's above mentioned paper. For a systematic comparison of the theories of Carchedi, Wright and Poulantzas, see W. Johnston and M.D. Ornstein, 'Social Class and Political Ideology in Canada', unpublished paper, York University, Toronto. Canada.

6 What follows has been dealt with in detail in G. Carchedi (1977, especially chapters 1 and 4).

7 W. Clement provides an interesting example of how workers are transformed into the collective labourer (see 1979).

8 In a previous writing (1977) I spoke of the global capitalist, a term which could generate some dangerous confusion because it could imply that all those who perform globally the function of capital are in fact capitalists. For example, R. Crompton and J. Gubbay define capital 'in the modern firm not ... as a set of people, top managers and major shareholders, but *[as]* a complex structure of roles defined in functional terms' (1977, p.70). The term global non-labourer seems to be much better suited.

9 Notice that for us a complete definition of a social class can be given only when the economic, political, and ideological aspects are considered. To avoid confusion, we refer to the economic identification of classes when only this aspect is considered. When the economic identification of classes is attempted and when its determinant core is considered then all three aspects of the production relations must be taken into account. J. Scott mistakes thus my position when he argues that 'Carchedi argues that the capitalist class is "defined" as the category of persons performing the function of capital, but that the bourgeoisie is "identified" as those members of the capitalist class who performs *only* the capitalist function' (1979, p.111).

10 Thus, of all the criticisms which can be moved to my theory, the most mistaken is that I define the middle class in terms of distribution relations. According to K.K. Schaeffer (1976) 'the structuralist Carchedi' is one of those authors 'who use wage-earners as a class determination'! The content of my article, which, by the way, is called Reproduction of Social Classes at the Level of Production Relations, is completely misinterpreted by this author. In any case, if misinterpretation of Carchedi might not be a dramatic problem for the struggle of the (American) proletariat, misinterpretation of Marx's thought is, of course, a much more serious matter. Just one example: for Marx, capitalist accumulation, i.e. production of profit, occurs just because labour power is paid its full exchange value and yet (and this is its use value) produces a value higher than its own exchange value. Now compare with Schaeffer's Marx: 'Labour power, without a surplus population standing behind it, and a reserve army in front of it, would be valued at its value and capital accumulation could not occur' (p.94).

11 1975, p.118. Also, according to Mandel, the third technological revolution presents the following three characteristics: (a) a shortening of the turnover time of fixed capital; (b) a great acceleration of technological innovations; (c) an enormous increase in the costs of major projects (1975, p.483).

12 This is the mistake of those who conflate the function of capital with, for example, all the activities in the commercial sphere (see, for instance, Urry, Johnson, etc.). Those agents who work in the commercial enterprise, and in general in all non-productive enterprises, can perform both the global function of capital and the function of the collective worker and thus have a contra-dictory location in the class structure in terms of production

relations. To define all those who are employed in a commercial
enterprise as performing the function of capital means in fact
conflating once more non-labour and unproductive labour. For
example, T. Johnson, while finding my project, as he puts it,
'worthwhile in its attempt to theorize the extension of the
function of capital' (1977, p.232), considers realization as a
function of capital, thus conceptualizing the 'new petty
bourgeoisie', in the realm of realization rather than of
production (p.218).

13 V. I. Lenin, Collected Works, no.1, pp.176-7.

14 E. Mandel (1975, pp.310 and ff.).

15 M. Zeitlin (1980).

16 1967a, p.178.

17 This approach, which remains within Marx's own theoretical frame,
has the advantage, on A. Cutler, B. Hindess, P. Hirst, and
A. Hussain's analysis, of not having to revert to the 'displacement of the question of the source of profit, and the essentiali-
zation of labour associated with it', i.e. to the throwing
overboard of all basic tenets of Marxism, in order to make
'possible the recognition of the effects of investment decisions,
innovations in the technique and methods of production organization as changes in the productivity of the process initiated by
capital' (1977, p.258-9). The point of view of the totality,
or societal production process, is necessary for the distinction
not only between productive and unproductive labour but also
between labour and non-labour. The critique that Marx's use
of the categories 'labour' and 'non-labour' is absurd since
'the "non-labourer" performs definite functions which are
technically necessary to production' (p.261) and thus that
'Carchedi's position is simply absurd' (pp.302-3) misses the
point that for Marx concrete labour cannot be used as a divide
between labour and non-labour or between productive and unproductive labour and that thus whether a job is useful or
necessary for the production process or not cannot function as
such a divide. (Moreover, I have clearly spelled out (1977)
that, contrary to what these authors seem to say at p.302, the
purchase and sale of commodities is not a part of the function
of capital but of unproductive labour.) That the positions
inscribed in the global function of capital are a condition of
existence of production and as such productive is a typically
functionalist standpoint. These authors' departure with great
fanfare from Marxism is in fact a tacit landing in functionalist
land. Marx's analysis is built upon the recognition that the
non-labourers are necessary for the capitalist production
process (just as unproductive labourers are) and yet do not
produce wealth.

18 When capital centralization takes the form, as especially after
the Second World War, of interlocking directorates, real
ownership might not be clearly localized in just one person,
or family, or even kinship group for a certain company but
might be personified by directors who sit on a number of boards.
This means that not only - as it is well known - the majority
of stocks is not needed any longer in order to have real
ownership; the necessary amount of stocks (percentage of capital)

keeps decreasing because a stock holder can become the dominant one, if he does not own enough shares, either through inter-locking directorates, or through coalitions with holders of stocks of the business aimed at. (See S. Norich, Interlocking Direc-torates, in M. Zeitlin, 1980, p.93.) Therefore, the real owner is not necessarily one person: it can be a family, a kinship group, or a coalition or alliance of capitalists. J. Scott (1975) submits evidence concerning the transition 'from "personal" to more "impersonal" forms of possession and control', i.e. from individual, personal, to finance capital. For the purposes of our discussion, it is enough to point at this further evidence of the correctness of the Leninist analysis without going into the question of whether industrial capital dominates bank capital or vice versa.

19 While real ownership of the means of production gives the right to the appropriation of surplus value, non-ownership implies having to provide surplus non-labour (in case the agent performs the function of capital). Partial real ownership implies thus neither the former advantage (appropriation) nor the latter disadvantage (the being the object of extraction of surplus non-labour) since the executive is usually paid a value in terms of labour time higher than the time provided as non-labour.

20 'It is therefore no longer necessary for the capitalist to perform the labour of superintendence himself...; the mere manager, who has no title whatever to capital ... performs all the real functions of the investing capitalist as such; only the functionary remains and the capitalist disappears from the process of production as a superfluous person' (K. Marx, 'Capital', vol.III, quoted in Bottomore, 1956, pp.153-4).

21 The same principle allows us to collocate also the old middle class on the capitalist side. The small capitalist who, no matter how much of his time is devoted to performing the function of labour, owns the means of production, is still a capitalist even though in terms of production relations he is a hybrid, he is a carrier of contradictory aspects of the capitalist production relations. This applies therefore also to the top managers even if they at times might perform the function of the collective worker. There is no question thus in the present work, as well as in a previous one (1977), contrary to what G. Salaman seems to think, of including 'experts and managers within the bourgeoisie on the grounds not of their owning property' but because they perform the global function of capital (1981, p.255). Also, the objection moved by the same author that 'the notion of the separation of ownership and control is invalid ... [because] it is in sociological terms doubtful if it is possible to make any clear-cut distinction between senior managers and the capitalists - i.e. the owners. Senior managers are usually from wealthy sections of society; they are frequently themselves owners of shares; and they pay themselves high fees and salaries out of profits' (p.243), points at most at practical difficulties in the carrying out of concrete research, not at a theoretical impossibility. In this, Salaman follows F. Parkin (1979, chs 2 and 4) who, however, transforms my emphasis on the importance of the functional

elements into disguised Weberianism by transforming my
definition of social classes into one purely in terms of the
functional aspect and by re-interpreting this latter in terms of
the Weberian concept of authority.

22 For a typology of Marxist theories on the middle classes and
managers see E.O. Wright, 1980a. However, the view submitted
here does not fit in any of the four categories presented by
Wright. R. Miliband, in his 'Marxism and Politics' (1977, ch.2)
collocates the managers in the capitalist class but on the basis
of an insufficient and incomplete analysis which is based on the
concept of productive labour on the one hand and on the concept
of ownership of the means of production on the other. There is,
in Miliband, no distinction between real and legal ownership
and between function of capital and function of labour. Thus,
for Miliband, even the top managers, the whole of the managerial
apparatus, is part of the collective labourer. But then, is the
individual capitalist, when performing the work of management,
a labourer? Marx's answer is emphatically negative. Even
worse is the position of A. Cutler et al., who also lump together
top managers and workers in one and the same class (1977, ch.12).
The absurdity of their position implies also a community of
interests which leads to an old acquaintance of Marxism: social
democracy.

23 Moreover, it is incorrect, methodologically, to base an argument
on a case limit.

24 We refer, of course, for sake of simplicity, to a corporation
engaged in a pure capitalist production process, where non-labour
is not a channel for realization of surplus value.

25 For a review of the relevant literature see M. Zeitlin (1974).

26 1980, p.9.

27 Various Authors (1976, p.44).

28 1974, p.1101.

29 P.1100.

30 This section has appeared as G. Carchedi (1979).

31 E. Mandel (1975).

32 And which is different from the old type of migration which,
until 1880, originated from 'civilized' countries such as
England, Germany, and partly Sweden. See V.I. Lenin, 'Collected
Works', no.19.

33 Op. cit., p.325. More on this below.

34 It is thus the internationalization of the acquisition of labour
power rather than of production which makes it possible for
capital to operate the international transfer of labour power.
This point seems to have been missed by C. Palloix: 'The process
of internationalization of capital and production, the basis for
the development of the multinational firms, gave rise on an
ever-increasing scale to world-wide mass automatic production.
Labour processes came to be definable only on an international
scale, and hence there arises a new worker, viz. the *mass-worker*,
bound to the vicissitudes of the multinationals, i.e. to the
movements of the internationalization of capital' ('Various
Authors', 1976). We will not probe the concept of mass-worker
but simply assert that this concept, as used in 'workerist'
circles, rests basically on (1) an a-dialectical notion of the

dequalification of labour and (2) an economistic deduction of class consciousness and struggle from this process of dequalification. For an example of such a concept see K. Heinz Roth in A. Serafini (1974). This concept of mass-worker has played and continues to play an important role in post-1968 Italy, not only in the original 'workerist' movement but nowadays also through the group Potere Operaio, in the Autonomia Operaia movement which, in the words of A. Mangano, 'considers the antagonistic consciousness expressed by the workers' insubordination as already "completely political" and which conceives of the process of proletarianisation as fully completed, to the extent that it [Autonomia Operaia] describes the entire capitalist social formation as a huge factory, the social factory' (1978, p.81). This book's chapter 3 is a cogent and well taken critique of Trontism and of its 'left-wing' and 'right-wing' labour elaborations from a non-PCI optic. This notion of mass-worker influences all the contributions (not only Roth's) to the book edited by A. Serafini. We will strive towards an interpretation of migration and more generally of labour power mobility, neither in economistic nor in 'workerist' terms, i.e. we will strive towards an analysis within the framework of a concept of dialectical determination in which the superstructural moments are given their proper role.

35 With the exception of Italy which, however, though it remains a country exporting labour power, begins to show signs of seasonal use of foreign, basically African, workers.

36 Objections to this thesis are dealt with below.

37 1976, p.8. C. Meillassoux also stresses the temporary character of migration when he writes of a new form of migration, that of 'rotating migrants' who return home after two to four years of work in the host country, coming back again for further stints of work over a period of twelve to twenty years, and later being replaced in this role by their children. He also notes the saving in reproduction costs which this entails for the host country. See his contribution in: Union Generale des Travailleurs Senegalais en France (1975). Two important conclusions can be drawn which, however, we can mention only in passing. First, following V. Parlato, we should distinguish in the labour power-importing countries three sectors making up the labour market, i.e. the free market (indigenous, naturalized and permanent workers), the controlled market (made up of yearly, seasonal and commuting workers), and the black market (irregular or illegal workers). See Preface, in V. Moioli, 1976, p.15. However, as we will attempt to show later on, we cannot talk of complete separation or segmentation of the national labour market. Second, the collective worker is now made up of two sectors, the indigenous and the foreign one. In turn the latter one is split into two sub-sectors, the relatively permanent and the highly temporary one (which is subjected to the ebb and flow of the conjuncture much more than the permanent one).

38 See, for example, R. Penninx and L. van Velzen (1976, no.21, pp.231-63).

39 As to the branches of industry in which foreign workers tend to be employed, it is difficult to generalize. In France and

Germany they seem to occupy large sectors of dequalified jobs in the dynamic sectors of the economy. In Holland they seem to be concentrated in the stagnant branches of industry.

40   At this point the limited geographical scope of this section deserves to be stressed again. The mechanism of labour power migration characteristic of late capitalism in Europe is a product of the needs of monopoly capitalism in that phase in that region, and is not necessarily the principal mechanism of meeting those needs in all other countries under its domination. In the USA, for instance, recent work has shown the importance of the criminalization of migrant labour as a control mechanism which has some parallels which, but is certainly different from, the migrant labour system of Western Europe (see in particular A. Portes, 1978, pp.1-48). A systematic analysis would have to take into account, among other specific features of the American situation, such things as the low level of unionization of US workers, the relatively deep penetration of the US working class by bourgeois ideology and especially racism, and the scope for internal migration of capital within the USA (notably to the South). The study of other countries, such as Japan or Canada, would no doubt reveal other important aspects of the general phenomenon.

41   It is not methodologically correct to consider the total number of licences in order to analyse the buffer function of foreign labour power, as it is also not correct to deduce from a constant increase in the permanent licences a trend towards a permanent form of migration. As we will see in more detail further down, given that migration is still relatively recent and still partly determined by structural causes, a more permanent sector of immigrant workers is still in the making. We do not have data on the rate of rotation within the temporary sector in Holland. Data for other European countries will be given further down and it supports our hypothesis.

42   Incidentally, we only touch on the question of the advantages and disadvantages of migration. If we were to embark on such an analysis, we would have to make a distinction, at least as far as Europe is concerned, between workers coming from EEC countries, the 'centre', i.e. basically Italians, and workers coming from the periphery. Each country of immigration establishes fictitious ideological differences, and minor differential treatments to substantiate these differences, in an obvious attempt to fragment the working class. But capital's plans encounter the foreign workers' combativeness which is rooted in the common condition of super-exploitation.

43   These are, of course, the main characteristic elements, which do not exclude the presence of other elements as well.

44   In A. Serafini (1974, p.79).

45   1972, p.105.

46   A. Sivanandan (1978, p.4).

47   A. Sivanandan (1976, p.256).

48   M. Dogo, in A. Serafini (1974).

49   Data elaborated from P. Kammerer (1976, p.78).

50   J.M. Oroval Planas et al. (1974, p.74).

51   Y. Moulier, in A. Serafini (1974).

52 P. Kammerer (1976, p.82).

53 Op. cit., pp.83-4.

54 Thus, it is correct to stress, as V. Moioli (1976, p.30) does
concerning Switzerland, that 'The present aim of Swiss employers
is by no means an almost total elimination of foreign labour
power. This operation is not only impossible but actually quite
unthinkable for an economy which has grown and developed precisely
at the expense of migrant workers. The penalty for such an
operation would be a vertical decline of the economy. Rather,
the aim is that of a sensible and articulated reduction and
regulation of the migrant army, according to the needs of capital
and through new forms of control, selection and stabilisation'.
We should not forget that what the state carries out is not solely
an economic but also an ideological and political selection.

55 M. Nikolinokos (1975, p.12).

56 See S. Castles and G. Kosack, (1973).

57 Op. cit., p.177

58 Sometimes state recruitment of foreign labour power is preceded
by free recruitment through privately owned enterprises; e.g. in
France from 1924 to 1945, a privately owned society (the S.G.I.)
in practice centralized all recruitment. See L. Gant (1972, p.13).
In 1945 the state took over this function and created the O.N.I.

59 In Various Authors (1978, p.199).

60 In Germany this agency is the Bundesanstalt für Arbeit. In
France, as we have seen above, this agency is the O.N.I. The
O.N.I., however, has not always functioned as it was supposed
to, at first taking up the function of regulating a posteriori
illegal immigrant labour power. But all possibilities of
regularization have been eliminated since 1973. Now 'the supplies
and demands of jobs must be sent to the O.N.I. which determines
the flux of entries, the rules and working of the economic and
political imperatives' (T. Sawyer, 1973, p.37).

61 The basic purpose of this law was to entice foreign workers to
leave West Germany by paying them a bonus of 5,000 DM - the
carrot instead of the stick.

62 And we should not forget the co-ordination of the various
national police forces both among the states importing labour
power and between the countries signing bilateral agreements.
See L. Gant (1972, p.97). In this connection we should remember
that the countries of the periphery usually have authoritarian
or fascist regimes which, besides leaving the workers exposed to
the abuses of the country of immigration, prevent - through their
own organizations such as the Amicale for the Moroccans and the
Grey Wolves for the Turks - their participation in the political
and trade union life of the country of immigration. Such regimes
do not object to these workers being hired on the basis of short-
term, renewable contracts and disposed of if necessary.

63 T. Sawyer (1973, pp.27-34).

64 For one of these forms, the rent-strike, see ibid., p.39. For
numerous data on the participation of foreign workers in the
class struggle in West Germany from 1955 to 1975, see P. Kammerer
(1976, part II, ch.4). See also, for other European countries,
A. Serafini (ed.) (1974), passim.

65 Ibid., p.74.

66 Ibid., p.5.
67 Ibid., p.37. But - to take only one example, Switzerland -
    only one year after Y. Noulier's essay appeared, 'in addition to
    the 200,000 [foreign workers] expelled or repatriated in the
    course of 1975, one can also count 32,000 unemployed (foreign
    workers)' (V. Moioli, 1976, p.26). As V. Parlato wittily
    observes in the preface to this book, the foreign workers can
    be considered as the Foreign Legion of the industrial reserve
    army.
68 Op. cit., p.149.
69 We think here, for example, of A. Cutler, et al. (1977). For
    these authors, these are probably idle questions since the concept
    of determination in the last instance is in their view nothing
    more than a theoretical obstacle. In fact, these authors' claims
    notwithstanding, the renouncing of this and other basic elements
    of Marxism amounts to its theoretical liquidation.
70 1976, p.194.
71 Ibid., p. 195.
72 However, it would seem that de Gaudemar's reasoning is strongly
    influenced by the implicit assumption of a high economic
    conjuncture and full employment; even more important, as a cause
    of labour power movement, than badly paid jobs, is the lack of
    jobs, i.e. unemployment.
73 Ibid., pp.194-8.
74 Ibid., p. 176.
75 In P. Kammerer (1976, p.152).
76 If anyone still doubts the idiocy of proposing emigration or,
    which is the same, forced repatriation, as a cure for unemploy-
    ment, let him ponder on P. Cinanni's point that the south of
    Italy, after a century of massive migration, is still as poor
    or poorer. See P. Cinanni (1974, pp.91 and ff.).
77 M. Castells (1975, p.39).
78 1976, p.189.
79 See 'Capital', Marx, 1967a, p.641.
80 1976, ch.9.
81 1973, p.141.
82 1976, p.235.
83 As far as South European and North African countries are
    concerned, see T. Dietz (1977, p.40).
84 S. Bologna, in Various Authors (1976, pp.68-91).
85 This is the dominant, characteristic form of migration. Just
    as in the case of capital movements, other forms of mobility
    not only still exist but play also an important role. Moreover,
    that this form of migration has become dominant after World War
    Two in Western Europe does not imply that it cannot be found in
    previous periods. In Holland, a country where the capitalist
    mode of production developed very slowly, temporary migration
    can be found already in the 1820s. 'It is important, for the
    spreading and the taking over of forms of action and experiences
    of struggle, that sometimes large groups of foreign workers were
    engaged in the laying out of roads, of railroads, and of canals
    and in peat-cutting. These workers came principally from Germany
    but also from Belgium and France' (G. Harmsen and B. Reinalda,
    1975, p.33). We thus do not agree with M. Castells's thesis

that 'immigration is not a conjunctural phenomenon linked to the manpower needs of expanding economies but a structural tendency characteristic of the current phase of monopoly capitalism' (1975, p.44). For us, migration is both permanent and conjunctural, but it is a specific type of temporary, conjunctural migration which characterized post-Second World War monopoly capitalism. The distinction is important because it is a prerequisite to inquire not only into the specific ways these two sectors of the foreign labour power act on the rate of surplus value of the 'host' country but also into the possible political and ideological manoeuvres of the state vis-à-vis the foreign workers. Thus, for Castells, 'the advantage of immigrant labour for capital stems precisely from the specificity of their inferior position in the class struggle, which derives from the legal-political status of immigrants. From the point of view of capital, this status can be modified in minor ways, but not transformed, because it is the source of the basic structural role of immigration' (p.53). Now, if this is true, and will probably remain so, for the fluctuating sector, it need not be so — and is already not so in some countries — for the permanent sector. The capitalist state can give this latter sector a good deal in the way of political equality. This happens through the integration of the permanent foreign worker into the status quo of the 'host' country. No matter how integration is defined — and Roy Jenkins's definition in 1966: 'not as a flattening process of assimilation but as equal opportunity accompanied by cultural diversity in an atmosphere of mutual tolerance' (A. Sivanandan, 1976, p.360) is still nowadays a very popular concept with the 'liberal' sectors of the national bourgeoisies — it will never be, at least in the schemes of capital, a class integration but always an a-political integration. What the British state has managed to do vis-à-vis the black West Indians ('they had remained parallel in terms of culture, they had merged in terms of class', A. Sivanandan, 1976, p.365) is already becoming a political and ideological model for the various Western European bourgeoisies. For all of them hold the same guiding principle: 'the strategy is to defeat the class, the tactic is to divide it' (see A. Sivanandan, 1978, p.7).

86   For Germany, see K. Heinz Roth, p.127. In Holland, recent legislation (1976) has further strengthened the limits imposed upon the immigrant workers' freedom to change and choose their jobs. For a brief summary of the 1976 Wet Arbeid Butenlandse Werknemers (according to which the work licence is given by the state to the entrepreneur who then gives it to the worker on a strictly personal and nominal basis; this licence is in other words valid only for that worker and thus makes him totally dependent upon 'his' entrepreneur for a period of three years) see R. Penninx and L. van Velzen (1977).

87   De Gaudemar is wrong when he states that 'This "freedom" of the labour force transforms itself into its opposite as it enters the labour market' (1976, p.259).

88   G. Carchedi (1977, especially ch.4).

89   Note that bourgeois sociology mistakes technical mobility for social mobility.

90 G. Carchedi (1977, chs 1 and 4).
91 Op. cit., p.159.
92 K. Marx (1967a, p.171).
93 We will not enter here into the discussion of this problem i.e. of the determination of the coefficients of reduction of different types of complex labour to simple labour and of the relation between these coefficients and wage differentials. For a treatment of this problem see A. Roncaglia (1974, pp.1-12).
94 1967a, pp.171-2.
95 P. Cinanni (1974, p.37).
96 Castells (1975, pp.46-7).

BIBLIOGRAPHY

ABENTROTH, W. (1972), 'A short history of the European working class', London, New Left Books.

ABERCROMBIE, N. (1980), 'Class, Structure and Knowledge', Oxford, Basil Blackwell.

ACKERMAN, J.S. (1949), Gothic Theory of Architecture and the Cathedral of Milan, 'The Bulletin of Art', vol.XXXI.

ALBURY, R., PAYNE, G., SUCHTIRS, W. (1970), Naturalism and the human sciences, 'Economy and Society', vol.10, no.3, pp.367-79.

ALTHUSSER, L. (1970), 'For Marx', New York, Pantheon.

ALTHUSSER, L. and BALIBAR, E. (1970), 'Reading Capital', London, New Left Books.

ANDERSON, P. (1976), 'Considerations on Western Marxism', London, New Left Books.

ASSMANN, G. et al. (1978), 'Wörterbuch der Marxistisch-Leninistischen Soziologie', Berlin, Westdeutscher Verlag.

BADIOU, A. (1975), 'Théorie de la Contradiction', Paris, Maspéro.

BALIBAR, E. (1974), 'Cinq Études du Matérialisme Historique', Paris, Maspéro

BARACCA, A. (1974), I concetti di lavoro e energia nell'Inghilterra del XVIII° secolo, 'Sapere', July-August.

BARACCA, A. (1980), 'Manuale Critico di Meccanica Statistica', Catania, CULC.

BARACCA, A. (1981), Dalla macchina di Watt alla macchina di Carnot, Milan, forthcoming.

BARACCA, A., and BERGIA, S. (1975), 'La spirale delle alte energie', Milan, Bompiani.

BARACCA, A., CILIBERTO, S., LIVI, R., LORINI, A., PETTINI, M., RUFFO, S., and RUSSO, A. (1980), Research programme on science and society: Germany and the United States 1870-1940, 'Radical Science Journal', n.10, pp.120-31.

BARACCA, A., and LIVI, R. (1976), 'Natura e Storia, Fisica e Sviluppo del Capitalismo nell'Ottocento', Florence, D'Anna.

BARACCA, A., LIVI, R. and RUFFO, S. (1979), Le tappe dello sviluppo della teoria dei quanti nel quadro della seconda rivoluzione industriale e delle contraddizioni del capitalismo nel primo dopoguerra, 'Testi e Contesti', Part I, n.2, p.5 (1979); Part II, n.3, p.51 (1980).

252

BARACCA, A. and RIGATTI, R. (1974), Aspetti dell'interazione tra
scienza e tecnica durante la rivoluzione industriale inglese del
XVIII secolo, Part I, La nascita dei concetti di lavoro e di energia,
'Il Giornale di Fisica', XV, 144; Part II, Sviluppi della macchina
a vapore, 'Il Giornale di Fisica', XV, 206.
BARACCA, A. and ROSSI, A. (1974), 1789, prassi e organizzazione della
scienza, 'Sapere', October.
BARACCA, A. and ROSSI, A. (1976), 'Marxismo e Scienze Naturali', Bari,
De Donato.
BARACCA, A. and ROSSI, A. (1978), 'Materia e Energia', Milan,
Feltrinelli.
BARACCA, A., RUFFO, S. and RUSSO, A. (1977), Scienza, industria e
lotta di classe, 'Praxis', no.18-19.
BARACCA, A., RUFFO, S. and RUSSO, A. (1979), 'Scienza e Industria
1848-1915', Bari, Laterza.
BARAN, P. and SWEEZY, P. (1966), 'Monopoly Capitalism', New York,
Monthly Review Press.
BARLETTA, G. (1978), 'Marxismo e Teoria della Scienza', Bari, Dedalo
Libri.
BARNES, B. (1974), 'Scientific Knowledge and Sociological Theory',
London, Routledge & Kegan Paul.
BATTIMELLI, G. (1974), Etere e relatività, 'Sapere', November.
BEER, J.J. (1959), 'The Emergence of the German Dye Industry',
Illinois Studies in the Social Sciences, 44, Urbana, University of
Illinois Press.
BENTON, T. (1981), Realism and Social Science, 'Radical Philosophy',
Spring, no.27.
BERGIA, S. (1973), Historical note to the volume of G. Cortini,
'La Relativita Ristretta', Turin, Loescher.
BERGIA, S. (1978), 'Einstein e la Relatività', Bari, Laterza.
BERGIA, S. (1979a), El cuanto de luz y la dualidad onda-particula
en las investigaciones de Einstein sobre la radiacion, in
R. Rodriguez and S. Hojman (eds), 'Einstein, el Hombre y su Obra',
proceedings of the Jornadas Einsteinianas, Puebla, UNAM-Nuova
imagnen.
BERGIA, S. (1979b), On the birth of special relativity, in 'Einstein,
a Centenary Volume', London, Heinemann, for The International
Commission on Physics Education.
BERGIA, S. and FANTAZZINI, P. (1979), Il ruolo dell'analogia nella
individuazione delle leggi fisiche: la 'lex Naturae' di Wren per
l'urto elastico, 'Il Giornale di Fisica', XX, p.287.
BERGIA, S. and FANTIZZINI, P. (1980), Dalla regolamentazione delle
acque alle leggi dell'urto centrale elastico: una rivalutazione
dell ruolo di Giovanni Poleni nella disputa delle forze vive, 'Il
Giornale di Fisica', XXI, '.46.
BERGIA, S. and FANTIZZINI, P. (1982), La descrizione dei fenomeni
meccanici in termini energetici nell'opera di John Smeaton, Part I,
Dalle ruote ad acqua ai teoremi dell'impulso e delle forze vive;
Part II, Un modello per l'urto elastico e il suo controllo
sperimentale, 'Il Giornale di Fisica', forthcoming.
BERNAL, J. (1976), 'Sociale Geschiedenis van de Wetenschap',
Nijmegen, SUN.
BHASKAR, R. (1975), Feyerabend and Bachelard: two philosophies of
science, 'New Left Review', November-December.

BHASKAR, R. (1978), 'A Realist Theory of Science', Hassocks, Sussex, The Harvester Press.
BHASKAR, R. (1979), 'The Possibility of Naturalism', Hassocks, Sussex, The Harvester Press.
BHASKAR, R. (1980), Scientific Explanation and Human Emancipation, 'Radical Philosophy', Autumn, no.26.
BHASKAR, R. (1982), Emergence, Explanation and Emancipation, forthcoming in P. Secord (ed.), 'Consciousness, Behaviour, and Social Structure', London, Sage Publications.
BINNS, P. (1973), The Marxist Theory of Truth, 'Radical Philosophy', Spring, no.4.
BINNS, P. (1974), The triviality of Althusser, 'Radical Philosophy', Spring, no.7.
BLOOR, D. (1976), 'Knowledge and Social Imagery', London, Routledge & Kegan Paul.
BOGGS, C. (1976), 'Gramsci's Marxism', London, Pluto Press.
BOLDRIGHINI, C. and MARCHETTI, F. (1977), Lo sviluppo della matematica alla fine del secolo XIX: il problema dei fondamenti e la formalizzazione hilbertiana, in E. Donini, A. Rossi and T. Tonietti (eds), 'Matematica e Fisica: Ideologia e Strutura', Bari, De Donato.
BOTTOMORE, T.B. (ed.) (1956), 'Karl Marx, Selected Writings in Sociology and Social Philosophy', New York, McGraw-Hill.
BRAVERMAN, H. (1974), 'Labour and Monopoly Capital', New York, Monthly Review Press.
BRINKMANN, H. (1978), 'Zur Kritik der Widerspiegelungstheorie', Lahn-Giessen, Focus Verlag.
BUCHARIN, N., et al. (1971), 'Science at the Crossroads', London, Frank Cass.
BUICK, A. (1975), Joseph Dietzgen, 'Radical Philosophy', Spring, no.10.
CARCHEDI, G. (1977), 'On the Economic Identification of Social Classes', London, Routledge & Kegan Paul.
CARCHEDI, G. (1979), Authority and Foreign Labour: Some Notes on a Late Capitalist Form of Capital Accumulation and State Intervention, 'Studies in Political Economy', no.2, Autumn.
CARCHEDI, G. (1981), Review article of E.O. Wright: Class Structure and Income Determination, 'Science and Society', Fall.
CARCHEDI, G. (1983), Class Analysis and the study of social forms in G. Morgan (ed.), 'Beyond Method: A Study of Social Research Strategies', forthcoming.
CARDWELL, D.S.L. (1971), 'From Watt to Clausius', London, Heinemann.
CARNOT, L. (1783), 'Essai sur les Machines en Général', Paris.
CARNOT, S. (1824), 'Reflections sur la Puissance Motrice du Feu', Paris, English translation Dover Publications, 1960.
CASTELLS, M. (1975), Immigrant Workers and Class Struggle in Advanced Capitalism, 'Politics and Society', 5.
CASTELLS, M. and DE EPOLA, E. (1976), Epistemological practice and the social sciences, 'Economy and Society', vol.5, no.2, May.
CASTELLS, S. and KOSACK, G. (1973), 'Immigrant Workers and Class Structure in Western Europe', Oxford University Press.
CERRONI, U. (1978), 'Lessico Gramsciano', Rome, Editori Riuniti.
CICCOTTI, G., et al. (1976), 'L'Ape e l'architetto', Milan, Feltrinelli.
SICCOTTI, G. and DONINI, E. (1975), Sviluppo e crisi del meccanicismo da Boltzmann a Planck, 'Sapere', October.

CICCOTTI, G. and JONA LASINIO, G. (1973), Il progetto della ricerca, 'Scientia', vol.108.

CINANNI, P. (1974), 'Emigrazione e Unità Operaia', Milan, Feltrinelli.

CLEGG, S. and DUNKERLEY, D. (1980), 'Organization, Class and Control', London, Routledge & Kegan Paul.

CLEMENT, W. (1979), Capitalism and the Working Class Mechanization and Automation in Canada's Mines, unpublished paper, Brussels.

COLLETTI, L. (1975), Marxism and the Dialectic, 'New Left Review', September-October.

COLLIER, A. (1978), In defence of epistemology, 'Radical Philosophy', Summer, no.20.

COOLEY, M. (1981), 'Architect or Bee?', London, J. Goodman & Son.

COOMBS, R. (1978), Labour and monopoly capital, 'New Left Review', no.107.

CORJAT, B. (1979), 'L'Atelier et le Chonometre', Paris, C. Bourgeois Editeur.

COT, J.P. and MONNIER, J.P. (1974), 'Pour une sociologie politique', Paris, Seuil.

COUNIHAN, T. (1976), Epistemology and science, Feyerabend and Lecourt, 'Economy and Society', vol.5, no.1.

CRAIB, I. (1977), Lukács and the Marxist Criticism of Sociology, 'Radical Philosophy', Summer, no.17.

CROMPTON, R. and GUBBAY, J. (1977), 'Economy and Class Structure', London, Macmillan.

CUNEO, C.J. (1980), State mediations and class contradictions in Canadian unemployment insurance, 'Studies in Political Economy', no.3.

CUTLER, A. et al. (1977), 'Marx's Capital and Capitalism Today', vol.1, London, Routledge & Kegan Paul.

CUTLER, T. (1978), The Romance of 'Labour', 'Economy and Society', vol.7, no.1, February.

DAVIES, M. (1980), The Barren Marriage of American Labour and the Democratic Party, 'New Left Review', November-December.

DE GAUDEMAR, H. (1976), 'Mobilité du travail et Accumulation du Capital', Paris, Maspéro.

DELLA VOLPE, G. (1969), 'Logica come Scienze Storica', Rome, Editori Riuniti.

DE MARIA, M. (1980), Ristrutturazione industriale e innovazione tecnologica negli anni '20 in USA, in 'Fisica e Società negli anni '20', Milan, CLUP-CLUED.

DE MARIA, M. and LA TEANA, F. (1979), I primi lavori di Schroedinger sulla meccanica ondulatoria e la nascita delle polemiche con la scuola di Göttingen-Copenhagen sull'interpretazione della meccanica quantistica, presented at the International School of History of Science, 3rd Course, Erice; forthcoming in 'Fundamenta Scientiae'.

DE MARIA, M. and LA TEANA, F. (1981), Il contributo di Dirac alla nascita della meccanica quantistica (1925-27), 'Fundamenta Scientiae', forthcoming.

DE MARIA, M. and SEIDEL, R.W. (1979), The Scientist and the Inventor, 'Testi e Contesti', vol.4.

DE MARZO, C. (1978), 'Maxwell e la Fisica Classica', Bari, Laterza.

DEWS, P. (1977), Misadventures of Dialectics, 'Radical Philosophy', Autumn, no.18.

DIETZ, T. (1977), De Migratie van Arbeid en Kapitaal tussen het Middelandse Zeegebied en de EEG, unpublished paper.

DOBB, M. (1971), 'Studies on the Development of Capitalism', Italian translation, 'Problemi di Storia del Capitalismo', Rome, Editori Riuniti.

DOBB, M., HILL, C., HILTON, R., PROCACCI, G., SWEEZY, P.M. and TAKAHASHI, H.K. (1978), 'The Transition from Fuedalism to Capitalism', London, New Left Books.

DONINI, E. (1978), La meccanica quantistica tra Germania e USA, 'Sapere', July-August.

DONINI, E. (1979), Scienze a Weimar, un nodo storico, 'Testi e Contesti', n.1.

DONINI, E. (1980), Aspetti scientifici e di contesto storico nel passaggio della meccanica quantistica agli Stati Uniti, in 'Fisica e Società negli anni '20', Milan, CLUP-CLUED.

DOWIDAR, M.H. (1974), 'L'économie politique, une science sociale', Paris, Maspéro.

DRAGSTEDT, A. (ed.) (1976), 'Value: Studies by K. Marx', London, New Park Publications.

DURKHEIM, E. (1964), 'The Division of Labour in Society', London, Macmillan.

DURKHEIM, E. (1966), 'The Rules of Sociological Method', Chicago, The Free Press.

DURKHEIM, E. (1970), 'Suicide', London, Routledge & Kegan Paul.

EDGLEY, R. (1976), Reason as Dialectic, 'Radical Philosophy', Autumn, no.15.

EMERY, F.E. (ed.) (1981), 'Systems Thinking', Harmondsworth, Penguin, vol.1.

EMMANUEL, A. (1972), 'Unequal Exchange', New York, Monthly Review Press.

ENGELS, F. (1970), 'Anti-Dühring', New York, International Publishers.

ENGELS, F. (1976), 'Dialectics of Nature', Moscow, Progress Publishers.

FETSCHER, I. (1976), 'Der Marxismus, Seine Geschichte in Dokumenten', vol. 1, Munich, R. Piper & Co. Verlag.

FEYERABEND, P. (1975), 'Against Method', London, New Left Books.

FINOCCHIARO, M.A. (1981), Testi e Contesti: Quaderni di Scienze, Storia e Società, book review, 'Isis', 72, 2, 262, p.300.

FISTETTI, F. (1977), 'Lenin e il Machismo', Milan, Feltrinelli.

FORMAN, P. (1979), 'Kausalität, anschaulichkeit, and Individualität; or How Cultural Values Prescribed the Character and Lessons Ascribed to Quantum Mechanics, paper presented at the Workshop on Growth of Quantum Mechanics, Lecce, September.

FOUCAULT, M. (1969), 'Il Sapere e la Storia', Milan, Savelli.

FRANK, A.G. (1969), Functionalism and dialectics, 'Latin America: Underdevelopment or Revolution', New York, Monthly Review Press.

FRANTSOV, G.P. (1975), 'Philosophy and Sociology', Moscow, Progress Publishers.

GANI, L. (1972), 'Syndicats et Travailleurs Immigrées', Paris, Éditions Sociales.

GERTH, H.H. and MILLS, C.W. (1977), 'From Max Weber', London, Routledge & Kegan Paul.

GEYMONAT, L. (1973), Neo-Positivist methodology and dialectical materialism, 'Science and Society', Summer.

GEYMONAT, L. (ed.) (1980), 'Critical Leninista del Presente', Milan Feltrinelli.

GEYMONAT, L. (ed.) (1981), 'Lavoro Scienza Potere', Milan, Feltrinelli.
GIDDENS, A. (ed.) (1972), Emile Durkheim, 'Selected Writings',
Cambridge University Press.
GILLESPIE, C.C. (1971), 'Lazare Carnot Savant', Princeton University
Press.
GIOANNINI, A. (1978), Popperismo di sinistra, 'Praxis', April.
GLUCKSMAN, M. (1974), 'Structuralist Analysis in Contemporary Social
Thought', London, Routledge & Kegan Paul.
GODELIER, M. (1973), 'Horizons, Trajets marxistes en anthropologie',
Paris, Maspéro.
GOLDBERG, S. (1970), in McCormmach (ed.), 'Historical Studies in the
Physical Sciences', Philadelphia, University of Pennsylvania Press.
GOLDMAN, L. (1972), Is There a Marxist Sociology? 'Radical Philosophy',
January, no.1.
GRAMSCI, A. (1971), 'Prison Notebooks', New York, International
Publishing Co.
GRAMSCI, A. (1975a), 'L'Ordine Nuovo, 1919-1920', Turin, Einaudi.
GRAMSCI, A. (1975b), 'Quaderni dal carcere', Turin, Einaudi.
GREEN, F. and NORE, P. (eds) (1979), 'Issues in Political Economy',
London, Macmillan.
HALFPENNY, P. (1980), book review of R. Bhaskar, The Possibility of
Naturalism, 'Sociology', vol.14, no.4, November.
HAMLYN, D.W. (1970), 'The Theory of Knowledge', London, Macmillan.
HAHN, E. and HAUG, F. (1971), 'Kritiek op de burgerlijke sociologie',
Nijmegen; SUN.
HARMSEN, G. and REINALDA, B. (1975), 'Voor de Bevrijding van de
Arbeid', Nijmegen; SUN.
HEGEL, G.W.F. (1975), 'The Science of Logic', Oxford University
Press.
HELBERGER, G. (1974), 'Marxismus als Methode', Frankfurt am Main,
Fischer Athenäum Taschenbuchen.
HERIVEL, J. (1975), 'Joseph Fourier', Oxford, Clarendon Press.
HESSEN, B. (1931), The social and economic roots of Newton's
'Principia', in 'Science at the Cross Roads', London, Kniga.
HILLS, R.L. and PACEY, A.J. (1972), The measurement of power in the
early steam driven textile mills, 'Technology and Culture', vol.13.
HOBSBAWM, E.J. (1975), 'The Age of Capital', London, Weidenfeld &
Nicolson.
HOHENBERG, P.M. (1967), 'Chemicals in Western Europe 1850-1914',
Chicago, Rand McNally & Co.
HOLZ, H.H. (1972), 'Tendensen in het europese Marxisme', Nijmegen,
SUN.
ISRAEL, G. (1977), Un aspetto ideologico della matematica
contemporanea: il 'Bourbakismo', in E. Donini, A. Rossi and
T. Tonietti (eds), 'Matematica e Fisica: Struttura e Ideologia',
Bari, De Donato.
ISRAEL, G. and NEGRINI, P. (1973), La rivoluzione francese e la
scienza, 'Scientia', I-II and III-IV-V-VI.
JOHNSON, T. (1977), What is to be known? The structural determination
of social class, 'Economy and Society', vol.6, no.2.
JOHNSTON, W. and ORNSTEIN, M.D. (1979), Social Class and Political
Ideology in Canada, unpublished paper, York University of Toronto.
KAMMERER, P. (1976), 'Sviluppo del Capitale e Emigrazione in
Europa: la Germania Federale', Milan, Mazzotta.

KEAT, R. and URRY, J. (1975), 'Social Theory as Science', London, Routledge & Kegan Paul.

KLEIN, R. (1968), 'Greek Mathematical Thought and the Origin of Algebra', M.I.T. Press.

KLEIN, M.J. (1966), Thermodynamics and quanta in Planck's work, 'Physics Today', 19, November.

KLEIN, M.J. (1963), Einstein's first paper on Quanta, 'Natural Philosopher', 2, 59.

KLEIN, M.J. (1965), Einstein, specific heats and the early quantum theory, 'Science', 148, 173.

KLEIN, M.J. (1967), Thermodynamics in Einstein's thought, 'Science', 157, 509.

KNEE, C. (1979), Connections, 'Radical Science Journal', no.9, pp.100-11.

KORCH, H. (1980), 'Die Materieauffassung der Marxistisch-Leninistischen Philosophie', Berlin, Dietz Verlag.

KOYRE, A. (1957), 'From the Closed World to the Infinite Universe', Baltimore, Johns Hopkins Press.

KUHN, T. (1970), 'The Structure of Scientific Revolution', University of Chicago Press.

KRIGE, J. (1979), Revolution and discontinuity, 'Radical Philosophy', Summer, no.22.

KUHN, A. and WOLPE, A. (1978), 'Feminism and Materialism', London, Routledge & Kegan Paul.

LACLAU, E. (1977), 'Politics and Ideology in Marxist Theory', London, New Left Books.

LACLAU, E. (1979), 'Democratic antagonism and the capitalist state', paper presented at the E.C.P.R. Conference, Brussels.

LAKATOS, I. and MUSGRAVE, A. (eds) (1970), 'Criticism and the Growth of Knowledge', Cambridge University Press.

LANDES, D.S. (1969), 'The Unbound Prometheus', Cambridge University Press.

LANZA, A. (1980), Taylorismo, fordismo e movimento di riorganizzazione industriale negli USA, 1890-1920, 'Testi e Contesti', n.2.

LECOURT, D. (1975), 'Marxism and Epistemology', London, New Left Books.

LECOURT, D. (1977), 'Proletarian Science? The Case of Lysenko', London, New Left Books.

LEFEBVRE, H. (1968), 'Dialectical Materialism', London, Cape.

LEFEBVRE, H. (1971), 'L'Idéologie Structuraliste', Paris, Antropos.

LEITHÄUSER, T. and HEINZ, W.R. (eds) (1976), 'Produktion, Arbeit und Sozialisation', Frankfurt, Suhrkamp.

LENIN, V.I. (1963), 'What "The Friends of the People" are and how they fight the social democrats', 'Collected Works', no.1, Moscow, Progress Publishers.

LENIN, V.I., 'Materialism and Empirio-Criticism', 'Collected Works', no.14.

LENIN, V.I., 'A "Scientific System of Sweating"', 'Collected Works', no.18.

LENIN, V.I., 'Capitalism and Workers' Immigration', 'Collected Works', vol.19.

LENIN, V.I., 'The Taylor System - Man's Enslavement by the Machine', 'Collected Works', no.20.

LENIN, V.I., 'A Caricature of Marxism and Imperialist Economism', 'Collected Works', no.23.

LENIN, V.I., 'The Immediate Tasks of the Soviet Government', 'Collected Works', no.27.

LENIN, V.I. (1965), 'Report on the Tax in kind delivered at the Meeting of Secretaries and Responsible Representatives of the R.C.B(B) Cells of Moscow and Moscow Gubernia, 9 April, 1921', 'Collected Works', no.32, Moscow.

LENIN, V.I., 'Purging the Party', 'Collected Works', no.33.

LENIN, V.I., 'Philosophical Notebooks', 'Collected Works', no.38.

LENIN, V.I. 'Original Version of the Article "The Immediate Tasks of the Soviet Government"', 'Collected Works', no.42.

LIEBKNECHT, K. (1976), 'Studies over de Bewegingswetten van de Maatschappelijke Ontwikkeling', Baarn, Het Wereldvenster.

LILIENFELD, R. (1978), 'The Rise of Systems Theory', New York, John Wiley & Sons.

LINHART, R. (1976), 'Lenine, les Paysans, Taylor', Paris, Seuil.

LORINI, A. (1979), Il passaggio del principio di efficienza dallo 'Scientific Management' alle scienze sociali negli Stati Uniti, 1890-1920, 'Testi e Contesti', n.1.

LORINI, A. (1980), 'Ingegneria Umana e Scienze Sociali negli USA (1890-1920)', Florence, D'Anna.

LUKÁCS, G. (1971), 'History and Class Consciousness', London, The Merlin Press.

LUPORINI, C. (1975), Reality and Historicity: Economy and Dialectics in Marxism, 'Economy and Society', vol.4, nos. 2 and 3.

MACCACARO, G.A. (1977), 'Sapere', March (special issue in his memory).

McLACHLAN, H.V. (1980), Popper, Marxism and the nature of social laws, 'The British Journal of Sociology', vol.XXXI, no.1, March.

MAGEE, B. (1973), 'Popper', London, Fontana/Collins.

MAIGNIEN, Y. (1975), 'La division du travail manuel et intellectuel', Paris, Maspéro.

MAITAN, L. (1977), Su alcune deformaxioni del metodo marxista nella estrema sinistra italiana, 'Praxis', no.14-15.

MANDEL, E. (1975), 'Late Capitalism', London, New Left Books.

MANGANO, A. (1978), 'Autocritica e Politica di Classe', Edizioni Ottaviano.

MANTOUX, P. (1971), 'Industrial Revolution in the XVIIIth Century', Italian trans., 'La Rivoluzione Industriale', Rome, Editori Riuniti.

MAO TSE-TUNG, (1966), Where do correct ideas come from? 'Four Essays on Philosophy', Peking, Foreign Languages Press.

MAO TSE-TUNG, (1967), 'On Contradiction', 'Selected Works', vol.1, Peking, Foreign Languages Press.

MARCHETTI, F. (1977), Il metodo assiomatico nella matematica moderna, 'Sapere', May.

MARTYNOW, A. (1930), Die Theorie des Beweglichen Gleichgewichts der Gesellschaft und die Weichselbeziehungen zwischen Gesellschaft und Milieu, 'Unter dem Banner der Marxismus', vol.IV, no.1.

MARX, K. (1967a), 'Capital', vol.1, New York, International Publishers.

MARX, K. (1967b), 'Capital', vol.II, New York, International Publishers.

MARX, K. (1967c), 'Capital', vol. III, New York, International Publishers.

MARX, K. (1969c), 'Theories of Surplus Value', vol.1, Moscow, Progress Publishers.

MARX, K. (1973), 'Grundrisse', Harmonsworth, Penguin.
MARX, K. and ENGELS, F. (1969a), 'Selected Works', no.1, Moscow, Progress Publishers.
MARX, K. and ENGELS, F. (1969b), 'Selected Works', Vol.2, Moscow, Progress Publishers.
MARX, K. and ENGELS, F. (1970a), 'The German Ideology', New York, International Publishing Co.
MARX, K. and ENGELS, F. (1970b), 'Selected Works', no.3, Progress Publishers.
MARXISTISCHE AUFBAUORGANISATION (1973), 'Die Krise der Kommunistische Parteien', Munich and Erlagen, Trikont-Verlag.
MEHRTENS, H. and RICHTER, S. (eds) (1980), 'Naturwissenschaft, Technik und Ideologie', Frankfurt, Suhrkamp.
MEILLASSOUX, C. (1972), From reproduction to production, 'Economy and Society', vol.1, no.1.
MENDELSOHN, E. et al. (eds) (1977), 'The Social Production of Scientific Knowledge', Dordrecht, Reidel.
MEPHAM, J. (1973), Who Makes History? 'Radical Philosophy', Winter, no.6.
MEPHAM, J. and RUBEN D.-H. (eds) (1979), 'Issues in Marxist Philosophy', vol. III, Hassocks, Sussex, Harvester Press.
MILIBAND, R. (1969), 'The State in Capitalist Society', London, Weidenfeld & Nicolson.
MILIBAND, R. (1977), 'Marxism and Politics', Oxford University Press.
MOIOLI, V. (1976), 'Made in Italy', Rome, Alfani Editore.
MORGAN, G. (1980), Paradigms, Metaphors and Puzzle-Solving in Organization Theory, 'Administrative Science Quarterly', December.
MORGAN, G. (ed.) (1983), 'Beyond Method: A Study of Social Research Strategies', forthcoming.
MULKAY, M. (1980), The Sociology of Science in the West, 'Current Sociology', vol.28, no.3, Winter.
MURRAY, D. (1979), Utopia or Phantasy, 'Radical Philosophy', no.22.
MUSSON, A.E. and ROBINSON, E. (1969), 'Science and Technology in the Industrial Revolution, Manchester.
NEUMANN, M. (1976), 'Methoden der Klassenanalyse', Europäische Verlaganstalt.
NIKOLINAKOS, M. (1975), Notes Towards a General Theory of Migration Under Capitalism, 'Race and Class', XVII, no.1
NOBLE, D. (1977), 'America by Design', New York, Knopf.
NORMAN, R. (1976), On Dialectic, 'Radical Philosophy', Summer, no.14.
NORMAN, R. and SAYERS, S. (1980), 'Hegel, Marx and Dialectic: A Debate', Hassocks, Sussex, Harvester Press.
OROVAL PLANAS, J.M. et al. (1974), El Dificil Retorno, 'Cuadernos para el dialogo', Madrid, Mayo.
PANCALDI, G. (1980), The history and social studies of science in Italy, Country Report, in 'Social Studies of Science', London and Beverly Hills, Sage, vol.10, p.351.

PARLIAMENTARY PAPERS

SAMUELSON, B. (1867-8), 'Industrial Progress and Instruction of Working Classes in France, Switzerland, Germany, etc.', vol.LIV, p.69.

'Report on Paris Universal Exhibition, 1867: Reports from Commissioners', vol. XXX (1867-8).

'Report on the Selected Committee Appointed to Enquire the Provisions for Giving Instructions in Theoretical and Applied Sciences to Industrial Classes; Report from the Selected Committee on Scientific Instruction', vol.XV (1867-8).

'Second Report of the Royal Commission on Technical Instruction', vol.XXIX (1884).

'Report on a Visit to Germany with a View to Ascertaining the Recent Progress of Technical Education in that Country', vol. LXXXVIII, p.403 (1897).

BAKER, J. (1900), 'Report on Technical and Commercial Education in East Prussia, Poland, Galicia, Silesia and Bohemia', vol.XXII, Part II, p.349.

ROSE, F. (1901), 'Report on the Chemical Instruction in Germany and the Growth and Present Condition of the German Chemical Industries', vol.LXXX, p.147.

ROSE, F. (1902), 'Supplementary Report on Chemical Instruction and Chemical Industries in Germany', vol.CIII, p.33.

PARKIN, F. (1979), 'Marxism and Class Theory: A Bourgeois Critique', London, Tavistock Publications.

PATTON, P. (1978), Althusser's epistemology: the limits of the theory of theoretical practice, 'Radical Philosophy', Spring, no.19.

PAUL, H.-H. (1978), 'Marx, Engels und die Imperialismus - Theorie der II Internationale', Hamburg, VSA Verlag.

PENNINX, R. and VAN VELZEN, L. (1976), Kaste Vorming in Nederland? 'Te Elfder Ure', no.21.

PERLINI, T. (1974), 'Gramsci e il Marxismo', Milan, CELUC.

PLANTY-BONJOUR, G. (1968), 'The Categories of Dialectical Materialism', Dordrecht, Reidel.

POPPER, K. (1959), 'The Logic of Scientific Discovery', London, Hutchinson.

POPPER, K. (1963), 'Conjectures and Refutations', New York, Harper Torchbooks.

POPPER, K. (1972), 'Objective Knowledge', Oxford University Press.

PORTES, A. (1978), Migration and Underdevelopment, 'Politics and Society', 8, no.1.

POULANTZAS, N. (1973), 'Political Power and Social Classes', London, New Left Books.

POULANTZAS, N. (1974a), 'Fascism and Dictatorship', London, New Left Books.

POULANTZAS, N. (1974b), 'Les Classes Sociales dans le capitalisme aujourd'hui', Paris, Seuil.

RADDER, H. (1980), Realisme in Natuur - en mens wetenschappen, 'Krisis', no.2, October.

RANCIÈRE, J. (1974), On the theory of ideology, 'Radical Philosophy', Spring, no.7.

RAVETZ, J.R. (1971), 'Scientific Knowledge and its Social Problems', Oxford, Clarendon Press.

RAYMOND, P. (1978), 'L'Histoire et les Sciences', Paris, Maspéro.

REE, J. (1976), Philosophy in China, 'Radical Philosophy', Summer, no.14.

REINFELDER, M. and SLATER, P. (1978), Review article, 'Capital and Class', no.6, pp.126-39.

REY, P.P. (1973), 'Les Alliances de Classes', Paris, Maspéro.
RONCAGLIA, A. (1974), The Reduction of Complex Labour to Simple Labour, 'Bulletin of the Conference of Socialist Economists', 9.
ROSSI, A. (1971), 'Sapere', October.
ROSSI, A. (1973), Le due strade della fisica, 'Scientia', VII-VIII and IX-X-XI-XII (1974).
ROSSI, A. (1974), Le nuove tecnologie in Inghilterra tra '700 e '800, 'Sapere', August-September.
ROSSI, A. (1975), 'Popper e la Filosofia della Scienza', Florence, Sansoni.
ROSSI, A. (1976), Boscovich e Faraday, 'Physis', nos.3-4.
ROSSI, A. (1977a), Epistemologia e prassi scientifica, Part I, 'Sapere', January-February; Part II, 'Sapere', September.
ROSSI, A. (1977b), L'esperimento di Joule sull'equivalente meccanico del calore e il secondo principio della termodinamica, 'Physis'.
RUBEN, D.-H. (1977), 'Marxism and Materialism', Hassocks, Sussex, The Harvester Press.
RUSSO, A. (1982), Fundamental research at Bell Telephone Laboratories. The discovery of electron diffraction, 'Historical Studies in the Physical Sciences', forthcoming.
SALAMAN, G. (1981), 'Class and the Corporation', London, Fontana.
SAWYER, T. (1973), Immigration: le blocage de la mobilité autour du bassin mediterranéen, 'Critique de l'économie politique', July-September.
SAYERS, S. (1976), The Marxist Dialectic, 'Radical Philosophy', Summer, no.14.
SAYERS, S. (1980), Forces of Production and Relations of Production in Socialist Society, 'Radical Philosophy', Spring, no.24.
SCHAEFFER, R.K. (1976), A Critique of the "New Class" Theorists: Towards a Theory of the Working Class in America, 'Social Praxis', vol.4, no.1-2.
SCOTT, J. (1979), 'Corporations, Classes and Capitalism', London, Hutchinson.
SERAFINI, A. (ed.) (1974), 'L'Operaia Multinationale in Europa', Milan, Feltrinelli.
SIVANANDAN, A. (1976), Race, class and the state. The Black Experience in Britain, 'Race and Class', XVII, 4.
SIVANANDAN, A. (1978), From Immigration Control to indirect repatriation, 'Race and Class', XX, 1.
SKILLEN, T. (1978), Post-Marxist Modes of Production, 'Radical Philosophy', Summer, no.20.
SLATER, P. (ed.) (1980), 'Outlines of a critique of technology', London, Ink Links.
SMEATON, J. (1759), An experimental enquiry concerning the natural powers of water and wind to turn mills and other machines depending on a circular motion, 'Philosophical Transactions', 51, p.100.
SMEATON, J. (1776), An experimental examination of the quantity and proportion of mechanical power necessary to be employed in giving different degrees of velocity to heavy bodies from a state of rest, 'Philosophical Transactions', 66, p.450.
SMEATON, J. (1782), 'Philosophical Transactions', 15, p.298.
SMEATON, J. (1812), 'Reports of the late John Smeaton', London.
SMILES, S. (1861-2), 'Lives of the Engineers', and 'Lives of Boulton and Watt', London.

SMITH, N. (1980), Symptomatic silence in Althusser: The Concept of Nature and the Unity of Science, 'Science and Society', Spring.
SOHN-RETHEL, A. (1978), 'Mental and Manual Labour', London, Macmillan.
SORG, R. (1976), 'Ideologietheorien', Cologne, Kiepenheur & Witsch.
STARNBERGER STUDIEN 1, 'Die Gesellschaftliche Orientierung der Wissenschaftlichen Fortschritts', Frankfurt, Suhrkamp.
STEPHENS, J.D. (1979), 'The Transition from Capitalism to Socialism', London, Macmillan.
TARSITANI, C. (1972), Il superamento teorico e Critico dell'elettro-dinamica dell'azione a distanza nell'opera di Hertz, in 'Alcuni Aspetti dello Sviluppo delle Teorie Fisiche 1743-1911', Piza, Domus Galilaeiana.
TONIETTI, T. (1976), Il dibattito sui fondamenti della meccanica quantistica, 'Sapere', January.
TONIETTI, T. (1980), La meccanica quantistica nel contesto matematico: cambiamenti di punti di vista e qualche aspetto istituzionale, in 'Fisica e Società negli anni '20', Milan, CLUP-CLUED.
TRIBE, K. (1973), On the Production and Structuring of Scientific Knowledge, 'Economy and Society', vol.2, no.4.
TRONTI, M. (1966), 'Operai e Capitale', Turin, Einaudi.
UNION GENERALE DES TRAVAILLEURS SENEGALAIS EN FRANCE, 'Qui est responsable du Sous-Development', Paris, Maspéro, 1975.
VAN DOOREN, W. (1977), 'Dialektik', Amsterdam.
VARIOUS AUTHORS, (1976), 'The Labour Process and Class Strategies', CSE, no.1.
VARIOUS AUTHORS (1977), 'Gramsci: un'eredità contrastata', Milan, Edizioni Ottaviano.
VARIOUS AUTHORS (1978), 'Contro l'autonomia della politica', Turin, Rosenberg & Sellier.
VARIOUS AUTHORS (1979), 'Geschichte der Dialektik, 14. bis 18. Jahrhundert', Berlin, Dietz Verlag.
VARIOUS AUTHORS (1980), 'Zur Konkreten Utopie gesellschaftlichen Arbeit', Offenbach, Verlag 2000 GmbH.
WEBER, M. (1949), 'The Methodology of the Social Sciences', Chicago, The Free Press.
WEBER, M. (1958), 'The Protestant Ethic and the Spirit of Capitalism', University of California Press.
WEBER, M. (1964), 'The Theory of Social and Economic Organization', Chicago, The Free Press.
WEBER, M. (1968), 'Economy and Society', New York.
WEIGHTS, A. (1978), Weber and "Legitimate Domination", 'Economy and Society', vol.7, no.1, February.
WHITAKER, R. (1979), Scientific Management Theory as Political Ideology, 'Studies in Political Economy', no.2, Autumn.
WILLIAMS, K. (1975), Facing Reality: A Critique of Karl Popper's Empiricism, 'Economy and Society', vol.4, no.3.
WRIGHT, E.O. (1978), 'Class, Crisis and the State', London, New Left Books.
WRIGHT, E.O. (1979), 'Class Structure and Income Determination', London, Academic Press.
WRIGHT, E.O. (1980), Varieties of Marxist Conceptions of Class Structure, 'Politics and Society', no.3.
WRIGHT, E.O. and LEVINE, A. (1980), Rationality and Class Structure, 'New Left Review', September-October.

ZAHAR, E. (1973), Why did Einstein's programme supersede Lorentz's? 'The British Journal for the Philosophy of Science', 24, pp.95-123 and 223-62.
ZEITLIN, M. (1974), Corporate Ownership and Control, the Large Corporation and the Capitalist Class, 'American Journal of Sociology', vol. 79.
ZEITLIN, M. (ed.) (1980), 'Classes, Class Conflict and the State', Cambridge, Mass., Winthrop.
ZIMBALIST, A. (1979), 'Case Studies on the Labour Process', New York, MR.

INDEX